**Ruin and
Resurgence
1939–1965**

1939-1965

Ruin and Resurgence 1939-1965

R. C. MOWAT, M.A. **(Oxon)**
Senior Lecturer in History
Oxford College of Technology

HARPER COLOPHON BOOKS
Harper & Row, Publishers
New York and Evanston

RUIN AND RESURGENCE: 1939-1965. ©
1966 Blandford Press Ltd.

Printed in the United States of America.

This book was originally published in 1966 by
Blandford Press, Ltd., 167 High Holborn, London, England, and is here reprinted by arrangement.

First HARPER COLOPHON edition published
1968 by Harper & Row, Publishers, Incorporated, 49 East 33rd Street, New York, N.Y.
10016.

Library of Congress Catalog Card Number:
68-27869

Contents

v

List of Illustrations

28 Churchill at the Council of Europe, Strasbourg.
29 Monnet and Schuman.
30 Adenauer and de Gaulle.
31 A clover-leaf intersection on the autobahn at Frankfurt-am-Main, Germany.
32 Monorail, Dortmund, Germany.
33 The Church of St Canisius, Berlin.
34 Eden.
35 Spaak.
36 Mendès-France.
37 Khrushchev.
38 Pope John XXIII.
39 The Queen with President Lübke in Germany, May 1965.

LIST OF MAPS
Drawn by A. Spark

ACKNOWLEDGMENTS

The illustrations have been reproduced by permission of the following:

   1–5, 5–12, 14–19   Imperial War Museum
   3–4, 13, 21, 26–27, 35–39   Camera Press
   20, 22–25, 28, 34   Radio Times Hulton Picture Library
   29   Paul Popper
   31–33   German Embassy

Extracts from books are reprinted by permission of the publishers, as mentioned in the footnotes.

Foreword

On the short period of European history 1939–65 there is a vast and growing number of books and documents. To make the treatment of the subject more manageable I have tried to restrict myself to the history of Europe proper, while well aware that even to define the limits of 'Europe' is difficult. The fact that British domestic history has been largely omitted is not because I regard Britain as outside Europe, but because that side of British history has already been treated in a volume in a parallel series. It is however impossible to regard contemporary European history except as an integral part of world history, and for this reason it has been necessary to treat aspects of the history of other continents. At the same time limitations of time and space dictated that these aspects, and even some of the themes of what is incontestably European history, had to be treated sketchily. This fact may explain certain omissions or the highly generalized approach of some sections.

A book of this scale, and written at this time, cannot in any case set out to be exhaustive on any topic, and certainly not definitive. We are too near the events to make final judgments on many issues, our perspective is too short, and daily more information is becoming available, together with works of research and specialized studies which will affect the interpretations of future historians. I have naturally treated more fully than others those episodes or questions which seemed to me particularly interesting or which have tended to be neglected.

I am most grateful to all those people who have helped me in various ways, by reading the book, or part of it, in typescript or proof, and offering advice or corrections which have frequently been invaluable. If the result is less worthy than it should have been, the fault is entirely mine, as is the responsibility for inaccuracies and other blemishes. Particularly I would like to thank Professor M. E. Howard, Professor Agnes Headlam-Morley, Professor C. L. Mowat, Mr G. D. Lean, Captain G. R. Waymouth, R.N., Air Vice-Marshal D. N. K. Blair-Oliphant, M. Gérard d'Hauteville, Dr O. Davies, Mr Philip Woolley, Herr Fritz Hirschner, Priv. Doz. Dr Arno Sachse, Stud. Ass. Ernst Melbach, and, in connection with the tedious but essential work of transcribing, typing and indexing, Mrs A. V. Burnley, and members of my family. I owe much to the courtesy and helpfulness of the staff at the Bodleian Library and the Library of St Antony's College, Oxford, and am indebted to both these institutions for the facilities they have afforded me. Also, it is only fair to add that without the forbearance, advice and assistance of my publisher, Mr Richard Harman, and his staff, this book could scarcely have seen the light of day.

Oxford, September 1965.   R.C.M.

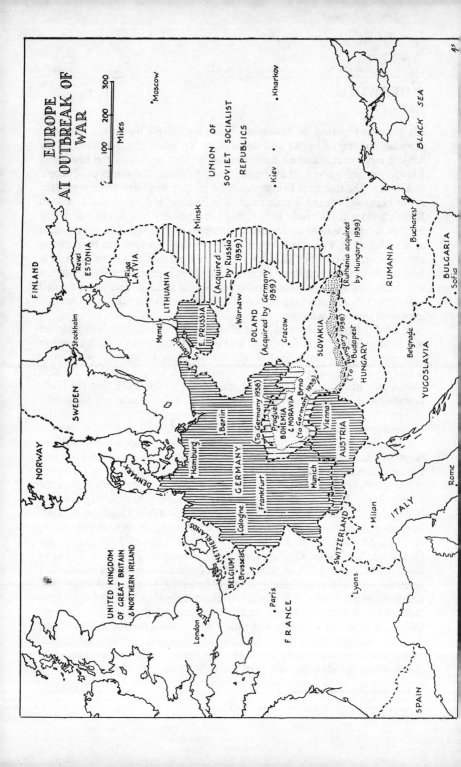

EUROPE
AT OUTBREAK OF
WAR

100   200   300

Miles

FINLAND

NORWAY

SWEDEN

• Stockholm

• Revel
ESTONIA

• Riga
LATVIA

LITHUANIA

• Memel

E. PRUSSIA

UNION OF

SOVIET SOCIALIST

REPUBLICS

• Moscow

• Minsk

(Acquired
by Russia
1939)

• Warsaw

POLAND
(Acquired by Germany
1939)

• Kiev

• Kharkov

DENMARK

• Hamburg

• Berlin

GERMANY

• Cologne

NETHERLANDS

• Frankfurt

(To Germany 1938)

Prague
BOHEMIA
& MORAVIA

• Cracow

SLOVAKIA

(Ruthenia acquired
by Hungary 1939)

Brno
(To Germany 1939)

BLACK SEA

UNITED KINGDOM
OF GREAT BRITAIN
& NORTHERN IRELAND

BELGIUM
• Brussels

London

Munich

Vienna
AUSTRIA

• Budapest

(To Hungary 1938)

HUNGARY

RUMANIA

• Bucharest

BULGARIA
• Sofia

• Paris

FRANCE

SWITZERLAND

• Milan

• Lyons

ITALY

Belgrade

YUGOSLAVIA

• Rome

SPAIN

1: The War: First Phases
(Poland to Norway)

In August 1939 Hitler was determined to make war on Poland. His preparations were complete and he would not be denied his prey. Austria and Czechoslovakia had been incorporated in the Nazi empire. From the jumping-off points which these acquisitions gave him, together with those in East Prussia, Poland could be attacked from three sides. From the fourth side, her eastern frontier, there was no salvation for Poland either. The Molotov–Ribbentrop Agreement of 23 August 1939 opened the way to a Russian occupation of eastern Poland up to what was approximately the 'Curzon Line' of the abortive 1919 arrangements.

The German army had been expanded from the highly efficient but diminutive force, officially only 100,000 strong, of the Weimar Republic, into the most powerful fighting machine in the world. Seventy-five divisions—over a million troops—were drawn up, poised to spring, along Poland's frontiers, while the Luftwaffe could dispose of a vast superiority of fighter and bomber planes.

The German General Staff had gladly accepted Hitler's help, first in the secret rearmament of the Reich in defiance of the Treaty of Versailles, then—after Hitler had repudiated the treaty—in its open rearmament from 1936 onwards. The senior officers, still mainly of the Prussian Junker caste, were ready to agree with part of Hitler's programme, while repudiating or at least ignoring much of his ideology.[1] Their doubts about his leadership mainly concerned the timing of his moves regarding the Rhineland, Austria and Czechoslovakia, and about the wisdom of his ultimate aims. But these had been largely overcome by his flair for exploiting the psychological weakness of the democracies. The resulting successes had made Germany once again

[1] Their reserve in regard to Hitler and National-Socialism was partly due to their feeling that they had failed to uphold their code of honour by not taking action against the Nazis for their murder of General von Schleicher on 30 June 1934.—K. Demeter: *Das Deutsche Offizierkorps* (Bernard & Greite Verlag, 1962); 142. See also this author's discussion of the 'crisis of confidence' in the Officers' Corps.

the most formidable of the European powers, with an extent of territory greater than that of Bismarck's Reich—and all without fighting a war.

The officers' caste hoped for another bloodless success over Poland, another *Blumenkorso* as in Austria and the Sudetenland, when the invading army had been greeted with flowers and rapturous rejoicing. The officers were eager to try out their war-machine if necessary, but the more far-sighted among them were fearful lest a campaign in Poland, however swift and successful, might lead on to another two-front war which could prove even more disastrous for Germany than that of 1914–18.

Ever since the British guarantee to Poland (31 March 1939) Hitler too had some doubts on this point. These, however, did not become serious even when the British Ambassador brought him a letter from the Prime Minister Neville Chamberlain on 23 August, stating categorically that 'no greater mistake could be made' than to assume 'that intervention by Great Britain is no longer a contingency that need be reckoned with'.[1] Despite these words Hitler assumed that Britain, in the event, would not intervene, though he was even more afraid that 'at the last minute some swine or other'—presumably Chamberlain again—'will produce a plan of mediation', and rob him of a triumphal entry at the head of his army into the conquered country, as Munich temporarily had in the case of Czechoslovakia. The generals who expected another Munich over Poland were disappointed. Hitler's proposals for settling Germany's account with Poland were produced only at the last moment (30 August) purely for propaganda purposes, after it had already been decided that Poland would be attacked at dawn on 1 September.[2] 'I needed an alibi,' Hitler explained later, 'especially with the German people, to show them that I had done everything to maintain peace.'[3] The Poles never even saw the proposals. The attack, originally timed for the 26th, had been put off once on Hitler's learning of the signature of the Anglo-Polish Pact of Mutual Assistance on the 25th, and of the Italian decision—communicated the same day—to postpone intervening on Germany's side. But these were merely last minute hitches. An incident was staged

[1] British Blue Book (cmd. 6106), No. 56.
[2] British Blue Book, (cmd. 6106), No. 92.
[3] P. Schmidt: *Hitler's Interpreter* (Heinemann, 1951), 153.

THE WAR BEGINS 3

by the S.S. on the Polish frontier on the night of 31 August (a faked attack on the German radio station at Gleiwitz), and at dawn the next day the invasion began.

Poland was swiftly crushed. It was the first demonstration of the Blitzkrieg which was to be so successful elsewhere. While motorized infantry and panzers poured across the frontier at nine different points, Stukas dive-bombed the defenders, their impact of terror being heightened by the whistles in the wings of the machines. Caught before mobilisation was complete, the Poles were weaker than the Germans in manpower and far weaker in *matériel*,[1] and whatever chance they may have had of keeping the Germans longer at bay was thrown away by the mistaken strategy—later repeated to his cost by Hitler in Russia—of attempting to hold on to the outlying areas of the country. The Germans had complete superiority in the air, having bombed the Polish Air Force practically out of existence before the planes could leave their runways. Only when the remnants of Poland's armies, still fighting magnificently, formed a ring around Warsaw, were the Germans seriously held, but the capture of the capital, already a foregone conclusion, was hastened by the entrance on 17 September 1939 of the Soviet army into eastern Poland, in accordance with the bargain struck by Ribbentrop with Molotov four weeks previously in Moscow. This incursion the Poles had no troops left to oppose. Warsaw fell on 27 September.

The Poles had pinned their all on an intervention in the west by France and Britain, which might have drawn off sufficient forces to save them. Such a move was not however contemplated by the French High Command, who were in charge of the strategy of the Western Allies. Indeed, up till 3 September, it had seemed problematical whether Britain and France would intervene at all, and it was for their continued paralysis that Hitler had been hoping.

Three and a half years previously, following the policy of 'appeasement', the British government had vetoed the proposal by France to march her army against the German troops whom Hitler sent to occupy the Rhineland in March 1936—the last occasion on which he could easily have been stopped, and had urged France to break her

[1] Poland's 'offensive plans were of 1918 vintage and dependent on a mass of heavy artillery that could not be ready until the sixteenth day'.—*The Listener*, 3 September 1964, B. H. Liddell Hart: *Generalship in the Second World War*, 333.

treaty engagement with Czechoslovakia in support of that country against Germany in 1938. It was not surprising that France needed a good deal of encouragement this time to come in with England in defence of Poland, particularly since the circumstances were far less favourable for the Western powers than on any previous occasion.

With some prodding however the French agreed, but their morale was low and their military doctrine mistaken. After reoccupying the Rhineland the Germans had constructed the Siegfried Line which, though fairly formidable, was no more than an improvisation compared with the solidity and permanence of the Maginot Line. The forces which held it in September 1939 were relatively light, while most of the Wehrmacht was engaged in the east. But an offensive had never been seriously considered by the French; their thinking was dominated by the trench-warfare of Verdun and the Somme; even tank attacks such as those of 1918, let alone the use of airborne forces, had no place in their strategic planning. They believed in static warfare, with the magnificently equipped Maginot Line as a type of fortification superior to trenches. For them it was to be a war of attrition. Germany would be immobilized on the Rhine and blockaded by sea. Cut off from essential supplies she would be unable to maintain her superiority in weapons in the face of the steady increase of Allied material strength. Eventually the preponderance of weight on the Allied side would make possible a knock-out blow against Germany. Meanwhile a slight incursion into the area of Trier was all that the French attempted at the hour of Poland's desperate need, a symbolic gesture only, since the forces were withdrawn as soon as the German divisions returned from Poland to the Siegfried Line.

The only war of movement which the French envisaged was in the event of a German advance to outflank the Maginot Line by marching through Belgium and Holland. But as was proved in the following year, the French High Command were ill-prepared to parry such a violent blow.

Britain declared war at 11 a.m. on 3 September,[1] and France a few hours later, but for over eight months an unhealthy calm brooded over the Western front, the period of the 'phoney war'. Artillery exchanged fire, and there was patrolling activity, but as if by mutual agreement no major operation was launched by either side.

[1] Followed eventually by all the Dominions.

Hitler intended to move against France immediately Poland was knocked out, while carrying on a peace-offensive. This was designed to persuade France and Britain that as they had been unable to achieve the object for which they had declared war, they had better accept the *fait accompli*, and make peace with a view to some kind of permanent settlement of Europe 'before millions of men are sent uselessly to their death'. In fact this so-called peace offer of 6 October was merely a cover for preparations to attack in the west, encouraging the Western powers in their passivity while appeasing opinion at home, since the Germans themselves, for the most part, were opposed to the continuation of the war. Hitler realized that there was virtually no chance of its leading to serious talks with the Allies; he had already informed his generals (27 September) that he intended to attack in the west, and despite their opposition, he shortly announced the 12th of November as the date when operations should begin.

A ding-dong struggle ensued between Hitler and his General Staff, who believed that a much longer interval was necessary before their forces could be built up to adequate strength in the west. But Hitler was now convinced of his military as of his political genius. When his Commander-in-Chief, von Brauchitsch, indicated that the new formations of the Wehrmacht were not up to the battle-worthy standards of their 1914–18 predecessors, Hitler poured such stinging rebukes on him that he returned to his headquarters in a state of near collapse. From then on Hitler worked increasingly through the Higher Command of the Defence Forces (O.K.W. = *Oberkommando der Wehrmacht*) which he had set up in distinction from the Higher Command of the Army (O.K.H. = *Oberkommando des Heeres*)—regarding the latter as merely a body to translate his directives into operational effect. The O.K.W. itself, under the servile Keitel (an officer of no great capacity) became the Führer's military cabinet. Thus the worst principles of command organization reasserted themselves, after decades when a succession of General Staff officers from Scharnhorst onwards had done their best to set up a united command, first for Prussia, then for Germany as a whole.

These arrangements heralded the growing intervention of Hitler in the direction of the war, not merely in planning strategy, but even down to the details of tactics and supply. This was indicated during the phoney war when Hitler worked behind the back of O.K.H. on a strategy for attacking in the west proposed by General von Manstein, and secretly prepared the attack on Denmark and Norway as an 'O.K.W. war' from which O.K.H. was entirely excluded, So that though the generals of O.K.H. had their way in postponing a further campaign until the spring—largely because weather conditions made an earlier offensive impracticable—they gradually lost direction of the war to Hitler and his immediate *entourage*. The fact that both campaigns were brilliantly successful finally established Hitler in his own estimation as a military genius superior to any of the generals or experts.

Meanwhile Russia was consolidating her position in the east. During late September and early October 1939, the three Baltic republics, Estonia, Latvia and Lithuania which had achieved independence from Russia after the First World War, were forced to accept Russian bases, a prelude to their later incorporation into the Soviet Union. Stalin was also eager to widen Russia's twenty-mile glacis north of Leningrad (thereby eliminating the Mannerheim Line), and to gain control over the Gulf of Finland by acquiring a base at Hangö as well as some islands. He also had an eye on the nickel-producing area at Petsamo in the far north. The Finns were ready to talk, but jibbed especially at leasing Hangö, and negotiations at Moscow broke down.

On 30 November the Russians attacked Finland at five points and their planes bombed Helsinki and Viborg. Then the world was treated to the astonishing spectacle of the diminutive (3,800,000 population) but robust republic standing up to, and for a time worsting the Soviet Goliath. Better trained for winter warfare, more mobile, and fighting for their national existence, the Finnish ski troops caused chaos on the Russian lines of communication, trapping and destroying some 200,000 men.[1] But the effort could not be kept up. Stalin put in a new commander (Timoshenko), changed his strategy and directed the entire Russian thrust at the Mannerheim Line. After the heaviest bombardment since Verdun, the line cracked, Viborg was invested and the Finns were forced to retire (12 March 1940). At that moment France and Britain were negotiating with Norway and

[1] L. L. Snyder: *The War. A Concise History 1939–1945* (Hale, 1962), 73. See also J. Erickson: *The Soviet High Command* (Macmillan, 1962), especially pp. 503 seq. for the effects of Stalin's purges of Army High Command and officers generally on its efficiency; and pp. 542 seq. for its performance in the Finnish War.

Sweden for the passage of 100,000 troops to come to Finland's relief —an event which, if consummated, would have brought the Western Allies into the grotesque position of tackling both the great totalitarian powers at once. They were saved from this result by the hesitations of Oslo and Stockholm, and the inevitable Finnish collapse. Finland forfeited all that Russia had demanded, and more—all her territory round Lake Ladoga (as well as the Karelian Isthmus itself), Viborg, Petsamo, Hangö (on lease), and the islands. The Finns' only gain was to be spared the imposition of the puppet government of Kuusinen, which had been set up on the Karelian border, but which failed to evoke any response among the solidly patriotic Finns.

Hitler's threatened attack in the west had been so long delayed that Chamberlain was mistaken enough to say at the beginning of April 1940 that Hitler had 'missed the bus'.[1] On the advice of Grand Admiral Raeder, Hitler had secretly prepared his campaign, thereby forestalling a similar operation which Churchill was urging. German warships had been violating Norwegian coastal waters, and German merchantmen had been using them as a safe neutral corridor for carrying the vital iron-ore from Narvik, where it was brought from the Swedish mines at Kiruna.

During the Finnish War the Allies were preparing to bring in a force of 100,000, not merely to succour the Finns, but to deny the Germans the ore, and to secure bases in Sweden and Norway from which Germany might be attacked. Stalin's fears of Allied intervention made him bring the war to a close just before these plans could be executed, but they still presupposed at least a measure of consent from Norway and Sweden for their fulfilment, which had not been forthcoming.

After the Finnish War the Allies reshaped their plans, to start with the mining of Norwegian waters. There was a further objective besides denying the Germans passage through 'the Leads': it was expected to provoke a German invasion of Norway, or at least speed it up, for such an attack was anticipated. The Germans on their side wished to secure their ore and communications, and at the same time throw the British blockade far out into the northern seas.

[1] Speech, 5 April 1940, to Central Council of the National Union of Conservative and Unionist Associations—quoted in W. S. Churchill: *The Second World War* (Cassell, 1954), I, 461.

The two sets of plans matured at exactly the same time.[1] German merchantmen and warships were already conveying six divisions, or waiting outside the ports which were due to be seized on 9 April. The Allies began laying their mines on the 8th. The German plan was speedy, effective and successful. The Allies, except at Narvik, showed themselves hesitant and ill-prepared for the German blow which they had anticipated. They were not helped by the similar delays and hesitations of the Norwegian government in laying mines and mobilizing the army during the days before the attack, even when clear intelligence had notified its coming.

Both Norway and Denmark had maintained an impeccable neutrality. Denmark was entirely defenceless. Norway was scarcely better prepared, but her shore-batteries and a few ships inflicted a sharp reverse on the German Navy in the Oslo Fiord, sinking the heavy cruiser *Blücher*, the training-ship *Brummer*, and damaging other vessels. Oslo soon fell, however, to air attack, covering a thrust by German troops who were landed up the coast. The other main cities followed. Only Narvik was recaptured by the Allies after the British navy sank the German supply-ships and their protecting destroyers, but it was found too difficult to defend it after the invasion of France (it was evacuated in June 1940). The Germans ruled Norway for five years, partly through their stooge, Major Vidkund Quisling and his handful of renegades in the *Nasjonal Samling*.[2]

The crisis in the west precipitated a change of government in Britain. Bitter discontent throughout the country at the disasters and evident unpreparedness for the Scandinavian campaign was reflected in Parliament. During the debate of 7 May Chamberlain in particular

[1] The *Altmark* episode of 16 February 1940, which brought the Allies to the point of decision about bringing troops to Scandinavia, was the occasion for Hitler's 'effective decision' to implement the plan of campaign which had been prepared, largely by Admiral Raeder and the Navy, since mid-December. The *Altmark* was a German auxiliary warship to which 299 British seamen had been transferred from the *Graf Spee*, just before it had been sunk in the River Plate in December 1939.—T. K. Derry: *The Campaign in Norway* (H.M.S.O., 1952), 13, 17. For the Allied mistakes, especially deficiencies in intelligence work, see the same, pp. 233 seq.

[2] There was however a gain for the Allies in the balance of sea-power, which stood Britain in good stead when later fighting the Axis alone. The *Gneisenau* and *Scharnhorst* were torpedoed, 'and the loss in cruisers and destroyers was such that at the end of June Germany's naval forces in these categories were reduced to a total of one 8-inch cruiser, two light cruisers and four destroyers. There was also a loss of merchant shipping which Hitler noted as an additional problem in relation to Operation Sea-Lion' (Derry, 231). Further, 300,000 troops were tied down uselessly in garrison duties.

was subjected to a tirade of criticism from members of his own party which far outdid the censures of the opposition, culminating in Leo Amery's thunderous quotation from Oliver Cromwell's speech to the Long Parliament:—'You have sat too long here for any good you have been doing. Depart, I say, and let us have done with you. In the name of God, go!'

Although the government secured a majority of 81, over 30 Conservatives voted with the opposition, and a further 60 abstained. It was an undoubted vote of censure on the government. Chamberlain decided to retire from the premiership in favour of the Foreign Secretary, Lord Halifax, but the latter deemed it impracticable to lead the government from the House of Lords. The mantle fell of necessity on Churchill, under whom the Labour and Liberal leaders agreed to serve in a National government.

'During these last crowded days of the political crisis my pulse had not quickened at any moment,' Sir Winston tells us.[1] 'I took it all as it came. . . . But as I went to bed at about 3 a.m. I was conscious of a profound sense of relief. At last I had the authority to give directions over the whole scene. I felt as if I were walking with destiny, and that all my life had been but a preparation for this hour and for this trial. . . . Therefore, although impatient for the morning, I slept soundly and had no need for cheering dreams. Facts are better than dreams.'

[1] *The Second World War*, I, 526–7. Churchill's position since the outbreak of war had been that of First Lord of the Admiralty and, since April 1940, Chairman of the Military Co-ordination Committee.

2: The Fall of France and the Battle of Britain

Germany Seizes Holland

On the very day that Churchill was appointed Prime Minister, the long delayed tornado swept over the west. It had long been evident that in the event of an attack the Germans could only outflank the Maginot Line if (as in 1914) they violated the neutrality of Belgium and possibly also of Holland. But Belgium had contracted out of her obligations under the Locarno Agreement, and though there had been staff talks between France and Belgium, these had been entirely non-committal, and no adequate arrangements had been made for bringing the French and British armies into line alongside the Belgians in the event of a German violation of their territory. Still less was any arrangement made with the Dutch, who despite repeated warnings of an imminent attack clung to their neutrality in the vain hope that it would be respected. Their confusion of thought and lack of logic was illustrated by the statement made by the Netherlands Foreign Minister, Dr. van Kleffens, in his apologia, *The Rape of the Netherlands*.[1] 'If we had previously entered into conversations with the Allies, the German Intelligence Service would without any doubt whatsoever have got hold of it, the result of which would have been an immediate German attack provoked by an act of ours. That would simply have amounted to suicide.'

The Minister was mistaken in thinking that any action by the Dutch, however provocative, would have made the slightest difference to Hitler in his choice of time and place for an attack. In his strategic thinking Hitler paid no attention to such considerations. The only consideration for him was the strength of the opposing forces. The principle 'united we stand', if translated into an effective alliance with France and Britain, backed by powerful defences, might have saved Belgium and Holland, at least for a time.

The warnings of the Dutch military attaché in Berlin were based

[1] Hodder and Stoughton, 1940, 118.

on up-to-the-minute data provided by his friend, Hans Oster, one of the opposition officers of the German General Staff. These warnings were no more effective in changing the policy of the Netherlands government than was the dramatic revelation of Germany's war-plan in the case of the Belgian government. On 10 January 1940 a German plane force-landed at Mechelen in Belgium; its two occupants were captured together with the plans of the forthcoming campaign through Belgian territory, which they had no time to destroy. Though the consequence was a more intensive effort by the Belgians to secure their defences, there was even then no further co-ordination with France, Britain and Holland.

Von Manstein's strategy, accepted by Hitler, departed from the principles of the 1914 Schlieffen Plan. It was to direct the main weight of German armour against a point, at Sedan, which was not covered by the Maginot Line (whose fortifications ended some distance to the east), and which was only weakly held since the French had considered a German attack impracticable—particularly with tanks—through the hilly and heavily wooded Ardennes. Further, the Germans realized that, if the Allied armies were to swing out in defence of Belgium and Holland, as they were certain to do once those countries had been attacked, the hinge of the movement would be at or near Sedan. To break the line at this point would therefore mean disrupting the whole Allied advance, while outflanking the Maginot Line and forcing its defenders to fight in reverse.

General Gamelin realized the disadvantages which the Allied armies would face if they were tempted out of their shell, as he put it,[1] and were obliged to conform to a war of movement which the Germans desired but for which the French were not prepared. However, the Dutch and Belgian armies would make a sizeable addition to the Allied forces, if only their staying power was adequate.

Numerically the Dutch army was slightly superior to the German invaders, but inferior in all other respects. Even the preparations to mine threatened bridges were inadequate, and many were captured intact. As in the case of Poland, the air force was immediately knocked out, and the combination of Stukas, tanks and motorized infantry was irresistible. Terror-bombing, notably of Rotterdam,

---

[1] A. Maurois: *Why France Fell* (Lane, 1940), 93. Gamelin was Commander-in-Chief of the Allied armies.

completed the confusion. After four days the Dutch Royal Family and government left for London, and military resistance ceased.

The German Invasion of Belgium and France

The Belgians were less successful than in 1914 in holding their frontier defences. After one day of fighting the fortress of Eben Emael was in German hands, and the Belgians were falling back on the Albert Canal. The Allied armies hurrying to their assistance tried to form a front from Antwerp to the Maginot Line, but the German advance could not be stemmed. While refugees crowded the roads and made organized troop movements difficult, the panzers were thrusting through at Sedan, outflanking the newly improvised line, and seizing bridgeheads across the Meuse. Even when the Allies fell back on the positions prepared during the winter of the 'phoney war' they were unable to stand. With the destruction of Corap's Ninth Army on their right they had no defensible flank, while on their left the Germans pressed heavily on the French forces around Antwerp and the roads to the Channel ports.

The British Expeditionary Force, which had begun with a meagre six divisions in September 1939, had now been reinforced to thirteen.[1] Although it held Arras and the surrounding area for several days, its position soon became untenable, and its commander, Lord Gort, was obliged to order its retreat on Dunkirk (25 May).

Before this decision was taken the French made an abortive effort at a counter-attack. The difficulty was to gather a last-minute strategic reserve in the south and co-ordinate its punch northwards with the B.E.F. and those French forces which were now virtually cut off in Belgium and Flanders. When Churchill went over to Paris to consult with the French government on 16 May he was dumbfounded to learn from General Gamelin that there was no strategic reserve. Gamelin was dismissed on the 19th, and General Weygand, who was rushed back from commanding the Army of the Levant, was put in his place. A further delay ensued while Weygand countermanded Gamelin's last order—already several days too late—to the effect that the northern armies should force their way back towards the Somme, while the French Second and newly-formed Sixth armies were to

[1] But no armoured division among them.—Liddell Hart, *The Listener*, 3 September 1964, 333.

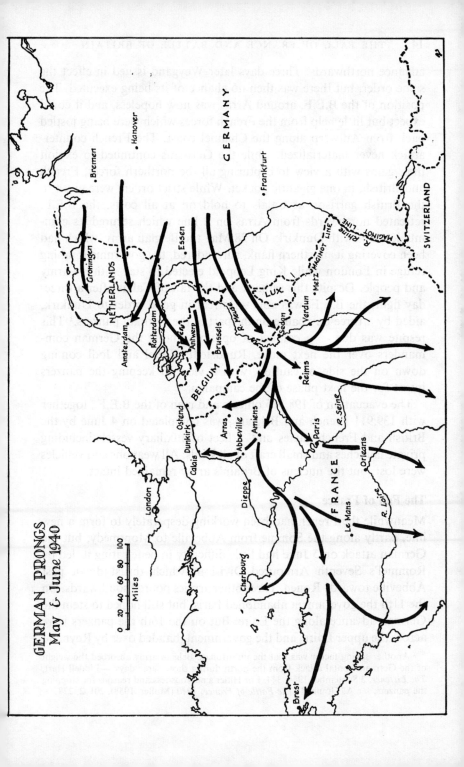

GERMAN PRONGS
May & June 1940

advance northwards. Three days later Weygand issued in effect the same order, but there was then no chance of its being executed. The position of the B.E.F. around Arras was now hopeless, and it could expect but little help from the French forces which were being jostled back from Antwerp along the Channel coast. The French counter-attack never materialized, while the Germans continued to exploit their gains with a view to capturing all the northern forces, French and British, in one gigantic pocket. While strict orders were given to the British garrison at Calais to hold on at all costs, the B.E.F. retreated northwards from Arras on a line which secured its communications with Dunkirk. On 28 May the Belgian army, which had been covering its northern flank, surrendered, the government taking refuge in London while King Leopold elected to stay with his army and people. Despite this setback and the fall of Calais after a three-day fight, the B.E.F. was able to retreat in good order to Dunkirk, aided by a three-day pause on the part of the German panzers.[1] This respite was due to a conflict of opinion among the German commanders over the next move, Rundstedt, Keitel and Jodl coming down on the side of caution, with a view to keeping the panzers intact for the next phase of the campaign.

The evacuation of 198,315 officers and men of the B.E.F., together with 139,911 French and Belgians, was completed on 4 June by the British and French navies and a fleet of auxiliary vessels including private launches and small craft of all kinds. All weapons and vehicles were lost, but the nucleus of Britain's army remained intact.

The Fall of France

Meanwhile the French had been working desperately to form a new line, partly along the Somme from Abbeville to Montmédy, but the German attack on 5 June had little difficulty in penetrating it, led by Rommel's Seventh Armoured Division, which thrust down past Abbeville towards Rouen. Three other armies poured southwards. On the 11th the government abandoned Paris, but still hoped to stem the German advance along the Loire. But on the 16th the panzers were across the upper Loire, and the government, handed over by Reynaud

[1] Another saving factor was that the unfortunate Belgian army absorbed the weight of the German frontal attack from the north during those same days'.—Liddell Hart, *The Listener*, 3 September 1964, 344. For Hitler's nervousness and reasons for stopping the panzers, see A. Goutard: *The Battle of France, 1940* (Muller, 1958), 201–2, 228.

to the 85-year-old Marshal Pétain, asked for an armistice on the following day. This was signed on the 22nd at Rethondes, stage-managed by Hitler in the same railway carriage where the German envoys had been obliged to sue for peace in November 1918. It was Hitler's hour of triumph, and he broke into a dance of joy.

Mussolini had waited until the issue was certain, and on 10 June launched his army against the French in the Alps, without, however, any success. Italy signed an armistice on June 25.

What were the reasons for the French defeat? These were partly material, partly moral. In terms of effectives, the Germans sent in 140 divisions against an Allied total of 121, if the weak and scarcely mobilized Belgian and Dutch armies are included.[1] In *matériel*, how-ever, the Allies were weaker, not so much in quantity of weapons (though this was the case in the air), but in quality. Although on paper the French had near-parity in tanks compared with the Ger-mans (2,400), the former were heavier and slower and were adapted for a different role to the panzers, that is, to aid the defence. They were split up into companies and even smaller sections, without the same integration which the Germans enjoyed with artillery and anti-tank weapons, and scattered along the entire front. 'As a result of this dispersal of potential strength, the entire Ninth Army on the vital Sedan sector possessed a total of three tank battalions to oppose the armoured corps of Guderian which alone boasted in excess of a thousand vehicles. The fault lay in dispersal, not "in hopeless numeri-cal inferiority".'[2] Guderian's comment was: 'the French tanks were better than ours in armour, guns and number, but inferior in speed, radio-communication and leadership. The concentration of all

[1] Royal Institute of International Affairs: *Survey of International Affairs 1939–46, The Initial Triumph of the Axis* (1958), 8.

[2] R. D. Challener in *Modern France* (ed. E. M. Earle, Princeton, 1951), 410. The figure does not include light reconnaissance tanks. Challener says: 'At most the Germans enjoyed a one-sixth superiority in armoured vehicles.' See also Capt. B. H. Liddell Hart: *The Other Side of the Hill* (Cassell, 1951 ed), 125. Challener's figures in his book *The French Theory of the Nation in Arms* (Columbia University 1955), 262, is that the French had '2262 modern tanks, 540 tanks of older models, and 743 armoured cars, while the Germans possessed 3,469 tanks'. He says, 'there was near-parity in much of the other equipment utilised by the ground forces'—though not in aircraft. He concludes that 'The French theory of war was as important a cause of defeat as material considera-tions or quantities of armament', especially the theory of the nation in arms, which, as applied, meant that no division could attain its war-strength without the recall of reserv-ists. All war plans were based on the assumption of delay in taking action—part of the general approach which was defensive, not offensive. (pp. 264 seq.)

armoured forces at the decisive spot, the rapid exploitation of success, and the initiative of the officers of all degrees were the main reasons for our victory in 1940.'[1]

The French strategic doctrine acted adversely on morale. 'The gunners settled down in the Maginot Line like apartment-house janitors, trailing about the corridors in slippers, playing innumerable games of cards under the silent guns, and with it all yawning from morning to night. . . . To dress men in uniform and then abandon them to inaction is a mockery. It is transforming war, a grand and terrible thing, into a masquerade.'[2] There were indeed examples of valour and heroic actions, there was a part of the Maginot Line whose defenders refused to surrender at the time of the armistice, but in general the French army had not the *élan*, the toughness, or the individual sense of responsibility that had been achieved on the German side.

Though the B.E.F. acquitted itself well, it was too small for the role which it had to undertake. As in 1914 it proved possible to build and train a small, efficient fighting force, but the British contribution, in terms of manpower, was so small as to be almost derisory. Having lost their weapons at Dunkirk the army was left with rifles, broomsticks and a handful of A.A. guns for the defence of Britain under threat of Nazi invasion. Had it not been for the navy and the R.A.F. —a minimum of twenty-five squadrons had been kept by Churchill out of the fighting in France—the fate of the island would have been sealed.

When it came to the Battle of Britain Göring was unable to translate his promises regarding the Luftwaffe into effect, but his Luftwaffe field-divisions, like the Waffen S.S. divisions of Himmler, did not show their weaknesses of training and leadership until the Russian campaign. The German commanders, officers and N.C.O.s showed all their accustomed flair, and the ordinary *Feldgrau* proved himself as outstanding a soldier as in previous wars. It was in this rather than in weight of *matériel* or superior strategy that the quality of the Wehrmacht told. As von Manstein put it: 'In the German Wehrmacht it had been found possible, with the help of the new means of warfare, to reacquire the true art of leadership in mobile operations. Indivi-

[1] Liddell Hart: *The Other Side of the Hill* (Cassell, 1948), 125.
[2] J. Dutourd: *The Taxis of the Marne* (Eng. trans. Secker and Warburg, 1957), 20, 22.

dual leadership was fostered on a scale unrivalled in any other army, right down to the most junior N.C.O. or infantryman, and in this lay the secret of our success.'[1]

While Gamelin was ineffective and often out of touch with General Georges, his commander in the field, and other subordinates, the politicians were divided among themselves. Reynaud carried on a bitter feud with Daladier (whom he ousted by one vote from the premiership on 18 March 1940), and Daladier could never agree with Herriot, the elder statesman of his own Radical-Socialist Party. Furthermore, as André Maurois has shown, both Reynaud and Daladier were under the influence of their respective mistresses, and this had an untoward effect at critical moments on their nerves and their decisions, and had a part in provoking their bitter rivalry. 'It is certain that the private lives of some of our statesmen impaired their public usefulness,' writes Maurois. . . . 'Few of these attached great importance to their sentimental or sensual intrigues; but events were to prove that these intrigues could nevertheless place nations in jeopardy. . . . The quarrels of the Ministers and the lack of any leader capable of imposing unity on the nation deprived the armies of their last chance.'[2]

Britain Alone

In Britain, essential unity was secured after Churchill's assumption of the premiership. Chamberlain continued with the leadership of the House of Commons and membership in the War Cabinet until his death in October. This War Cabinet of five, set up by Churchill on the model of Lloyd George's War Cabinet of 1916–18, consisted, besides Chamberlain, of Lord Halifax (Foreign Secretary), and the two Labour leaders, Clement Attlee and Arthur Greenwood. It was in constant touch with the service Ministers and the Chiefs of Staff. 'There was an integral direction of the war . . . (which) . . . soon settled into a very few hands. In spite of the turbulence of events and the many disasters we had to endure, the machinery worked almost automatically, and one lived in a stream of coherent thought capable of being translated with great rapidity into executive action.'[3]

[1] E. von Manstein: *Lost Victories* (Methuen, 1958), 63.
[2] *Why France Fell* (Lane, 1940), 67, 87.
[3] Churchill, op. cit., II., 16.

This was essential in dealing with the successive crises which broke
on the new administration—the breaching of the French line, the
defeat of Holland and Belgium, Dunkirk and the collapse of France.
Swift and painful decisions were necessary. Backed by a united
cabinet, Churchill made several visits to France. When he flew to
Tours on 13 June 1940, he could hardly find the French government,
so great was the disorganization. The British offer of common citizenship and complete unity, political and military, with which to confront Hitler and fight on from Africa and Britain, was spurned. As
the defeatist elements in the French government gained control, their
desire was to be free of all obligations to Britain. Not merely did they
abandon their agreement never to treat for a separate peace, but they
refused to move the government to Africa, or give adequate guarantees that the French navy would not be turned against Britain.

To neutralize those units of the French navy which were at Oran
in Algeria, Churchill ordered a squadron under Admiral Somerville
to enforce their removal either to British ports or a more distant
French port such as Martinique; or failing that they were to be destroyed. On the refusal of the French Admiral of these terms, the
British squadron opened fire: one battleship was blown up and two
others were beached (3 July, 1940). 'This was a hateful decision, the
most unnatural and painful in which I have ever been concerned.'
Churchill wrote later.[1] 'The French had been only yesterday our dear
Allies, and our sympathy for the misery of France was sincere. On
the other hand, the life of the State and the salvation of our cause
were at stake. It was Greek Tragedy.'

There was little time however for regrets. An intensive programme
was already being implemented to raise and arm a large army and the
auxiliary Home Guard, and to turn Britain into an impregnable
fortress. Meanwhile across the Channel there was a pause. Enemies
might be defeated, but supposing they failed to treat for peace? The
bitter experience of Napoleon at Boulogne or at Moscow might once
again be repeated with Hitler playing, even less adequately, the Na-
poleonic role. Hitler aspired to realize the dreams which had bemused

[1] Churchill, op. cit., II, 200. The battleship *Richelieu* at Dakar was also disabled. In
retrospect it can be said that this action did more harm than good, through the enormous bitterness it aroused in France, and the consequent difficulty in bringing about
co-operation with the French authorities in North Africa at the time of the landings
there in 1942—which for this reason had to be made under American auspices.

the German General Staff in the First World War. The first part of
this programme, outlined in *Mein Kampf*, had been carried out to the
letter, up to the elimination of France. For the next stage Hitler
envisaged an agreement between Germany and the British Empire
(that 'greatest political achievement of the Teutonic peoples'), whereby they should divide the world between them, Germany being then
free to smash Russia as she had smashed France and seize the living-
space in the Ukraine and elsewhere so necessary for the dynamic
Master-Race.

As for the fighting troops, they believed the war was over. A victory
parade in Paris was planned, after which demobilization was assumed.
Peace-feelers to Britain were put out. On 19 July 1940 Hitler proclaimed in the Reichstag: 'In this hour I feel it to be my duty before
my own conscience to appeal once more to reason and common sense
in Britain as much as elsewhere. I consider myself in a position to
make this appeal, since I am not a vanquished foe begging favours,
but the victor, speaking in the name of reason. I can see no reason
why this war need go on. I am grieved to think of the sacrifices it
must claim. . . . Possibly Mr Churchill will brush aside this statement of mine by saying it is merely born of fear and doubt of final
victory. In that case I shall have relieved my conscience in regard to
the things to come.'[1]

In fact the offer *was* brushed aside. It was not even deemed worthy
of a parliamentary debate, and before Lord Halifax rejected it in his
speech of 22 July, the British press and B.B.C. had scotched it 'without any prompting from His Majesty's Government'.[2]

Operation Sea-Lion

There was nothing for it but to bring matters to the test of a war for
which there were no adequate preparations. No plan had been made
for immediately exploiting the fall of France by pressing on with an
invasion of Britain while she was disorganized and virtually unarmed
—still better for initiating the assault on Britain while France was
reeling though not yet prostrate. June and July were largely wasted.
The Germans had no landing-craft; they had neither built the warships nor destroyed those of Britain on a sufficient scale to secure

[1] Quoted Churchill, op. cit., II, 229.   [2] Ibid., 230.

supremacy in the Channel even for the relatively brief period necessary to launch an invasion force, let alone for following it up with the
massive reinforcements and supplies which would be needed. All
Admiral Raeder could promise, and that rather dubiously, was the
establishment of a narrow sea-lane across the shortest line from the
French to the English coast, flanked by protecting minefields and
submarine supports. But even this could only be carried out if the
Royal Air Force were first destroyed and the Navy partially crippled,
since otherwise small craft covered from the air could tear the minefields apart and wreck the entire scheme—in consequence of which
the German army, as Raeder pointed out, might go to the bottom too.
Despite these pessimistic views Operation Sea-Lion was prepared by
the Germans, originally timed to be launched not later than 15
September, 1940.

The Battle of Britain

All depended on the Luftwaffe securing the mastery of the air. Göring
was ready to take on this task and win the laurels of success. The
offensive opened in mid-July, gaining momentum until by August the
Luftwaffe had 2,669 aircraft available—over a thousand bombers,
346 dive-bombers and 1,288 fighters. The operational aircraft in
Britain were less than half this number: 1,176, of which 501 were
bombers and 675 fighters, though over the period July to October the
average strength of the fighters on the opposing sides was much nearer
equality—the figures for British fighters being 980 compared with
1,200 for the Germans.[1] On the fighters the brunt of the battle fell,
since (though the bombers did good work on concentrations of German shipping and their communications), Göring's fleets of bombers
with fighter escort had mainly to be dealt with. The heaviest daylight
raid was attempted against the industrial districts of northern England
by a hundred bombers escorted by 40 Messerschmitt 110 fighters
(the faster 109s could not be used because of the distance), it being
assumed that the full fighter strength of the R.A.F. had already been
engaged in the south. But the seven Hurricane and Spitfire squadrons

[1] Churchill II, Appendix C, 644. As Churchill explains, fewer fighters were actually
available on both sides on any given day. *R.I.I.A. Survey, The Initial triumph of the
Axis* (1958), p. 13 gives figures: Germany 1,361 bombers, 1,308 fighters; Britain 471
bombers, 714 fighters. By October, the Germans lost 1,733 aircraft, The British 915.
(See also Snyder, 123.)

stationed at northern airfields for just such an emergency did deadly work—30 German planes were shot down; British losses were two pilots injured.[1]

Nonetheless the tide of battle swung against Britain from 24 August to 6 September, though the Germans failed to press their advantage by destroying the airfields of Fighter Command and the communications system on which it entirely depended. 466 fighters were destroyed with a loss of 231 pilots killed or wounded, for whom there were only inexperienced or partially trained replacements.

The Luftwaffe was, however, switched to night attacks on London and railway centres, giving Fighter Command a much-needed breathing-space. When the Germans made their culminating effort on 15 September they lost 56 planes against the R.A.F.'s loss of under 40.

Churchill records the scene on that day at No. 11 Group H.Q.

The Group Operations Room was like a small theatre. . . . We took our seats in the Dress Circle. Below us was the large-scale map-table, around which perhaps twenty highly-trained young men and women, with their telephone assistants, were assembled. Opposite to us, covering the entire wall, where the theatre curtain would be, was a gigantic blackboard divided into six columns with electric bulbs, for the six fighter stations, each of their squadrons having a sub-column of its own.

Presently the red bulbs showed that the majority of our squadrons were engaged. A subdued hum arose from the floor, where the busy plotters pushed their discs to and fro in accordance with the swiftly-changing situation. Air Vice-Marshal Park gave general directions for the disposition of his fighter force, which were translated into detailed orders to each Fighter Station by a youngish officer in the centre of the Dress Circle, at whose side I sat. . . . The Air Marshal himself walked up and down behind, watching with vigilant eye every move in the game, supervising his junior executive hand, and only occasionally intervening with some decisive order, usually to reinforce a threatened area. In a little while all our squadrons were fighting, and some had already begun to return for fuel. All were in the air. The lower line of bulbs was out. There was not one squadron left in reserve. At this

[1] The importance of radar in the defence of Britain is evaluated by Snyder (p. 123): 'A major factor in winning the Battle of Britain . . . was the development by a British team of physicists from Birmingham University of the resonant cavity magnetron, a new and powerful device that became the heart of all radar equipment.'
It should also be added that fighting in the R.A.F. were Polish, French, Czech and Belgian pilots.

moment Park spoke to Dowding at Stanmore, asking for three squadrons from No. 12 Group to be put at his disposal in case of another
major attack while his squadrons were rearming and refuelling. I now
asked: 'What other reserves have we?' 'There are none,' said Air Vice-
Marshal Park. In an account which he wrote about it afterwards he
said that at this I 'looked grave'. Well I might. What losses should we
not suffer if our refuelling planes were caught on the ground by further
raids of '40 plus' or '50 plus'! The odds were great; our margins small;
the stakes infinite.[1]

At the time Britain's victory was magnified, since German planes
shot down were claimed by more than one fighter, and the tonic
effect of the success (and of other air-battles) was therefore greater
than the real facts warranted. But in effect 15 September was decisive,
since two days later Hitler postponed 'Sea-Lion', the preliminary to
calling it off for the year and its abandonment in 1941. Göring did
not give up hope of a great air victory until 27 September, but thereafter

> though London received its full share, the German effort was spread
> by day and night in frequent small-scale attacks on many places.
> Concentration of effort gave way to dispersion; the battle of attrition
> began.[2]

Well could Churchill say, 'Never in the field of human conflict was
so much owed by so many to so few'.

For Hitler the war against Britain was something of a sideshow.
Only briefly he believed in the possibility of a knock-out blow against
the obdurate island. If she could not be knocked out her powers of
resistance might be nullified. After the postponement of 'Sea-Lion'
the blitz on London and other cities continued with full vigour.

The attack on Britain's communications at sea were intensified
though here Raeder complained that his requests for building up
strength, notably in submarines adequate to throttle Britain, were not
fully implemented. Hitler was never whole-hearted in the attempt to
bend Britain to his will. His real objectives lay in the east.[3]

---

[1] Churchill, II, 293–6.

[2] Churchill, II, 298.

[3] The flight of his deputy as Party leader, Rudolf Hess, to Scotland in May 1941,
when Hess gave himself up to the authorities in order to start negotiations, was a dramatic but purely personal initiative by Hess, disowned by Hitler, and was without consequences.

3: Hitler Prepares to Attack Russia

Scarcely had the armistice been signed with France than Hitler began preparations to attack Russia. At one moment in July 1940 he wished to leave Britain alone, and at once begin moving his forces to the east. He was dissuaded from this by the fact—as his advisers pointed out—that several months would have to elapse before the supply-lines and depots were ready in Poland, and the build-up of forces completed.

Negotiations with Franco and Pétain

While the attempt was made to bring Britain to her knees, the Führer entered on a phase of intense diplomatic activity, notably his interview with Franco on 23 October and with Pétain the following day. The aim was to thwart Britain's access to the Mediterranean from the west by a combined German–Spanish attack on Gibraltar, and go on to occupy the Azores, Canaries, Madeira and the Cape Verde group of islands, and so deny them to the British as a possible jumping-off point for a further attack. But Franco, who had brought the Spanish Civil War to a conclusion only in 1939 was in no mood for further adventures, besides being impressed by the reality of Britain's continued resistance. The price he asked was too high for Hitler, who found himself for the first time worsted in an encounter with a fellow-dictator.

The demands of Franco to which Hitler did not wish to accede concerned transfers of Morocco and other French African territory to Spain. Hitler did not want to antagonize the government of Vichy France, since he wished France to enter his 'new order' as the defender of North Africa against Britain. In his talks with Hitler at Montoire, Pétain made promises to Hitler in this sense, but with little intention of fulfilling them—'it will take six months to discuss this programme,' he is reported to have said, 'and another six months to forget it.'[1]

Ten days previously (4 October) Hitler had met Mussolini on the

---

[1] Quoted in A. Bullock: *Hitler* (Odhams, 1964), 606.

Brenner, and explained his strategy (to which the Duce objected) of winning over France. No word had passed then of Italy's Balkan aspirations. In a last effort to assert an independent policy, Mussolini ordered the attack on Greece for 28 October. This action, undertaken 'not merely without Hitler's agreement, but in flat contradiction of his wishes . . . was an event which affected the whole future of the war'.[1]

Italy Attacks Greece

For the time being this diversion did not affect preparations for 'Barbarossa', the code-name for the attack on Russia. At this point Hitler threw over the shrewder strategy outlined in *Mein Kampf*, to oppose Russia only when Germany should have her hands free in the west. While intensifying the preparations against Russia, Hitler still hoped to secure an outlying glacis against Britain and against possible American intervention by persuading Franco to agree to implement the proposed plan for Gibraltar and the Atlantic islands in the winter of 1940–1. But Franco's caution was strengthened by the successful counter-attack of the Greeks against the Italians, and the British thrust against the Duce's forces in North Africa (December 1940). The original plan of barring the western approaches to the Mediterranean had to be abandoned after the British advances had brought them to Benghazi, with the capture of an entire Italian army 113,000 strong (6 February 1941).

The consequence of the Italian attack on Greece was the implementation of the British guarantee to that country given in April 1939. While the able strategy of General Papagos and the fighting spirit of his troops secured the defeat of the Italians, and even the capture of the Italian base at Koritza in Albania (22 November), a British Mission and some token forces were sent to their support. Most important, Suda Bay in Crete was turned over to the British navy as a base. This might eventually prove a threat to the German flank in the Balkans, which Hitler was in process of strengthening in preparation for his attack on Russia.

[1] Bullock, page 606. Mussolini wrote to Hitler on 19 October while Hitler was on his visits to Franco and Pétain, and the letter 'seems to have followed him around. When he received it he proposed a meeting in Florence for the 28th, but the attack on Greece began that morning.' (Churchill, II, 471.)

Hitler Secures Control of Rumania, Hungary, Bulgaria

Rumania, which had rejected the British guarantee offered by Chamberlain in April 1939, had since moved closer into the German orbit. She had been obliged to cede Bessarabia and the Northern Bukovina to Russia in July 1940, and was ready to accept a German guarantee, with a promise of 12 divisions to implement it. At the same time she suffered a severe blow in the amputation of most of Transylvania and its transfer to Hungary under terms dictated by Ribbentrop at Vienna (August 1940). The national resentment was however directed against King Carol, who was forced to abdicate in favour of his son Michael, while General Antonescu, a strong pro-Nazi, became Prime Minister and virtual dictator. Thereafter Rumania was an obedient satellite, providing Germany with its coveted oil, and serving as a base for the build-up of the forces destined for the invasion of Greece.

On accepting German support in her claims on Rumania, Hungary was firmly tied to Germany. Over Bulgaria a fierce diplomatic conflict was waged with Russia, which determined Hitler more firmly than ever to persist in the aim of eliminating Russia as a factor in European affairs. Hitler demurred to Molotov's request that Russia should guarantee Bulgaria, as an equivalent to Germany's guarantee to Rumania, and succeeded in checkmating the Russian attempts to secure a decisive influence over Bulgaria's affairs. On 28 February 1941 German forces entered Bulgaria from Rumania.

Hitler Crushes Yugoslavia and Greece

To complete his communications with Greece, Yugoslavia had also to be brought into line. Here Hitler expected to win again by diplomacy rather than force. Even before the war Yugoslavia under the Regent Paul had been drifting into the German orbit. Now, in February and March 1941, it was not difficult to persuade the Regent and his government to line up with Germany in the Pact of Vienna, in return for the bribe of Salonika, which was to be wrested from Greece. But the government reckoned without the spirit of the people. With wide popular backing, a group of officers expelled the Regent and his ministers, and seized power in the name of the 17-year-old Peter II.

Hitler's wrath was terrible. Without waiting to see whether he could secure his ends by less violent methods, he determined 'to destroy Yugoslavia militarily and as a national unit',[1] and to that end postpone the start of the campaign against Russia for a period of up to four weeks. Eleven days later, on 5 April, German forces crossed the frontiers while the Luftwaffe began a three-day blitz designed to destroy utterly the capital, Belgrade. This was 'Operation Punishment', which Hitler ordered to be carried out with 'merciless harshness'.

With Yugoslavia in his grasp, Hitler's way was clear for the attack on Greece. Despite the hurried despatch of New Zealand troops and some further R.A.F. support, the Nazi tide could not be stemmed. By 27 April 1941, the Germans were in Athens. The King and government had fled to Egypt. About half the British forces got away, being evacuated from various of the smaller ports, many of them to Crete.

The Seizure of Crete

Churchill later complained that Crete had not been adequately fortified during the period since November 1940 when the navy had occupied Suda Bay, but the difficulties of withstanding the airborne attack which the Germans mounted on 20 May were probably too great in any case for the meagre British forces in the Mediterranean. German seaborne forces were severely mauled by the navy—at the cost of two cruisers and three destroyers sunk, and the battleship *Warspite* and other units severely damaged.

The Italian navy was immobilized in consequence of Admiral Cunningham's air–sea attack on Taranto of 11 November 1940, when three battleships had been torpedoed and much other damage done. But without adequate air defence—Crete being too far for support from Britain's air bases in North Africa, while covered from German airfields in Greece—the island could not be held against a massive attack by an airborne army. German losses were severe, but those troops who succeeded in landing were able to seize Maleme airport, through which their strength could be built up for ousting the rest of the British defence. By 27 May the operation was completed. Sixteen thousand and five hundred British Imperial troops were evacuated, more than half the force.

Though General Student, director of the air operations, pressed

[1] Quoted in Bullock, 635.

Hitler for further such attacks on Cyprus, the Suez Canal and later on Malta,[1] Hitler had no intention of becoming too involved in the Mediterranean or Middle East. Just before the attack on Yugoslavia, Hitler authorized an armoured division under Rommel to be sent to North Africa to bolster the Italian position. With a surprise offensive brilliantly executed, Rommel had by 12 April driven the British out of Cyrenaica and was within a few miles of the Egyptian frontier. But the reinforcements for a decisive blow were denied him, since Hitler was determined to launch 'Barbarossa' at the latest on 22 June. That date had been long enough postponed on account of the operations in the Balkans and Crete—too long, as the event showed, to make it possible to fell the Russian giant before winter intervened in defence of Moscow and Leningrad.

[1] Liddell Hart: *The Other Side of the Hill*, 243.

4: The Invasion of Russia

Russia Tries to Keep the Peace

At dawn on 22 June 1941, 164 divisions of German and satellite troops moved across the Russian frontier. On the Russian side everything had been done to maintain the relations which had been established by the Soviet–German Agreement of August 1939, and so avert the threatened blow. On the German side the deception of friendly relations had been continued—deliveries of German goods under the Agreement had been kept up until almost the last moment. The Russians punctiliously honoured their side of it in this respect until the invasion began. Hitler may have been right in fearing that one day the Russians might attack; but on 22 June their armies were drawn up in purely defensive positions.

Like the Western governments, Stalin feared to provoke Hitler or give him an excuse for attack. He believed war with Germany was inevitable, but hoped to postpone it at least till the following year.[1] Even after the panzers had crossed the frontier he and Molotov were still making futile attempts to contact Berlin in order to negotiate.

The German Attack

The Germans had signally underestimated the Russians' fighting qualities and equipment, based on the poor showing of the Soviet army in Finland.[2] They did not realize that they had nearly 1,000 T-34 tanks, 'at that time the best fighting tank in existence'.[3] Nonetheless

[1] A. Werth: *Russia at War 1941–1945* (Barrie and Rockliff, 1964), 122–3.

[2] There were good grounds for much of the German estimates. 'The drafts assigned to formations in the frontier areas lacked "even basic training" in the use of weapons they would employ. Not one of the basic measures of reform and re-organization had been completed among the troops stationed in the frontier districts. . . . The Red Army had not yet recovered from the effects of the purge. . . .' J. Erickson: *The Soviet High Command 1918–1941* (Macmillan 1962), 579 seq.

[3] Colonel-General Sepp Dietrich, quoted M. Shulman: *Defence in the West* (Secker and Warburg, 1947), 63. Dietrich's figure of 2,000 is wrong. The T-34's had only begun to arrive in the frontier districts shortly before the invasion. All the up-to-date planes and most of the older ones were destroyed on the ground. On these points and others connected with Russian unpreparedness, see Werth, 131 seq. Werth also stresses the

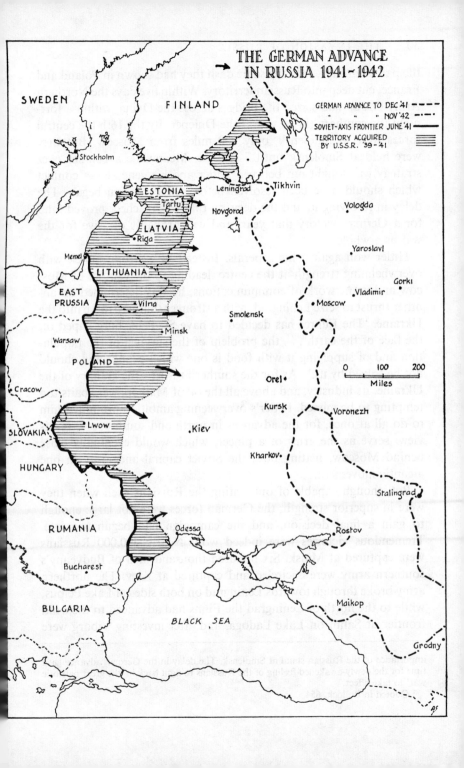

THE GERMAN ADVANCE
IN RUSSIA 1941~1942

GERMAN ADVANCE TO DEC '41 — — —
     "   "   " NOV '42 —·—·—
SOVIET-AXIS FRONTIER JUNE '41 ———
TERRITORY ACQUIRED
BY U.S.S.R. '39 - '41

SWEDEN

FINLAND

Stockholm

ESTONIA
Tartu

Leningrad   Tikhvin

Novgorod

Vologda

LATVIA
Riga

Yaroslavl

Memel

Gorki

LITHUANIA

Vladimir   • Moscow

EAST
PRUSSIA
Vilna

Smolensk

Warsaw   • Minsk

0   100   200
Miles

POLAND

Orel •

Cracow

Kursk •   Voronezh

Lwow

Kiev

SLOVAKIA

Kharkov •

HUNGARY

Stalingrad

RUMANIA   Odessa   Rostov

Bucharest

Maikop

BULGARIA   BLACK   SEA

Grodny

AS

the panzer groups, with the same dash they had shown in Poland and France, cut deep into Russian territory. Within five days the Northern Army Group had seized the bridges across the Dvina, within a fortnight the southern thrust was at the Dnieper. By the 16th the central forces were at Smolensk, only 200 miles from Moscow. But they were held at Smolensk until 7 August. Meanwhile a conflict over strategy was fought out between Hitler and his generals—a conflict which should have been resolved before the campaign began. The delay in resolving it, and the decision that was reached, proved fatal for a German victory that year, and was probably decisive for the war as a whole.

Hitler won against his generals. Instead of a strong punch with overwhelming strength at the centre, leading to the capture of Moscow and its network of communications, he was determined on another thrust to seize Leningrad, with a stronger southern drive into the Ukraine. 'The Führer has decided to have St. Petersburg wiped off the face of the earth . . . the problem of the survival of the population and of supplying it with food is one which cannot and should not be solved by us.'[1] As for the southern thrust—the granary of the Ukraine, its industry, and above all the oil of Maikop, were baits too tempting to be missed. Hitler's overweening ambition prompted him to do all at once, for the advances in north and south could, in his view, serve as the arms of a pincer, which would eventually close behind Moscow, netting both the Soviet capital and army in one gigantic movement.

But, though capable of outfighting the Russians even when they were in superior strength, the German forces were not large enough to gain a final decision, and the campaign had begun too late. Tremendous victories were indeed won. Nearly 300,000 Russians were captured at Minsk. Six hundred thousand men of Budyenny's southern army were encircled and captured at Kiev. The northern army broke through towards Leningrad on both sides of Lake Peipus, while to the north of Leningrad the Finns had advanced to their old frontier at Salmi on Lake Ladoga, and after investing Viborg were

---

importance of the Russian stand at Smolensk. The delay in the German advance gave time for the newly-awakened feeling of the Russians to fight back in 'the great patriotic war' to take effect.

[1] Quoted in Bullock, 654.

working their way along the western shores of the lake. By 20 August Leningrad was in imminent danger.

The Failure Before Moscow

But failure to concentrate at any one point jeopardized the Germans' chances. Von Bock's central army was reinforced at the beginning of October. Though another 'Cannae' was brought off around Vyasma and Bryansk with the capture of 600,000 Russians, Bock's strength was not sufficient for an encirclement of Moscow, or a successful assault on it, in the face of growing Russian concentration and fierce resistance. At the same time von Leeb in the north was instructed to capture Leningrad and link up with the Finns, while von Rundstedt was to clear the Crimea and advance beyond Rostov to the Caucasus. Rundstedt and his staff laughed in amazement at these orders, 'for winter had already come and we were almost seven hundred kilometres from these cities'.[1]

On the rest of the front also winter came earlier than had been expected. The autumn rains had slowed the advance; to the mud was added the snow, on the night of 6–7 October. Driven on by von Bock, who desired to emulate the successes in the south, the troops struggled forward to within a few miles of the almost beleaguered city.

> On December 2nd von Bock ordered a third and last effort. It carried the attackers at the furthest point to within the very suburbs of the city. The towers and eagles of the Kremlin gleamed against the leaden sky before the eyes of the weary, battling German *Feldgrauen*. But the Russian workers poured out of their factories and fought in defence of the Holy City of the Revolution with sledge-hammers and even with bare fists. The tide turned back upon itself. . . . The Battle of Moscow had been fought and lost, the field-grey columns turned sullenly westwards, never again as free men to come within sight of the Kremlin towers.[2]

On 6 December the Russian counter-offensive under Marshal Zhukov began. Though, after some confusion and wavering, the Germans held their line, they were beaten back at several points. The threat to Moscow was averted.

[1] Quoted in Bullock, 655.
[2] J. Wheeler-Bennett, *The Nemesis of Power* (Macmillan, 1953), 522.

5: Anglo-American Strategy and the War at Sea

America and the War

The failure of the German attack on Moscow took place at the same time as another decisive event. At the moment when, on 7 December, the Russian counter-attack at Moscow was developing, aircraft of the Japanese fleet came out of the morning mists of the Pacific to bombard the American fleet at Pearl Harbour.

Hitler had long been attempting to bring the Japanese into the war, but against Britain, not the U.S.A. As a member of the Tripartite Pact, Japan was engaged to come into the war only if her partners were the victims of aggression. However, approving the blitz tactics of the Japanese, and without much further reflection, Hitler at once declared war on America. He had realised that an ultimate confrontation with her as the ally of Britain was almost inevitable, but his failure to delay this event was due, in large part, to his complete under-estimate of the forces which America could bring to bear. He was also exasperated by the fact that America was already virtually at war without having declared it. America was thereby brought into Europe, and after the war it was clear that she had come to stay.

For some time America had been Britain's ally in all respects short of shooting—and even some shooting had already occurred. Slowly President Roosevelt had weaned America from isolation, aided by the spectacular success of Hitler, and the growing realization among Americans that Britain constituted their first line of defence against the German peril. They could not afford to sit by while Britain was under heavy attack, or was being threatened with strangulation by the U-boats. With this as the dominant mood in America in the autumn of 1940, Roosevelt was able to carry through the deal whereby 50 destroyers of the First World War were handed to Britain in exchange for 99-year leases by America of bases in the West Indies (September 1940). This was followed in March 1941 by the Lend-

Lease Act, at a time when Britain's assets for purchasing war-goods and supplies on the 'cash-and-carry' basis[1] were running down—in effect a blank cheque for as big a draft as Britain wished to make. For Britain in her hour of need it was, as Churchill described it, 'the most unsordid act in the history of any nation'.[2]

The Defence of Britain's Sea-lanes

At the time of the Battle of France British war-time imports reached their maximum, but thereafter they fell off as sinkings of British merchantmen increased. The Germans had their bases for submarines and surface raiders all along the coasts from the North Cape to the Bay of Biscay, and the French Navy was no longer working with the British to safeguard the vital routes. 'The only thing that ever really frightened me during the war,' wrote Churchill, 'was the U-boat peril.'[3] Without the Southern Irish bases, given up only a year before the war, it was increasingly difficult to provide adequate escorts for convoys across the breadth of the Atlantic, or air cover against the Focke-Wulfs. Losses rose to a peak during the week ending 22 September 1940, when they exceeded those of the darkest period in 1917 during the First World War.

It was with the greatest relief therefore that the British government welcomed the steady extension eastwards of the American 'Security Zone'. In April 1941 it was extended to a line drawn along the meridian of 20° west, which thus became 'the virtual sea frontier of the United States'.[4] Britain had already occupied Iceland at the time of the German invasion of Denmark, while Canada had established a base in Newfoundland and the Americans in Greenland. In July 1941 the Americans took over the Iceland base, and thereafter escorted convoys, including British and other non-American ships, as far as Reykjavik, an arrangement which gave relief to Britain equivalent to over 60 destroyers and corvettes.[5]

[1] By the Neutrality Act of May 1937, the President could authorise the export of goods—but not arms and ammunition—to a belligerent who could ship and pay for them.

[2] In Parliament, quoted Churchill, II, 503.   [3] Churchill, II, 529.

[4] Churchill, III, 122.   [5] Churchill, III, 399.

The Atlantic Charter

In August 1941 the historic meeting of Churchill and Roosevelt took place at Placentia Bay, Newfoundland.

> As soon as the customary naval courtesies had been exchanged I went aboard the *Augusta* and greeted President Roosevelt, who received me with all honours. He stood supported by the arm of his son Elliott while the National Anthems were played, and then gave me the warmest of welcomes. . . .
> On Sunday morning, August 10th, Mr. Roosevelt came aboard H.M.S. *Prince of Wales* and, with his Staff officers and several hundred representatives of all ranks of the United States Navy and Marines, attended Divine Service on the quarterdeck. This service was felt by us all to be a deeply moving expression of the unity of faith of our two peoples, and none who took part in it will forget the spectacle presented that sunlit morning on the crowded quarterdeck—the symbolism of the Union Jack and the Stars and Stripes draped side by side on the pulpit; the American and British chaplains sharing in the reading of the prayers; the highest naval, military, and air officers of Britain and the United States grouped in one body behind the President and me; the close-packed ranks of British and American sailors, completely intermingled, sharing the same books and joining fervently together in the prayers and hymns familiar to both.[1]

The fruit of this meeting was the publication of the Atlantic Charter,[2] and the closest co-ordination of the two forces that was possible within the limits of their not yet being Allies.

> The profound and far-reaching importance of this Joint Declaration was apparent. The fact alone of the United States, still technically neutral, joining with a belligerent Power in making such a declaration was astonishing. The inclusion in it of a reference to 'the final destruction of the Nazi tyranny' . . . amounted to a challenge which in ordinary times would have implied war-like action.[3]

The War at Sea, 1941–3

In fact America was already practically a belligerent on the side of Britain. In October 1941 there were two engagements between them and the U-boats, in the latter of which an American destroyer was sunk and a hundred of her crew lost.[4]

---

[1] Churchill, III, 383–4.
[3] Churchill, III, 394.
[2] See note at end of chapter.
[4] Bullock, 662.

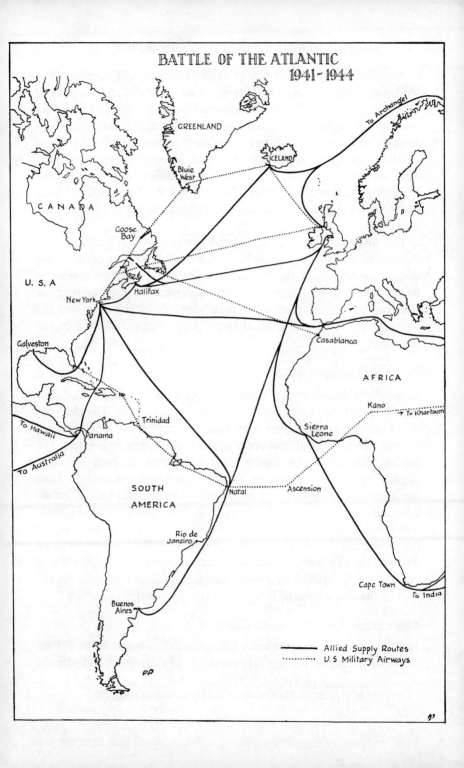

BATTLE OF THE ATLANTIC
1941~1944

GREENLAND

ICELAND

To Archangel

Bluie
West

CANADA

Goose
Bay

U. S. A

New York

Halifax

Galveston

Casablanca

AFRICA

Kano

To Khartoum

To Hawaii

Panama

Trinidad

Sierra
Leone

To Australia

SOUTH
AMERICA

Natal

Ascension

Rio de
Janeiro

Cape Town

To India

Buenos
Aires

—— Allied Supply Routes
········ U.S Military Airways

America's entry into the war as a full participant in December 1941 led before long to a vast stepping-up of war-material and supplies of all kinds, not only to Britain but also to Russia, but for the time being the sinking of Allied shipping continued to increase heavily. From January to June 1942 sinkings were nearly as heavy as for the whole of 1941, and exceeded the entire Allied ship-building programme.[1] Though the acceleration of American shipbuilding led to their balancing current losses with new shipping by May 1942, U-boat depredations were not brought adequately under control until a year later.

The long struggle was prolonged because the American navy delayed in establishing convoys in the Caribbean and other areas, despite the lessons of the North Atlantic. Also the Allies developed heavy bombing of Germany at the expense of air protection for shipping—a serious mistake in that 'shortage of shipping was the controlling factor in all allied strategic purposes almost to the end of the war'[2].

Conflicts Over Strategy

In principle Roosevelt and Churchill were agreed to finish the European war first, but events placed this decision in doubt. The chiefs of the American armed forces were eager to strike an immediate blow against Germany, and believed it could best be done in Europe. The British temporized, fearful of losing American support for their position in the Mediterranean. They were not strong enough to force the Americans' hand, though in 1942 they could block a cross-Channel operation, since the brunt of it, in manpower and shipping, would have fallen on them, in view of the lapse of time required for the American build-up to become effective. But British prestige declined in the months between Pearl Harbour and Alamein, a decline which resulted in a corresponding lack of readiness on the part of the Americans to listen to British proposals.

Japan Seizes Europe's Pacific Colonies

The feebleness of the resources left to Britain wherewith to defend her eastern Empire was quickly revealed. The Japanese had already

---

[1] Churchill, IV, 176.
[2] S. W. Roskill: *The Strategy of Sea-power* (Collins 1962), 180.

established themselves in Indo-China after the fall of France. After Pearl Harbour they rapidly subdued Hong-Kong, and worked their way down the Malayan Peninsula with a weight of air support and a driving-power completely unexpected by their opponents. On 10 December 1941 the crack battleship *Prince of Wales* and the modernized battle-cruiser *Repulse* were sunk by air attack in Malayan waters, and by the end of January 1942 the Japanese were at Johore, facing the landward side of Singapore. As an attack had never been envisaged from that side by the planners of the multi-million base, it was left practically open and exposed. Its few and mostly obsolete planes had little chance against the Japanese, and after a week of fighting Singapore surrendered with over 100,000 men (15 February).

India was in turmoil with Gandhi and other leaders demanding immediate independence; with the Japanese striking north through Burma and apparently poised for attack on Ceylon,[1] India's future seemed to be in doubt. In the Middle East, Rommel, despite reverses, was still installed in Libya, and though the Italian East African empire had been liquidated by the British and South Africans, the nightmare of a link-up between Germans and Japanese in the neighbourhood of Suez haunted British minds. Forced out of Wake Island and the Philippines, the Americans had their own embarrassments in the Pacific, and were unable to do much to help the Dutch with the remnants of British and Australian forces in the defence of the East Indies. The fate of these was decided by the destruction of the Allied fleet (Dutch, British, Australian, American) in the battle off Sourabaya (26 February 1942).

The Machinery of the Anglo-American Alliance

During these darkest hours the Anglo-American Alliance as an effective instrument of victory was strengthened by the growing friendship and trust between Roosevelt and Churchill. There was no greater contrast to this relationship than the 'brutal friendship' between Hitler and Mussolini, the Führer's bullying, the Duce's cringing, and the deceptions which the two practised on each other. Soon after Pearl Harbour Churchill spent three weeks with Roosevelt at the White House (with a brief visit to Canada) and during this period the meeting of minds became complete.

[1] In fact the Japanese were in doubt what to do next.

This unity at the top tided the Alliance over the crucial period of mid-1942 when divergent views between the American and British Chiefs of Staffs nearly led to a breakdown in the joint prosecution of the war. Thereafter the united war-effort of the two powers got into its stride. The Chiefs of Staffs themselves became an integrated body, forging policy in the Combined Chiefs of Staffs Committee, usually meeting in Washington, though also at the regular high-level conferences at Casablanca, Quebec and elsewhere. When at Washington, the British Chiefs of Staff were represented by the Joint Staff Mission under Field-Marshal Sir John Dill, until his death in November 1944.

These representatives were in daily, indeed hourly, touch with London, and were thus able to state and explain the views of the British Chiefs of Staff to their U.S. colleagues on any and every war problem at any time of the day or night. . . . Decisions once reached and approved by the Heads of Governments were pursued by all with perfect loyalty. . . . There was never a failure to reach effective agreement for action, or to send clear instructions to the commanders in every theatre. Every executive officer knew that the orders he received bore with them the combined conception and expert authority of both Governments. There never was a more serviceable war machinery established among allies.[1]

But it proved impracticable to have a Russian representative on this body. 'Effective contact with Russia relied, in fact, entirely on Heads of Government. . . . The absence of effective machinery [reflected] in part the impotence of all Russian authorities but the very highest.'[2]

This unity of organization presupposed a unity of aim, and took some time to secure. The Chiefs of Staffs had first to thrash out strategy in their separate British and American joint committees before the process could be completed in the combined Chiefs of Staff Committee where a single master-strategy was forged for the Alliance as a whole. In the British Joint Staffs Committee the Prime Minister and his Chiefs had first to achieve unity before their findings could be brought forward by the British representatives at Washing-

[1] Churchill, III, 608–9. Sir Alan Brooke, the Chief of the Imperial General Staff, also came to regard the organization as 'the most efficient that had ever been evolved for co-ordinating and correlating the war strategy and effort of two allies'. [Quoted in A. Bryant: *The Turn of the Tide* (Collins, 1957), 316.]

[2] J. Ehrman: *Grand Strategy, History of the Second World War*, Vol. 5, ed. J. R. M. Butler (H.M.S.O., 1956), 24.

ton—'though the Prime Minister constantly strove to persuade [the Chiefs of Staff] to adopt his strategic views, and brought to bear on them all his remarkable powers of oratory, invective and persuasion, he would never overrule the Chiefs of Staff's unanimous opinion on any purely military matter'.[1] The contrast with Hitler and his harassed generals is striking.

Roosevelt, too, allowed a large freedom to his own Chiefs of Staff, though as Commander-in-Chief of the American forces he had the final say. It was his decision which determined the pattern for the grand strategy of the Allies throughout the war. For the first seven months of 1942 this decision had not been taken. While General Marshall and his American colleagues clung to the idea of a major stroke on the continent that very year, such as the seizure of Cherbourg and the Cotentin, the British were equally clear that the right move was in North Africa. But this was precisely the area where British prestige sank abysmally. After a forward move to Benghazi in November 1941, General Auchinleck was forced to retreat to Gazala and Bir Hacheim (covering Tobruk) in January 1942.

The Decision for North Africa

Cut off from the support which could have come from air bases at Benghazi or further west, Malta now had to submit to its hardest ordeal. Supplies for the garrison and population were running out, and there was the greatest difficulty in delivering fighter planes and munitions. Axis air superiority over the central Mediterranean meant that Allied convoys could scarcely be run any longer, whether from east or west. Of 17 ships despatched in June 1942, only two reached harbour. The garrison was down to half rations and the plight of the island was desperate. Conversely the essential supply convoys for Rommel were arriving regularly, since Allied light naval forces were no longer able to deny him this route from their base in Malta.

Before Auchinleck had finished his build-up in the desert, Rommel attacked at the end of May. Frustrated at first, he withdrew into a bridgehead which thrust into the British defence-system. He sprang forward again early in June, finally worsting the British in the tank battles around the 'Knightsbridge' communications centre.

At this point Churchill paid his second war-time visit to America,

[1] Bryant, op. cit., 320.

discussing among other things how to develop work on the atomic bomb. He was at the White House when 'a telegram was put into the President's hands. He passed it to me without a word. It said, "Tobruk has surrendered with twenty-five thousand men" (the figure being later revised to 33,000). . . . I did not attempt to hide from the President the shock I had received. It was a bitter moment.'[1] Surprise and consternation were great that this fort, which had recently stood a six months' siege, had so suddenly fallen.

North Africa was clearly the focus. While the Americans at once despatched 300 Sherman tanks and a hundred self-propelled guns to Egypt, the British retreat to Alamein was completed, and there Rommel was held, only 70 miles from Alexandria. His effort had at least diverted Axis strength from Malta, which held on successfully. But even with the necessity of seeking a decision in North Africa the American chiefs were not convinced of turning it into a major theatre until July. Doubtful of British morale and intentions, those who had always hankered after giving the war in the Pacific priority pressed their views with renewed vigour. It was only Roosevelt's decision in mid-July which determined the issue—'a decision to try once more to make the alliance effective in action. Seldom in history has a choice so important for the fate of nations and peoples presented itself so sharply, so urgently, so personally'.[2] Everything was to be subordinated to a dual thrust in North Africa, by the British from Egypt and the Americans from Morocco. It was at about the same time that Stalin made the equally momentous decision to hold Stalingrad, which was the turning-point on the eastern front.

The same midsummer of 1942 saw the turning-point of the war in the Pacific, when on 4th June at the Battle of Midway four of Japan's aircraft carriers were sunk. But in the Atlantic and the Arctic Ocean the sea-lanes were still in jeopardy. In the week of 7–14 July 400,000 tons of Allied shipping were sunk, a rate of losses which was more than double that at which they could be made up. After 23 ships out of 34 had been sunk in the convoy P.Q. 17 from Iceland to Archangel early in July, Churchill cancelled these convoys until September.

It was not until May of the following year that the U-boat menace was reduced to manageable proportions, after tremendous efforts by

[1] Churchill, IV, 343, 344.
[2] R.I.I.A. Survey, America, Britain and Russia, 1941–6, 194.

the Allies (early in 1943 the Germans sunk 96 ships in 20 days). The tide was turned by bringing five 'Atlantic Support Groups' into action against the submarines, including escort carriers of a new type. These were able, in particular, to fill the 'air gap' south of Greenland. The Support Groups 'were controlled from the headquarters of the Western Approaches Command at Liverpool, and as soon as a threat appeared to be developing against a particular convoy one or more of them was sent to reinforce its escort'.[1] The Germans lost 41 U-boats during May, and on the 23rd withdrew the rest of them from the Atlantic battle-ground. In December 1943 Grand Admiral Dönitz admitted that 'the enemy has rendered the U-boat war ineffective', but the long delay in achieving this result made it impracticable to open the 'Second Front' in France, so urgently demanded by the Russians, before 1944.

NOTE

THE ATLANTIC CHARTER
JOINT DECLARATION BY THE PRESIDENT AND THE PRIME MINISTER
August 12, 1941

The President of the United States of America and the Prime Minister, Mr. Churchill, representing His Majesty's Government in the United Kingdom, being met together, deem it right to make known certain common principles in the national policies of their respective countries on which they base their hopes for a better future for the world.

First, their countries seek no aggrandisement, territorial or other.

Second, they desire to see no territorial changes that do not accord with the freely expressed wishes of the peoples concerned.

Third, they respect the right of all peoples to choose the form of government under which they will live; and they wish to see sovereign rights and self-government restored to those who have been forcibly deprived of them.

Fourth, they will endeavour, with due respect to their existing obligations, to further the enjoyment by all States, great or small, victor or

[1] S. W. Roskill: *The Strategy of Sea Power* (Collins, 1962), 195.
'The main explanation of this sucess lay in the use of radar-equipped search planes which were able to harass U-boats when they lay on the surface recharging their batteries.'—*R.I.I.A. Survey* 1941–6, 220. See also Churchill, V, 11; Roskill: *The War at Sea*, (History of the Second World War, H.M.S.O., 1960), 37 seq., and (in the same series) *Grand Strategy*, V, 3.

vanquished, of access, on equal terms, to the trade and to the raw materials of the world which are needed for their economic prosperity.

Fifth, they desire to bring about the fullest collaboration between all nations in the economic field, with the object of securing for all improved labour standards, economic advancement, and social security.

Sixth, after the final destruction of the Nazi tyranny they hope to see established a peace which will afford to all nations the means of dwelling in safety within their own boundaries, and which will afford assurance that all the men in all the lands may live out their lives in freedom from fear and want.

Seventh, such a peace should enable all men to traverse the high seas and oceans without hindrance.

Eighth, they believe that all the nations of the world, for realistic as well as spiritual reasons, must come to the abandonment of the use of force. Since no future peace can be maintained if land, sea, or air armaments continue to be employed by nations which threaten, or may threaten, aggression outside of their frontiers, they believe, pending the establishment of a wider and more permanent system of general security, that the disarmament of such nations is essential. They will likewise aid and encourage all other practicable measures which will lighten for peace-loving peoples the crushing burden of armaments.

6: The War in Russia, 1941-4

Hitler and the Winter War 1941-2

Though the vast Allied effort to supply Russia gradually had its effect, it had no decisive influence on the events of the winter of 1941-2.[1] At Moscow and elsewhere along the front the Russians had the advantage of shorter supply lines, and of equipment and clothing for a winter campaign. In these the Germans were almost entirely lacking. With amazing perversity, Hitler had persisted right up to December 1941 in believing that the war in the east was virtually over; he had said so publicly at the beginning of October—'the enemy in the east has been struck down and will never rise again'.[2] But though sorely smitten, Russia would not admit she was dead. It was only by the most gigantic effort of will-power that Hitler could force his commanders and troops to hold their ground, whereas prudence and the Generals counselled retreat. 'With the valour of ignorance and the zeal of a fanatic, [he] withered their hesitation with the fierce blaze of his fury.'[3]

Not only was the line held, but as the campaigning season of 1942 drew near, the German armies were found in a posture which even permitted renewed advance. The line had indeed been retracted in some places, especially where troops were disabled by frost-bite on a large scale. But by ignoring the appalling sufferings of his men, Hitler had once more accomplished a miracle. For this he took full credit, and the abilities of his generals sunk even lower in his estimation. To them 'he displayed a ruthlessness and a brutality' . . . which even they had never witnessed in him before. His Commander-in-Chief, von Brauchitsch, was reduced 'to the status of a messenger-boy'.[4]

[1] 'It was not until 1943 that large amounts of weapons, food and military transport for the West became available for the day-to-day support of Russian troops.' *R.I.I.A. Survey. America, Britain, and Russia*, 1941-6, 219.
[2] Bullock, 654.
[3] Wheeler-Bennett, 523.
[4] Wheeler-Bennett, 523.

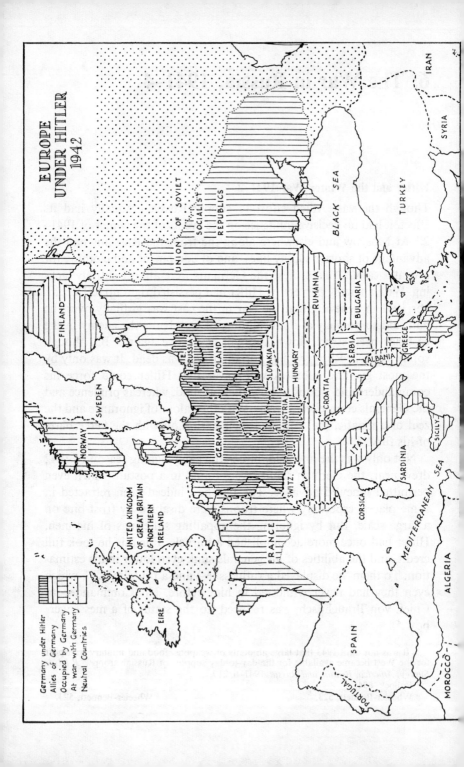

EUROPE
UNDER HITLER
1942

Germany under Hitler
Allies of Germany
Occupied by Germany
At war with Germany
Neutral Countries

FINLAND

NORWAY

SWEDEN

UNION OF SOVIET
SOCIALIST
REPUBLICS

EAST
PRUSSIA

POLAND

UNITED KINGDOM
OF GREAT BRITAIN
& NORTHERN
IRELAND

EIRE

GERMANY

AUSTRIA

SLOVAKIA

HUNGARY

SWITZ.

FRANCE

CROATIA

SERBIA

RUMANIA

BULGARIA

ALBANIA

GREECE

BLACK SEA

TURKEY

IRAN

SYRIA

ITALY

CORSICA

SARDINIA

SICILY

MEDITERRANEAN SEA

SPAIN

PORTUGAL

MOROCCO

ALGERIA

The Tide Turns Against Germany

To this fact the subsequent mistakes which lost Germany the war were primarily due. Total victory for Germany was now virtually impossible in any event, since she was steadily losing the advantages of the new types of weapons developed on a mass-scale before the production of similar or superior weapons by her opponents had got into its stride. Now, however, the huge productive forces of the U.S.A. were being mobilized against her. This, added to the weight of the redeployed industries of Britain and the U.S.S.R., geared entirely to war production, was bound to overbear the efforts, extraordinary though these were, of German industry, even when directed by the genius of Albert Speer, and drawing on the labour of millions of prisoners and of workers from the subjugated lands.

The balance of morale was also turning in favour of the Russians. They had been dispirited by the Germans' stupendous advance, the loss of great cities, of the whole Ukraine with its rich agriculture, and of the great industrial complex in the Donetz Basin. Entire armies had fallen to the Nazi onslaught. Now, however, confidence had returned. The Germans had been held—they had even been thrown back. Man for man the Russian had shown himself as good a soldier as the German, in some circumstances even better. Though more stolid than the German, and lacking the same sense of responsible initiative which inspired German N.C.O.s as well as officers, the Russian showed himself more adaptable in his use of ground, and unsurpassable in his staying power and in his ability to dispense with all those adjuncts in supply and transport to which the armies of more civilized states are accustomed.

By now Stalin had recovered his nerve, and was himself directing his armies.

His leadership was by no means confined to the taking of abstract strategic decisions, at which civilian politicians may excel. The avid interest with which he studied the technical aspects of modern war, down to the minute details, shows him to have been anything but a dilettante. He viewed the war primarily from the angle of logistics . . . to secure reserves of manpower and supplies of weapons, in the right quantities and proportions, to allocate them and to transport them to the right points at the right time, to amass a decisive strategic reserve

and have it ready for intervention at decisive moments—these operations made up nine-tenths of his task.[1]

Hitler's Military Leadership

Time for Hitler was fast running out. His only hope of attaining a
peace not completely disastrous for Germany was to knock Russia
out by a series of blows concentrated on her weakest spots. But this
he was not prepared to do. His dogma of not surrendering an inch
of ground made it impossible to withdraw and regroup his forces. The
efforts of his armies continued to be dispersed; though victories were
won, none of them was decisive.

Hitler had a formidable memory and a remarkable grasp of facts
and figures—numbers of tanks, guns, planes, etc., that were operational or available for this part of the front or that—figures for the
production of such items, figures for the enemy's strength. This helped
him to have a picture of what was going on, and what could be done
over a large range of possibilities. He could sometimes see more
clearly than his generals (in holding the line in Russia in the winter
of 1941–2 many of them admitted later that it had probably been the
only way to stop a panic). But he was bemused by figures. Numbers
came to mean everything—more weapons and more divisions were
the answer, he came to believe, to every problem, even if the divisions
were created merely by dividing existing ones. The weight of the big
battalions directed by a ruthless will became for him the secret of
victory. 'For the art of war,' says von Manstein, 'he substituted a
brute force.'[2]

In his earlier victories, particularly over France, it had been his
political flair as much as any strategic ability which had secured a
quick decision—he could assess the strength of a country's morale,
and his sense of timing had always been good. In those days he still
left most of the work to his generals, but in Russia he interfered more
and more, finally taking over the job of the Commander-in-Chief
himself. It was here that his deficiencies were shown up. With all his
quickness and keen intelligence, he lacked 'military ability based on
experience'; he had not had, like von Manstein who makes the criticism, 'a real training in strategy and grand tactics'.[3]

[1] I. Deutscher: *Stalin* (O.U.P., 1961), 470.   [2] *Lost Victories*, 280.
[3] *Lost Victories*, 275–6.

Increasingly Hitler became divorced from reality. He refused to consider the true position either of the enemy with his growing resources or of the German armies and their relatively declining strength. He could quote figures for this and that, but months after the Allied bombing of Berlin and the other German towns had been going on, he had no conception of the havoc they had wreaked. When he returned from his eastern H.Q. to Berlin in November 1944 he was appalled at the ruins he saw around him.

Though in the spring of 1942 Hitler's armies were standing, battered but unbowed, along a line stretching from Leningrad to the Crimea, 'he could not bring himself to stake *everything* on success'[1] and hurl them in a concentrated drive against the Russians' most vital spot. The Caucasus still lured—von Rundstedt was to make for the oilfields; another army under von Manstein in the Crimea had to secure its right wing by clearing the peninsula and capturing Sebastopol. A third was directed towards Stalingrad. With a spectacular drive, von Rundstedt in July recaptured Rostov, which he had evacuated in December, and thrust on towards Maikop and Grozny. In the Crimea the Kerch peninsula was cleared, and with well-directed hammering Sebastopol was overwhelmed. The thrust towards Stalingrad also made considerable progress. By capturing Voronezh (also in July) the Germans cut the communications between Moscow and the Caucasus. Though temporarily denied the crossing of the Don, they were over it in August with the capture of Kalach, only 70 miles from Stalingrad at the nearest point of the Volga's westerly bend.

Stalingrad

By the end of the first week of September the German Sixth Army under von Paulus was at the western limits of the city, with the Fourth Panzer Army at its south. Hitler's directive was to capture Stalingrad at all costs, and by breaking this vital communications centre, to roll up the whole of Russia's front. Stalingrad, stretching for 35 miles along the western bank of the Volga, was also important economically: the Dzerzinsky Tractor Factory which had turned out 60,000 tractors in 1939 had, in 1941, been switched to the production of tanks. But almost above everything else, prestige was involved in the capture of the former Tsaritsyn, defended by Stalin against the

[1] *Lost Victories*, 276.

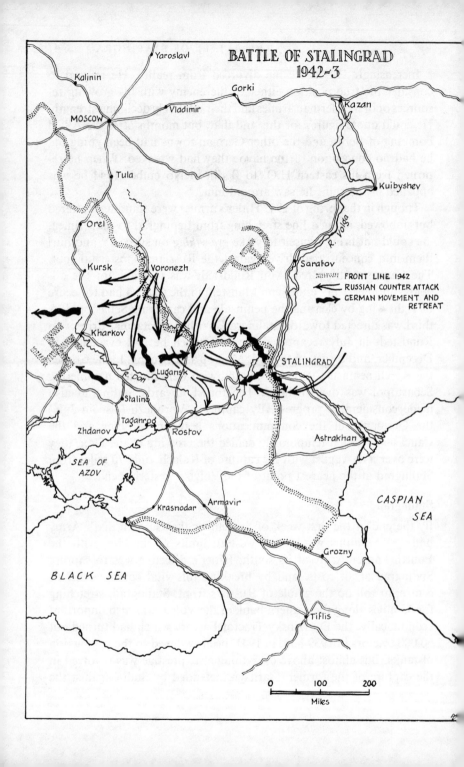

BATTLE OF STALINGRAD
1942-3

Yaroslavl

Kalinin

Gorki

Vladimir

Kazan

MOSCOW

Tula

Kuibyshev

Orel

R. Volga

Kursk

Voronezh

Saratov

FRONT LINE 1942
RUSSIAN COUNTER ATTACK
GERMAN MOVEMENT AND RETREAT

Kharkov

Lugansk

STALINGRAD

R. Don

Stalino

Taganrog

Zhdanov

Rostov

Astrakhan

SEA OF
AZOV

CASPIAN
SEA

Krasnodar

Armavir

Grozny

BLACK SEA

Tiflis

0   100   200
Miles

Whites in 1918, a city celebrated in Soviet lore, to which Stalin had given his name.

The defence of Stalingrad stiffened, with Zhukhov, the saviour of Moscow, in charge of the Russian front,[1] and Chuikov directing the operations in the city itself (September). Stalingrad's modern blocks of factories were defensible by a determined force. Its numerous gullies descending to the river could be disputed yard by yard, and by the river it could be supplied—even to some extent when, after 26 October, the Germans brought the last remaining ferry under fire at 400 yards.[2] By that date the attacking armies of some 250,000 men were besieging a force a quarter of its strength in the central area to which the defenders had been driven. This was the *Tennisschläger* or tennis racquet, as the Germans called it from its shape, six square miles in extent.

Here every foot was fought for, blocks and factories changing hands as the tide of battle ebbed and flowed. By November the Germans in the city had been fought to a standstill, and the Russians were poised for an assault on the exposed flanks of the besieging force.

Then the besiegers became the besieged. The German Eleventh Army which, on completion of its task in the Crimea, might have been used as a strategic reserve, was dissipated. The Germans had no other reserve, and through the gaps in their line to north and south of Stalingrad, the Russians came pouring, sweeping away the Third Rumanian Army guarding the left wing of the Germans, and the Fourth Rumanian Army guarding its right. The latter, together with elements of the Fourth Panzer Army, were squeezed back towards the city against the German Sixth Army, the whole of the German forces being shortly encircled by the Russian tanks, which had penetrated in depth on both their wings. 220,000 Germans[3] were now besieged by a greatly superior force, whose pincers had met at Kalach on 21 November, denying the Germans the vital bridge over the Don (the Russians had captured it intact).

Now began the long agony of the Sixth Army. With short rations for only twelve days, augmented inadequately by a sketchy air-lift

[1] His name has been expunged from Soviet accounts of Stalingrad. Marshal Chuikov does not mention his name in his book. See Deutscher, 483 n.

[2] Marshal V. I. Chuikov: *The Beginning of the Road* (MacGibbon and Kee, 1963), 195.

[3] von Manstein's higher estimate, 296.

hastily organized by Göring, it held out until the end of January. Hitler's order of no retreat was obediently fulfilled. All attempts by a relieving army under von Manstein from the south-west failed. On 31 January 1943, von Paulus was promoted Field-Marshal—'there is no record in German history of a Field-Marshal being taken prisoner,' said Hitler.[1] The same day von Paulus capitulated with the remnant of his emaciated, frost-bitten troops. 'Thereby [was] brought to a useless conclusion perhaps the most monumental isolated example in military history of deliberate and wasteful sacrifice of human life.'[2]

The Russian Push to Poland

Had the Russians not been anxious to have an overwhelming super-iority over the beleaguered Sixth Army to make sure of their prey, they would have been able to deploy sufficient forces to push down towards Rostov and cut off the German army in the Caucasus. By delaying to withdraw from this area, even after the fate of Stalingrad was sealed, Hitler continued to present the Russians with the oppor-tunity which, if thoroughly exploited, might have led to a total German collapse. This danger was only narrowly averted, after the annihilation of the Rumanian, Hungarian and Italian divisions on that front, by the staying power and toughness of the German troops. They were directed by Kleist in a feat of extrication fully as difficult as that which had faced the British command at Dunkirk.

Elasticity of defence might still have worn down the Russians before the Allies were able to launch the 'Second Front' in the West, but this was just what Hitler would not allow. Any withdrawal, even the smallest, had to have his personal sanction. The inelasticity which had proved fatal to the French in 1940 was now disastrous to the Germans. Timoshenko's offensive at Kharkov was indeed held, and the city, lost by the Germans in February 1943 was recaptured by them in March, but their counter-offensive at Kursk petered out. Meanwhile the build-up of troops and weapons continued on the Russian side—despite the hazards of the Arctic seas round the German-held north of Norway. British convoys brought supplies through to Murmansk, while a route for the growing volume of American supplies was organ-ized by way of Persia. The thousands of lorries and jeeps, and the millions of boots brought mobility to the Russians' effort. In war-

---

[1] Bullock, 890.   [2] Wheeler-Bennett, 534.

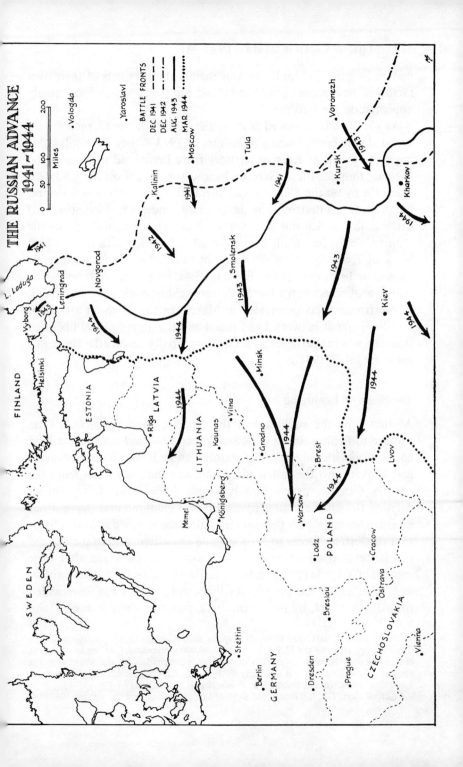

THE RUSSIAN ADVANCE
1941~1944

BATTLE FRONTS
DEC 1941 ----
DEC 1942 -·-·-
AUG. 1943 ————
MAR 1944 ········

Miles
0   50 100   200

SWEDEN

FINLAND

Helsinki

Vyborg

L. Ladoga

Leningrad

Novgorod

ESTONIA

LATVIA
Riga

Memel

LITHUANIA
Kaunas

Vilna

Königsberg

Grodno

Minsk

Brest

POLAND
Warsaw

Lodz

Lvov

Stettin

Breslau

Cracow

Ostrava

GERMANY
Berlin

Dresden

Prague

CZECHOSLOVAKIA

Vienna

Vologda

Yaroslavl

Moscow

Kalinin

Tula

Smolensk

Kiev

Kursk

Voronezh

Kharkov

material—guns and tanks—it was mainly the products of their own factories, now reorganized far behind the front, which increasingly appeared on the battlefield.[1]

As the Russians moved over to the offensive, the Germans were thrust slowly back. During the winter of 1943-4 they were still holding on to a belt of Russian territory from Leningrad to Odessa (the Crimea, though still in German hands, was cut off on the landward side). Bit by bit the Ukraine was liberated, now a vast desert—cities, factories, farms destroyed by the Germans under a ruthless scorched-earth policy which did not stop at flooding the coal-mines of the Donetz. Stalin had a superiority of 60 divisions, which he was able to swing from one point on the front to another, dealing a massive blow now here, now there. Early in 1944, in a series of tremendous battles around Kiev, the Germans were pushed back towards Poland, whose frontier was penetrated in March. In the north an attack on a 120-mile front between Lake Ilmen and Leningrad at last liberated that city, where the siege had been only partially raised after the nightmare winter of 1941-2.

The Siege of Leningrad

At that time the sufferings of the city beggared description. The capture of Schlusselburg on 8 September 1941 had cut the last land connection with the rest of the country, and a little later the Germans had broken into the last fortified line less than ten miles from the city. A German penetration had only been avoided by Hitler's decision to halt the armoured assault on Leningrad and starve it out by encirclement.[2] That this attempt failed was partly due to the diversion of German forces to Moscow and elsewhere, and to the dogged resistance of the Red Army, which halted the Germans after their capture of Tikhvin (9 November). Above all it was due to the fortitude and stolidity of the population in bearing with conditions which turned Leningrad, by New Year 1942, into the semblance of a city

[1] B. H. Liddell Hart: *The Other Side of the Hill*, (Cassell, 1948), 331. According to Chuikov, op. cit., 369 the U.S.A. sent about 14,000 planes and 7,000 tanks to Russia during the war. Bryant, 324 n. 'Under the agreement made with the Kremlin in the autumn of 1941, Britain was to supply by June '42, 2,250 tanks, 1,800 aeroplanes and 1,800 Bren-gun carriers.' *British War Production.* (H.M.S.O., 119.)

[2] Liddell Hart, 278; L. Goure: *The Siege of Leningrad* (Stanford Univ. Press, 1962), 94.

already dead. In fact over a million—a third of the population—died in the course of the siege.

The death-blow to Leningrad might have come from the north, but the Finnish army halted at their old frontier, Mannerheim resolutely refusing to co-operate in an assault on the city, as he considered himself to be under an old pledge to the Russians that Finland should never constitute a threat to their northern capital. This left Lake Ladoga as the Russians' remaining back door to Leningrad, and across it a few supplies were brought by shipping until an ice-road was organized in November 1941. Though supplies by this route increased to a total of 3,000 tons per day, these—by no means all of food—were not enough to make much difference to the rations until February 1942. In December 1941 rations were down to 150 grammes of heavily adulterated bread, and practically nothing else. With supplies of fuel exhausted, the electricity was cut except for a few party and administrative offices, street-cars stopped, and most water ceased to flow. People went to work because factories were a social unit, representing often more security than the home, though with power cut off little work could be done. People came to work to die—they died everywhere. Hospitals, without light or heat were places where the sick had little hope, and where 'the medical staff could barely stand on their feet through hunger, cold and hard work'.[1] 'Dystrophy' as it was called (extreme weakness through hunger), the sub-zero cold, attendant diseases, claimed their vast daily toll. 'Most survivors seemed to be only a short step behind those they were burying. The inhabitants were either grotesquely swollen with hunger or shrunken to skeletons. Diarrhoea with bleeding, and scurvy assumed epidemic proportions, as did heart and respiratory diseases. . . . Everyone suffered from dizziness; most people could walk only with great difficulty. People were often afraid to sit down lest they should be unable to stand up again.'[2]

Moscow's resistance saved Leningrad. Hitler could not concentrate sufficient forces at both spots. At the same time that the Germans failed before Moscow they were beaten back from Tikhvin (8 December 1942). This ended the threat of encirclement, but the Russian offensive from January to mid-March 1942, failed to free the city, after penetrating 35 miles into the German lines. The Germans were

[1] Goure, 162.   [2] Goure, 220.

able to turn the tables by encircling the Second Assault Army and destroying it in June of that year. But though the siege continued, conditions for the populace gradually improved, while considerable numbers were evacuated, until the Russians finally liberated the city after a siege of nearly three and a half years.

7: Grand Strategy:
The 'Second Front' and the Balkans

Conflicts Over Strategy

In every strategic move which the Allies contemplated, important political decisions were involved. The decision to land in North Africa forced the question of relations with the Vichy Government of France to the fore, and underlined the need to choose between the rival claims of Generals de Gaulle and Giraud for leadership of 'Free France'. But far more decisive for the future of a large part of Europe was the advance of the Red Army towards Poland and the Balkans, and the prospect of Anglo-American strength being brought to bear on the destiny of south-east Europe.

The position of General Marshall and other American Chiefs of Staff was clear—they wished the war to be won as quickly as possible with the minimum expenditure of lives. With the political consequences they were not concerned. Admiral King and the American naval staff were indeed not much concerned about the European theatre at all, and their tendency was constantly to deflect the general effort to the Pacific. The difficulty of mounting amphibious operations in the Mediterranean was largely that so much of Allied naval strength, and particularly of landing-craft, was deployed in the Pacific.

Even at the darkest hour of Russian defeats in 1941 Stalin never lost sight of his further objectives. Though at first so hardly pressed that he was willing for British and (later) American forces to operate alongside his armies under their own command, he did not refrain from demanding that Britain should commit herself to recognizing Russia's 1941 frontiers as established by his deal with Hitler in 1939, with particular reference to Russia's annexation of the Baltic states.[1] This was the burden of his conversations with Eden, when the latter visited Moscow in December 1941. Churchill was disgusted at this

[1] H. Feis: *Churchill, Roosevelt, Stalin* (Princeton 1957), 11. See also *Foreign Affairs*, January 1951, Sumner Welles: *Two Roosevelt Decisions*.

bare-faced attempt at violating the Atlantic Charter, to which Stalin
had just recently acceded.

Stalin had no interest in upholding the principles of the Charter.
He had reverted to the traditional policy of Russia, to secure the
northern capital, to regain the Baltic provinces, to recover the Western
Ukraine and Byelo-Russia from Poland, and to dominate that country thereafter. Bessarabia and Northern Bukhovina were to be recovered from Rumania, and a commanding position to be gained in
the Balkans. How far all these aims were clear in Stalin's mind in
1941–2 is speculative; his attitude was empirical and opportunist. He
was clear on restoring the Great Russia of the Tsars, both in the Far
East as in the west. The 'aspirations' of the Pan-Slav days, the claims
on the Straits, and the determination to dominate Central Europe
became actual as the liberated areas were occupied by the Russians,
whose hands were left free by Anglo-American commitments elsewhere.

Stalin himself was perfectly clear where these Anglo-American commitments should mainly lie—in the west, and specifically through the
speedy opening of a second front at the nearest convenient point on
the continent opposite England. Churchill at one time favoured
Norway as a possible landing-point in Europe, but military and naval
considerations indicated a cross-Channel assault as the only feasible
operation for the purpose. Stalin consistently and warmly backed
this project. The last thing he wanted was a diversion of Anglo-
American strength towards his hitherto undeclared sphere of influence
in the Balkans.

Finally decisions on this point only became urgent as operations
in the Mediterranean developed. Marshall had reluctantly concurred
in the North African strategy, after Roosevelt's decision of July 1942,
anxious lest it would increasingly absorb the Allied effort, with the
consequent postponement of the cross-Channel enterprise. Churchill
on the other hand, though eager to strike across the Channel, which
he hoped would be possible in 1943, wanted involvement in the
Mediterranean to be maximum—a major stroke, not just a side-show
on a minor scale.

The North African Landings

For many months it seemed as if Churchill might have his way. The initial stages of the Anglo-American occupation of North Africa, in November 1942, were successful. The British Eighth Army under Montgomery held Rommel's last assault at Alam Halfa, which began on 31 August 1942, then turned the tables in the great tank battle of El Alamein from 23 October to 5 November, forcing Rommel to a retreat which brought him, by January 1943, to the Mareth line defending the eastern entry to Tunisia. From the other side the Americans approached, landing at Oran, Casablanca and Algiers on 8 November 1942, from which points they speedily reduced French resistance which ended with an agreement made by the Vichy leader, Admiral Darlan.[1] But Hitler's decision to defend Tunisia, sending large reinforcements (which faulty Allied co-operation against Axis convoys failed to stem), delayed the completion of the conquest by four months. Not until 12 May 1943 were the last Axis troops over-borne, with the surrender of 160,000 at Cape Bon.

Italy Knocked Out

This delay, together with the still un-mastered U-boat threat in the Atlantic, made the cross-Channel assault impracticable for 1943. The alternative was to push on in the Mediterranean, with the landings on Sicily in July 1943. The object was to knock Italy out of the war, then strike eastwards towards Yugoslavia, where Tito was pinning down 50 Axis divisions. To this apparently logical development, employing divisions which could not yet be used in France, Marshall and his colleagues had no obvious objection to make—though as he had forecast, a far larger quantity of troops, shipping and supplies of all kinds than the British estimated, came to be absorbed by the Mediterranean theatre.

For Mussolini, Rommel's failure to penetrate to Alexandria had been a sign that the war in the Mediterranean was lost. The Duce had returned to Italy dispirited, an ailing and disillusioned man, 'his face grey and ashen, the cheeks sunken, his look troubled and tired, his mouth expressing a sense of bitterness'.[2]

---

[1] Shortly afterwards assassinated, 24 December 1942.
[2] G. Bottai (one of the opposition Fascist leadership), quoted in F. W. Deakin: *The Brutal Friendship* (Weidenfeld and Nicolson, 1962), 41.

Hitler made one more attempt, at Feltre on 19 July 1943, to put life into Mussolini and the Italian alliance—an attempt which was fruitless because Mussolini had already been discussing with his entourage how to extricate Italy from the war (though he could not bring himself to admit to Hitler that Italy could not fight on).[1] His followers however could no longer wait on his indecision. Count Dino Grandi succeeded in calling a meeting of the Fascist Grand Council, the first since 1939. A motion which he presented was carried by 19 votes against 7, to the effect that the powers exercised by the Duce should be restored to the relevant governmental institutions, and that command of the armed forces should revert to the King (25 July 1943). This move by the discontented Fascist leaders fused with another plot hatched in court circles. After a visit to the King, Mussolini found himself under armed guard in an ambulance, soon to be confined as a prisoner in a mountain resort in the Abruzzi. The King vested his powers in Marshal Badoglio, who at once put out feelers for an armistice, while trying to maintain the impression to the Germans that the war would be carried on.

But though Italy was knocked out of the war, and the way prepared for her 'co-belligerency' with the Allies, Hitler would not allow these gains to be easily come by, and his despatch of German forces to secure the front in Italy slowed the Allied advance up the peninsula to a painful crawl. The bridgehead behind the German lines which the Allies seized at Anzio (22 January 1944) was contained, and over five months of hard fighting were required to break the German resistance at Monte Cassino (January–May 1944). Rome fell on 4 June 1944.

Mussolini had been rescued from his internment at Gran Sasso (12 September 1943) by the daring stroke of Colonel Otto Skorzeny with 120 gliderborne parachutists (a stroke however of small value, since the fallen Humpty-Dumpty, though made puppet head of a dwindling 'Socialist Republic' in North Italy, could not be put up on his wall again). An Allied occupation of Italy in autumn 1943 might have given good grounds for the attempt to strike through Yugoslavia (where co-operation was hoped for from Tito's partisans) and the Ljubljana Gap into Hungary. But by May 1944—the date eventually settled for the cross-Channel operation—General Alexander and his

[1] Deakin, 408.

American colleague, Mark Clark, were still to the south of the rich industrial and agricultural plain of Lombardy. The island-hopping plan in the Aegean had also been abandoned. Cos and Leros, captured by the independent initiative of the British Middle East Command under General Maitland Wilson, were recaptured by the Germans (October–November 1943), and the attack on Rhodes never materialized.

The Teheran Conference

Decisions adverse to a Balkan strategy had in fact already been taken at the meeting of Roosevelt, Churchill and Stalin at Teheran in November 1943.[1] Here for the first time the great war-leaders were gathered together—Roosevelt and Churchill, aristocrats both of them, confronting the parvenu successor of the Tsars of All the Russias. Different as their views might be in detail, in general the outlook of Roosevelt and Churchill was similar. No wide mental gulf divided the heir of the prosperous long-established families of the east coast of America (Delanos and Roosevelts were among the seventeenth-century pioneers from Holland),[2] and the descendant of the Dukes of Marlborough, himself the son of Lord Randolph Churchill and his American wife, Jennie Jerome. Though Roosevelt was a left-of-centre liberal, and Churchill a traditionalist, if imaginative conservative—neither term being fully applicable in a party sense —the gap between them was as nothing compared with the abyss which divided the two of them from the son of the Georgian cobbler who had made himself absolute ruler of the Soviet Union. Stalin's peasant suspiciousness, his background of conspiracy and plot, his ruthless uprooting of the Russian masses, and his destruction of several millions of them in the process—both during the collectivization drive and in the vast purges of the thirties (purges which made him the only rival, in this grisly sphere, of Hitler, Himmler and their accomplices)—all this together with his dedicated atheism and his semi-Asian standpoint, set him apart from his Anglo-American collaborators, who were to be his keenest rivals as constructors of the world to be.

What Roosevelt wished to demonstrate at Teheran was not this

---

[1] 28 November–1 December 1943.
[2] The Delanos were French Huguenots who came to America via Holland.

rivalry but the sense of common interests. With this object he was prepared to play down his partnership with Churchill in the pursuit of understanding with Stalin. It was a delusion similar to that which had befuddled Chamberlain with Hitler. After Teheran Roosevelt ruefully admitted that he could not understand the Russians— he couldn't tell 'a good one from a bad one',[1] but at the time he believed that behind the coarse outlandish exterior of Stalin, and below his unplumbable reserve, there lay the lineaments of a good American. Even if Stalin could not be a gentleman any more than Hitler, he might at least respond as one New Dealer to another, with a generous deal this time embracing the world.

To this end Roosevelt refused to give colour to Russian suspicions of hatching schemes privately with Churchill. He accepted Stalin's invitation to live in the Russian embassy compound, and refused Churchill's invitation to lunch. He even embarked on a strategy of teasing Churchill at the conference meetings and making fun of him in order to effect some kind of breakthrough and make a human contact with Stalin. Eighteen months previously Roosevelt had told Churchill that he could 'handle Stalin better than either your Foreign Office or my State Department'.[2] But the necessity of wooing Stalin, whom he found tougher than expected, led to a widening of the rifts which existed between American and British policy in the interests of seeking a wider solidarity with Russia. 'Churchill's tireless advocacy of his own strategic concepts [were] more than ever taxing to his patience. . . . Roosevelt now felt sure that, to use his own term, Stalin was "getatable", despite his bludgeoning tactics and his attitude of cynicism toward such matters as the rights of small nations, and that when Russia could be convinced that her legitimate claims and requirements—such as the right of access to warm-water ports— were to be given full recognition, she would prove tractable and cooperative in maintaining the peace of the post-war world.'[3]

Decision Against the Balkans

Harry Hopkins, as a social worker on relief administration in New York at the time of the New Deal, and subsequently as head of the

---

[1] Frances Perkins: *The Roosevelt I Knew* (Hammond, 1947), 72.
[2] Letter of 18 March 1942, Churchill, III, 177.
[3] R. E. Sherwood: *Roosevelt and Hopkins* (Harper, 1948), 798–9.

Works Progress Administration, had become the intimate confidant and aide of the President. He had done much to cement Roosevelt's friendship with Churchill, and along with Roosevelt could enter into Churchill's ideas and show some sympathy for them, but when these conflicted with grand strategy, as most Americans understood it, Hopkins was the first to block them. When Roosevelt raised the question at the first meeting at Teheran, on Churchill's initiative, as to a possible operation across the Adriatic towards Rumania, Hopkins quickly knocked it down.

In any case 'nothing could have been further from the plans of the U.S. Chiefs of Staff'.[1] Stalin naturally stuck out for the alternative of a landing in the South of France, directed from Italy, to accompany the major blow of a cross-Channel assault. But, though this became accepted Allied policy, Churchill did not give up his schemes till the last moment. After Teheran, he attempted fruitlessly in a meeting with President Inönu (at Cairo, 4–6 December 1943) to persuade Turkey to enter the war and open the way for speedier help to Stalin, and for more effective bombing of the Rumanian oilwells and other targets in Hitler's Europe. Even after D-day and the beginning of the invasion on the Normandy coast, he bombarded Roosevelt with a series of messages, to the effect that the value of an attack through the South of France was as nothing compared with that of a thrust eastwards to Vienna. Though General Clark agreed with this assessment, Marshall and Eisenhower opposed, and Roosevelt backed them with a final 'no'.[2]

This was not quite the end of the story. In August 1944 Stalin's refusal to help the insurgents in the Warsaw rising was the red light which showed up his real intentions in eastern Europe. That autumn when bottlenecks in transport and supply prevented sending divisions which were trained and waiting in America to Europe, Churchill proposed that two or three divisions be sent to reinforce Fifth U.S. Army in Italy—the Allied forces there having been much weakened because of sending a proportion of their strength to the South of France. The Gothic Line was broken in September, and this success could have been exploited, not merely in order to pin down larger forces which might have been used elsewhere, but to make possible a move into the Balkans (British forces landed in Greece in the first

[1] Sherwood, 780.   [2] Feis, 344–6.

week of October). The American veto on this plan was perhaps inevitable, but 'by refusing to employ the American reserve divisions
anywhere except in Western Europe, where they could not all be
brought into action quickly, Marshall and his colleagues were failing
to exploit the great strategic flexibility which the Allies enjoyed
through their command of the sea'.[1]

By this time it was already too late to act effectively in the Balkans.
The Russians took the step which the Americans had jibbed at,
securing Rumania and Bulgaria in September, and advancing up the
Danube Valley to Belgrade which they entered on 20 October 1944.
Even if Churchill had won his point, difficulties, possibly insurmount-
able, might have been revealed in working with Tito on his own
ground, while the political complications with Russia might well have
proved endless. But the political issues of the decision were never
thrashed out; it was made ostensibly on military grounds alone.[2]

'Unconditional Surrender' (Casablanca)

The Teheran conference was not Roosevelt's first meeting with
Churchill outside America. The two leaders had met in January of
the same year, 1943, at Casablanca. There Cossac[3] was set up, the
combined command and planning organization which was to work
out the plan for invading France. It was there also that the announcement was made that 'unconditional surrender' alone would be
accepted from the enemies of the Atlantic alliance. This was originally
Roosevelt's idea, based on his reading of events of the American
Civil War, and also on his view that the Germans' acceptance of the
armistice in 1918 on the terms of President Wilson's Fourteen Points
had made possible the myth that they had never been defeated. The
phrase came out suddenly at a press conference, but it was not un-
premeditated (Roosevelt had been advised to declare this policy by
his Subcommittee on Security Problems) and Churchill hastened to
associate himself with it. It was agreed that such a pronouncement

[1] C. Wilmot: *The Struggle for Europe* (Fontana paperback, 1952) 622.
[2] Feis, 347. According to Feis, pages 101–2, Churchill wished to discuss political
decisions at the Casablanca conference, but Roosevelt refused. Also regarding
Eden's visit to Washington 12–30 March 1943, when policy was discussed—'no-one
suggested that military strategy be adjusted to serve the political purposes and settlements in mind'. (Feis, 122). It is also clear that until the time of Teheran Churchill
was so concerned with, first defending Britain, and then in winning the war, that he
had not the time or energy to bring the wider political questions much under review.
[3] Chief of Staff to the Supreme Allied Commander (Designate).

was necessary to prevent Stalin from thinking that the Western Allies would do deals with Germany or Italy at Russian expense.[1] It is doubtful whether the announcement achieved much. It was naturally used by Nazi propagandists to keep the Germans resisting to the bitter end. Stalin, though he made the formula his own, protested to Roosevelt about it on these grounds.[2]

The Polish Question

Of all the problems that plagued repeated conferences, none was more difficult than Poland. Britain had gone to war ostensibly on behalf of Poland, yet from the earliest talks with the Russians it was clear that they would not allow liberated Poland to have the same frontiers as before. They demanded approximately the Curzon Line as their frontier with Poland, not even allowing her the indisputably Polish town of Lwow, or the oilfields in that area. In recompense Stalin was prepared to allow Poland most of East Prussia and all German territory as far west as the Oder and western Neisse. Such an arrangement, unless freely agreed by the Polish Government in London, and sanctioned by the eventual peace conference, could only be made in breach of Britain's pledges not to recognize war-time gains made by force, and specifically that of 30 July 1941, not to recognize 'any territorial changes which have been effected in Poland since August 1939'.[3] But, without reference to the Polish Government, Churchill at Teheran agreed on the Curzon Line as Poland's future frontier in the east, with compensation for her in the west for the loss of territory involved. Roosevelt bowed to Churchill's initiative in this matter; only the Poles were left to make their untimely objections unsupported.[4]

---

[1] *Grand Strategy*, VI, 4.

[2] Deutscher, 501. See also Elliot Roosevelt: *As He Saw It* (Duell, Sloan & Pearce, 1946), 117; J. L. Snell: *Dilemma over Germany* (Hauser Press, 1959), 16–19.

[3] Text in E. J. Rozek: *Allied War-time Diplomacy; a Pattern in Poland* (Wiley; Chapman and Hall, 1958), 159–163.
In the House of Commons, 5 September 1940, Churchill stated: 'we do not propose to recognize any territorial changes which take place during the war, unless they take place with the free consent and good will of the parties concerned.' (Hansard, vol. 365, 40). See also S. Mikolajczyk: *The Pattern of Soviet Domination* (Sampson Low, 1948), 49, 310.

[4] Rozek. After Teheran Eden assured Mikolajczyk that, though the Russians wanted the Curzon Line as the boundary, nothing had been agreed (Mikolajczyk, 53). Churchill, however, on 20 January 1944, told him of the arrangement that had been made (p. 56).

The Katyn Graves and the Warsaw Rising

The London Poles embarrassed their friends, as well as further antagonizing the Russians, by demanding investigation under Red Cross auspices into the origin of the mass graves of Polish officers, discovered in April 1943 at Katyn near Smolensk. They suspected that these officers—either captives or refugees after Russia's 1939 occupation of Eastern Poland—had been murdered by the Russians, who however insisted that the atrocity was the work of the Germans. In any case these graves threw light on the disappearance of several thousand Polish officers who were known to have been in Russia, but who could not be traced for service in the Polish army which had been formed in the Middle East, and which subsequently fought with distinction in North Africa and Italy. While the Katyn crisis was boiling the London Poles suffered a serious loss through the death in a plane crash of their Premier, General Sikorsky (4 July 1943), who was respected by the Russians more than his successor, the Peasant Party leader Mikolajczyk—though he too was a man of integrity, and realist enough to go some way in satisfying the Russians' territorial demands.

The most ghastly episode in the Polish struggle with Stalin was the Warsaw rising, which lasted over two months, from 1 August–2 October 1944. As the Russian army approached the city, the leader of the Polish underground, General Bor-Komorowski, eager to effect the liberation of the capital by the Poles themselves, ordered the long-prepared rising to begin. The General, however, had failed to make contact with the Russians—a difficult task in the circumstances—but this is not enough to explain the sudden halting of the Soviet troops (Stalin's explanations of special German pressure outside Warsaw and elsewhere on the front cut very little ice).[1] Not only did the Russian troops fail to support the rising, and their air force arrive too late, but Stalin refused use of the Poltava airfield by British and American planes in organizing a shuttle service from North Italy to drop

[1] Though Deutscher says (p. 523): 'Rokossovsky's army had been stopped at the Vistula and then thrown back. . . . It may be, it is indeed very probable, that Rokossovsky, repelled by the Germans, was unable to come to the rescue of Warsaw, and that Stalin, just conducting major offensives on the southern sector of the front . . . could not alter his strategic dispositions to assist the unexpected rising.' For General Bor-Komorowski's account, see his book, *The Secret Army* (Gollancz, 1950).

supplies to the hard-pressed Poles. Six weeks after the rising began, the Russians occupied the Praga suburb of Warsaw, but went no further. After a fearful agony in which the Germans killed thousands of Poles and destroyed most of the remaining buildings in the already shattered city, the struggle was abandoned—three months later the Russians 'liberated' the city themselves. It seems that 'the Soviet government had decided to grasp the chance afforded by the Warsaw tragedy to so cover the London government with blame as to destroy it in the eyes of the Poles within the country'.[1]

The Germ of the United Nations

'Death to the German invader' was the grim refrain of every broadcast from war-time Moscow, and the fact that the Russians were killing more Germans than the British and Americans put together during most of the war was a constant challenge to Roosevelt and Churchill to confront German power directly by the cross-Channel assault. Stalin's demands for a 'second front now' were difficult to fob off; and the democratic leaders were aware that the more troops they put into action the more likely were they to make their voices felt in the eventual settlement of Europe.

Meanwhile attempts were made by Roosevelt to buy Stalin off from his territorial claims by including Russia in a general post-war scheme for security to be guaranteed by the great powers. In May 1942 Roosevelt threw out to Molotov, during the latter's visit to Washington, a number of ideas as to how the peace should be guaranteed by America, Russia and Britain, with China as a somewhat uncertain fourth, and how trusteeships, in which Stalin might be interested, should be established over islands and the territories of colonial powers. In a private conversation with Stalin at Teheran, Roosevelt enlarged further on this theme: an international organization should be established consisting of forty or more countries, with executive power residing in two committees, of which the most important was that dubbed by the President 'the Four Policemen'— Russia, America, Britain and China. Stalin's comment was that he doubted whether China would have much power at the end of the war; in any case his main interest was in keeping Germany down. An organization which could do this would be useful, but Stalin showed

[1] Feis, 385.

himself little interested in the principles which might underlie such an organization, or the policy which the United Nations (the phrase was already being used)[1] might pursue towards the vanquished and the smaller states. His attitude was that as long as he got what he wanted for Russia, the British and Americans could get what they wanted for themselves.

[1] The Declaration of United Nations was signed between America, Russia and Britain on New Year's Day, 1942.

NOTES

1. CHURCHILL'S PRESSURE ON EISENHOWER TO HAVE LANDINGS IN THE SOUTH OF FRANCE SWITCHED TO BALKANS:
'Although I never heard him say so, I felt that the Prime Minister's real concern was possibly of a political rather than a military nature. He may have thought that a post-war situation which would see the Western Allies posted in great strength in the Balkans would be far more effective in producing a stable post-war world than if the Russian armies should be the ones to occupy that region. I told him that if this were his reason for advocating the campaign into the Balkans he should go instantly to the President and lay the facts, as well as his own conclusions, on the table. I well understood that strategy can be affected by political considerations, and if the President and the Prime Minister should decide that it was worth while to prolong the war, thereby increasing its cost in men and money, in order to secure the political objectives they deemed necessary, then I would instantly and loyally adjust my plans accordingly. But I did insist that as long as he argued the matter on military grounds alone I could not concede validity to his arguments.'
(Gen. D. D. Eisenhower: *Crusade in Europe* (Heinemann, 1948), 311).
2. Sumner Welles' conclusion about the general trends of policy is:
'The position so confidently and firmly taken by the British and American Governments in January 1942 was wholly at variance with the course which they later actually pursued, and ... this change of policy in a matter of vital significance apparently was not due to a conscious decision by either of them. They seem to have been drifting into a fundamental modification of policy without any realistic apprehension of all its implications.'
(*Foreign Affairs*, January 1951, 191.)
3. On Roosevelt at Teheran see W. C. Bullitt: *The Great Globe Itself* (Macmillan 1947), ch. 1.
4. A useful summary of the strategic decisions and of the work of the conferences where they were made, can be found in A. Russell Buchanan: *The United States and World War II* (Harper and Row, 1964), Vol. 2, ch. 14 (pp. 297 seq.), 'The Statesmen at War'.

8: From the Normandy Assault to Hitler's Suicide

The Battle of Normandy

At midnight 5–6 June 1944, the assault began against Hitler's Atlantic Wall in Normandy. The build-up for this gigantic operation had been proceeding for months, preparations being perfected in the light of the raids against St Nazaire (26–27 March 1942) and Dieppe (17 August 1942). The main bottleneck was in landing-craft. It needed all the exertions of General Eisenhower (commander of the operation) to have enough of these built, and to extract them from Admiral King.

These and other preparations could not be completed by the original date, 1 May. The delay of five weeks was more of a disadvantage for the Allies than for the Germans. Rommel had taken over command of the coastal sectors between Holland and the Loire in February, under general command of von Rundstedt, and was doing much to bring them into a high state of preparedness. The Atlantic Wall was being made an increasingly formidable obstacle, and Rommel's dispositions for holding the Allies at or near the Wall and driving them back into the sea, were rapidly taking shape. Another advantage, which the Allies lost by delay, was the weather—perfect for the operation during May, it broke early in June, and culminated in the great storm of 19–23 June, the worst June storm on that coast for forty years.

The delay was however put to good use by the Allied air forces, whose strategic bombing of Germany considerably reduced the production of petrol and other essential supplies, and of these only a small proportion could be moved to the battle areas since Allied bombing caused a near paralysis in communications. At the same time the bombing was designed as part of an elaborate scheme to give the impression that the attack was to be expected, not in Normandy, but between the Pas-de-Calais and the Seine. Though Hitler's intuition was for Normandy, Rommel continued to expect the attack farther

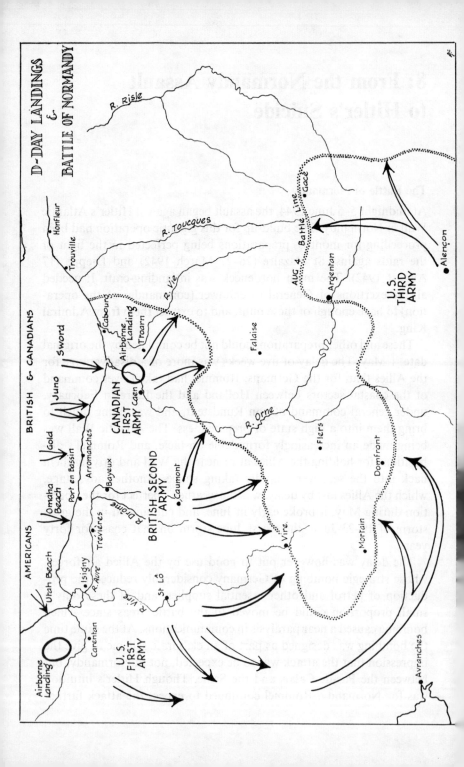

D-DAY LANDINGS
&
BATTLE OF NORMANDY

R. Risle

Honfleur

Trouville

R. Toucques

R. Vie

Cabourg

Airborne
Landing

Troarn

SWORD

JUNO

GOLD

BRITISH & CANADIANS

Arromanches

Port en Bessin

Bayeux

CANADIAN
FIRST ARMY

Caen

R. Orne

Falaise

AUG. 4 Battle Line

Gacé

Argentan

Alençon

U.S.
THIRD
ARMY

Flers

OMAHA BEACH

AMERICANS

Utah Beach

Airborne
Landing

Carentan

Isigny

R. Aure

Trévières

R. Drôme

St Lô

R. Vire

Caumont

BRITISH SECOND ARMY

Vire

Domfront

Mortain

U.S.
FIRST
ARMY

Avranches

north, and kept the larger proportion of his divisions in that area. On D-day the Allies secured almost complete surprise for their initial assault, Rommel himself having gone away to Germany. Long after it began he continued to regard it as a feint in preparation for the real thrust in northern France.

A fleet of 5,300 ships, supported by 12,000 planes, carried 150,000 men and 1,500 tanks across the Channel, where they landed on a 60 mile front. Before the first landing craft and amphibious tanks came in to the beaches, parachute troops had been dropped at both ends of the landing area to secure bridges and other key points. 'Flail tanks' to beat pathways through minefields, and all manner of specialized equipment had been brought (much of it invented for the occasion) to deal with the difficulties which were expected.

These were mostly used by the British—the Americans, usually so partial to gadgets, believed that dash and weight would make such aids irrelevant. This was one reason for their high losses on 'Omaha' beach, the other being that the terrain particularly favoured the defenders who directed a sustained and murderous fire against them. Nevertheless this beach, like the others, was seized, and with hard fighting the Americans, Canadians and British were able to link up along a frontage which, by the fifth day after the assault, was 80 miles long and stretched 20 miles inland at its farthest point.

The colossal task of supplying the 16 divisions now ashore was undertaken by relays of ships which unloaded their cargoes on the beaches, in the small ports as they were captured, and later in the artificial 'Mulberry' harbour at Arromanches which had been pre-fabricated and part carried, part ferried across the channel (the American Mulberry was blown away in the storm of 19–23 June). Tankers were pumping petrol through pipe-lines to the shore, later to be supplemented by the pipe-lines of 'Pluto' (pipe-line under the ocean), which brought oil direct from the Isle of Wight to France. With some justice Stalin could say of the operation, in his congratulatory letter to Churchill that 'the history of warfare knows no other like undertaking from the point of view of its scale, its vast conception, and its masterly execution'.[1]

The Germans were rightly sensitive about the Pas-de-Calais area, since here the sites had been prepared for launching the V1 flying

[1] Letter of 11 June 1964, quoted in Churchill, VI, 8.

bombs against London. But though much damage was done (2,500
buildings were destroyed) and there were over 20,000 casualties (about
a quarter being fatal), morale was unaffected and the war-effort un-
impaired. Further damage and casualties were caused by the V2
rockets in August in London, Liége and Antwerp. By then the V1
launching-sites had been overrun and those for the V2 were under
constant attack by land and air, and their effectiveness was greatly
diminished.

The need to retain the means of using these and other 'secret
weapons', on which Hitler pinned his hopes for still winning the war,
was a main determinant of his strategy during these months of doom.
The other was his fanatical obstinacy for holding the line at every
point. Still directing operations from Rastenburg in East Prussia,
with an occasional visit to the west, Hitler re-emphasized his costly
doctrine to every general on every front, and attempted to lay down
the procedure in detail for every situation. This meant that, though
the Germans formed a hard crust around the Normandy bridgehead,
once it was broken they had no reserves with which to arrest an
Allied advance until it reached the obstacles of the Siegfried Line,
the Rhine and the islands and inundations of Holland. It was the
French strategy of 1940 in reverse—this time it was the Germans who
had no strategic reserve.

Montgomery commanded the invasion forces under the over-all
direction of Eisenhower. His colleague commanding the American First
Army was Bradley, not technically under his orders, but accepting
his 'operational control' largely because Montgomery was admitted
to be 'a master in the methodical preparation of forces for a formal
set-piece attack'.[1] Montgomery (at least during this period) used his
authority with 'wisdom, forbearance and restraint'.[2] These qualities
he needed in full measure to curb the impatience of the other commanders, even at one time of Eisenhower himself, as he built up a
powerful thrust by the British and Canadians around Caen. This
drew the bulk of the German troops against him in that area, which
enabled the Americans to break out against lighter resistance to the
east. They drove across the base of the Cotentin peninsula, going on

[1] Eisenhower: *Crusade*, 423.
[2] General Omar Bradley: *A Soldier's Story* (Henry Holt, 1951) 319–20. 'I could not
have wanted a more tolerant and judicious commander', he adds.

to the capture of Cherbourg on 26 June (though the port was so damaged that it could not be used until August). This was followed by the capture of the strong-point and communications centre of St Lô (18 July), from where a sledge-hammer blow was struck on a 6,000 yard front against the German forces to its west.

A terrible battle of attrition ensued. The Americans themselves lost nearly a thousand casualties a day during the twelve days fighting for St Lô—but parallel losses on the German side could not be so easily sustained. Dempsey with the Second British Army was pinning down 14 divisions and 600 tanks near Caen; the Luftwaffe had almost disappeared from the skies; and the high hedgerows of the Bocage country ceased to be so formidable a defence as soon as an American sergeant found a way of welding four steel teeth on the front of a Sherman tank, converting it into a 'Rhinoceros'. After an air bombardment which knocked out 70 per cent of the defenders and most of their front-line panzers, the Americans moved forward as the Rhinos cut through earth and roots and restored mobility to the battle. On 27 July the German front crumbled, and Bradley was able to exploit the opportunity by sending Patton's VIII Corps through the gap. Patton moved fast through Avranches and was into Britanny by the end of the month.[1]

The way to Paris was now open. Caen had been captured on 10 July, but there were large German forces to its south and east. Hitler's only hope was to withdraw them immediately to the Seine. By keeping them where they were, with orders to mount a counter-attack for regaining Avranches, he risked another Stalingrad. A vast enveloping movement was effected by the Allies, after Montgomery had broken the 'hinges' of the German defences near Caen.[2] 100,000 German troops were squeezed into the Falaise pocket, with little hope of escape. Hitler relieved the Commander-in-Chief West, von Kluge, who committed suicide—he had relieved von Rundstedt after the latter's failure to stem the landings. Rommel was out of action with wounds after his staff car had been shot up from the air on 19 July—he too later committed suicide.

Hitler's standfast orders and control of strategy gave little latitude to the new and vigorous commander, Model, to extricate his troops from the melée. For this it soon became. 'The battlefield at Falaise

[1] Wilmot, 440–453.   [2] Montgomery: *Memoirs* (Collins, 1958), 260.

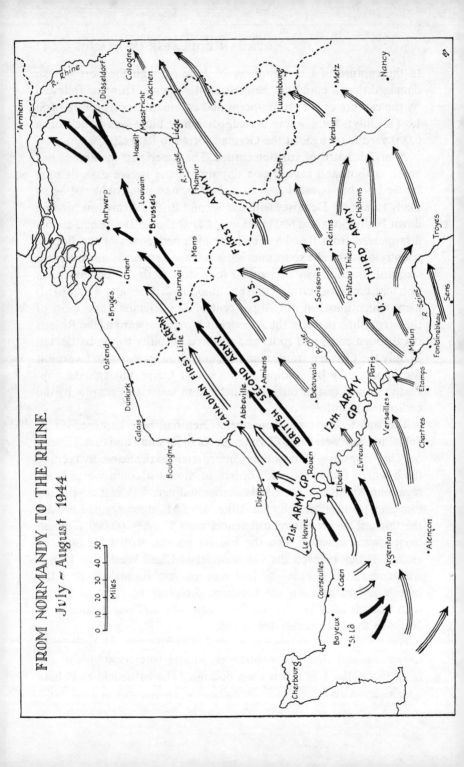

FROM NORMANDY TO THE RHINE
July ~ August 1944

Miles
0 10 20 30 40 50

Arnhem
R. Rhine
Düsseldorf
Cologne
Aachen
Maastricht
Hasselt
Liège
R. Meuse
Namur
Louvain
Antwerp
Brussels
Ghent
Mons
Tournai
Bruges
Ostend
Lille
Dunkirk
Calais
Boulogne
Dieppe
Abbeville
Amiens
Beauvais
Oise
Soissons
Reims
Château Thierry
Châlons
Troyes
Sens
R. Seine
Fontainebleau
Étampes
Chartres
Versailles
Paris
Evreux
Elbeuf
Rouen
Le Havre
Courseulles
Caen
Bayeux
St Lô
Alençon
Argentan
Melun
Sedan
Verdun
Luxembourg
Metz
Nancy
Cherbourg

FIRST ARMY (U.S.)
THIRD ARMY (U.S.)
12th ARMY GP
SECOND ARMY (BRITISH)
CANADIAN FIRST ARMY
FIRST ARMY
21st ARMY GP

was unquestionably one of the greatest "killing grounds" of any of the war areas,' wrote Eisenhower. 'Roads, highways, and fields were so choked with destroyed equipment and with dead men and animals that passage through the area was extremely difficult. Forty-eight hours after the closing of the gap I was conducted through it on foot, to encounter scenes that could be described by Dante. It was literally possible to walk for hundreds of yards at a time, stepping on nothing but dead and decaying flesh.'[1] Eight infantry divisions and two panzer divisions were captured almost intact. In all some 50,000 Germans were captured and 10,000 killed, though some of the German armour and most of the senior commanders made their escape by a corridor cut through the Canadian line by the panzers. The fact that the disaster was not on the scale of Stalingrad saved German morale—shaken as it was by the attempt of 20 July on Hitler's life[2]— and enabled it to recover sufficiently for the war to be prolonged until the following spring. But with mopping-up operations east of Mortain on 19 August the Battle of Normandy came to its end.[3]

Arnhem

Leaving the strongly held ports, like le Havre and Brest, to be captured later, the bulk of the Allied forces streamed north and west, capturing an entire army group (25,000) near Mons while liberating Belgium, and freeing Paris (25 August). At this stage Montgomery urged that one strong thrust be made north-eastwards across the lower Rhine outflanking the Siegfried line and assaulting the Ruhr before winter fully set in. There was a chance that the war might be ended that year. But the denial to the Allies of many ports for so long, and their complete wrecking before abandonment, enormously aggravated the problem of supplying several armies which were constantly extending their lines of communication. Even after the capture of Antwerp with its docks intact, the Germans continued to hold the islands in the estuary of the Scheldt. A long and grim campaign by the Canadians was necessary before the islands were finally cleared (9 November).

[1] *Crusade*, 306.
[2] See below. It was in consequence of Rommel's connivance with the *Putsch* that he was forced to commit suicide on Hitler's orders.
[3] Montgomery: *Memoirs*, 263.

Montgomery believed that for such a thrust to be successful, the advancing armies to his south would have to be halted. But this plan did not suit the Americans, and in particular was anathema to the flamboyant and pushful Patton commanding the American Third Army. Eisenhower, though approving Montgomery's strategy, was inhibited in carrying it out because of possible press and public reactions in America should the American armies be halted in order to enable the British to deliver the knock-out blow. Furthermore, due to an accident, he was immobilized for a crucial period far behind the battle areas. When the build-up for Montgomery's northern blow eventually began the best autumn weather was nearly over, and it was not possible to bring up sufficient supplies to give the Allies the needful superiority.

Though something of a gamble, Montgomery's plan for opening a northern route around the end of the Siegfried line nearly succeeded. Three divisions (two American, one British) were to land by parachute and form a corridor fifty miles long by seizing bridges over the Maas, Waal and Neder Rijn at Eindhoven, Nijmegen and Arnhem, besides over five other waterways. Another airborne division was to come in as soon as an airfield had been captured, while ground forces were to blast their way through to relieve and expand the bridgeheads. The scheme was, however, frustrated by bad weather, which held up the despatch of supplies and reinforcements, by mistakes such as dropping the paratroops too far from the Arnhem bridge, and by bad luck such as the fact that both the German commanders, Model and Student, were in the combat area at the moment of attack, and able to take immediate and personal control of the defence. Also an armoured division was resting at Arnhem at the time. Though the thrust up to Nijmegen succeeded, the hard-won bridgehead at Arnhem had to be abandoned after eleven days of bitter fighting. Less caution on the part of some of Montgomery's commanders, and more dash by some of their troops, might have overcome the difficulties.[1] But, having held the attack, the Germans recovered their morale. Rundstedt set himself not merely to build a stable line, but to prepare a winter assault which could turn the tables on the Allies.

[1] 'It was most unfortunate that the two major weaknesses of the Allied High Command—the British caution about casualties and the American reluctance to concentrate —should both have exerted their baneful influence on this operation which should and could, have been the decisive blow of the campaign in the West.' Wilmot, 605.

The Ardennes 'bulge'

This was the Germans' last fling. Their object was to repeat the Ardennes breakthrough of 1940, then strike northwest towards Liége and Antwerp. Somehow 28 divisions had been gathered for this attack, but of varying quality. The shortage of fuel-oil due to Allied bombing, and of other supplies as Germany's industrial empire shrank, were bound to reduce mobility and staying-power. Nevertheless, the attack when it came surprised the Americans by its punch and speed (16 December), and within a day had penetrated 20 miles into Belgium. For a week the 'bulge', extending in the direction of Namur, increased, but its 'shoulders' were held, while Bastogne stood, though beleaguered, in the middle of the German path. Montgomery, to whom Eisenhower now gave control of the northern sector, headed the German advance away from the danger-spots, and with co-ordinated movements from north and south brought it to a halt by Christmas. Though the Americans had nearly 80,000 casualties, it was for the Germans an even greater disaster than Ludendorff's reverse on the Black Day of the German army in August 1918.

The Last Phase in the West

From then on it was, for the Germans, merely a question of patching the crumbling fronts, but Hitler failed to use the forces which were available. Large armies were standing around—40 divisions[1] in the Courland pocket on the Baltic, others in Norway and Denmark. Hitler refused all advice for shortening the eastern line and concentrating on the defence of Germany. Chiefs of Staff and commanders were changed with bewildering rapidity—new units with fantastic names were formed from police, sailors, the Luftwaffe and half-grown boys. Though continuing to fight with extraordinary determination, and confronted with their country's utter ruin, the Germans were powerless to do more than stave off collapse. 'Unconditional surrender' and the area bombing of the great cities convinced many that there was as little hope in giving in as in prolonging a desperate resistance.

Although resistance in many places was stiff, the western defences of the Reich crumbled more quickly than expected as the Allied assault developed. At Remagen the railway bridge across the Rhine

[1] Wilmot, 712.

was captured intact (7 March 1945). A fortnight later another bridge-head was seized south of Mainz, while in the north Montgomery's Army Group effected the crossings which had been so much contested in the Arnhem battles in September. General Model tried vainly to organize the defence of the Ruhr, which was completely encircled by the Allies (1 April). While 18 American divisions were detailed for the mopping up in the Ruhr (325,000 Germans were eventually captured), the remainder of the Allied forces were freed for the drive towards the east.

Stalin Stakes His Claims

By this time the Germans were mainly concerned to hold off the Russians in the east, where on 12 January they had begun an offensive which brought them from the Vistula to the Oder, within striking distance of Berlin. For political reasons Churchill was eager for the Western Allies to push through quickly to Berlin, and penetrate in other sectors as far to the east as possible, particularly into Austria and Czechoslovakia. Occupation zones had already been demarcated between the Allies, but—partly for prestige and partly to have some bargaining power against the Russians—Churchill wanted the Western powers to liberate the capitals concerned and to hold as much terri-tory as possible before the eventual withdrawals behind the zonal boundaries took place.

The need to hold a strong bargaining position *vis-à-vis* Stalin was becoming increasingly plain the less dependent he became on Allied support. The main bond of union between Russia and the Western powers had been the common struggle against Germany. Now that Germany's utter defeat was imminent, the question at issue had become the control of middle and eastern Europe. On this Stalin had always had his eyes fixed, even at the darkest hour—as his talks with Eden in December 1941 showed—when the Germans had been at the gates of Moscow and Leningrad. His great anxiety was lest the West-ern Allies should gain some advantage through German readiness to negotiate with them while the Germans held off the Russians in the east. Though attempts to deal with the points at issue, especially over Poland, were made at the Yalta Conference in February 1945, the compromises for the most part were unsuccessful and mutual sus-picions increased.

Politics and Strategy

Both on account of the American decision against the north-eastern thrust into the Balkans from Italy, and the agreement on occupation zones, the main Russian aims had already been conceded. It was now clear that where the Russians were in occupation they were going to direct affairs as they pleased, without reference to the Atlantic Charter, Western commitments (notably to Poland) or even agreements recently entered into with the West. There was sense therefore in Churchill trying to move the Western armies as far eastwards as possible before the fighting stopped, if only as a means of exerting some pressure on the Russians, particularly in regard to the joint occupation of Berlin and Vienna, and inter-zonal arrangements for feeding the captured populations.

Churchill never proposed altering the occupation zones as they had been agreed,[1] but this clearly would have been a possibility—and at least the lot of the inhabitants would have been less harsh than it was when their areas were taken over immediately by the Russians. But Marshall and Eisenhower looked at all questions from a purely military point of view—the need to bring about the total collapse of the German armies with the least possible loss of Allied lives. This, added to exaggerated assessments of German strength (in which Montgomery also shared), led to undue caution as to the possibility of capturing Berlin instead of leaving it to the Russians. Bradley thought it would cost 100,000 casualties, and that this was a high price seeing that most of the territory to be fought for in order to seize Berlin would be handed over to the Russians anyway.

The Occupation Zones

The basis of the agreement on the occupation zones had been worked out in the summer of 1943 by a British committee presided over by Attlee—three areas roughly equal in extent, Russian in the east, British in the north, and American in the south, with a joint occupation of Berlin. The Russian zone would extend to within 100 miles of the Rhine. This project had at the time been considered somewhat

[1] 'I never suggested going back on our word over the agreed zones provided other agreements were also respected.' Churchill, VI, 445.

academic. Roosevelt did not like it—he wished the Anglo-American sphere to extend as far east as Berlin, the boundary to run from Stettin in the north via Berlin to the Czechoslovak border at Eger and so southwards along it to Ulm, leaving Dresden, but not Leipzig, to the Russians. Another major change which he favoured was that the American zone should be in the north, the British in the south.

But these proposals and counter-proposals got stuck in a low-level committee at Washington, which was itself paralysed by conflicting pressures from the War Department and the State Department, and which failed to pass on the President's views to the British.[1] Later (February 1944) the Russians accepted the British proposals *en bloc*, and drew up their own detailed plan for the inter-allied occupation of Berlin. At the second Quebec conference (September 1944), Roosevelt abandoned his plan and accepted the British proposals for the boundaries of the Soviet zone, since they had been accepted by the Russians, and also those for the British zone to be in the north— apparently in consideration of Churchill's acceptance (temporarily) of the Morgenthau plan for 'pastoralising' Germany, though stringent undertakings were imposed to safeguard American access to their zone from the sea. The Americans were to control the ports of Bremen and Bremerhaven, and to have 'access through the (other) western and north-western seaports and passage through the British-controlled area'.[2] 'Accurate delineation' of this arrangement was to be under- taken later—all of which careful planning contrasted with the failure to pay adequate attention to similar questions of access to Berlin, which was to lie 120 miles within the Soviet zone.

Eisenhower agreed with Stalin that Berlin was now of little military importance[3]—though later Stalin thought it worth while to mass a million men on a 200-mile front to secure its capture. Eisenhower therefore launched his main thrust south of Berlin towards Leipzig and Dresden. Churchill, after appealing to Roosevelt, had to give way. Roosevelt was already failing in health, and Marshall, who strongly backed Eisenhower's 'non-political' approach, replied on his behalf. Churchill had to be content with a non-political strategy,

[1] J. E. Smith: *The Defence of Berlin* (Johns Hopkins Press 1963) 20–1 et seq.
[2] Part of section 34 of the Combined Chiefs of Staff Report, quoted Churchill, VI, 142.
[3] Churchill VI, 402; Eisenhower, 433–6; Wilmot, 789. See also *World Politics*, IV, April 1952, 368, F. L. Pogue: *Why Eisenhower's Forces Stopped at the Elbe*.

though it included a push by Montgomery to Lübeck, which would enable the British, not the Russians, to liberate Denmark (2 May).

Surrender Negotiations

By then negotiations with German commanders in Holland and Northern Italy had already begun. Although in Holland the commander would not surrender his forces as long as fighting continued elsewhere, a local arrangement was made whereby supplies for the Dutch (who were in severe straits from hunger and cold in areas still under German control), would be brought in under Red Cross auspices. In return for the Allies halting their advance the Germans agreed not to flood the remaining land and to cease oppressing the people.

On the Italian front similar moves for an armistice produced violent Russian reactions. The S.S. General Wolff sought contact with the British and Americans through Switzerland, and though the Russians were immediately informed of meetings of which the sole aim was to confirm Wolff's credentials and powers, they accused the Western Allies of negotiating a surrender behind their backs which would release German forces for fighting against them elsewhere, and would let 'the Anglo-American troops . . . advance into the heart of Germany almost without resistance on the part of the Germans'.[1] Roosevelt's exchanges with Stalin ended on a bitter note—he was too weak to draft the final reply (5 April 1945) and let Marshall do it for him, but he approved the letter whose last paragraph expressed his anger: 'I cannot avoid a feeling of bitter resentment toward your informers, whoever they are, for such vile misrepresentations of my actions or those of my trusted subordinates.'[2] A week later he was dead.

In view of this extreme touchiness and suspicion on the part of the Russians, Eisenhower realized that he had to move with the greatest caution in arranging surrenders of the German forces. Contact was made between Russian and American troops at Torgau on 25 April. Thereafter the German forces were pressed together between the Western and Russian armies. Eisenhower had decided not to advance beyond the Elbe (except in the extreme north), and to insist that all Germans facing east should surrender to the Russians, and should

[1] Stalin to Roosevelt, 3 May 1945, quoted in Churchill, VI, 392.
[2] Quoted in Churchill, VI, 394.

not attempt to negotiate a surrender to the Anglo-American forces instead. Further, any general surrender was to be signed jointly by all the Allied commanders (or their deputies). These arrangements were scrupulously observed, from the moment when the Germans began sending emissaries across the lines to Montgomery's and Eisenhower's Headquarters. On 4 May Montgomery accepted the surrender of all the German forces in north-west Germany, Denmark and Holland, and on the 7th the surrender of the remaining forces was signed at Eisenhower's Headquarters at Rheims—an occasion that was marred by a last-minute Russian insistence that the official ceremony of signing should take place the following day in Berlin.[1]

The End of Hitler

By this time Hitler was dead. Since 16 January 1945 he had been at the Chancellery at Berlin, and for the last weeks of his life spent most of the time underground in the concrete bunker in the garden (containing office, bedrooms, kitchen, etc.). He was prematurely aged. His face was thin and ashen, his figure that of a bent old man, his left hand and the whole left side of his body shook and trembled. His hoarse voice quavered, his metallic eyes were covered with a film of exhaustion.[2] This was the man who kept an obsequious court underground while above his head Berlin was bombed and shelled into ruins, and the other great cities of the Reich were shattered, in a holocaust of death and disaster which overtook soldiers and civilians alike. 'World conquest or ruin'[3] had been his slogan. Now at last forced to admit defeat he was prepared for the whole of Germany to go down into destruction with him. Such was the hold that he still kept on his former followers that when a man like Speer set himself to preserve what could be saved from the wreck, instead of obeying Hitler's orders to destroy, he could only act by subterfuge; and he made the dangerous trip to Berlin after it had been entirely surrounded by the Russians, to ask his Führer's pardon.

---

[1] For details about these negotiations, see H. Feis: *Between War and Peace* (Princeton, 1960), 6–18.

[2] H. R. Trevor-Roper: *The Last Days of Hitler* (Pan Books, 1952), 77; Bullock, 766.

[3] Trevor-Roper, 54. Hitler said to Speer: 'If the war is to be lost, the nation also will perish. This fate is inevitable. There is no need to consider the basis even of a most primitive existence any longer. On the contrary it is better to destroy even that and to destroy it ourselves.' Trevor-Roper, 88.

Increasingly divorced from reality, Hitler still shuffled about the bunker with maps in his hand, or pored over them on a table, ready to explain to anyone who would listen his latest plan for saving Germany. For at times his hopes revived. The only consistent point to which he held was that he would stay in Berlin and commit suicide there before being captured by the Russians. Still in his last days subject to rages and uttering torrents of impassioned speech, he bitterly denounced his generals and colleagues, the army and the Luftwaffe—everyone was incompetent or had deserted him. He abandoned responsibility for further conduct of the war, in a terrible scene on 22 April, and petulantly said that the generals could apply to Göring for orders, and that Göring could do the negotiating with the enemy. But when Göring (now at Berchtesgaden) asked for confirmation of this point, he dismissed him from all his offices and had him and his staff put under arrest.

Göring, Bormann,[1] Himmler and others who were, or once had been close to Hitler, were living in the same unreal world. Each one attempted by intrigue against his rivals to take over power from the stricken master—as if there would be power to inherit or share in the general collapse of the Third Reich. With the waning of Hitler's dominating will, the light shone momentarily on the private empires which his minions had built up, before these too disappeared.

Eventually, on 29 April, Hitler dictated his political testament, in which Grand-Admiral Dönitz, latterly in command of the north German zone, was appointed as his successor. Thereafter everything went in ceremonial fashion. Hitler married Eva Braun, his mistress, who had refused to leave the bunker; a reception was held, champagne was drunk; formal farewells were paid by Hitler to his personal staff, and to Goebbels, to his women secretaries and cook; finally he committed suicide along with his bride, and the bodies were burned in the Chancellery garden (30 April 1945). Goebbels and his wife followed his example, after poisoning their children; Bormann disappeared while trying to escape; Himmler committed suicide when he fell into the hands of the British, as did Göring when on trial at Nuremberg. So ended Hitler's Reich; and Europe began to rebuild itself from the ruins.

[1] Hitler's Party Secretary. Himmler was also dismissed for negotiating with the enemy.

9: Heavy Bombing

When Hitler shot himself in the Chancellery bunker he left Germany a land of ruins. These ruins were made by the Allied bombers, a high proportion of them in the last months of the war.

Bombing in 1939–40

At the start of the war, as if by a mutual pact, both sides refrained from bombing each other's cities. The mass destruction of the great centres of population, which many had expected immediately war began, did not take place. The Luftwaffe's strength was mostly employed in support of the ground forces and, in Poland, in annihilating the enemy air force. Parts of Warsaw suffered from bombardment, but until the air attack on Rotterdam in May 1940, Western cities had been scarcely touched. A few purely military or naval objectives were attacked. The R.A.F. spent most of its hours over Germany in dropping leaflets on the inhabitants.

Chamberlain had been frustrated in his attempts to prevent the outbreak of war, but as long as he was Prime Minister he wholeheartedly set himself to limit its effects. In any case Bomber Command of the Royal Air Force did not possess the ability, in terms of aircraft and bomb-loads, to do anything effective even against Germany's most obvious targets, its large industrial towns. This was proved when Churchill took over the Premiership and a more aggressive attitude was shown. Especially after the fall of France Bomber Command was regarded as providing a means of 'getting at' Germany, which had become extremely difficult to do in other ways. Much of its strength was directed against the ports from which the invasion of Britain was expected to be launched. Such forces as it had left over for raids on objectives in Germany had only nuisance value. They were an incentive for the Germans to improve their air raid precautions, which before long, in most cities, reached a high state of efficiency.

The Moral Issue

Some of the leading clergy and laymen, well known for their religious or humanitarian principles (such as Lord Salisbury), raised the moral issues connected with the bombing of population centres. Few would cavil at damage done to civilians or their property in raids directed against military and industrial objectives; whereas deliberate attacks on built-up areas as the main targets could be regarded as making war not merely on men engaged in war-production, but on women and children as well. They involved the justification of terror as an instrument of war and opened a chapter of the most extreme barbarism in history, which the massacres of Genghiz Khan or the destruction of Magdeburg in the Thirty Years War can scarcely be said to rival.

The only equivalent to the complete flouting of the values of civilization, which was implicit in the heavy bombing policy of the Allies, was in the grotesquely brutal actions of the Nazis themselves, particularly in Poland, Yugoslavia and Russia, and in the corresponding excesses of the Red Army and the rigours of the Soviet Occupation.

The moral issue was however ignored. It was assumed, before war began, that if war came it would be total, that it could scarcely be limited in any appreciable degree, and that it might well bring about the decline, or even the end, of civilization. A few could perceive that the policy of the economic blockade, relentlessly pursued by the Ministry of Economic Warfare [1] from the earliest days of hostilities, was equally and inevitably directed also against all civilians, including women and children, especially if the blockade reached a degree of effectiveness like that of the First World War.

In any case the bombing of Rotterdam and later the 'blitz' on London, Coventry and other cities, supplied the justification for many of the British people—if any were needed: the Germans had to be paid back in their own coin. It was immaterial who 'started it' (in fact the British attempted area bombing, albeit ineffectively, against German cities in May 1940, before the Germans unleashed the blitz on London). As one M.P. wrote to the Minister for Air, Sir Archibald Sinclair,[2] 'I am all for the bombing of working-class areas in

[1] See W. N. Medlicott: *The Economic Blockade* (History of the Second World War, H.M.S.O., 1952). Ch. 22: 'Assessment and perspective' (Vol. II, p. 630).
[2] Later Lord Thurso.

German cities. I am Cromwellian—I believe in "slaying in the name of the Lord", because I do not believe you will ever bring home to the civil populations of Germany the horrors of war until they have become tasted in this way'—a similar sentiment to that expressed more tersely by many an Englishman under the blitz.

Sinclair's reply was that he was 'delighted to find that you and I are in complete agreement about ... bombing policy generally'.[1] In public he took a different line, steadfastly denying that attacks on the German population were being made with a view to breaking morale. 'He usually, and on public occasions invariably, suggested that Bomber Command was aiming at military or industrial installations as, of course, it sometimes was. He did not conceal that severe and sometimes vast damage was done to residential areas, but he either implied, or on some occasions said, that all this was incidental and even regrettable. Only in this way, he explained ... could he satisfy the enquiries of the Archbishop of Canterbury, the Moderator of the Church of Scotland and other significant religious leaders whose moral condemnation of the bombing offensive might, he observed, disturb the morale of Bomber Command crews.' [2]

Among those responsible in Britain and America for the direction of the war, the moral issue was not considered when decisions were being made as to whether 'area' or 'precision' bombing was to be the policy.[3] The simple criterion was which form of attack would have the greatest effect in disrupting Germany's war-effort and in weakening her will to resist, this being weighed in relation to the striking power and technique available to the planes at the time. When in 1940–2 it was found by experience that precision bombing, whether by day or night, was unable to produce worth-while results, the logical conclusion was to go for area bombing in the hopes of lowering morale and—even if on the side—striking a blow at military or industrial objectives.[4]

[1] The extracts from the M.P.'s letter and from Sinclair's reply are quoted in Sir Charles Webster and Noble Frankland: *The Strategic Air Offensive against Germany 1939–1945* (History of the Second World War, H.M.S.O., 1961), III, 115.

[2] Ibid., 116.

[3] 'The moral issue was not really an operative factor. The choice between precision and area bombing was not conditioned by abstract theories of right and wrong nor by interpretations of international law. It was ruled by operational possibilities and strategic intentions.' (*The Strategic Air Offensive*, II, 22.)

[4] E.g., Memo of Sir Charles Portal (Chief of the Air Staff) to Sir Norman Bottomley

The Strategy of Area Bombing

This policy was warmly embraced by Sir Arthur Harris, who became Commander-in-Chief of Bomber Command in February 1942. 'His power of command and unshakable determination . . . distinguished him as a giant among his contemporaries.' His very defects, though 'serious and inconvenient' to others, were but one aspect of the intense concentration with which he pursued his aim—his 'habit of seeing only one side of a question and then exaggerating it', his 'tendency to confuse advice with interference, criticism with sabotage and evidence with propaganda'.[1] His personal contact with Churchill, whose war-time residence of Chequers was only a short drive from Bomber Command H.Q., made him a formidable adversary to the opponents of his policy.

To prove his point Harris organized the bomber raid on Lübeck in March 1942, whose inner city on its island—a medieval glory of half-timbered houses—was a compact, visible and inflammable target, with a high density of population to the acre. The old Hanseatic city, with its romanesque Cathedral, its Marienkirche, its medieval salt-house, and many other art treasures, was totally destroyed. Thanks to good precautions, the loss of life was lower than might have been expected. An almost equally destructive raid on Rostock where (incidentally) the Heinkel aircraft works were hit, served as another proof of the effectiveness of area attacks, and the thousand bomber raids on Cologne and Essen (May and June 1942) clinched it. Thereafter, though the policy swung from area bombing to precision targets, the attempts to sap German morale by striking at the cities became accepted policy. It was written into the Casablanca directive of January 1943, though this was interpreted by Harris in a way which somewhat strained the meaning of the original. It was held to be vindicated by the destruction of a large part of Hamburg in the seven successive raids of July and August 1943.

The sweltering weather and drought of those summer days had converted Hamburg into a tinder-box. Excellent visibility and new

---

(Deputy Chief of the Air Staff), 15 February 1942: 'Aiming points are to be the built-up areas, *not*, for instance, the dockyards or aircraft factories.' (*The Strategic Air Offensive*, I, 324.)

[1] *The Strategic Air Offensive*, III, 80.

radar and anti-radar devices [1] had enormously increased the effectiveness of the attack. The fires started were on such a scale that they linked up to form a blazing inferno at the heart of Hamburg, the first of those fire-storms [2] which asphyxiated more people than were burnt, and whose heat made it impossible for rescuers even to approach the devastated areas. This bonfire of a city, presaging the atom-bomb attacks on Japan, was repeated at Wuppertal (May 1943), Kassel (October 1943), later at Stuttgart, Darmstadt and elsewhere. On these occasions shelters became death-traps. Those fleeing were often scorched to death by white-heat from the sea of flame behind them.

Berlin, though heavily and continuously bombed, escaped the fate of the fire-storm. More spread out, more solidly built and better defended than many other cities, it survived amidst its rubble as the recognizable capital of the Reich.

As the war continued, industrial targets were often hit, sometimes incidentally in an area attack, often deliberately aimed at. The *Pointblank* plan of June 1943 laid down the priorities, particularly attacks on German fighters and on the oil and other industries on which they depended. The policy of the 8th U.S. Air Force was precision bombing, whose daylight raids, though of considerable effect, were too costly to be continued after the autumn of 1943.[3] They were only resumed when long-range fighters and the weakening of the Luftwaffe had given the Allied planes command of the air.

Precision bombing was also required of R.A.F. Bomber Command when it came under Eisenhower before and during the invasion of Europe. Its efforts were then largely directed, with evident success, against communications, concentration areas and other objectives whose destruction would weaken the Wehrmacht's mobility and resistance. When in the autumn of 1944 it regained its virtual autonomy, it reverted to its policy of area bombing—the aim, as Harris put it, being the destruction of two and a half of Germany's largest towns per month.[4] In addition, some of the smaller towns were (in con-

---

[1] One of the most effective devices was 'Window'—slips of metallized paper which, dropped in quantity, jammed the radar defences. Its use had been postponed for many months for fear lest the Germans would use it against British defences.

[2] See note at end of chapter.

[3] The raid on the Schweinfurt ball-bearing works cost 198 aircraft destroyed or seriously damaged.

[4] *The Strategic Air Offensive*, III, 82.

junction with the U.S.A.F.) demolished if they lay in the path of the advancing armies: Jülich was 97 per cent destroyed, and Düren totally.[1] But the most fearsome ordeal was reserved for Dresden.

The Bombing of Dresden

'Operation Thunderclap' was planned as a last morale-shaking blow against Germany. 'The time might well come in the not too distant future,' declared the British Chiefs of Staff in July 1944, 'when an all-out attack by every means at our disposal on German civilian morale might be decisive.'[2] The moment for this blow was defined by Sir Charles Portal as that when the Nazi system was on the point of collapse. 'This opportunity to enforce surrender may be a fleeting one; if it is not seized either the extremist elements may succeed in rallying the Army for a further stand or the collapse may spread so rapidly that central government ceases to exist.'[3] He suggested that, with a view to maximum devastation, the entire attack might be concentrated on a single big town other than Berlin and one hitherto relatively undamaged.[4]

This was supported by Churchill, who in January 1945 favoured 'basting the Germans in their retreat from Breslau'. What this meant in effect—though it may not have been intended by Churchill, was an all-out attack not merely on the inhabitants of the town concerned, but on the thousands of hapless refugees fleeing from the Russian advance in the east. In the latter part of January 1945 seven million Germans prepared to move westward from Silesia. Deprived of their able bodied menfolk at the last minute by a Gauleiter's decree, this mass of humanity began its long trek under the worst conditions, 'carrying all their remaining chattels in boxes and bags and camping out in the open air night after night in spite of the below-zero temperatures'.[5] The Gauleiter's decree also accounted for the disproportionately high number of women killed in the raid on Dresden. The Silesian capital, Breslau, was evacuated on 21 January of its

[1] H. Rumpf: *The Bombing of Germany* (Muller, 1963), 142. Only six houses were left intact.

[2] *The Strategic Air Offensive*, III, 52.

[3] Memo of 1 August 1944 (ibid., 54).

[4] Ibid., 55. As Sir Arthur Harris says 'the attack on Dresden was considered a military necessity by much more important people than myself'.—Sir A. Harris: *Bomber Offensive* (Collins, 1947), 242.

[5] D. Irving: *The Destruction of Dresden* (Kimber, 1963), 81.

remaining women, children and old folk. 'As the existing train service was hopelessly inadequate, over 100,000 people had to set out literally on foot.'[1]

In this way the 630,000 population of Dresden was vastly swollen. The city had no particular importance industrially; partly for this reason, and partly on account of its eastern location, it had not previously been bombed. One of the most beautiful cities in Europe, its inhabitants believed its immunity was due to the fact that the German bombers had spared Oxford.

Its fame as an architectural treasure-house did not deter the planners from putting 'Thunderclap' into effect. Although they did not know it, the target was almost open, since the city's anti-aircraft defences had been dismantled to meet more urgent needs elsewhere. With its well worked out 'Pathfinder' and 'Marker' Techniques, and the various radar and other navigational aids perfected during the war,[2] the first fleet of 250 aircraft had no difficulty in finding its target on the night of 13 February 1945. Three hours later, when the city was already a blazing inferno, 529 Lancasters flew in. Rescuers and their relief supplies who had been heading towards the city were overwhelmed in this second holocaust. Of the thousands of tons dropped in this attack 75 per cent were incendiaries, the rest blockbusters and other high explosives. The final blows were dealt by the American daylight raid of the next day, 14 February.

'By this time . . . the civilian population was completely stunned by the weight of the blow which had hit Dresden. Just a few hours before, Dresden had been a fairy-tale city of spires and cobbled streets, where it had been possible to admire the crowded shop-windows in the main streets, where the evening hours had not brought the gloom of total black-out, where the windows were still unbroken and the curtains had not been removed, a city where the evening streets had been full of people thronging home from the Circus, Opera, or the scores of cinemas and theatres which, even in these days of 'total war', had been still playing. Now total war had put an end to all that. . . .'[3]

The American raid 'finally brought the people to their knees'—not the bombs of the Flying Fortresses, but the Mustang fighters 'which

[1] Irving, 84.

[2] The Germans' early warning system had by now been overrun—hence defence in depth on their part was impossible.

[3] Irving, 180.

suddenly appeared low over the city, firing on everything that moved, and machine-gunning the columns of lorries heading towards the city. One section of the Mustangs concentrated on the river banks where masses of bombed-out people had gathered'.[1]

The raids on Dresden were in fact part of a pattern, an orgy of destruction, seemingly for its own sake, undertaken as if by some fearful Frankenstein released in the heart of Europe. Cathedral cities with their thousand-year, irreplaceable buildings, and their more recent but equally noble baroque glories, were committed to the flames with virtually all their people. Such was the fate of Würzburg, and of the medieval town of Hildesheim, 'with its four magnificent churches and its great store of art treasures'.[2] Nordhausen, Potsdam —the list might have continued indefinitely had not the war's ending intervened—its ending being scarcely, if at all, hastened by this catalogue of annihilation.

Balancing the Account

At the time of writing it is difficult to pick up a charred limb or a human bone in the neighbourhood of what was not long ago a scene of devastation. But if some twentieth-century Peterkin were to find such a relic and ask his grandfather 'what good came of it at last?'[3] the question might be hard to answer.

On the negative side, destruction and death on a scale, which in many cases can never be measured. Nobody knows how many were killed in the raids on Hamburg or Dresden. In Dresden people were burnt to death, or more often (probably 75 per cent) asphyxiated when the fire-storm raged above and around them, trapped in the cellars, in the underground shelters, in the station subways, in the crowded refugee trains or even in the open. For weeks it was impossible to approach some of the areas on account of the heat or to enter cellars, where the temperatures had risen over 1,000°. In a vast number of cases identification was impossible, despite the heroic and typically thorough efforts of the rescue workers, many of them girls of the K.H.D. (*Kriegshilfsdienst*)[4] and the volunteer and auxiliary

---

[1] Irving, 180.   [2] Rumpf, 151.

[3] R. Southey: *After Blenheim.*

[4] 850 of these were killed in the raids on Dresden. The figure for the total number of killed is between 60,000 and 250,000 (Rumpf, 157).

officials. Pyres and mass-graves had not received all the victims before
the Russians arrived in the city on 8 May 1945, the last day of the
war.

In fact, Dresden did not yield one day sooner to its enemies on
account of the raids than if it had been spared. Did this apply to the
Reich as a whole?

Usually after a big raid—as in the case of Dresden—transport was
quickly restored,[1] and even factories which had been hit often resumed working fairly soon, unless damage to the actual machinery
had been severe. Estimates of reduced production in consequence of
raids in the first half of the war were invariably wide of the mark.
Lübeck's production was back to 90 per cent within a week, the
Heinkel works at Rostock made a 'brilliant recovery'. Cologne, after
the thousand-bomber raid, was functioning normally within a fortnight: only a month's production was reckoned to have been lost.
In Hamburg the labour force was reduced by 10 per cent, but in five
months production of armaments recovered, though not of other
goods.[2] As the war went on and destruction became more severe,
production correspondingly suffered, but the efforts of Albert Speer
as Armaments Minister were so successful as to bring about a rising
curve of production for aircraft, tanks and other necessities of war
until autumn 1944. Considering the generally disappointing results,
in terms of lowering production, of precision raids (even when the
objectives were attained) such as those by the R.A.F. on the Möhne
and Eder dams,[3] or by the U.S.A.F. on the Schweinfurt ball-bearing
works, it is not surprising that area bombing achieved no greater
success in this sphere.

On the other hand, though Speer achieved the 'miracle' of raising
German war-production until late in the war, undoubtedly production would have risen more, and more quickly, had it not been for the
bombing attacks.[4] The estimate made at the time by Allied intelli-

[1] Through rail traffic was restored in three days. The marshalling yards had received
little damage and the main bridge was intact.
[2] *The Strategic Air Offensive*, II, 261. Rumpf, 85.
[3] The failure to breach the third (Sorpe) dam offset considerably the success in
breaching the other two.
[4] It can be argued that some of the early destruction *helped* production. 'The loss of
"a few desks and telephones" released Germany's industry from the harassing bonds
of bureaucratic over-organization, and allowed it to get on with its job without interference'—Rumpf, 169. Speer stated that war production would have been 30 per cent

gence that Germany lost between 7 per cent and 10 per cent production between March 1943 and March 1944 turned out to be 'not far from the truth', though, of this, armaments production counted for only 5 per cent, and a good deal less in the first quarter of 1944.[1] The subsequent attacks on Germany's oil industry were successful in greatly reducing the mobility of the Wehrmacht, while the lack of fuel made it impossible to train pilots and aircrews on the necessary scale, and contributed to grounding the Luftwaffe. Already the need to increase fighter-defence prevented Germany from building a strategic bombing force.[2] The German night-fighters which were developed were highly effective, but the army did not have the air-support in the latter part of the Russian war which it otherwise might have had, and the same applied, even more disastrously for the Germans, in their attempt to stop the Allied invasion in the west. On the other side, the powerful support which bombing gave the invasion army made its task far less costly in casualties, and possibly made the difference between success and failure.[3]

In the important attacks on V-bomb sites, on the rocket development centre at Peenemunde, on U-boat pens and other naval objectives (for instance the *Tirpitz*) it was precision bombing which counted. The area attacks stand or fall largely on their effectiveness in shortening the war by undermining morale.

Allowing that, in the circumstances of 1942 'area bombing was operationally inevitable',[4] there was far too much wishful thinking in the decisions to pursue it. From the beginning of the war until near the end 'the cardinal error of intelligence was the description of the German economy as tightly stretched and in decline when it was, in reality, resilient, cushioned and increasingly productive, and of the German people as exhausted, disaffected and liable to panic and revolt when, in reality, and on the whole, they were vigorous, calm, stoical and loyal'.[5] A shattering blow, such as the destruction of

---

higher but for Allied bombing. Medlicott, II, 640. J. K. Galbraith: *The Affluent Society* (Hamilton 1958), 128: "It is a distinct possibility that the attack on Hamburg increased Germany's output of war material and thus her military effectiveness."

[1] *The Strategic Air Offensive*, II, 251, 252.   [2] Ibid., 297.

[3] Sir Arthur Harris makes the point rather curiously: 'Without the intervention of Bomber Command the invasion of Europe would have gone down as the bloodiest campaign in history unless, indeed, it had failed outright—as it would undoubtedly have done.' (*Bomber Offensive*, 269.)

[4] *The Strategic Air Offensive*, III, 300.   [5] Ibid., 302.

Hamburg, aroused fears in the minds of Speer and some others that it might not be possible to continue the war. But such fears were temporary. The essential virtues of the German character never shone more clearly than during this ordeal—courage, tenacity, steadiness and a high degree of self-help and communal responsibility. Even Dresden did not break morale—there was evidence that, if anything, it promoted a determination to stick it out until the end, whatever the end might be, for between 'unconditional surrender' and mass destruction, between the erasing of cities by the Allies from the west and the advancing Red Army from the east, there seemed little to expect or hope for either from heaven or earth. 'What kept people on their feet was the desperate situation itself. . . . The suffering caused by the devastation of Germany's towns was the cement which not only held them together but held them to a state for which they no longer felt any enthusiasm. And the catastrophe which descended on Dresden aroused a last desperate effort among the exhausted masses.'[1]

From the standpoint of rough justice the Germans might be said to have reaped where they had sown, but the justice, if such it was, was so rough as to fall largely on those who had no responsibility whatsoever for Germany's crimes. But the partial or total destruction of eighty cities, the loss of 600,000 civilian lives (as against 60,000 in Britain during the whole of the blitz), the maiming of another 800,000, and the infliction of immeasurable suffering, has been regarded by some as a kind of requital.[2]

Hitler, Goebbels and the rest of the Nazi hierarchy never viewed it in this light. It was not realized outside Germany that to destroy them, or break their fanaticism, was the only means of shortening the war. The unleashing of total destruction on Germany's cities large and small, one after another could not by itself produce the desired effect. The war only ended when the Russians had nearly reached Hitler's bunker in the heart of Berlin. His suicide, along with his handing power to Dönitz, alone produced the conditions for an armistice.

[1] Rumpf, 205. Sir Arthur Harris confirms this view: 'The idea that the main object of bombing German industrial cities was to break the enemy's morale proved to be wholly unsound' (*Bomber Offensive*, 78). He asserts however that Dresden was a suitable target as a communications and industrial centre.
[2] Rumpf, 164.

These considerations in no way invalidate the incalculable cold courage of pilots and crews as they fought their way to their objectives, through conditions of weather, 'flak' and fighters which were often murderous. For the Commonwealth it was an inspiring effort of co-operation, a high proportion of those serving in Bomber Command being from overseas, not to mention the considerable number from other European countries (nearly a thousand from Poland). The Empire Air Training Scheme supplied the means of putting the air armadas into action. But the losses were heavy—over 57,000 officers and men died while serving in the Command, while over 9,000 were wounded. These men, and those of the U.S. Air Force who gave their lives or their limbs, were the flower of their countries. The losses, though low in relation to those inflicted, are high in comparison with those suffered by the land-forces. The British Army, between Dunkirk and Arnhem, had only slightly higher casualties, of whom 63,000 were killed.

The Atomic Bomb

If bombing has to be done there is logically no stopping point between the smallest hand-bomb or incendiary and the hydrogen bomb with its power of massive destruction. In pursuit of this logic another great international, and largely Anglo-American enterprise was undertaken, the creation of the atomic bomb. Scientists who had fled from Germany, many of them former students of the Danish physicist Niels Bohr, joined with the brilliant group in England which Professor Ernest (later Lord) Rutherford had gathered at Cambridge. The American government took over the British project and placed it under the direction of J. R. Oppenheimer at the University of Chicago and at Los Alamos, New Mexico. This vast co-operative venture belongs to the history of the world, rather than to that of Europe, as does its horrifying sequel in the bombing of Hiroshima and Nagasaki. It is the story of the bomb that, within a margin of a few weeks, might have obliterated what was left of Berlin.

NOTES

1. A secret German official document, quoted by Sir Arthur Harris in *Bomber Offensive* (page 174), describes a fire-storm as follows: 'Through the union of a number of fires, the air gets so hot that on account of its

decreasing specific weight, it receives a terrific momentum, which in its turn causes other surrounding air to be sucked towards the centre. By that suction, combined with the enormous difference in temperature (600–1000 degrees centigrade) tempests are caused which go far beyond their meteorological counterparts (20–30 degrees centigrade). In a built-up area the suction could not follow its shortest course, but the overheated air stormed through the streets with immense force taking along not only sparks but burning timber and roof beams, so spreading the fire farther and farther, developing in a short time into a fire typhoon such as was never before witnessed, against which every human resistance was useless.'

2. Details about German war-production and the efficacy of Allied bombing can be found in the testimony of Albert Speer during his trial at Nuremberg, printed in *The Trial of German Major War Criminals—Proceedings of the International Military Tribunal sitting at Nuremberg, Germany* (H.M.S.O., 1951), vol. 17, pp. 2 seq.

In production, total war-effort was achieved only in August 1944. There was a steady rise in production up to autumn 1944. During 1944 Speer was able to re-equip completely 130 infantry divisions and 40 armoured divisions—two million men. 'This figure would have been 30% higher had it not been for the bombing attacks.' The production peak for munitions was August 1944, for aircraft September 1944, for ordnance and U-boats, December 1944. 'Here too, however, bombing attacks retarded the mass production of these new weapons, which, in the last phase of the war might have changed the situation to a great extent' (p. 26).

From 12 May 1944 onwards, when fuel plants became targets for concentrated air attacks, the situation became 'catastrophic. Ninety per cent of the fuel was lost to us from that time on. . . . Our new tanks and jet planes were of no use without fuel' (p. 26).

3. The effect of heavy bombing on morale can be gauged from some of the entries by Goebbels in his diary. '*May 25, 1943*. The night raid by the English on Dortmund was extraordinarily heavy, probably the worst ever directed against a German city. . . . Reports from Dortmund are horrible. The critical thing about it is that industrial and munitions plants have been hit very hard . . . Schaub . . . had received reports from Bochum and Dortmund indicating that morale was lower than ever before. The reports are somewhat exaggerated, but we must recognize that the people in the west are gradually beginning to lose courage. Hell like that is hard to bear for any length of time, especially since the inhabitants along the Rhine and Ruhr see no prospect of improvement.'—*The Goebbels Diaries*, ed. L. P. Lochner (Hamilton, 1948), 311.

10: The German Resistance

The war ended with Germany prostrate, divided, occupied and, in part, devastated. There was no government except that which the occupying powers could provide. Of the opposition to Hitler which might have eventually formed a new government for Germany, the largest number had been killed—most of them after the failure of the attempt on Hitler's life of 20 July 1944.

The Opposition to Hitler

This plot had been the culminating point of the efforts of those who had wished to bring about a change of government in Germany during the war. Although the opposition to Hitler had been widespread, it had been largely inarticulate, and ranged from the 'non-Nazis' and the critics of the régime who were prepared to take no overt action, to those who were prepared to risk all in overthrowing what they had come to regard as a disastrous and monstrous tyranny. Of those who acted individually, none hoped to do much more than make a protest which might ultimately have practical consequences, but which could not affect the existing situation.

From 1933, practically the only hope for overthrowing the régime lay with the army; it depended on a sufficient number of senior army officers being ready to organize a coup. Initiative and backing could come from civilians, but short of a revolt among Hitler's own 'Praetorian Guard' of the S.S. and élite units, it had to come from the other element in the state with actual physical power, the armed forces.

This does not deprive of significance the immense and unconditional sacrifices of individuals and non-military groups in taking their stand for the right against what they came to recognize as evil enthroned in the state. Among the communists who stood against Hitler there were many inspired by a genuine idealism—though as a party the communists were thrown off balance by the Molotov-

Ribbentrop agreement of August 1939. Those who were in prison before that date mostly remained there, despite the agreement. Their comrades who were still at liberty resumed anti-Nazi activities after Hitler declared war on Russia. Communists gained power over the other prisoners in several concentration camps, and even began clandestinely to collect arms, but not in sufficient quantity to effect their own release before the war ended. Many were slowly done to death in the camps, others were eventually murdered, as was Ernst Thälmann in Buchenwald (August 1944).

Social-democrats and other opposition parties had their martyrs too. Of the religious groups some of the toughest resisters were to be found among the Jehovah's Witnesses, who refused to swear oaths, do military service, and acknowledge 'State and Führer'. Several thousand were sent to concentration camps before the war started, their women being taken to Ravensbrück and their children scattered. Some were shot in batches, all were given particularly brutal treatment, but save in a few cases the S.S. failed to break their spirit. The case of youthful resisters who paid the ultimate penalty has a special poignancy, such as Hans and Sophie Scholl. These students of Munich University severed their connections with the Nazi Youth organizations, and, in the winter of 1942-3, duplicated leaflets claiming freedom of thought and attacking the Nazi oppression of Jews and Poles, and other excesses. Arrested by the Gestapo, the Scholls and one of their friends, Christopher Probst, freely admitted their actions, and after a brief imprisonment were executed.

The Scholls came from a Protestant home—their mother was a Deaconess in the Evangelical Church. But in general the Protestants, fragmented into numbers of sects, were ill-placed for concerting opposition, and the tradition of the Evangelical Church, going back to Luther, was of dependence on (even subservience to) the state. Concentration on personal religion and on maintaining the life of the Church as something which was 'not of this world', had brought the bulk of Ministers and laity to the position of accepting the actions of the state authorities as not being their concern. But there were many who sooner or later came to realize that their version of rendering to Caesar the things that are Caesar's had put power over all the external actions of life—even of private life—into the hands of evil men. Many began to realize this fact only when the state supported the 'German

Christian' movement, and enforced the appointment of its leader Ludwig Müller as Bishop in September 1933, an event which split the Evangelical Church, as it was designed to do. (The German Christians tried to prove that Christ was an 'Aryan' who had been killed by the Jews, and that the Old Testament, being Jewish, was at best largely irrelevant.)

Of those who resisted, some, like Bishop Wurm of Württemberg and Bishop Meiser of Bavaria, managed to hold their own till the end of the war, making constant protests to the authorities (for instance against the treatment of Jewish Christians, and the take-over of Church groups by the Nazis), despite warnings and periods of imprisonment. Some, like Pastor Niemöller, were imprisoned but survived, others were done to death with the utmost cruelty, accepting their tortures as re-living the sufferings of Christ on the cross. Such was Pastor Paul Schneider, whose outspoken criticisms brought him into trouble in the first year of Nazi rule, and who was killed in Buchenwald in July 1939 after nearly two years of the most brutal and degrading treatment

Catholics, too, resisted as individuals. In Germany the protest of the Roman Catholic Church as a whole was muted, apart from Pius XI's encyclical of March 1937, *Mit Brennender Sorge*, which criticized the Nazis' racial doctrines and their failure to observe the Concordat of July 1933. The weakness of the Catholic position lay in having made the Concordat at all, for in making it the Vatican was taking the lead in giving recognition to the Nazi state—and it gained few benefits from it, since Hitler had no intention of respecting the guarantees for Church autonomy which it contained (only five days after concluding it, Hitler dissolved the Catholic Youth League). But, with or without backing from the Vatican, the Catholic Church gave its martyrs and men of faith. There was Father Bernhard Lichtenberg, Dean of St Hedwig's Cathedral, Berlin, who publicly prayed for the Jews, and died on the way from his Berlin prison to Dachau. There was the priest, August von Rathenau, murdered in Dachau for trying to prevent Polish girls from being beaten up and raped, and Father Otto Müller, tortured to death in Berlin-Tegel gaol for helping Jews to escape from the Nazis. There were the lion-hearted Bishops, Cardinal Faulhaber of Bavaria, and Clemens Count von Galen of Münster, whose outspokenness and tenacity brought them such

powerful support from their flocks that the Nazis held back from
bringing them to book.

The Kreisau Circle

Individual protests and martyrdoms had their value, but organized
attempts to overthrow the régime came near to changing the course of
history. The core of this resistance was Christian, and some clergy,
like the Jesuit Father Delp and the Protestant theologian and pastor
Dietrich Bonhöffer, were connected with these attempts. Not all the
members of the Kreisau circle, with whom they were in touch, were
ready to overthrow the régime. Its leader, Count Helmut von Moltke,
great-grand-nephew of the famous Field-Marshal, himself much
travelled, and with close English connections,[1] brought many men of
different backgrounds into the meetings on his Kreisau estate where
the future of Germany and Europe was discussed. Moltke died rejoicing that he had not been actively involved in the planning of a
coup—that he stood before Freisler, the President of the People's
Court 'not as a Protestant, not as a landowner, nobleman or Prussian,
not even as a German—but as a Christian and nothing else'.[2]

Friends and relatives of Moltke's, like Count Peter Yorck von
Wartenburg and Adam von Trott zu Solz, took a more active part in
the conspiracy, as did Social Democrats like Julius Leber and trade
unionists like Jakob Kaiser. The link between the Kreisau Circle and
the army officers who attempted Hitler's overthrow was important—
'whereas the generals had to organize action against Hitler, Kreisau
produced the moral and intellectual ideas which gave them
faith and sense of purpose'.[3] Their Christian faith inspired these men.
'Where [the decision] came out of the genuine compulsion of faith,
the Opposition dared to appear more openly in the light, to speak
more boldly and clearly, and to go more confidently to martyrdom
than any other section of the resistance.'[4] Bonhoeffer could take the
radical step, at a secret church conference at Geneva in 1941, of pray-

---

[1] His mother, *née* Dorothy Rose-James, was from South Africa. 'Through his mother
he had come to love England and English liberalism, and he had English godfathers for
both of his sons.'—R. Manvell and H. Fraenkel: *The July Plot* (The Bodley Head, 1964),
52.

[2] Quoted in T. Prittie: *Germans Against Hitler* (Hutchinson, 1964), 227.

[3] Prittie, 225.

[4] G. Ritter: *Carl Goerdeler und die Deutsche Widerstandsbewegung* (Deutsche Verlags-
Anstalt, Stuttgart, 1954), 106.

ing for the defeat of Germany: 'Only through a defeat can we atone for the terrible crimes which we have committed against Europe and the world.'[1] He believed that a necessary step in bringing about the moral purging of Germany was the elimination of Hitler.

The attempt could only be undertaken by the officers, who alone had some chance of access to Hitler, and who could organize the take-over of the various military headquarters and of the civilian centres of government. But most of the senior officers after 1939 were too concerned with their professional tasks and their personal careers —they were understandably absorbed in the business of directing their highly efficient fighting machine in the greatest war in history— a war with whose objectives, at the start at any rate, many of them were in agreement.[2] They had also put themselves morally in a weak position for overthrowing Hitler by having allowed him to use his private army, the S.S., for murdering Röhm and the many others who were 'liquidated' in the blood-bath of 30th June 1934, and for shortly afterwards taking a personal oath of loyalty to Hitler in the place o that to the German state. This oath, in the minds of most officers, had about it something of the sanctity which attached originally to the oath of fealty to the Prussian monarchs, and which could not easily be broken.[3] This, and the withdrawal from ultimate responsibility for the use of force within the state—as against the state's external enemies—which their neutrality of 30 June 1934 signified, had prepared the way for the degrading subservience to Hitler of the officers' corps as a whole.

The Military Opposition

This position, however, had not been accepted by all the officers (most of the resisters among them were from old Junker families with generations of service to the Prussian Crown). The former Commander-in-Chief, von Hammerstein, was ready to stake all on overthrowing Hitler, as were Ludwig Beck, until 1938 Chief of the General

---

[1] H. Rothfels: *The German Opposition to Hitler* (Wolff, 1962), 135.

[2] See Manstein, 287.

[3] According to L. von Hammerstein (son of General von Hammerstein), and one of the younger officers who took part in the attempted coup of 20 July 1944, 'neither he nor his comrades were concerned about their oath to Hitler, whom they regarded as a criminal and the destroyer of their country. The oath, he said, was only used as an alibi by those who were too cowardly to face the issue of loyalty.' (Manvell and Fraenkel, 234.)

Staff, Field-Marshal von Witzleben, in 1942 commanding the army in the west, General Olbricht, head of the Army Office in Berlin, General Hans Oster of the Central Counter-Intelligence Office of O.K.W., and General Henning von Tresckow, who in 1941 became Chief of Staff to von Bock's Central Army Group in the east. Admiral Canaris, head of the Abwehr (Intelligence Security Department) gave fullest cover to the conspirators (Oster, for instance, came directly under his orders). Many other higher officers, and various of the commanding generals—latterly Rommel himself and Speidel his Chief of Staff— were either privy to or supporters of one or another of the plots to get rid of Hitler from 1936 onwards.

It was not a matter merely of killing Hitler—the need was also to seize control, and at the same time make contact with the Allies. Von Trott (a former Rhodes Scholar with friends in England and America) had been active in attempting to bring about an understanding be- tween the Opposition and the Western democracies both before and after the outbreak of war. Planning for a coup to overthrow Hitler and stabilize Europe in agreement with the Western powers had reached an advanced stage in 1938 just before the Munich Agreement put *finis* to that particular attempt. The Western Governments showed themselves cautious and even cold towards such approaches, and these became increasingly difficult with the ending of the 'phoney war' in 1940, and the proclamation of unconditional surrender as the Allied objective at Casablanca in January 1943. Nevertheless the attempts continued, notably through the visits of Dietrich Bonhoeffer and Dr Hans Schönfeld (a representative of the World Council of Churches) to the Bishop of Chichester (George Bell) at Stockholm in May 1942, with the subsequent, but fruitless exchanges between the Bishop and Foreign Secretary Eden (June–July 1942).[1]

The basis of a possible settlement was agreed by most conspirators as a return to the 1919 frontiers, and a move towards a limitation of national sovereignty in Europe, in other words something like a federal approach. But as late as 1944 some of them, notably the leader on the civilian side, Karl Goerdeler, believed that Germany might keep something of what the Third Reich had gained in territory. Goerdeler, former Lord Mayor of Leipzig (1930–7) and Price Commissioner in the German Government under the Nazis (1934–5), represented the

[1] Rothfels, 134–7; Prittie, 122–3.

conservative element in the opposition. With all the virtues and some of the limitations of a Prussian he was a staunch nationalist and backed the Nazis until 1936, when he moved over to whole-hearted opposition. He was one of the essential links between the Kreisau circle and the military conspirators, and would have become Chancellor had they succeeded.

Plots Against Hitler

Of the various plots which developed, part were concerned with killing Hitler and his accomplices, part with seizing control, initially in Berlin, Vienna and Paris. When General von Hammerstein was recalled to active duty in September 1939 he attempted to lure Hitler to his headquarters at Cologne in order to arrest him there, but Hitler did not oblige. There were other individual attempts before a large-scale conspiracy was organized. Early in 1941 Tresckow took on to his staff Fabian von Schlabrendorff, a lawyer who had been an active anti-Nazi since his student days in the late twenties. The two became the centre of a far-ramifying conspiracy, worked out as 'Operation Flash', involving Witzleben, and enough of the officers in key positions at Berlin and the other capitals to make the success of a coup probable. In August 1941 they planned to seize Hitler on a visit to Bock's Headquarters near Smolensk, but found him far too carefully guarded. Further opportunities were few—the Führer 'had a peculiar scent for personal danger',[1] constantly changed his plans, and seemed to bear a charmed life. Tresckow worked continually on von Kluge, Bock's successor, to bring him to the point of action, and Goerdeler visited him to this end late in 1942.

The next year presented the most favourable opportunities. Attempts to get Hitler to visit the Headquarters at Smolensk at last succeeded, and the plotters placed a time-bomb, disguised as a parcel of brandy-bottles, on the plane for his return journey (13 March 1943). But the plane arrived safely, and Schlabrendorff, retrieving the package, found that 'the fuse had worked; the glass globule had broken; the corrosive fluid had consumed the retainer wire; the striker had operated; but—the detonator cap had not reacted'.[2] Several other attempts, some of which came near to success, might

---

[1] Fabian von Schlabrendorff: *Revolt against Hitler* (Eyre and Spottiswoode, 1948).
[2] Schlabrendorff, 85. See Note at end of chapter.

have shortened the war by one or two years and saved many of the fearful consequences which ensued from its prolongation.

By this stage a newcomer to the plot, Colonel Claus von Stauffenberg, had already begun to take a leading part. He was a 37-year-old noble from Württemberg, devoted to poetry and the arts, a magnificent horseman—formerly in the crack Bamberger Reiter Regiment—an Apollo among men; at the same time a devout Catholic whose robust faith impelled him take up the cudgels against the total barbarism of Hitler and his minions. Though of an old monarchist family his sympathies were all-embracing, and he looked to a generous inclusion of socialist and popular elements in the rehabilitated government of the Reich. He had shown himself to be at one with Tresckow and Schlabrendorff during a spell on the eastern front, where he had worked with them in building Russian units as the nuclei of an anti-Soviet resistance movement.[1] His decision to take an active part in the conspiracy came while recovering from serious wounds suffered in Tunisia early in 1943. With one eye, one arm, and only two fingers and a thumb on his remaining hand, he re-applied for active service and was taken on by General Olbricht as his Chief of Staff in the Home Army Headquarters at Berlin.

His first task was to overhaul and perfect the arrangements for seizing Berlin, Paris and other key-points as soon as another attempt on Hitler's life succeeded. To this end 'Operation Valkyrie' was devised as an official plan in the event of a mutiny by the S.S. or by some of the millions of foreign slave-workers now in Germany: a code-word announcing Hitler's death was to set the operation going. Secondly, Stauffenberg undertook the task of killing Hitler himself. As Chief of Staff to General Fromm commanding the Home Army (June 1944) he could gain access to the Führer's conferences, at one of which he planned to dispose of Hitler with a time-bomb concealed in his briefcase. Despite the Allied landings, Tresckow agreed that the attempt should be made 'at any cost. Even should that fail, the attempt to seize power in the capital must be undertaken. We must prove to the world and to future generations that the men of the German resistance movement dared to take the decisive step and to hazard their lives upon it. Compared with this object, nothing else matters.'[2]

An opportunity for the attempt was provided by a conference, at

[1] See pp. 105, 120.   [2] Schlabrendorff, 131.

the Obersalzburg in Bavaria (11th July), but it was called off because though Hitler was there Himmler and Göring were not present. The next occasion, at Rastenburg, (15th July) led to the preliminary code-word for Valkyrie being given in Berlin—it had to be halted when Hitler left the conference early, though troops had already begun to move into Berlin. On the third occasion (20th July), Stauffenberg actually exploded the bomb in the conference room at Rastenburg, but though Hitler was badly bruised and his right arm temporarily paralysed, he miraculously escaped alive.

Stauffenberg, who left the conference chamber just before the explosion, flew back to Berlin convinced that the first part of his mission was accomplished. General Fellgiebel, in charge of the communications branch of Hitler's headquarters, was to send the final code-word to Berlin as soon as the explosion took place, and then put the whole communications system out of action, so leaving Rastenburg isolated while the take-over at the capital was completed. He sent the code-word, but did not silence the communications centre, with subsequent fatal results.

Receiving the code-word at Berlin, Olbricht began to put Valkyrie in train, but he failed to persuade his superior, General Fromm, that Hitler was dead. Fromm managed to phone Field-Marshal Keitel at Rastenburg, and hearing that Hitler was alive attempted to halt Valkyrie altogether. He and some other officers were overpowered by Beck and his associates and put under guard while the conspirators attempted to carry on with Valkyrie by phoning the commanders in Berlin and elsewhere. Beck and Witzleben, coming to take over at the War Office, had however moved too slowly, and the conspirators failed to make a broadcast which might have brought them support throughout the country.

When Stauffenberg arrived at the War Office, nearly four and a half hours after leaving Rastenburg, not enough had been done. Calls to Paris and Vienna started the operation going there, but these were soon countermanded by Keitel from Rastenburg. Goebbels, who had not been arrested, spoke from his Berlin house over the phone to Hitler, and gained the support of Major Remer of the Guards Battalion, who moved his men to capture the conspirators in the Ministry of War. They found Fromm already freed by a counter-putsch of his pro-Nazi officers who had evaded the guard put over them by Olbricht. Stauffenberg was wounded and later despatched, Beck committed suicide. Fromm, by summary court-martial, decreed the death-penalty on the conspirators present. Olbricht and others were shot, and further executions were only halted by the arrival of the Gestapo who wished to secure information from those who were incriminated. News over the German radio at 9 p.m. that Hitler was still alive and would address the nation later, together with the orders from Berlin and the counter-orders from Rastenburg, had created confusion everywhere, in the course of which the S.S. were able to regain power with the aid of troops under officers who were either loyal to Hitler or who wished to conceal their part in the conspiracy.

In the various other centres where Operation Valkyrie had been started it was abruptly halted, except in Paris, where it achieved complete success under the leadership of the Military Governor, General von Stülpnagel, and General von Speidel. But von Kluge, Commander-in-Chief of the West, vacillated as he had vacillated before when, daily, Tresckow had wound him up like a clock, only to unwind again.[1] On hearing that Hitler was still alive he refused all support. With no backing except from the troops immediately in Paris, Stülpnagel was obliged to hand back power to the S.S. His attempt to commit suicide failed, and he was subsequently convicted before the 'People's Court' and hung.

Thus the last chance of saving Germany and a large part of Europe from nine more months of slaughter, torture and devastation failed by a hair's breadth—not primarily because the attempts on Hitler's life failed, but because too few of the leading generals wholeheartedly supported the aim of purging their country of this evil force which had gripped it. Hesitant, equivocal, and waiting on events, most, like Fromm and Kluge, were concerned to secure their own positions whatever the outcome of the various plots of which they, for the most part, were privy. The martyrdom of the men who made the attempts was also the martyrdom of Europe.

Most of the men involved in the conspiracies were tracked down by the Gestapo, imprisoned and tortured, and finally executed—often in the last days of the war—by slow hanging with other refinements of cruelty. Nearly 5,000 victims have been reckoned as Hitler's blood-

[1] Schlabrendorff, 65.

sacrifice for these events. Besides those killed by the S.S. many committed suicide, for fear of incriminating their friends while under torture. Of these Henning von Tresckow was one, whose words to Schlabrendorff before leaving on his last journey to the front are the most fitting epilogue of this audacious but ill-fated enterprise: 'Hitler is not only the arch-enemy of Germany, he is the arch-enemy of the whole world. In a few hours time I shall stand before God, answering for my actions and for my omissions. I think I shall be able to uphold with a clear conscience all that I have done in the fight against Hitler . . . God once promised Abraham to spare Sodom should there be found ten just men in the city. He will, I trust, spare Germany because of what we have done, and not destroy her. . . . The worth of a man is certain only if he is prepared to sacrifice his life for his convictions'.[1]

Speculation about a future which was never realized is no part of the historian's task. Most of the younger military leaders were *Ostpolitikers*, men who believed that a genuinely Russian resistance had to be built up in order to beat the Soviets: Stauffenberg and Tresckow played key parts in developing the *Osttruppen* as they grew under army auspices.[2] Though farther to the left than officers of the vintage of Beck or civilians such as Goerdeler, this younger group was no less anti-Soviet than they. Their vague ideas of turning the tables on Stalin by enlisting the support of anti-Soviet Russians and the dissident nationalities of the Soviet Union against him, in partnership with the Western democracies, was at that time illusory. Nor is it certain that the front so painfully formed against Hitler would have held. Goerdeler could stand neither the politics nor the personality of Stauffenberg, and his own ideas about Germany's future were equally, or more impracticable.[3] Had the resisters been successful the war would have ended in a different way; but whether they would

[1] Schlabrendorff, 145.
[2] A. Dallin: *German Rule in Russia* (Macmillan, 1957), 543 seq. For the outlook of Stauffenberg and the younger officers, (e.g. their detachment from the monarchist idea), see *Aus Politik und Zeit Geschichte* (Bundeszentrale für politische Bildung, Bonn, Germany), B 29/64, 15 July 1964 (articles, notably F. Carsten: *Nationalrevolutionäre Offiziere gegen Hitler*, p. 46).
[3] Goerdeler's aims for a settlement as late as March 1943 were: the frontiers of 1914 plus Austria, the Sudetenland and the South Tyrol; the frontier with France to run along the linguistic frontier, thus 'eliminating the old idea of fighting (*Kampf-begriff*) about Alsace-Lorraine' (Ritter, 587).

have formed a government which the Allies would have recognized, and so saved Germany from division, can only be a surmise.

NOTES

1. PASTOR PAUL SCHNEIDER

During much of this time he was in an unlit cell, with only the floor to sleep on, often an inch deep with water. Unlike other prisoners, he was not allowed to wash, and in consequence of frequent beatings his body was covered with festering sores, which were never dressed or treated.[1] The S.S. overseer, 'had him strung up by his arms, which were tied behind his back, from the bars of his cell window. His hands could be tied higher and higher behind his back, forcing his head down into a bent position. The Agony on The Cross was being re-enacted, but not as a single, awful ordeal. Schneider was strung up for hours at a time, day after day and week after week, as he fined down to a broken, bruised skeleton, clad in rags, and with his body crawling with lice.'

Moved to another cell, 'he prayed aloud, in a resonant voice which carried across the parade ground, filled with its human scarecrows . . . "Jesus said —I am The resurrection and the life"'.[2]

2. SCHLABRENDORFF

Schlabrendorff accepted the living martyrdom of falling into the hands of the S.S. and was one of the very few to survive and tell the tale. After standing up to questioning under various third-degree methods, he was tortured in four stages: 'First my hands were chained behind my back; then a contrivance was applied to both hands, which gripped all ten fingers separately. On the inner side of the instrument were spikes, which pressed against the finger tips. The turning of a screw caused the machinery to contract so that the spikes penetrated into the fingers.'[3] The same process was applied to his legs, by means of other spike-filled contrivances resembling stove-pipes into which his legs were thrust; he was then stretched on a rack, and finally trussed up and beaten unconscious. When he recovered the tortures were repeated in the same four stages. 'Those of us who had never before learned to pray did so now, and found that prayer and only prayer, can bring comfort in such terrible straits, and that it gives more than human endurance. We learned also that the prayers of our friends and relatives could transmit currents of strength to us.'[4] Later he was brought to a shooting range, where the exhumed body of Tresckow was displayed to him. However, he was not shot, but put on trial before the Peoples' Court, where his fate was postponed by the ceiling falling in during an air

---

[1] E. Kogon: *The Theory and Practice of Hell* (Secker and Warburg, 1950), 211.
[2] Prittie, 119 (The quotation from John 11 v. 25 has been emended).
[3] Schlabrendorff, 155.   [4] Schlabrendorff, 156.

raid on the Court President, who was standing with the files of the case in his hand.[1] Eventually he was liberated by the Americans.

3. THE CATHOLIC CHURCH AND NATIONAL SOCIALISM

For a survey of recent literature on the Catholic Church and National Socialism, see the article by J. J. Sheehan in *The Wiener Library Bulletin*, January 1965. His conclusion is: 'Catholic leaders, like most German bureaucrats, diplomats, generals and professors, lacked the political sophistication and values to detect the true nature of Hitler's movement. Like these others, the Catholics made an alliance with the new Nazi rulers that was based on partial agreement, illusory hope, misunderstanding and fear. Catholics, like almost all those who made such an alliance, then found that this initial compromise dulled the will and destroyed the opportunity for resistance at the same time that self-interest and self-delusion opened the way to collaboration.'

[1] Schlabrendorff, 164.

11: Nazi Colonization and the *'Untermenschen'*

The fate of Eastern Europe had been decided by the advance of the Red Army. The attempts of Roosevelt and Churchill in their meetings with Stalin at Teheran to exert some control over events in this area had failed. The blocking of Churchill's strategy for moving into the Balkans from Italy and the Eastern Mediterranean meant that practically the whole area was turned over to the Russians.

The Fate of the Baltic States

Little enough could have been done in any event for the peoples of the Baltic states, Estonia, Latvia and Lithuania. These flourishing republics with a total of six million people had been among the most successful ventures in state-building since the First World War. Having escaped from the control both of Tsarist Russia and of the German Baltic barons, and stimulated by their newly won and much prized freedom, they leaped forward in developing a nearly classless society, based on the hard work of their peasant farmers and the growing industry of their towns. The Estonians, akin to the Finns in language and origins, managed like them to maintain a stable democracy until occupied by Russia in 1940, though Lithuania in 1926 and Latvia in 1934 moved over to authoritarian régimes.

These peoples owed their independence to the fact that both Russia and Germany suffered defeat in the First World War. The Russian and German grip over Central and Eastern Europe weakened to the point where the victorious Allies were able to secure a drawing of frontiers at the Paris Peace Conference of 1919 which remained more or less fixed until 1939. But once Russia and Germany resumed their role as 'great' and aggressive powers it was to be expected that they would attempt to resume their sway over their formerly subject peoples. The only thing which stood in their way was the system of public law and international security maintained (partly through the League of Nations) by France and Britain. When the two Allies failed to main-

tain the system in the face of the rising might of Hitler, it was clear
that there was little hope of safeguarding the freedom, not only of the
Baltic peoples, but of all the states of Eastern Europe which lay between the upper and nether millstones of Germany and Russia.

Chamberlain had an inkling of this when he refused to bring Russia
into the negotiations over Czechoslovakia before Munich, and—
perhaps more justifiably—when he hesitated in 1939 to make an
agreement with Russia against Germany at the cost of giving Finland
and the Baltic States a 'guarantee' which would have carried with it
the right of the Russian army to march into their territories. A
guarantee on these conditions was refused by the Baltic states, which,
in a choice of evils, leaned rather towards Germany than Russia
(Estonia and Latvia signed non-aggression pacts with Germany in
May 1939).

These pacts did nothing to save them. Having been assigned to
Russia's sphere of influence by the Molotov–Ribbentrop Agreement,
the three republics had to submit to Russia's demands for the occupation of bases in October 1939. In June of the next year larger forces
of the Red Army moved in, along with three special representatives—
one for each republic[1]—who quickly arranged for puppet governments to replace the established régimes; these held faked elections
resulting in Chambers of Deputies which unanimously voted the incorporation of the three republics into the U.S.S.R. This was followed
by the deportation to Russia of political and cultural leaders deemed
antagonistic to the Soviets, and the thorough sovietization of life
began. Every political and cultural group was spied upon and in-
filtrated.

In Estonia seven thousand volumes of the University Library at
Tartu (dating back to the seventeenth century) were destroyed. Half
the factory machinery was sent to Russia, the other half feverishly
overworked to produce goods for the U.S.S.R. Questionings by the
N.K.V.D. preceded further deportations, which became increasingly
frequent, of politicians, officials, judges, clergy, many ordinary
citizens and farmers. Full-scale deportations began only just before
the German invasion, but 50,000 men, women and children were

[1] A. A. Zhdanov for Estonia, A. Vishinsky for Latvia and V. G. Dakanozov for
Lithuania. See H. Daniel: *The Ordeal of the Captive Nations* (Doubleday, New York,
1958), 41.

taken away under the most inhumane conditions in cattle trucks, without adequate food or water, and with no sanitary arrangements. The large crowds which assembled in the villages through which the trains passed were not allowed to come near to hand in food or drink. The journey, according to the account of a survivor, 'lasted one week. Many of us collapsed and died in the wagons for lack of water and food.' On arrival in Siberia the deportees had to make dug-outs in the still frozen ground. 'The majority of those arrested died during the winter of 1941–2.'[1] Many others were liquidated on the spot. In the prison at Tartu 192 men and women—teachers, actors, authors— were 'told to take their last bath before their promised release, had been made to strip and were then one by one shot down in cold blood'.[2] This was just one of many similar atrocities perpetrated by the Russians in the Baltic states before they fled in the face of the German advance.

With Hitler's attack on Russia in June 1941 the other millstone came into operation. Though bad enough, the German occupation of the Baltic states was less oppressive than it was in Poland and the Ukraine, whose Slav and Jewish inhabitants were classed by the Nazis as sub-humans, and whose lands were ear-marked for Aryan colonization. Most of the inhabitants of the three republics, on the other hand, were classed as Aryans or near-Aryans (though some dialectical skill by Himmler's ideologists was necessary to assert this, particularly in the case of the Estonians with their Finno-Ugrian background). But the Jews and known opponents of Nazism, together with those suspected of flirting with Communism during the Russian occupation, had to be liquidated, and this was carried through as ruthlessly in the Baltic states as elsewhere.[3] Many of the Jews did not attempt to escape, preferring to stay and take a chance. An old watchmaker of Tartu, 'the soul of honesty . . . said, shaking his head "who am I that the Germans should bother about such an

[1] A. Oras: *Baltic Eclipse* (Gollancz, 1948), 170–1.

[2] Oras, 192. Professor Oras describes the bombardment of Tartu by the Russians in the course of their retreat. 'Imagine Oxford or Cambridge burning fiercely for weeks. Think of St. Mary's, the Sheldonian Theatre, Magdalen Tower, King's College being consumed by flames under your eyes. The cultural treasures of Tartu were worth all these and more to us, since we had only one University town, one commanding intellectual centre. Now we saw it being annihilated bit by bit, utterly powerless to interfere.' 199.

[3] Oras, 220–1, etc.

old fogey?"' But he, together with the Jewish professors, teachers and
doctors, were all shot. 'A few more weeks passed; then their women
and children, who in the meantime had been used as scrub-women
and street-sweepers, had all gone the same way.'[1] The local S.S.
Commissioner could proudly declare that Estonia was *Jüdenfrei*.

Hitler's Colonization Schemes in Eastern Europe

A central theme of *Mein Kampf*, which Hitler constantly stressed to the
very end of his life, was the German need for expansion to the east
into those areas of Central and Eastern Europe as far as the Urals,
which were the rightful *Lebensraum* of the Nordic master-race. To
settle affairs with France and Britain—if possible without war—was
incidental to this 'grand design', for securing that free hand in the
East which was Hitler's main objective. 'The aim must still be to win
territory in the East for the German people', were among Hitler's last
words which he dictated for his Political Testament in the Chancellery
bunker at Berlin.[2]

To accomplish his vast scheme of colonization, Poland and Russia
had to be conquered and their peoples enslaved—no political
arrangements with either country which gave him less than this would
have satisfied Hitler in the long run. Details of the ultimate settlement
were left vague—for instance, what kind of Russian state might continue to exist *beyond* the Urals, though as the war went on blue-
prints for the conquered territories were worked out, and even began
to be applied in practice.

Extermination of the Jews

Part of the plan consisted in reducing the number of the existing inhabitants and so clearing the ground for German settlers. The Jews
were to be exterminated, while large numbers of Poles, Ukrainians
and Russians were to be hampered in reproducing themselves, by
breaking up families, separating the sexes, and encouraging abortions
and birth-control. Famines which were deliberately allowed to occur[3]

[1] Oras, 216–7.
[2] I. Kamenetsky: *Secret Nazi Plans for Eastern Europe* (Bookman Associates, New
York, 1961), 81.
[3] Transport difficulties no doubt aggravated the harshness dictated by policy. Kiev
under the Germans was supplied with only 30% of its minimum needs. In the Ukraine,

served the dual purpose of killing off large numbers of 'sub-humans' and of reducing their birthrate.

S.S. units under Himmler were allotted the task of carrying this policy into effect. To this end their personnel were given a rigorous ideological training and subjected to a conditioning process which killed the ordinary feelings of humanity and so hardened them for their murderous work. The numerous thugs and sadists who accumulated in the S.S. ranks needed little encouragement. Men who showed any weakness or sentimentality in the course of their training or while being tried out on the staffs of concentration camps were sent elsewhere, while running the risk of themselves suffering humiliating punishment and degradation.

One objective of the training was to fix a certain picture of Jews and Slavs as sub-humans firmly in the mind. 'The sub-human, this apparently fully equal creation of nature, when seen from the biological viewpoints with hands, feet and a sort of brain, with eyes and a mouth, nevertheless is quite a different, a dreadful creature, is only an imitation of a man with man-resembling features, but inferior to any animal as regards intellect and soul. In its interior, this being is a cruel chaos of wild, unrestricted passions, with a nameless will to destruction, with a most primitive lust and of unmasked depravity.'[1] The curious fact is that, in dealing with these so-called sub-humans that fine flower of the Aryan race, the S.S., became themselves sub-human: types of 'a horrible, thoughtless, soulless, gluttonous monster . . . a dreadful tool of destruction',[2] without pity, mercy or any of the finer sentiments of the human heart.

In Warsaw, after its capture in 1940, 400,000 Jews were herded into part of the city around the medieval Ghetto, enclosed in a high wall. They were badly overcrowded, and less than half the supplies needed to keep them alive were allowed through to them. Starvation did not do the work of death quickly enough. In 1942 310,322 Jews were taken away to extermination camps. In April 1943 the remaining

'the security Police not only stopped private efforts at securing food, even through the inevitable black market operations, but they also conducted an organized drive against all efforts of the local governments to provide relief for the population' (Kamenetsky, 146).

[1] From International Military Tribunal Document No. 1805, quoted in Kamenetsky.

[2] Stated by one of their number, an ex-member of the S.S. Division Leibstandart Adolf Hitler, who left it to join the Ukrainian underground and was subsequently killed—quoted in Kamenetsky, 41.

60,000, now walled into a reduced area 1,000 by 300 yards, were attacked by the S.S. in a three-day 'special action' under their Brigadeführer and Major-General of Police, Stroop, with tanks, artillery, flame-throwers and dynamite—weapons necessary to burn and bombard the victims out of the sewers and cellars in which they had sought their last refuge.[1] This was part of the implementation of the policy of race murder, the 'final solution' for 'the Jewish problem', for the Jews, along with Gypsies, chronic invalids and others, were to be slaughtered *en masse*. This was the policy worked out by Reinhardt Heydrich, S.S. leader and Chief of the Security Police, and agreed at a conference in Berlin in January 1942.[2]

'Resettlement' was the usual euphemism for dealing with the Jews. When they were taken off in batches they often had little idea of the fate in store for them. Sometimes they were sent to ghettos in the east whose inhabitants had previously been exterminated. Others were shot in desolate areas.

The *Einsatzgruppen* which had gone into Poland followed the combat troops into Russia. Their practice was to enter a village or town and call together the Jews for 'resettlement'. The Jews had to hand over their outer clothing and valuables. Only when they—men, women and children—were driven away to the place chosen for the 'action' and forced to dig their own mass-grave (unless an existing anti-tank ditch was used for the purpose) did they understand the purpose of their captors.[3]

Sometimes they were put into 'gas vans' which, with the exhaust gases from the engine, accomplished death in ten to fifteen minutes. But this method, being slow and expensive—as also were poison-injections—was superseded by the gas-chambers and crematoria of the 'extermination camps', of which the largest and most notorious was Auschwitz, organized for the purpose in 1942. Those arriving at these camps were not necessarily sent at once to the gas-chambers. A proportion were used for slave-labour (in circumstances which were calculated to kill before long in any case); some of the women were sent to the camp brothels. The rest were directed to the building

[1] W. L. Shirer: *The Rise and Fall of the Third Reich* (Secker and Warburg, 1963), 975–8.

[2] Shirer, page 959 seq.

[3] G. Reitlinger: *The Final Solution* (Valentine, Mitchell, 1953), p. 95 seq., where details of the scheme and methods of implementation are fully presented.

marked 'BATHS'—which, at Auschwitz, were harmless looking structures surrounded by lawns and flowers. An orchestra of girls played cheerful music, while the often still unsuspecting victims were escorted inside, with instructions to undress in preparation for taking a shower. Once they were inside the 'shower-room', as many as 2,000 in a batch, 'the massive door was slid shut, locked and hermetically sealed. Up above where the well-groomed lawn and flower beds almost concealed the mushroom-shaped lids of vents that ran up from the hall of death, orderlies stood ready to drop into them the amethyst-blue crystals of hydrogen cyanide, or Zyklon B. . . . It took some moments for the gas to have much effect. But soon the inmates became aware that it was issuing from the perforations in the vents. It was then that they usually panicked, crowding away from the pipes and finally stampeding towards the huge metal door.'[1] Special squads of the Jewish male inmates and S.S. *Sonderkommando* took over the work of extracting the gold from the teeth of the corpses and disposing of the latter in the vast crematoria where, in 1944 at Auschwitz, as many as 6,000 were consumed daily.

Death did not necessarily come quickly at Auschwitz or the other concentration camps. Some Jews survived for years, along with the political prisoners, men of religion and gaolbirds, who were their companions. Life in these camps has been described and analysed in detail.[2] For sheer brutality and sadism it is a story that has never been surpassed. The contrast is intense between the degradation of human beings who could inflict such suffering, and the fine flame of the human spirit which made it possible for men and women to survive tortures and brutalization of every kind. For hundreds of thousands in the camps death came as a merciful release. Many who survived were shattered in body and soul.

The Nazis and the '*Untermenschen*'

By various methods some four and a half million Jews were exterminated. Others besides Jews suffered this fate, but for most of the '*Untermenschen*' other less drastic if more lingering and painful methods of reducing numbers were applied. Prisoners of war were

[1] Shirer, 970.
[2] Notably in E. Kogon: *The Theory and Practice of Hell* (Secker and Warburg, 1950); also G. Reitlinger: *The S.S., Alibi of a Nation 1922–45* (Heinemann, 1950), Ch. 10.

allowed to die in droves from exposure, lack of supplies and medical care, and overcrowding—quite apart from the unavoidably bad conditions in which many Russian prisoners found themselves, especially in 1941, when they were being captured in enormous numbers. Prisoners of war, together with labourers recruited by more or less forcible methods for digging anti-tank ditches, for building or for armaments factories, were often worked to death on short rations— if they survived the manhunts, the long journeys in cattle-trucks, the beatings, epidemics and air raids. By the end of 1944 nearly five million workers had been 'recruited' for German industry—'not even 200,000 voluntarily' according to Sauckel, Hitler's Plenipotentiary for Manpower.[1] In October 1943, when the demand for labour was overwhelming, Himmler regretted that they had got rid of the sub-humans so quickly. 'At that time (1941) we did not value the mass of humanity as we value it today, as raw material, as labour. What after all, thinking in terms of greatness is not to be regretted, but is now deplorable by reason of the loss of labour, is that the prisoners died in tens and hundreds of thousands of exhaustion and hunger.'[2]

This was the Himmler who congratulated his S.S. men on the way they were doing their job. 'Most of *you* know what it means when a hundred corpses are lying side by side, or five hundred, or one thousand. To have stuck it out, and at the same time—apart from exceptions caused by human weakness—to have remained decent fellows, that is what has made us hard.'

Methods of Colonization

All this was in preparation for the future glorious plans of colonization. 'We shall colonise. We shall indoctrinate our boys with the laws of the S.S. . . . It must be a matter of course that the most copious breeding should be from this racial élite of the Germanic people. In twenty to thirty years we must really be able to present the whole of Europe with its leading class. If the S.S., together with the farmers, then run the colony in the East on a grand scale without any restraint, without any question about tradition, but with nerve and revolutionary impetus, we shall in twenty years push the frontiers of our Folk Community five hundred kilometres eastwards.'[3]

Such were the plans which Hitler worked out with Himmler and

---

[1] Quoted in Bullock, 695.   [2] Bullock, 696.   [3] Bullock, 698.

others of the Aryan élite. 'The German colonist ought to live on handsome, spacious farms. The German services will be lodged in marvellous buildings, the governors in palaces. . . . Around the city, to a depth of thirty to forty kilometres, we shall have a belt of handsome villages connected by the best roads. What exists beyond that will be another world in which we mean to let the Russians live as they like. It is merely necessary that we should rule them . . . We shan't settle in the Russian towns and we'll let them fall to pieces without intervening. And above all, no remorse on this subject! We're absolutely without obligations as far as these people are concerned. To struggle against the hovels, chase away the fleas, provide German teachers, bring out newspapers—very little of that for us! . . . For them the word "liberty" means the right to wash on feast days. . . . There's only one duty: to Germanize this country by the immigration of Germans, and to look upon the natives as Redskins.'[1]

This scheme was worked out in more detail by organizations such as Himmler's *Reichskomissariat* for the strengthening of Germandom and the Reich Office for Space Planning. It was a system of splitting up the conquered peoples by belts of colonies, which would lead to 'gradual strangulation (*Einkapselung*)'.[2] These belts were to lie along important lines of communication, whose road and rail junctions were to be surrounded by solid German settlements, which were also to be made throughout the 'outpost areas' of Estonia, the larger part of Latvia, and the Crimea. But owing to war conditions, and still more to the fact that Germans could not be found in sufficient numbers ready to uproot themselves and settle in the alien and unquiet East the scheme was only implemented in part.[3] In Lithuania some 20,000 Germans were settled. Sixty-five thousand Estonians were moved to Finland from the district of Ingria, but it was too late (winter 1943–4) to move any Germans in, even supposing some had been available.[4] Practically all Poland as far as the Ukrainian border was to be settled solidly with Germans. From mid-October 1939,

[1] *Hitler's Table Talk* (introduction by H. R. Trevor-Roper) (Weidenfeld and Nicolson, 1953), 25, 68, 69.

[2] Kamenetsky, 59.

[3] 'A general indifference of the German masses to becoming pioneer-peasants in the East may indicate that the *Lebensraum* concept, as Hitler conceived it, had not such a magic appeal to the German people as was reflected in Nazi official literature.' (Kamenetsky, 60.)

[4] A. Dallin: *German Rule in Russia*, (Macmillan, 1957), 281–2.

Poles and Jews were deported *en masse* from West Poland (which was annexed to Germany)—both from the countryside and large cities like Poznan.[1] Ethnic Germans were resettled there, many coming from territories farther east, such as the Lublin area, which were due to be colonized later.

In fact partisan activities made such colonization almost impossible. Even the Zamosc settlement, not far from Lublin, which was established in 1940, was constantly harassed by the displaced inhabitants (many of them had escaped to the forests when the Germans evicted them) and by other partisans, so much so that the Governor had to ask for its liquidation to be considered ('the problem of disbanding this settlement was finally solved by the advance of the Red Army, which occupied the area in July 1944').[2] In the Crimea German villages were established, and the German minorities in the towns were consolidated. But only one settlement was firmly established in the Ukraine, at Zhytomyr. The S.S. took over some large estates as nuclei for future colonization. For the rest, the *Kolkhozes* were kept going, as a convenient way of organizing the production of the '*Untermenschen*' until victory should release the potential colonists from the front.[3]

Conflicts of Policy Among the Herrenvolk

Maintaining the Kolkhozes meant undercutting the propaganda to the inhabitants by which they were promised the abandonment of the 'murderous Bolshevik system' and the ownership of their own land. But this was just one of many points where promises and policy conflicted. Policy in general was never unified. Germany's action in the East was a chaos of conflicting aims and ambitions. Tempted by occasional carrots, more often brutally treated, sometimes cajoled, frequently bullied, the inhabitants became increasingly sullen and bewildered, scarcely looking forward to a resumption of Soviet rule,

---

[1] 'The people to be deported received a notice which allowed them between twenty minutes to a few hours preparation. They were allowed to take only hand luggage weighing from 50–100 lbs. No valuables were allowed. . . . The ear-marked families were crowded into trains and either dumped in the *General-Government* or sent to Germany as slave-labour. . . . Polish evacuees were simply dumped at small railway stations or even on open fields and left to their own devices. Their compensation, shelter and means of livelihood never bothered the Germans.' (Kamenetsky, 53.)

[2] Kamenetsky, 65.

[3] Kamenetsky, 132. Ninety per cent of the Kolkhozes were kept going in the Ukraine.

but detesting the tyranny, exploitation and vacillation of their present masters.

While the army tried to deal with practical problems at or behind the front, and Himmler and others built or lost their empires farther in the rear, Hitler moved in a realm above these struggles. Only occasionally did he make policy decisions when appeal was made to him by one or another of the contesting parties. Such decisions re-inforced the *obiter dicta* regarding the colonial or sub-human status of the conquered with which he besprinkled his table talk.

' "The basic trait of Nazi administrative anarchy was the endeavour of anyone who felt strong enough, to do in his sector what he pleased." If totalitarianism has at times been justified in terms of the increased efficiency and co-ordination it is assumed to produce, the German experience, as is well illustrated in the Eastern question, disproves this allegation. Rarely was so much effort in governing spent on so chaotic yet well-planned an orgy of mutual throat-cutting.'[1]

Indulgence in this orgy began almost as soon as Alfred Rosenberg, the leading ideologist of the Nazi Party, took up his appointment as Commissioner for the Eastern European Region, before ever the in-vading armies had broken into Russian Territory. As a German from the *Baltikum* (he was born in Reval, Estonia), he instinctively championed the nationalities of the Russian Empire which he had known against the Great Russians who lorded it over them. For the Russians there could be no political future worth mentioning. In regard to them he agreed with Hitler in treating them as expendible sub-humans. But for the Baltic peoples, the Ukrainians, Caucasians and others Rosenberg had a scheme—to appeal to their national feel-ings, build them up into separate groupings, and so construct a ring of satellites around the eastern borders of the Reich. To this end he was ready to countenance 'soft' policies towards the Ukrainians and other nationals, encourage their own languages and cultures, and bind them to Germany by ties of loyalty and gratitude.

A weak personality, Rosenberg could not compete with the ruth-less ambitions of men like Bormann (Hitler's Party Secretary), Goebbels or—most powerful and sinister in this internecine war—Heinrich Himmler and his followers of the S.S. Erich Koch, as

---

[1] A. Dallin, 669. The quotation is from W. Petwaidic: *Die autoritäre Anarchie* (Hoffman and Campe, Hamburg, 1946), 18.

Himmler's man in charge of the Ukraine, though nominally coming under Rosenberg, pursued policies diametrically opposed to his own. Where Rosenberg wanted education right up to higher and university levels to be restarted, as part of his *Kulturkampf* against Moscow, Koch confined such activities to the lowest levels, and treated the populace as *Untermenschen* and nothing more. 'In Melitopol Koch publicly declared in the presence of a large Ukrainian audience that "no German soldiers would die for these niggers". In another village where . . . a peasant delegation tendered the Germans the traditional bread and salt, Koch thrust the presents out of their hands, screaming that they should not dare offer gifts to a German dignitary.'[1]

The Wehrmacht's Aims and Needs

This approach, together with naked exploitation for extracting food from the land and labour for the Reich, swiftly offset any benefits accruing from propagandist efforts directed to gaining co-operation from the inhabitants or desertions from the Soviet ranks. It also made nonsense of the army's attempts to secure order in its rear or auxiliary troops from among the millions of war prisoners. Not that the army leaders necessarily wanted a measure of fair dealing for prisoners or inhabitants for humanitarian reasons, though many of them undoubtedly did. It was a part of military security to maintain law-abiding inhabitants in the rear, sufficiently acquiescent in the rule of the conqueror not to join the partisans and saboteurs, and in a state of health which would not endanger the troops through outbreaks of epidemics. For this reason their teams of public health specialists restored drainage systems, hospitals and in some circumstances inoculated the inhabitants—a measure which particularly aroused Hitler's wrath. ('What a ridiculous idea to vaccinate them! . . . No vaccination for the Russians and no soap to get the dirt off them.')[2]

Expediency prompted the army to use prisoners as auxiliaries, most of them in low-grade work as ammunition carriers, cooks or drivers, some as translators or interpreters. As the number of these *Hilfswillige* or '*Hiwis*' increased, so the tasks allotted to them expanded. When the tide of war turned decisively against Germany and manpower shortages became acute, formations of these '*Untermenschen*' were even put into action alongside German troops. Grateful to find a

[1] Dallin, 163.   [2] *Hitler's Table Talk*, 319.

means of survival in place of a precarious existence in prison-camps or as deportees to Germany, the *Hiwis* for the most part served their German masters loyally.

This development took place unofficially. Though they became numerous (200,000 by the spring of 1942, half a million or more a year later), their status was for much of the war indeterminate and unacknowledged. The build-up of combat formations of *Osttruppen* only took place as German manpower shortages became acute. By then many of the indigenous peoples had been alienated. Though Azerbaijanis, Turkestanis and others were often most strongly anti-Soviet, they also suffered most from shootings by the S.S. since they were often taken for Jews.[1] Later a strange volte-face took place, straining ideological consistency to the breaking-point. The obviously non-Aryan Tatars and Turkestanis were ordered to be regarded as 'comrades and helpers',[2] while blond and blue-eyed Ukrainians were being remorselessly battered into the slavery befitting sub-humans. Gradually, as the war situation worsened, other nationalities (Armenians and Georgians) gained similar 'benefits', and were recruited into the eastern legions. Cossacks, too, were early recognized as descendants of 'Nordic and Dinaric' races, and eligible for military service with the Wehrmacht.

The most ambitious project of this kind was the army recruited from prisoners of war under the nominal command of the captured Russian general, Andrei Vlasov. A well-known and successful officer, he turned anti-Soviet after his capture in July 1942. He resoundingly criticized the inconsistency and consequent feebleness of German political warfare, to such effect that the intelligence officers who dealt with him brought him forward as a rallying point for an anti-Soviet resistance movement. Hitler opposed this development, but by late 1943 Germany's extremity was such that Himmler authorized the S.S. to build up 'Vlasov divisions'. Only when the fronts were crumbling was this 'army' sent into action, but its demoralized and bewildered commanders kept it away from the fighting. Eventually it was requested by the Czechs to help in the liberation of Prague—then as

---

[1] 473,000 men were exterminated as prisoners of war while under army command in Germany and Poland, and another half million 'were written off as exterminated . . . in occupied Soviet territory. . . . Wholesale execution after screening virtually ceased in February 1942.'—G. Reitlinger: *The House Built on Sand* (Weidenfeld and Nicolson, 1960), 94.   [2] Dallin, 272.

quickly asked to leave the city when it became clear that its presence would be a source of embarrassment with the arrival of the Red Army.[1] The promise of the Western Allies to hand over to the Soviet authorities all Soviet citizens at the war's end meant that there was no salvation for the *Osttruppen* either in the east or the west.

[1] Dallin, 657. See below, p. 178.

NOTES

1. Professor Viktor E. Frankl, who survived Auschwitz to become Professor of Neurology and Psychiatry at the University of Vienna, makes the following comments on his experience there: 'A human being is not one thing among others; things determine each other, but man is ultimately self-determining. . . . In the concentration camps . . . we witnessed some of our comrades behave like swine while others behaved like saints. Man has both potentialities within himself; which one is actualized depends on decisions not on conditions. . . . There is nothing in the world that would so effectively help one to survive even the worst conditions as the knowledge that there is a meaning to one's life.'—V. E. Frankl: *Man's Search for Meaning* (Hodder and Stoughton, 1964), 136.

2. 'Over five million Soviet soldiers fell into German hands in the course of the war. Of these, less than one million were released. . . . A total of two million men are known to have died in captivity, and another million are not accounted for. As the Allied armies closed in on the German heartland, barely one million survived in the camps.' (Dallin, 426). According to figures, admitted by the Germans, 3,700,000 died in their hands (Reitlinger, *The House Built on Sand*, 98).

12: The 'Liberation' of the Balkans

Eastern Europe had always been an area of fierce loyalties and hates, where the invading tribes who had poured in during the Dark Ages had continued their bitter antagonisms, their claims and counter-claims, into the modern world. Older peoples and groups had been submerged; frontiers which came into existence during the Middle Ages complicated the ethnic patterns: few nations but had their irredenta, their backward-looking visions of greatness which encouraged them to oppress their neighbours and claim their territory whenever they had the chance. Nor was religion a bond of unity. Christian was against Moslem, and the Christians themselves were deeply divided between Catholics, Orthodox and Protestants. Cleaving these old divisions, or reinforced by them, came the further conflicts of class, especially between landlords and peasants, while the Jews were sometimes regarded as an alien element within capitalist or bourgeois societies.

Czechoslovakia and Bulgaria Under Hitler

Hitler, who ruled by dividing and dominating, had a fair field for his ploughing. Before the war began Czech hostility to Poland had been encouraged by the forced cession of Teschen to the latter. The Slovaks had been urged to rebel against the Czechs—the issue which gave Hitler the pretext for the occupation of the Czech lands. Transylvania, a sure bone of contention between Hungary and Rumania, was partitioned, the larger part going to the former, by Ribbentrop's Vienna Award.

While Slovakia was given preferential treatment as a showpiece, being a friendly (though entirely dependent) state, the rump of the Czech state was largely de-nationalized. After carefully fostered riots in the autumn of 1939, student leaders and intellectuals were arrested, in many cases executed, and the Czech university was closed. A Germanizing policy was forced on the majority of the people, and the beginnings of a ribbon-colonizing scheme applied in areas where the people were considered racially too inadequate to be redeemed as Aryans. But the German settlers were found to be less efficient producers than the Czech farmers whom they ousted, and since the German policy also was to treat the country as a milch cow, the colonizing schemes languished.

In May 1942 the S.S. leader and Nazi strong man Heydrich was assassinated by Czech resisters flown in from Britain. Another and fiercer reign of terror was initiated, during which the villages of Lidice and Lezaky were razed to the ground, their men-folk shot and the women sent to concentration camps after their children had been torn from them. The Jews were carried off, thousands of young Czechs pressed for labour in Germany—for the rest a policy of getting maximum production from industry and land was resorted to, which involved keeping the people in sullen complaisance.

Bulgaria too suffered relatively less than most of its neighbours. Accepting the bribes of Yugoslav Macedonia and Greek Thrace as annexations, Bulgaria joined the Axis in March 1941. But because of her old ties with Russia her position was accepted as a non-belligerent partner in the war against Russia, which Hitler began a few months later. She also occupied some of the Serb areas of Yugoslavia. After the death of King Boris (who maintained his personal power to the end), in August 1943,[1] successive governments gradually moved towards making peace with the Allies.

There were however hesitations, since Bulgarian governments, of whatever colour, were eager to keep at least some of the recent territorial gains. While a delegation was seeking terms from the Allies in Cairo, Russia suddenly declared war on Bulgaria (5 September 1944). Stalin wished to demonstrate forcibly that Bulgaria was within his sphere of influence, and since American policy had prevented Allied forces from moving into the Balkans, there was nothing to prevent the Red Army entering Bulgaria—which it did, unopposed, on 8 September. Two days earlier the Bulgarian government had accepted the inevitable, declaring war on the Axis. It was now obliged to fight on the Russian side, its army advancing with the Russians to the capture of Belgrade, in which operations it lost thirty thousand dead.[2]

[1] A Regency Council was set up for the six-year-old King Simeon.
[2] H. Seton-Watson: *The East European Revolution* (Methuen 1950), 90–8.

The Red Army Enters the Balkans

The Red Army had entered Bulgaria from Rumania. Despite the affront to national pride of the Vienna Award, Rumania had been one of the closest and most effective allies of Germany in the war against Russia. Marshal Ion Antonescu, who had taken power after King Carol's abdication in September 1940, was convinced that closest collaboration with Germany was the way to recover Bessarabia and the Northern Bukovina from Russia, and also to regain at least part of the Transylvanian lands which had been handed over to Hungary—although Hungary was also an ally of Germany. To this end he exercised a military dictatorship on fairly humane lines. Jews and political opponents were not much molested, and the main opposition leader, Iuliu Maniu, of the National Peasant Party, was allowed his liberty, and periodically wrote strongly critical letters to the 'Conducator'.

The business men, large landowners and prosperous peasants were the main beneficiaries of the régime. The Rumanian army became increasingly involved in the Russian War. Its campaigning did not stop with the reconquest of Bessarabia and the Northern Bukovina, but it went on to occupy Odessa and territory up to the Bug (which was annexed to Rumania), and played a large part in the conquest of the Crimea. Several of its divisions were caught with the German Sixth Army at Stalingrad, and others were broken or badly mauled in the subsequent winter battles.

By 1943 casualties were reaching the half million mark, and the people were looking for a way of pulling out of the war. Maniu sent emissaries to the Allies in Cairo, but could not obtain terms which he thought satisfactory, since Russia insisted on regaining Bessarabia. Nor would the Western Allies act behind Russia's back by flying their troops into Rumania, as Maniu suggested. Attempts within the country to construct a 'Patriotic' or 'Popular Front', including the Communists, failed for the same reason.

The deadlock was eventually broken when a group of army officers and diplomats persuaded the young King Michael—who had long wished to escape from the German yoke—to arrest Marshal Antonescu and Professor Antonescu (the Vice-Premier), and declare the war against Russia at an end (23 August 1944). He gave the Germans an opportunity to withdraw peacefully from Rumania; instead they bombed Bucharest, aiming specially at the Royal Palace. They tried to restore Horia Sima and his 'Iron Guard' to power (they had been displaced by Antonescu three years previously after committing anti-Jewish outrages and political massacres). A full-scale campaign was necessary, alongside the Russians, to clear them out of the country, after which the campaign was continued in Hungary in the hope of regaining Transylvania. In the course of this fighting the Rumanians suffered another 150,000 casualties. King Michael was awarded the Order of Victory by Stalin, the highest Soviet decoration.[1]

In Hungary the pattern of events was similar. Admiral Horthy, Regent since the fall of the Hapsburgs, presided over a government drawn from the party of the 'establishment', which was in social background and attitude near to the whig-liberals of nineteenth-century Britain. Landowners and businessmen (among both of whom Jews were prominent or had intermarried) maintained an uneasy balance between their respective interests, opposed by the peasant small-holders under Ferenc Nagy and others, and the Communists who were still suffering from the oppression which followed their rising in 1919.

The government party's orientation was towards the West (the fact that Catholicism was the dominant religion played a part in this), and particularly towards Britain. Its hope was to keep out of the war, but the twin baits of Slovakia and Northern Transylvania, which it had swallowed when offered by Germany, had drawn Hungary to the latter's side—and a further bait was constantly dangled, that of re-ceiving the rest of Transylvania if Hungary became an obedient satellite (at the same time, Northern Transylvania was being held out as a bait to Rumania). Having let German troops have passage for attacking Yugoslavia in April 1941, it was only a step to declaring war, along with Germany, on Russia a few months later—a step which was encouraged by a bombing raid, probably faked, which the Russians were alleged to have made on the frontier town of Kosice.

Hungarian industry, which was not subjected to bombing until 1944, made an important contribution to Germany's war effort, and its army received heavy casualties in the fighting around Voronezh in

[1] Seton-Watson, 83–90. The figure for casualties in the fighting against the Axis is given as 168,591 in A. Cretzianu (ed.): *Captive Rumania* (Atlantic Press, London 1956), 20.

1942. The government party began looking to intervention by the Western Allies to get Hungary out of the war, especially after the collapse of Italy in the summer of 1943. But when no Allied attack developed across the Adriatic their hopes were dashed. As in the case of Rumania, Britain and America insisted that there could be no peace negotiations without Russia. Though making contact with the Russians and the local communists, Horthy hesitated too long. Early in 1944 the German grip on the country increased—oppression of the Jews and deportations were stepped up, and the German army prepared to defend Hungary against a Russian incursion from Bessarabia. When, with insufficient preparation, on 15 October 1944, Horthy declared a cease-fire and attempted to negotiate with the Russians, he mis-timed the move. Local fascists helped the Germans to seize the capital. The Palace was captured and Horthy deported.

Thereafter Hungary, and Buda-Pesth in particular, became a battleground between Germans and Russians, some of the Hungarian army continuing to fight with the former, the rest, under General Miklos, going over to the latter. 'The capital was besieged for two months. In one part of it the Germans and the Hungarian fascist gangs murdered and robbed and destroyed, in the other half the Red Army raped and robbed and murdered. Artillery pounded the historic citadel of Buda to pieces. No other European city except Warsaw suffered such horrors.'[1] In January 1945 the three Allies signed an armistice with Hungary in Moscow, but it was mid-April before the country was cleared of Germans and the government under General Miklos re-established at Buda.

Yugoslavia: Tito and the Partisans

Events followed a different course in Yugoslavia. There the overwhelming German attack in April 1941 had destroyed the army, wrecked half the capital, and temporarily numbed the people. Soon however two different resistance movements were operating. One was that of the Cetniks under General Mihailovich, the other that of the Partisans under the Communist leader Josip Broz, known as Tito.

Mihailovich was a regular officer who took to the hills with some companions, and built up an almost entirely Serb organization. On establishing communication with London, whither the King and

[1] Seton-Watson, 104–5.

government had fled, he was appointed Minister of War. But soon convinced by experience that attacks on the Germans produced savage reprisals quite incommensurate with the gains, he and his followers went on to the defensive, and even assisted the puppet government under General Nedich against the Partisans. This brought some of the Cetnik groups into active collaboration with the German and Italian occupying forces. Though British and American liaison officers were attached to them, and supplies were sent them by air-lift, before long the Cetniks were doing virtually nothing against the Axis forces, while concentrating on attacking the Partisans.

Mihailovich, like Nedich, was a good nationalist—at least a good Serb—but he did not believe that a free Yugoslavia, as he understood it, was compatible with the existence of Communism in the country. He was supported in this attitude by the Yugoslav government in London. The B.B.C. broadcasts, which the government directed, made his name known, and resistance fighters were attracted to his banner.

Many however soon left, transferring to the Partisans, when they found they were not getting the fighting against the Axis forces which they wanted. Tito was not afraid of German reprisals, costly though they were (in the first German anti-Partisan offensive the Germans burned seventeen villages and killed nine thousand hostages).[1] He continued to keep up the Partisan attacks which, by 1943, were occupying twelve Axis divisions. Through his leadership a national resistance network was built up, in which Croats, Slovenes and Serbs. besides other ethnic groups, were represented.

Tito himself came from an area on the borders of Croatia and Slovenia, where poverty and hunger were common among peasant families like his. A sergeant-major in the Austrian army in the First World War, he was captured by the Russians, and was freed in the general liberation of war-prisoners at the time of the 1917 revolution. He volunteered for the Red Army, became a Communist, and even-tually returned to his homeland, now Yugoslavia, where he was soon sentenced to five and a half years in prison (which became six when he attempted to escape), for disseminating subversive propaganda and organizing revolutionary activity. Later he spent some time at the Comintern Headquarters in Moscow, and in 1937 was made

[1] F. Maclean: *Disputed Barricade* (Cape, 1957), 155.

Secretary-General of the Yugoslav Communist Party. Besides his work there, he was given a major job in organizing recruits for the International Brigade during the Civil War in Spain.

What differentiated Tito from most other Communist leaders of the time was his independence of mind. The first impressions of Edward Kardelj, the Slovene schoolmaster who became one of his closest collaborators, on meeting him in 1934, was that 'he was not at all like the old-time Party leaders, who were nothing but bureaucrats. . . . He was well versed in Marxist theory, but, when you put a question to him, he did not always answer with a quotation from Marx, or Engels, or Lenin—he spoke in practical commonsense terms.'[1] He made a similar impression on Brigadier Fitzroy Maclean, who was parachuted into Yugoslavia as head of the British Mission accredited to him in September 1943. He was ready 'to discuss any question on its merits and, if necessary, to take a decision there and then. He seemed perfectly sure of himself; a principal, not a subordinate.'[2]

Another unusual characteristic in a Communist leader was his passionate national feeling. 'He reacted strongly to anything that, by the widest stretch of the imagination, might be regarded as a slight on the national dignity of Yugoslavia. . . . There were many unexpected things about Tito: his surprisingly broad outlook; his never-failing sense of humour; his unashamed delight in the minor pleasures of life: a natural diffidence in human relationships, giving way to a natural friendliness; a violent temper flaring up in sudden rages; a considerateness and a generosity manifesting themselves in a dozen small ways; a surprising readiness to see two sides of a question . . . yet . . . a man whose tenets would justify him in going to any lengths of deception or violence to attain his ends. . . .'[3]

By this date, autumn 1943, Tito could claim that there were 150,000 Partisans under his control. After many breath-taking escapes from Germans, Italians and Cetniks, he was in a strong position to organize an offensive. The Italian collapse had brought him a large windfall of arms and supplies, and the British Mission was now able to arrange for their regular replenishment, and the evacuation of wounded Partisans to base-hospitals in Italy. The island of Vis off the Dalmatian

[1] Quoted in Maclean: *Disputed Barricade*, 70.
[2] Maclean: *Eastern Approaches* (Cape-Reprint Society, 1951), 238.
[3] *Eastern Approaches*, 256.

coast became 'an Anglo-Yugoslav condominium',[1] where regular supplies could be brought in by sea and air, for distribution on the mainland.

Until spring of 1944 the Russians had given the Partisans no supplies, but only unpalatable advice (e.g. to avoid statements about communizing Yugoslavia).[2] Stalin even considered sending a misson to Mihailovich as late as the Moscow conference of October 1944.[3] He had been infuriated by the resolution agreed upon by Tito and his associates at Jagce in November 1943, when the National Committee of Liberation was set up with Tito—who assumed the title of Marshal —as Prime Minister and Minister of Defence. However, in February 1944 he sent a military mission to Tito, and a few Russian supplies were dropped by air in April.

Recognition of Stalin's partial disinterestedness in Yugoslavia—or perhaps coldness towards the independent-minded Tito—was expressed in his agreement with Churchill at the Moscow conference that Britain and Russia were each to have a 50 per cent interest in the country.[4] This agreement seemed to accord with the facts of the situation, as interpreted by Tito himself. In August 1944 he went to Caserta for a meeting with Churchill and General Wilson. In September—without notifying the British, and to Churchill's annoyance —he flew to Moscow for discussions with Stalin and the Politburo.[5] Though it went against the grain, Stalin felt obliged to accept Tito's conditions for co-operation with the Red Army in the march on Belgrade and for operations against the Germans in Hungary: the Soviet troops were to withdraw from Yugoslavia as soon as their tasks accomplished, and the Russians were to exercise no civil or administrative powers while in Yugoslavia.

As for the constitutional question, Stalin advised Tito to have the King back, at least for a time ('then you can slip a knife into his back at a suitable moment')[6] but Tito did not see the situation in this light. In June he had made an agreement with the new and moderate Premier of the London government, Dr. Subasich, which shelved the

---

[1] *Disputed Barricade*, 261.   [2] *Disputed Barricade*, 180.
[3] *Disputed Barricade*, 241.   [4] See below, pp. 132, 138.
[5] 'Tito, having lived under our protection for three or four months at Vis, suddenly levanted, leaving no address, but keeping sentries over his cave to make out he was still there.' Churchill to H. Hopkins, 12 August 1944, Churchill, VI, 200. See also *Disputed Barricade*, 291.   [6] *Disputed Barricade*, 284.

question of the Monarchy. After the Moscow meeting he continued the same policy, by arranging a government for Yugoslavia (now in process of being cleared of the Germans), of which the nucleus would be members of his Anti-fascist Council together with some drawn from Subasich's cabinet. The King was to be represented in Yugoslavia by a Regency pending a decision on his future by plebiscite (November 1944). Very unwillingly the King was obliged to accept this arrangement, just as earlier he had been obliged to dismiss Mihailovich as his Minister of War.

Before this arrangement was concluded Belgrade had fallen (20 October 1944), and with Tito's Partisans in control anti-monarchist demonstrations were encouraged. It was only after a lengthy struggle that King Peter consented to transfer his prerogatives to the Regency Council (which in any case was a shadowy affair). Though the united government eventually came into being (March 1945) Tito held all the cards, especially after the failure of the Cetniks and the overthrow of the puppet Fascist state of Croatia.[1]

One bone of contention which remained between Tito and the Western Allies as the fighting ended was Trieste. This Adriatic port, formerly the main commercial outlet of Austro–Hungary to the Mediterranean, had been annexed by Italy after the first World War. It was occupied by the Germans in 1943 and liberated by the Yugoslavs in 1945. But for the Italian inhabitants of the city it was no liberation, and their case was backed by the British and Americans. General Alexander, commanding the Allied troops in the area, forced the evacuation of the Partisans from the city itself, though they continued to hold the Slav-inhabited hinterland. Friction between the Allies in Zone A and the Yugoslavs in Zone B, as between their respective governments, remained as a sore point constantly in danger of becoming inflamed.

Greece: Britain and the Communists

Although the pattern of events was somewhat the same in Greece as in Yugoslavia, the end of the war-time story was different, in that an

---

[1] This had been set up by Ante Pavelic with Axis backing. Pavelic stood for the Catholic Croats, and his speciality was brutal attacks by his Ustash bands, including Croatian Moslems, against Orthodox churches and congregations.

anti-Communist government under British influence was in control from early 1945 onwards.

The resounding 'No' of General Ioannides Metaxas to the Italian ultimatum of 27 October 1940[1] and the successful resistance to the Italians which he organized, gave a large measure of support to his dictatorship at the end of his days, similar to the Yugoslav rallying behind General Simovitch's government after its defiance of the Germans in April 1941. Metaxas died in January 1941, before the German onslaught in April swept away everything for which he had stood. Thereafter with king and Government in exile, and resistance movements growing in Greece—notably guerillas on the mountains, of which the Communist-organized EAM/ELAS was far the strongest body,[2] there was little to prevent a development such as led eventually to Tito's domination of liberated Yugoslavia.

One difference lay in the fact that there was no Tito in Greece. The war-time leader, Siantos, though able, and popular among his following, was less shrewd—or cunning—particularly in the timing of his moves (such as the attempt to seize power throughout Greece in October 1943). A second influence was that the most important non-Communist guerilla body, EDES (National Democratic Greek Union) was republican in tendency, and not committed, as was Mihailovich in Yugoslavia, to what seemed at one time the declining star of the Monarchy. Further, its leader, Colonel Zervas, zealously fought the Axis, and co-operated unstintingly with the British (later Allied) Military Mission. His guerillas did not collaborate with the security forces of the collaborationist Premier Rallis, whose role corresponded with that of the Yugoslav Nedich.

Finally, the decisive factors were the close co-operation of the allies with Zervas and his EDES guerillas, and support of them against ELAS when the latter attempted to destroy them and seize control throughout Greece; the fact that Britain was in a position,

[1] The Italians did not wait for the answer before attacking on 28 October.
[2] An important achievement of the civilian Communist resistance through its labour organization (EEAM) was the prevention of the conscripting of workers for Germany (C. M. Woodhouse: *Apple of Discord* (Hutchinson 1948), 38). When the ELAS guerillas were persuaded to work with the non-Communist guerillas, they contributed to the success of the operations in 1943 which led to the Germans moving two divisions into Greece—part of the diversionary strategy of the Allies before the landings in Sicily (B. Sweet-Escott: *Greece, a Political and Economic Survey*, 1939–53 (R.I.I.A, 1954), 25). ELAS stands for People's Liberation Army; EAM: National Liberation Front.

through her access to Greece by sea, to intervene militarily when the Germans left, and defeat ELAS (even though the forces of Zervas and the other non-Communist groups were in fact destroyed); and the disinterestedness of Stalin at that time (winter 1944–5) in the Greek situation, signified by his acquiescing in Churchill's proposal at Moscow in October 1944 for Britain's share of influence in Greece to be 95 per cent, compared with the Soviets' 5 per cent only.

The Russians in any case had no forces available at the critical moment for sending to Greece, nor would this have been worth their while in view of the overwhelming antagonism it would have created against them on the part of the Western Allies. At the end of 1944 the goodwill of the Western Allies was worth much in enabling Stalin to achieve far more important objectives than control of the southernmost extremities of the Balkan Peninsula. The Red Army had its hands full north of the Balkans in taking over the Danube Valley and Central Europe as far west as the zonal boundaries.

Further, having shown little interest in, and having exercised as little direction of the Communist war-time effort in Greece as in Yugoslavia, the Russians were not impressed by the quality of the Communist-led guerillas when they sent a secret mission to investigate them in July 1944. This, together with their determination to apply in Greece (as elsewhere at that time) their tactics of forming 'Popular Front' governments led them to withdraw support from EAM's strategy, and to advise the Greek Communist leaders to fill the places reserved for them in the government of National Unity under Papandreou which was in process of being formed.[1]

The Moscow-directed phase of this policy of EAM, when there was co-operation with the other parties, was exceptional and of brief duration. Both before it and afterwards, EAM had been hard at work attempting to gain undivided control. It had attacked and destroyed the smaller non-Communist resistance groups—the turn of EDES for destruction was only postponed by the support which it enjoyed from the British Military Mission.[2] It had succeeded in gaining the entire arms—including valuable artillery—of the Italian Pinerolo Division

---

[1] Woodhouse, 197–9. W. H. McNeill: *The Greek Dilemma* (Gollancz, 1947), 121.

[2] The support was given not primarily on account of its political orientation, but because it was doing the job for which the support was necessary—fighting the Axis (Woodhouse, 139, 143. Major, later Colonel Woodhouse, was first deputy Head, then Head of the British Mission).

when its Commander, General Infante, turned it over to fight against the Germans at the time of the Italian armistice. Instead EAM made a local truce with the Germans and rushed the arms across the mountains in an attempt to destroy EDES while opportunity offered (a manoeuvre which failed). In October 1943 it attempted to seize control of Greece, on the assumption that the Germans were leaving (the plan failed when the assumption proved incorrect). In March and April 1944 it organized mutinies in the Greek divisions, which had been assembled and trained in Egypt, just before they were due to proceed to the Italian Front. In the concentration camps where the mutinous divisions had been sent for screening, the Communists continued to maltreat and even murder the non-Communists, in an effort to secure their control.

The phase of co-operation with the Papandreou Government ended in late November 1944. EAM, which already controlled the largest part of Greece, could have walked into Athens, as they walked into other towns, when the Germans eventually moved out—obliged to evacuate because of the threat to their rear posed by the Russian incursion across the north of the Balkan area through Rumania, Bulgaria and Yugoslavia. At that point (September 1944) still adhering to the Soviet line, EAM did not take this action, and let the British enter peacefully. But in November they lost patience when attempts were made to disarm them, along with EDES and the few other remaining non-Communist guerillas. Two army formations, the Rimini Brigade and the Sacred Squadron, now purged of their Communists, were to be moved from Italy to Greece—to EAM these were in effect armies of the Right, which could doubtless be used against them, especially when disarmed. They demanded that these formations be also disarmed, and on receiving a negative reply, took steps to seize the capital and the remaining areas not yet under their control (3 December 1944).

Athens was garrisoned by only a sketchy force of British troops although such a crisis had been foreseen, and to some extent provided for by Churchill.[1] General Scobie was firmly based on Salonika, and was able gradually to reinforce the Athens garrison, though at one time the area it held was reduced to little more than Constitution

[1] His plan, approved by Roosevelt, was to have 10,000 British troops ready for this contingency (Churchill, VI, 99,100).

Square. After five weeks' fighting Athens and Peiraeus were cleared (5 January 1945) and British forces and Greek regulars were extending their control over other areas of the country.

Something of a cross-current, though prominent as ostensibly the chief issue between Left and Right, was the position of the Monarchy —the perennial question of Greek politics. Though EAM was out to annihilate EDES, both were in favour of getting rid of the Monarchy. Churchill had disclaimed interest in the ideologies or political arrangements of the Greeks,[1] but it was well known that he favoured a constitutional monarchy, and that his sympathies were with George II as the man who, along with Metaxas, had the courage to stand against the Axis, and who had been a loyal ally of Britain throughout. On Christmas Eve, 1944, Churchill flew with Eden to Athens, and managed to shelve the question of the Monarchy by arranging for Archbishop Damaskinos to head a Regency, pending an eventual settlement. The King had reluctantly agreed not to return 'unless summoned by a free and fair expression of the national will'.[2] Papandreou resigned and General Plastiras—a strong republican—took his place. On 11 January ELAS accepted an armistice, and the terms were arranged with General Scobie. The British had suffered over a thousand casualties in fighting Greeks, at a time when both British and Greeks needed to be fighting Germans, and the country had been subjected to 'bitter suffering . . . the dynamiting of property, the ruthless destruction and extortion, the rounding up and execution of innocent hostages, the coercion of civilian population by terroristic methods in true Nazi style.'[3] For the Greek people the miseries of the winter rivalled those of 1941–2, when under Axis occupation, some 24,000 died of hunger.[4] Though the end of a chapter, January 1945 was not yet the end of their sufferings.

[1] Regarding Greece and Yugoslavia, 'In one place we support a King, and in another, a Communist . . . there is no attempt by us to enforce particular ideologies'. House of Commons, 25 May 1944, quoted by Woodhouse, 108.
[2] Churchill, VI, 279–90.
[3] Field-Marshal Smuts to Churchill, 30 December 1944, quoted Churchill, VI, 282.
[4] Mussolini's estimate, quoted in R.I.I.A. *Survey: Hitler's Europe*, 679.

13: Yalta and Potsdam: Anglo-American Rifts and Russian Intransigence

American Attitudes

Though Stalin (for whatever reasons) maintained his understanding with Churchill to allow Britain a free hand in Greece, the Greek crisis brought to the fore the rift between British and American policy. 'We felt the British Government had messed the whole thing up pretty thoroughly',[1] as Hopkins put it. To the Americans 'all that was apparent on the surface was that British troops, engaged in the task of "liberation", were killing Greek patriots who had been fighting the Germans, and it was even possible that the British were using American lend-lease weapons for this purpose.'[2] Admiral King went so far as to order Admiral Hewitt, the American Commander of the Mediterranean Fleet, not to permit any landing-craft to be used for transferring supplies to Greece—though Hewitt was himself under the command of General Wilson as Supreme Commander in the Mediterranean (Hopkins, critical as he was of British strategy, was fair enough to have Hewitt's order countermanded). American opinion on Greece only began to change when the first letters came through from Greeks to their relatives in the U.S.A., relating the horrors of the EAM attempts to gain control.[3]

American foreign policy had, ever since George Washington's famous directive, been based on the principle of non-involvement in the affairs of Europe. A cultivated detachment, fused with isolationism, made it possible to write off the politics of Europe—and particularly of Eastern Europe—as merely the narrow national egotism of the European powers exploiting the weaknesses of their smaller neighbours. Except among a few State Department experts and men like Ambassador Harriman and George F. Kennan who were particularly familiar with Russia, there was little understanding of the

[1] R. E. Sherwood: *The White House Papers of Harry L. Hopkins* (Eyre & Spottiswode, 1949), 833.
[2] Ibid., 832.   [3] Woodhouse, 105.

power factors involved in making or maintaining peace. Instead of seeking a balance of power most likely to be lasting and most favourable for the extension of American influence and the realization of American democratic ideals, Roosevelt and his associates (of whom Hopkins was the most important), hoped to secure their aims by personal diplomacy and the establishment of the United Nations.

In effect during the first 150 years of her national life America had left it to Britain to maintain a system which, if it failed to keep the peace in Europe, prevented, from 1814 to 1914, a war which might have involved America. When the system broke down and America was eventually involved in two wars originating in Europe, the system itself was condemned as well as Britain's supposedly mistaken role in world affairs. Two world wars had demonstrated that Britain's survival was necessary for the defence of America, but the corollary was denied that Britain, to be an effective ally in peace or in war, had to regain a position in Europe which would enable the Anglo-Saxon powers jointly to restore the balance which Britain alone had failed to maintain.

Thinking on this point was further befogged by the fact that George III's Britain had been the colonial power from which America had won her independence. Britain was accordingly regarded as being deeply imbued with a form of original sin from whose taint America, and even Russia, was regarded as mercifully free. Roosevelt gave out that he was certain that 'Stalin is not an Imperialist',[1] while Eisenhower professed to believe that Russia, like America, was unmarked by the stigma of empire-building by force.[2] As the war in Europe ended and the partnership of the 'Big Three' showed signs of breaking up, the Americans became fearful that Churchill's wiles might line them up 'in a bloc against Russia to implement Britain's European policy'.[3]

Truman, precipitated unexpectedly into the Presidency on Roosevelt's death (12 April 1945), shared these anxieties and turned to his predecessor's advisers, among them J. E. Davies, formerly Ambassador at Moscow—a warm, if superficial, admirer of the U.S.S.R.

---

[1] Roosevelt to Mikolajczyk, 7 June 1944 (S. Mikolajczyk: *The Pattern of Soviet Domination* (Sampson Low, 1948), 65.

[2] J. Biggs-Davison: *The Uncertain Ally* (Christopher Johnson, 1957, 92).

[3] Hopkins to Forrestal, 20 May 1945—Feis: *Between War and Peace* (Princeton, 1960), 4.

After being sent by Truman on a special mission to Churchill in May 1945, Davies reported back that Churchill 'was basically more concerned over preserving Britain's position in Europe than in preserving peace'. On this Admiral Leahy, confidential adviser to both Roosevelt and Truman, made the pregnant comment: 'this was consistent with our staff estimate of Churchill's attitude throughout the war'.[1]

It was obvious that Churchill was resisting gallantly and vigorously the unpleasant fact that his government no longer occupied its former degree of power and dominance in the world, and that he saw in the presence of the American army a hope of sustaining Britain's vanishing position in Europe. He feared that America's abandonment of Europe would leave Britain 'holding the bag alone'. In vain Churchill 'objected to the implicit idea that the new disputes now opening with the Soviets lay between Britain and Russia. The United States was as fully concerned and committed as ourselves.'[2]

Delusions and Disillusionment

Disillusionment began to set in soon after the Yalta Conference of the Big Three in February 1945, but for many months the Americans continued trying to implement Roosevelt's policy. This had been expressed by Roosevelt to Ambassador Bullitt earlier in terms of a 'hunch' that Stalin 'doesn't want anything but security for his country, and I think that if I can give him everything I possibly can and ask nothing from him in return, *noblesse oblige*, he won't try to annexe anything and will work with me for a world of democracy and peace.'[3] Although by the time of Yalta Stalin had already made a number of annexations, and although it was clear that his appetite was not yet sated, the policy of gaining his co-operation 'for a world of democracy and peace' was continued. This meant giving away other people's territory to Russia—accepting Russia's entitlement to Eastern Poland, the Baltic States and other areas which she had

[1] Fleet Admiral W. D. Leahy: *I Was There* (Gollancz, 1950), 443. (The first quotation is Leahy's version of Davies' conclusion.) Leahy adds, 'Davies felt that Russian knowledge of Churchill's attitude was responsible for the aggressiveness and unilateral action on the part of the Soviets since Yalta.' 444. See also Leahy's tribute to Churchill, 486–7.
[2] Churchill, VI, 503.
[3] *Life*, 30 August 1948, W. C. Bullitt: *How We Won the War and Lost the Peace*, 94; H. W. Baldwin: *Great Mistakes of the War* (Redman, 1950), 5. See also Bullitt: *The Great Globe Itself* (Macmillan, 1947), 13 seq.

already seized, as well as promising her lands and privileges in the future at the expense of China and Japan.

Though not officially dead, the Atlantic Charter had long since been buried. The best that Roosevelt and Churchill could hope for at Yalta was to gain some chance of freedom for the countries of Eastern Europe, at least in the form of free elections and especially for Poland, the defence of whom had been the original *casus belli* for Britain and France. The bargaining was hard, but Roosevelt and Churchill left Yalta with the conviction that they had gained real concessions on these points, and that if they had not got all they wished, the balance on the debit side was a fair price to pay for Russia's support in setting up the new world organization.

The Conflict over Poland

Poland was the main bone of contention. Stalin's claims to her territory as far west as the Curzon Line had already been decided by the Big Three, Polish opposition notwithstanding.[1] There was also the question of her government. Stalin insisted that the new Poland should have a government friendly to the Russians—and this meant in practice 'one completely dominated by them'.[2]

On these issues Stalin took an uncompromising stand. When the subject was raised he stood up—the only time he did so at the conference 'and made an impassioned statement'. 'You would drive us into shame,' he protested, if Russia were forced to accept less than her full claims. 'What will be said by the White Russians and the Ukrainians? . . . Poland has been the corridor through which the enemy has passed into Russia. Twice in the last thirty years, our enemies, the Germans, have passed through this corridor. It is in Russia's interest that Poland should be strong and powerful, in a position to shut the door of this corridor by her own force.'[3]

Stalin was not to be budged, and all that Churchill and Roosevelt could do was to attempt to secure minor adjustments of frontier, and to bring about some understanding between him and the exiled Polish government in London. This was difficult, partly because the

---

[1] Polish opposition had been restated at Moscow, October 1944, when Mikolajczyk joined Churchill, and Eden there (Mikolajczyk, 104–12). See above, p. 63.

[2] J. F. Byrnes: *Speaking Frankly* (Harper, 1947), 32.

[3] Byrnes, 29–31.

London Poles were as uncompromising as Stalin, determined to recover all of Poland with her 1939 frontiers, partly because Stalin had his alternative Polish government ready, composed of Polish Communists, whom he could place in power in the wake of the Red Army as it reconquered their land. This in fact is what he did, having installed them in Lublin, in July 1944.

After hours of stalling, Stalin and Molotov at last agreed that representative non-Communist Poles, like Mikolajczyk, from both within and outside Poland, should be included in the Lublin government, which could then be recognized by Britain and U.S.A., also that free elections should be held (Stalin said this could be done 'within a month').[1] The question of compensation which Poland should have in the west for territory surrendered to Russia in the east, was left in suspense: it should include Danzig and German territory as far as the eastern or western Neisse. According to a three-power declaration, 'the final delimitation of the western frontier of Poland should . . . await the Peace Conference'.

Yalta: Hopes and Realities

Agreement was also reached on a 'Declaration on Liberated Europe',[2] on Russian representation at the United Nations, on voting in the Security Council (the question of the veto had come to the fore) and on a French occupation zone in Germany. With these gains, the American and British delegations left Yalta in some elation, though Roosevelt was fatigued and frail—'tired and anxious to avoid further argument'.[3] Churchill's optimism was tempered with caution, but he felt convinced enough about the outcome of Yalta to assure the House of Commons: 'I know of no government which stands to its obligations, even in its own despite, more solidly than the Russian Soviet Government. I decline absolutely to embark here on a question of Russian good faith.'[4]

But a few more weeks sufficed to convince Churchill that his

---

[1] Churchill, VI, 333. In fact elections of a kind—not free elections—were held only in January 1947.

[2] See Feis: *Churchill, Roosevelt, Stalin*, 559–60.

[3] Baldwin, 81. There was also the 'Top Secret' Protocol: in return for Russia entering the war against Japan, she was to gain the Kurile Islands, the southern half of Sakhalin, the lease of Port Arthur, etc. (See Note p. 147 for the part played by Alger Hiss.)

[4] Churchill, VI, 351. Speech of 27 February 1945.

optimism was mistaken. A particularly flagrant case of Soviet bad faith was in luring General Okulicki, the successor of General Bor-Komorowski as commander of the underground army, together with fourteen leaders of all the political parties in Poland, to a meeting in Moscow for discussing the reconstruction of the Polish Government in accordance with the Yalta decisions. Though provided with a written safe conduct, all these men were held prisoner in Moscow, as admitted by Molotov on 4 May 1945. Eventually most of them were sentenced to terms of imprisonment varying from four months to ten years for 'diversionary tactics in the rear of the Red Army'.

The Division of Europe

On the same 4 May Churchill wrote to Eden, who was at the San Francisco Conference for establishing the United Nations, saying that the 'terrible things' which had happened during the Russian advance to the Elbe showed clearly the kind of domination which the Soviet government intended to impose on all the territories under its occupation. The withdrawal of the British and Americans from the areas which they then held within the zones ear-marked for the Russians 'would mean the tide of Russian domination sweeping forward 120 miles on a front of 300 or 400 miles. . . . What would in fact be the Russian frontier would run from the North Cape in Norway along the Finnish-Swedish frontier, across the Baltic to a point just east of Lübeck, along the at present agreed line of occupation and along the frontier between Bavaria and Czechoslovakia [1] to the frontiers of Austria, which is nominally to be in quadruple occupation, and half way across that country to the Isonzo river, behind which Tito and Russia will claim everything to the east. Thus the territories under Russian control would include all the Baltic provinces, all of Germany to the occupational line, all Czechoslovakia, a large part of Austria, the whole of Yugoslavia, Hungary, Rumania, Bulgaria, until Greece in her present tottering condition is reached. It would include all the great capitals of Middle Europe, including Berlin, Vienna, Budapest, Belgrade, Bucharest and Sofia. . . . The Russian demands on Germany for reparations alone will be such as to enable her to prolong the occupation almost indefinitely, at any rate for many years, during which time Poland will sink with many

[1] The original as printed in Churchill, VI, 438–9 reads 'Bavaria to Czechoslovakia'.

THE IRON CURTAIN
FEBRUARY 1948

other States into the vast zone of Russian-controlled Europe, not necessarily economically Sovietized, but police-governed.'

Churchill's Proposals

His conclusions were that the Allied occupation forces should not be withdrawn within their zonal boundaries 'until we are satisfied about Poland, and also about the temporary character of the Russian occupation of Germany, and the conditions to be established in the Russianized or Russian-controlled countries in the Danube valley, particularly Austria and Czechoslovakia, and the Balkans;' and that before the Allied, and particularly the American forces in Europe melted away, there should be a 'show-down' with the Russians at some point in Germany under American and British control.[1]

Churchill's analysis of Russian intentions and his pre-view of the Europe that was to come, was correct almost to the details. His urgent conviction that the Big Three should meet again, while the Allies still held a large part of Germany as a gage, eventually took effect—though the meeting was held at Potsdam in the Russian-controlled area, and not before the Allied forces had been pulled back within their zonal boundaries. This was despite Churchill's insistence with the Americans: the hangover of the old policy of trying to do business with the Russians by meeting their claims was still potent. Hopkins, sent by Truman to Moscow in May, came back with a glowing account of his achievements in face to face diplomacy with Stalin.[2] Truman was delighted and Stettinius 'excited'—the main achievement being that 'the San Francisco Conference had been saved'. Stalin and Molotov had been persuaded to abandon the use of the veto by a permanent Member to prevent a dispute coming before the Security Council, when it was not directly involved.[3]

Truman's Views

Truman and his associates came to Potsdam (15 July 1945) determined to play a mediatory role between the British and the Americans. Truman—brisk, efficient, warm in his sympathies, and (with all

[1] Churchill, VI, 438–9.
[2] Later he regretted not having had someone from the British side associated with him on this mission. In fairness it should be said that Hopkins was a very sick man and this was his last journey. He died in January 1946.
[3] Feis: *Between War and Peace*, 118.

his homespun Missouri manner) as shrewd as Roosevelt, in some ways shrewder in summing up men and situations—wanted quick decisions and an early end to the conference with its atmosphere of 'tuxedo, tails . . . preacher coat, high hat, low hat and hard hat as well as sundry other things'.[1]

Truman was a man who learnt quickly. Though he had Joseph E. Davies and other appeasers of the Soviets at his elbow during the conference, he was soon able to appreciate the truth of Churchill's grim warnings about Russian aims and the 'iron curtain' which they were drawing down on their frontier with the west.[2] Before Potsdam Truman had been 'trying to get Churchill in a frame of mind to forget the old power politics and get a United Nations organisation to work;'[3] but at Potsdam he noticed that Stalin 'would reduce arguments quickly to the question of power, and had little patience with any other kind of approach'.[4] Stalin's rude rejection of his pet project for internationalization of the Danube and other waterways ('Nyet! No, I say No!')[5] did much to convince Truman that 'the Russians were planning world conquest'.[6]

Potsdam and Poland

Stalin made it perfectly clear that the territory overrun by the Red Army was for the Soviet government to dispose of as it wished, any formula about leaving decisions to the peace conference being only a way of having the Soviet arrangements politely rubber-stamped. Truman and Churchill got nowhere in challenging Stalin and Molotov on their *fait accompli* of putting German territory west of Königsberg as far as the Oder and Western Neisse under Polish administration, or on the Russian annexations of the rest of East Prussia, of Ruthenia and other territories. They complained that Russia was unilaterally creating another occupation zone for Poland, besides prejudicing the decision of the peace conference, and aggravating the food problem in the rest of Germany by conniving at the expulsion of millions of German inhabitants from these areas into the zones of

[1] Letter to his mother and sister, 3 July 1945 in *The Memoirs of Harry S. Truman* (Doubleday, 1955), I, 331; (Hodder, 1955, I, 256).
[2] Churchill to Truman, 12 May 1945, Churchill, VI, 498.
[3] Truman (Doubleday), I, 246.   [4] Ibid., 275.
[5] R. Murphy: *Diplomat Among Warriors* (Doubleday 1964), 279.
[6] Truman (Doubleday), I, 412; (Hodder), I, 342.

the Western Allies. Stalin stated there were no Germans left there—they had already fled, but Churchill's information was that there were still two to three million Germans in the area between the Eastern and Western Neisse (which was the main bone of contention in the arguments as to where the western frontier of the new Poland should run).

Even if four million Poles from east of the Curzon Line had to be resettled in former German territory, it was a bad bargain for the Western Allies when they had to feed eight and a quarter million Germans expelled to make room for them. Their zones would be deprived anyway of the produce of what had formerly been Germany's best agricultural lands, those of the east, which had constituted 25 per cent of her pre-war arable area.[1]

The Russians fought hard to have their free hand in the east accepted, in return for what were practically nominal concessions, such as allowing the American proposal to go forward that Italy be granted membership of the United Nations. But—though largely disinteresting themselves from Italy and other countries within the Allied sphere—they were not prepared to give the Western Allies an entirely free hand in their areas. They demanded an Italian colony under mandate (Libya or the Dodecanese) and they wanted a 25 per cent control over the industry of the Ruhr with a view to obtaining what they considered their share of reparations.

Germany and Reparations

It was over the question of reparations that the Anglo-Saxons began to dig in their toes, since it was quickly recognized that even a modified version of the 'pastoralization' policy for Germany was incompatible with the necessity of enabling her to stand on her own feet economically, without vast sums being expended by the Allies merely to keep the people alive. What the Russians did in their own zone and in greater Berlin had to be regarded as their business—and they were busy removing all the industrial equipment which it was worth their while to carry away; but the Western Allies were increasingly loath to hand over also such equipment from their own zones, except what was directly for war production purposes.

'Pastoralization' had been dropped; Truman was against it; and

[1] Churchill, VI, 561–73.

1 Battle of Britain: British fighter-pilots 'scramble' to their Hurricanes.

2 Liberator Bombers were prominent in the heavy bombing of Germany. This actual aircraft 'Commando' was the personal plane of Winston Churchill.

3 Von Rundstedt.

4 Guderian.

German Wartime Commanders

5 Rommel with men of the Afrika Corps.

6 Tanks in action at El Alamein.

7 D-Day on the Normandy beaches.

8 Stalin, Roosevelt and Churchill at Teheran, Nov./Dec. 1943.

9 The Potsdam Conference, July 1945.

10 The liberation of Eindhoven, Holland, September 1944.

11 Tanks advancing through the rubble of Udem in Germany, February 1945.

12 Heavy bombing by a B29 Superfortress.

13 Armed with light machine guns, Soviet troops attack the German forces near the Red October plant in Stalingrad.

14 A V2 rocket leaving the firing table, during the bombardment of England.

15 The Mohne dam, Germany, breached by British bombs.

16 Rotterdam levelled by German bombs, 1940.

17 The concentration camp at Belsen, Germany.

18 Montgomery takes the surrender of the German Forces, Lüneburg Heath, 4 May 1945.

19 Churchill at the ruins of Hitler's bunker, Berlin, 1945.

20 Laval.

21 Tito.

22 Marshall and Bevin.

23 Hungary's fight for freedom in Budapest, 1956.

24 Burning of Stalin's portrait.

25 Russian officers and armour in Budapest

26 General Lucius Clay, the American High Commissioner to Germany (second from right), at the Berlin Wall.

27 President Kennedy with Willy Brandt, Mayor of West Berlin (on the President's left), at the Brandenburg Gate, Berlin, 1963.

28 Churchill at the Council of Europe, Strasbourg.

29 Monnet and Schuman.

30 Adenauer and de Gaulle.

31 A clover-leaf intersection on the autobahn at Frankfurt-am-Main, Germany.

32 Monorail, Dortmund, Germany.

33 Postwar architecture in Germany. The Church of St Canisius, Berlin.

34 Eden.

35 Spaak.

36 Mendès-France.

37 Khrushchev.

38 Pope John XXIII.

39 The Queen with President Lübke in Germany, May 1965.

its begetter, Morgenthau, resigned from the cabinet.[1] Stalin and Molotov however first held to their demand for twenty billion dollars worth of reparations from Germany (retreating later to eighteen or sixteen billion dollars) of which Russia should get half.[2]

When it was accepted that they should take what they wished from their zone, they stood out for a further ten or nine billion dollars worth from the other zones.[3] On being offered a percentage of such equipment as would not be necessary to Germany's peace economy, they haggled for a total figure in money value or tonnage, and demanded one-third of the shares in German industrial and transport companies in the western zones, and about one-third of German gold and assets abroad.[4] Ultimately they had to settle for much less, since Truman was determined that there should be no repetition of the post-1919 situation, when America paid 'the reparations bill for Europe'.[5] For all it was worth the principle was written into the Potsdam Protocol that payment of reparations was to be limited by the necessity of leaving Germany with enough resources to subsist without assistance from abroad.

A short way of dealing with the Russian demands was the proposal of the British delegation to make the satisfaction of the Soviet demands for reparations from the western zones conditional on the Russians accepting the western frontier of Poland which they and the Americans deemed right. But the Americans decided against this plan at the start of the conference—their tactic was to explore the possibility of compromise.[6] Recognition of the fact that the Russians had

[1] The 'pastoralization' plan had been largely inspired by Harry Dexter White, an undercover Communist who was special assistant to Secretary of the Treasury Henry Morgenthau, Jnr. (White was directly responsible for foreign affairs as they concerned the Treasury Department.) See J. L. Snell: *Dilemma over Germany* (Hauser Press, 1959), 64 seq.

[2] Feis: *Between War and Peace*, 255. The Russians maintained that the twenty billion dollars was approved at Yalta, but it had only been agreed by Roosevelt and Churchill to consider it as a basis for discussion. The Americans also opposed payments of reparations out of German production for a period of years, as artificially stimulating German industry in the wrong way.

[3] Later the Americans and British repeatedly demanded accounts from the Russians of reparations taken from their zone, both in capital goods and current production, in order to work out a level of industrial production common to all zones, and a co-ordinated economic policy, but the Russians refused. See also Foreign Affairs, January 1951, 300, P. Nettl: *German Reparations in the Soviet Empire*.

[4] Feis, op. cit., 265, Leahy, 493.

[5] Truman (Doubleday), I, 323; (Hodder), I, 248.

[6] Feis, 225.

already given away part of Germany to the Poles, was, however, the basis for the American decision—much resisted by the Russians—that reparations could no longer be exacted from the whole of Germany and then divided out. As against this start of dividing Germany economically was the statement in the Potsdam Protocol, agreed at the end of the conference, that Germany should be treated as one economic unit. Though the Russians did not apply the agreement, it provided the formal basis for the co-operation of the British and the Americans, and eventually of the French, in building a unified and thriving economy for a rehabilitated Western Germany.[1]

Britain's Decline

This development was still far in the future. As Potsdam ended, the war-time Allies were in disarray. Despite the setting up of the Council of Foreign Ministers as a body for working out the details of a final settlement, the Anglo-Americans were deeply divided from the Russians, and they were themselves at odds with the French (de Gaulle, not invited to Potsdam, refused to implement its decisions). Even the closest of the war-time partnership between Britain and America had gone, though the war in the Far East continued. On this point the Americans treated the Russians as principals, and their concern to get them into the war against Japan was one reason for the American failure to be uncompromising with Russia.

The British, though sharing with the Americans a sense of achievement over the successful proving of the atomic bomb (the prototype was exploded at Alamagordo on 16 July, 1945, the first day of the conference), were turning increasingly to concern themselves with their own problems of living standards and social welfare at home. Significant of the changing position of Britain as a world power were the agreements which the Americans were now making with the Russians regarding the Japanese War and the post-war settlement for China and the Japanese Empire, about which Britain was informed only after action was taken.

Churchill's Fall

Significant too of this trend was Churchill's fall. Ready to take a tough line with the Russians, he had welcomed, momentarily, with

[1] Murphy, 279.

jubilation the explosion of the atomic test-bomb. The bomb would 'redress our position—completely alter the diplomatic equilibrium which was adrift since the defeat of Germany'. It would be possible to say to the Russians, 'if you insist on doing this or that, well. . . .'[1] Such a policy was scarcely practicable, not least from a moral point of view, and there is no evidence that Churchill could have brought the Americans to pursue it. But by voting in Attlee and the Labour Government, over half the British electorate decided that rebuilding Britain on a socialist basis was preferable to retaining in office the commanding figure who might have made the Anglo-American alliance a more effective force in the post-war world than in fact it was.

The removal of this world figure by the declaration of the poll on 26 July 1945 was symbolic of Britain's incipient retreat from the position of a world power. The Potsdam Conference was not yet over. Churchill had brought Attlee to Potsdam in case the hand-over of power would be necessary. All the British delegation went to London on 25 July to await the outcome of the poll, and when Attlee and Bevin returned to Potsdam on the 28th instead of Churchill and Eden, the subsequent sessions were 'anticlimactic'.[2]

A new order was emerging, in which the duel of the super-powers, America and Russia, held the centre of the stage; and in the shadow of these combatants the peoples of Europe had to start a new chapter in working out their own salvation.

[1] Extract from diary of F. M. Lord Alanbrooke, 23 July 1945, in A. Bryant: *Triumph in the West 1943–1946* (Collins, 1959), 478.

[2] Murphy, 275.

NOTE

The part played by Alger Hiss at Yalta, where he was present as a State Department Adviser and participated in some of the drafting, is not precisely clear. His next important appointment was as Secretary-General of the San Francisco Conference which instituted the United Nations. He was subsequently convicted of perjury (21 January 1950) in denying that he had been a member of the Communist Party. There is a considerable literature on Hiss and the trial. Some of the books are:

Whittaker Chambers: *Witness* (Random House, New York, 1952).
Earl Jowitt: *The Strange Case of Alger Hiss* (Hodder and Stoughton, 1953).
A. Cooke: *A Generation on Trial* (Hart-Davis, 1950).

14: The End of Appeasement
(August 1945–June 1947)

Allied Policy

Despite Truman's conviction that 'the Russians were planning world conquest',[1] the Western Allies still hoped that the war-time co-operation with Russia would not fade away, and that, by making timely concessions to the Soviets over such issues as Poland, they might succeed in buying a measure of support for their concept of the new world order.

Truman's analysis of the Russians' ultimate intentions may have been correct; but their immediate aim was to consolidate the gains which the war had enabled them to make. What they wanted was acceptance of their absolute control over all the areas which they had 'liberated' or occupied, and this involved recognition of the puppet governments which they had set up or were in process of organizing. They also expected to keep Germany—the whole country, not merely their own zone—permanently weak and functioning at the lowest economic level, and they were prepared to make four-power control a reality on this basis. If the Anglo-Saxons would agree with them on these matters, they were prepared to allow them a free hand over all the remaining areas of the world where Russia had (as yet) no rights or claims. Stalin's attitude was, in fact, much the same as Hitler's had been, only instead of doing a deal with Britain, he was mainly concerned to do a deal with America.

Such agreement was impossible, because the Western Allies believed that in the post-war settlement the principles of democracy and self-determination should be applied, not merely that some lip-service be given them, as in the Soviet-dominated areas. Nor could they agree with the Russian policy for keeping Germany indefinitely as a subject and impoverished state. For reasons of mere humanity the Western Allies could not leave millions of Germans in a permanent condition of near-starvation. They could not face continuing to spend

[1] See above, p. 143.

enormous sums just to keep these Germans alive, without letting them have sufficient industry for export as well as for internal needs. The Russians might intend keeping Eastern Europe as a whole at a low economic level as part of their plan for subjecting it politically— but the Anglo-Saxons could not accept similar arrangements for Western Europe. Trade with Germany had been the life-blood of Holland; it was almost equally essential for economic health and a decent standard of living in Scandinavia, Switzerland and elsewhere.

Whatever the fate of Germany as a whole, the Russians believed that they had the right to exercise control in the areas which they occupied because they had the troops on the spot: in the face of this hard fact no other considerations mattered. When Churchill protested during the Potsdam Conference against the Russians' disregard of the Catholic outlook of the vast majority of the Poles, 'Stalin reflected a moment, stroking his moustache, and then asked the Prime Minister in a hard, even tone: "How many divisions has the Pope?"'[1]

As long as they thought that they still had some hope of winning America to their point of view (and particularly until the defeat of Japan made American co-operation less necessary) the Russians were prepared to show an amenable spirit. Such was the experience of General Clay as Eisenhower's Deputy in Berlin: 'In Germany and elsewhere the representatives of the Western countries met frequently with representatives of the Soviet Government in an atmosphere of outward good will. This good will was directed particularly towards the United States. General Eisenhower was received in Moscow in August 1945 with a warm and, I still believe, genuine welcome. In Berlin, Soviet representatives insisted that the headquarters of four-power government be established in the American sector. Likewise, they had refused to consider anyone other than General Eisenhower as the first chairman of the Control Council. Senior Soviet representatives exchanged visits with our senior representatives unaccompanied even by interpreters. There was evidence of Russian suspicion of the other occupying powers, but not of the United States. Even the inevitable incidents which resulted from the close proximity of our troops were not permitted to interfere with these relations.'[2]

[1] Leahy, 476.
[2] General L. D. Clay: *Germany and the Fight for Freedom* (Harvard University Press, 1950), 17.

Russian Tactics

While the Western Allies were loath to yield on the principles on which they believed the settlement should be based, they were ready to come a long way in making compromises with the Russian demands. But such compromises gave the substance to the Russians while keeping for the Allies only the shadow of face-saving professions, or a postponement before the *fait accompli* had to be accepted as inevitable. Hope that it would be possible to 'do business' with the Russians on this basis was kept alive by Stalin's 'occasional concessions to Western wishes, which nourished the belief that, though tough, he was not immovable'.[1] Long after the evidence pointed the other way, Byrnes (who took over from Stettinius as Secretary of State on 30 June 1945) believed that he could get favourable decisions from Moscow by personal contact with Stalin. Molotov gave the impression in conferences of being even tougher than Stalin, and less open to persuasion.

If they could not get what they wanted at once, the Russian tactic was one of postponement. Time was on their side. The troops of the Western Allies were quickly being brought home, while the Red Army stood to its arms, several million strong, throughout eastern and central Europe. The balance of power was therefore shifting decisively during those months in favour of Russia. Hence the endless and (for the West) frustrating conferences, in which little was done but talk, until the time came, in the Russian view, to present the West with *faits accomplis* which could not be reversed.

Ernest Bevin, as Britain's new Foreign Secretary, was at the start as hopeful as the Americans, though in manner gruff, tough and aggressive.[2] 'He still hoped . . . perhaps rather naïvely, that . . . "Left would be able to speak to Left."'[3] He too hoped for much from personal contact with Stalin, and in an interview with him offered to extend the twenty-year Anglo-Russian Alliance, negotiated during the war, into one for fifty years. There were occasions—the latest being the Foreign Ministers' Conference of March and April 1947, when he felt satisfaction, even jubilation, that, on account of

---

[1] Feis: *Between War and Peace*, 66.

[2] The assessments of Byrnes (*Speaking Frankly*), p. 79, and Leahy, op. cit., 490.

[3] Francis Williams: *Ernest Bevin* (Hutchinson, 1952), 242.

some real or apparent concession—the Russians were at last being reasonable.[1]

But such moments proved to be miasmas. Byrnes' experience was of the same order. At the first Council of the Foreign Ministers' meeting after Potsdam (September 1945) deadlock quickly ensued, which Byrnes attempted to break in December 1945, by offering Russia a four-power pact for forty years for keeping Germany disarmed. He did this by seeking a direct interview with Stalin, thus by-passing the Conference of Foreign Ministers, and the procedural question which Molotov had raised as a barrier there. But this attempt at personal diplomacy with Stalin proved no more successful than those of Hopkins and others had been. All it led to was a row with Truman, who was convinced of Russia's intransigence—'unless Russia is faced with an iron fist and strong language another war is in the making'.[2]

Change of Allied Policy

This was not yet American official policy, which was still to secure a settlement by negotiation with Russia, first in making peace treaties with Italy and the smaller ex-enemy states. Some progress was achieved over Italy in the Foreign Ministers' Conference of September 1945, before Molotov's blocking tactics brought it to a halt.[3] The Paris Peace Conference, which met in July 1946, produced little more than wrangling.[4]

The Western Allies could get no satisfaction on the major points of free elections in Eastern Europe, or even on rights of diplomatic staff and press correspondents to travel and report in Russian occupied areas. The Russians were busy eliminating all opposition in those areas to the puppet régimes which they had set up, from which all influences other than Communist were being rapidly eliminated. Eventually, confronted by the completed *fait accompli*, the Western Allies concluded that they had better accept the situation with as good a grace as possible, and use their recognition of these régimes

[1] The conference was from 10 March–24 April 1947 (R.I.I.A. Survey for 1947–8), 236.

[2] Truman (Doubleday), I, 552; (Hodder), I, 492.

[3] By refusing to continue the conference with the French and Chinese Foreign Ministers present.

[4] Some preparatory work for peace treaties, notably with Italy and the East European countries was carried out. See below, pp. 152, 171, 367.

(and implicitly the wholesale spoliations which the Russians had carried through) in order to buy what complaisance they could from the Russians for other issues still outstanding. On this basis peace treaties with Rumania, Bulgaria and Hungary were grudgingly signed in February 1947.

But by that date the consolidation of the Eastern bloc was virtually complete (incomplete only insofar as a rupture between Yugoslavia and Russia was developing beneath the monolithic surface). Molotov had kept the Westerners talking through week after week of frustrating and well-nigh fruitless conferences—now for both sides this method had reached the point of rapidly diminishing returns. On their side the Anglo-Saxons had now taken steps to contain the Russians at the limits which they had reached, and to bring order and prosperity to the areas where they could exert ultimate control. Increasingly Britain's weakness, material and to some extent moral, and her dependence on America, threw the onus of leadership on the latter. It was under American hegemony that the free nations of Europe began to recover economically and co-operate politically, in face of Russia's challenge to control ever wider areas as her power thrust outwards across the peripheries of the great Eurasian Plain which she dominated.

15: The Cold War and the Integration of Western Europe

Gradually the struggle in Europe took on the aspect of a struggle between the super-powers, America and Russia; indeed this struggle was only part of a wider, world conflict, since the areas which they respectively controlled were now coming to touch each other at every point around the world, from Sakhalin to Western Germany. Going or gone were the powers, formerly great, now at best only intermediate, who could cushion the shock of the confrontation of Russia and America. France, struggling to assert herself in Europe and to regain what she could of her realm in Indo-China and elsewhere, was riven by political divisions and tardy in recovering her economic health. Britain, divesting herself of empire in the Orient and retreating from the weight of responsibility in the Mediterranean, was increasingly compelled to invite America to take over the obligations which she could no longer undertake.

Yet for two years after Potsdam the brunt of the struggle with the Soviet Union was borne by Britain—or (to put it in other words) it was Britain and not the U.S.A. who came most often under fire from Russia. Acrimonious debates in the Security Council, where Russia began her long record with the veto, usually concerned some area where Russia was tangling with Britain, notably in the Middle East. In Europe, Greece was a sore kept running by Russia and her Balkan satellites: here Britain was challenged on keeping troops in the country, and her naval forces were molested by mines sown in the Corfu Strait (May and October 1946), while Russia vetoed a Security Council resolution which placed the blame on Albania. Turkey too was under heavy attack, beginning with the Russian demand for revision of the Montreux Treaty and for a base in the Dardanelles, together with the restoration to Russia of Kars and Ardahan. As Turkey was closely linked with Britain by the Anglo-Turkish Agreement of 1939, which its government regarded as the cornerstone of their policy, this challenge too was mainly directed at Britain.[1]

Bevin stood up to Molotov, at first so aggressively that his American colleagues wondered whether they would be able to get on with him themselves.[2] But he was aware of the growing weakness of the British position, and his aim was to seize the right moment in effecting the handover of British commitments to America in places where Britain could no longer carry the burden alone. For if Greece was a dependency of Britain, Britain was virtually a dependency of America, and this applied also to a greater or less extent to Britain's relations with Turkey and other countries. Britain could only recover to the point of being able to stand on her own feet, at least economically, if she divested herself of some of her responsibilities, and allowed America to take them over directly.

Until 1947 American policy was mainly concerned with preparing a withdrawal from Europe, but situations like Greece, which were deteriorating economically and politically, determined her further involvement. Truman himself was more convinced than the State Department of the need to peg Russian power at the Black Sea, safeguarding the Straits and opposing any turning of Turkey's flank through Greece. A further step was taken when America joined with Britain in 'observing' the Greek elections in March 1946 (which the Russians declined to do on the grounds that it constituted an interference with Greece's internal affairs).

In Germany co-operation between the two powers developed rapidly as it became plain that the British could not long continue to support the burden of feeding the inhabitants of their zone—occupation costs were estimated as rising to more than £80 million in 1946-7.[3] The only alternative was to initiate a policy which would economize occupation costs and enable Germany to become self-sufficient. If no policy to this end could be agreed with the Russians—and by the latter part of 1946 it was clear that this was the case—then Britain and America, perhaps with France, would have to take such action as was open to them within their own zones.

---

[1] C. M. Woodhouse: *British Foreign Policy Since the Second World War* (Hutchinson, 1961), 15–17.

[2] Byrnes, 79. 'We soon came to admire his bluntness and directness,' he adds.

[3] Britain could not maintain an adequate food-ration as it was—there was some starva-

The first obvious step was to unify the western zones for economic purposes, which would effect a considerable saving. The French, who had been consistently obstructing Anglo-American policy in Germany would not come in (though they did so later),[1] but in the face of Russian protests the economic fusion of the British and American Zones ('Bizonia') took place on 1 January 1947.

Towards Rehabilitating Western Germany

This was the first step in rehabilitating Western Germany, and eventually bringing her into the Western Alliance. Since the breaking up of the Dönitz government at Flensburg a few days after the German surrender, there had been no government for Germany other than that supplied by the victorious Allies. The functions of government were to be carried out by the Allied commanders, 'each in his own zone of occupation, and also jointly, in matters affecting Germany as a whole'[2]—in the latter case deliberating together in the Allied Control Council seated at Berlin. But the Council was incapable of applying a policy for Germany, because its members disagreed on what that policy should be. Policies proposed by the British or Americans, such as a plan for running the railways on a national basis, foundered in the face of opposition—usually from the French. Having been kept away from Potsdam, and therefore having not accepted the principle agreed there of administering Germany as a single economic unit, the French asserted their right to manage the affairs of their own zone without reference to the Control Council, and vetoed British and American plans which aimed at the rehabilitation of Germany as a whole. Since the Russians disagreed with any policy of restoring Germany's economy, they merely had to sit back and watch these French actions for blocking the Anglo-American plans.[3]

---

tion and much under-nourishment aggravated by the acute housing shortage and breakdown of services.

[1] Economic fusion of the American Zone with those of any other governments who would come in was offered by Byrnes at the Foreign Ministers' Conference at Paris in July 1946. (Byrnes, 195).

[2] Statement by the Governments of the U.K., the U.S.A., the U.S.S.R., and the Provisional Government of the French Republic on Control Machinery in Germany, 6 May 1945.

[3] L. D. Clay: *Decision in Germany* (Heinemann, 1950), 42. See also D. Middleton: *The Struggle for Germany* (Wingate, 1950), 70.

It is possible to argue that had it not been for this French policy, economic administration of Germany as a unit might have been achieved, which would have had the effect of weakening the Russian grip on the East Zone. But if the French had not carried out this policy it is probable that the Russians would have done it themselves. The Russian line, in the first months after Potsdam, that they favoured central administrative agencies for Germany, may have been a blind.

General Clay, who was deputy to Eisenhower and his successor on the Control Council, and subsequently Military Governor of the American Zone, thought that there might have been a chance during the first six months after Potsdam for creating such agencies; the Western powers could then have struggled within the framework of these agencies for a common economic policy for Germany. Sooner or later, he concluded, Russian policy would have jeopardized this development, but it might have been more difficult for Russia 'to have split a Germany in which central agencies were directing affairs everywhere'.[1]

The policy of America and Britain to bring about a common economic administration for Germany, and promote recovery by pooling the resources of the different zones was first made public by Byrnes in a speech at Stuttgart in September 1946. It marked the change from pulling down to building up the West German economy, and promised progress in handing political responsibility to the Germans on a democratic basis. It also promised continued participation of America in such a policy, and a pledge that she would not retreat before the demands of Russia. Perhaps the most acceptable of the many statements on that occasion, which brought about a rebirth of hope in a possible future for millions of Germans, was Byrnes' statement that 'as long as an occupation force is required in Germany, the army of the United States will be part of that occupation force'.[2]

Russia's policy was not opposed to unifying Germany as an administrative and economic unit, as long as she could keep the country weak and make large gains for herself, by exacting the oft-demanded ten billion dollars of reparations out of current production. As a corollary, Molotov insisted that the Ruhr should be under

---

[1] Clay: *Decision in Germany*, 131.
[2] Speech of 6 September 1946. Byrnes, 188–91; Clay: *Decision*, 80–1.

Four-Power control, that is that the Soviet Government should be in a position to veto any rise in production above what it considered the correct level, and would have a major say in the apportionment of whatever product there was. This was Russia's preferred solution of the German question, and Molotov continued fighting hard for it from the moment in July 1946 when the economic fusion of the zones was first proposed by the Americans.[1]

Molotov's counter-proposal was the fusion of all the zones, not only economically, but also politically. At the conference of Foreign Ministers in Moscow in March 1947 he proposed the setting up of a provisional German government, with a centralized state based on the Weimar Constitution. He soon indicated the way in which he hoped such a state would come under Soviet control, by advocating (2 April 1947) the inclusion in such a government of the various Communist-front organizations in Germany. This proposal to set up the beginnings of a provisional government with centralized agencies was not far removed from a similar British plan also mooted at the Moscow conference. But it was unacceptable to the Western powers, because Molotov would not retreat from linking it with the demand for ten billion dollars' worth of reparations. He would not hear of a compromise, proposed by the new American Secretary of State, General Marshall, which would have allowed the Russians reparations for a certain period from a number of specified factories.

Molotov's refusal to entertain any such compromise 'convinced many members of the United States delegation that it was no use trying to negotiate with the Russians on the critical question of reparations'.[2] The cold anger of Marshall and others of the American delegation spurred them to abandon the former policy of seeking Germany's unity through negotiations with Russia. Instead Marshall took a new course in building up a government in Western Germany which would be acceptable to the Anglo-Saxons.[3]

Until then there had been no intention of developing a German administration with political responsibilities for the Bizone. According to the Potsdam Protocol essential central administrative agencies

---

[1] It had been suggested by General Clay in a report to the American War Department of 5 May 1946 (Clay: *Decision*, 731).

[2] Middleton, 136.

[3] Ibid., 140–1; W. Millis (ed.): *The Forrestal Diaries* (Cassell, 1952), 261.

were to be set up, headed by German state secretaries under the supervision of the Allied Control Council. But as the Council could not reach agreement on implementing this for Germany as a whole, it had been necessary to carry through such arrangements as were possible on a zonal basis. The revival of local government and the setting up of *Länder* (sometimes translated 'states') in the Western zones were not designed to prejudice the development of central institutions; but when the central institutions failed to materialize, the *Länder*, ultimately reorganized, became the basis of the German Federal Republic.

The Marshall Plan

While these political developments in regard to Germany were maturing, far-reaching steps had been taken, on American initiative, to rebuild Europe's economy. The Americans believed that recovery, to be effective, must be linked with a measure of integration. A return to the pre-war 'autarky' and international economic anarchy would mean a Europe enfeebled, subject to crises, and more or less dependent on America.

The idea was sound, but it conjured up Russian fears that this rebuilt economy would be controlled by America. The Russians were even suspicious of UNRRA (The United Nations Relief and Rehabilitation Agency), although it aimed only at satisfying the most elementary needs of the destitute and starving millions left in the wake of the war. They refused to allow it to operate in Eastern Germany.

In the period immediately following the end of hostilities, when hopes of a new era of international co-operation were still high, East European countries, and the Soviet Union itself, were represented on some of the commissions and bodies which were founded at the time —the European Coal Organization, the European Central Export Organization, and the Economic Commission for Europe (a child of the United Nations Economic and Social Council). But these bodies possessed but an advisory or token value: at best they stimulated thought, particularly among the Americans, as to what should really be done to make recovery effective.[1]

---

[1] Notably the plan of the American economist W. W. Rostow, then Assistant Chief of the German-Austrian Economic Division of the State Department. See M. Beloff: *The United States and the Unity of Europe* (Faber, 1963), 10.

This thinking bore fruit when it became plain, during the severe winter of 1946–7, that Europe would not recover without a new level of American aid and planning. This was the moment for which Bevin had been waiting, to begin turning over some of Britain's commitments to America. After the sudden cutting off of Lend-Lease (21 August 1945)[1] Britain had been sustained by the $3,750 million line of credit, negotiated with the American Treasury by Lord Keynes. But the dollar had become inflated, and by 1947 what was left of the loan had only 60 per cent of its original value.[2] Britain could no more hope to sustain Greece and Turkey than she could her zone in Germany, let alone regain a position of economic strength which would enable the pound sterling to become convertible to dollars.[3] On 24 February 1947 Bevin informed the American Government that Britain could not continue giving aid to Greece after the end of the current financial year (in five weeks time), and later made it clear that this applied also to Turkey.

These shock tactics produced an agitated note from Marshall asking if this represented a major policy change for Britain. Bevin replied that he believed support for Greece and Turkey, as well as Persia and Italy, was essential for the defence of the free world, but that America would have to bear a larger part of the burden.[4] Truman, who had long been concerned about Russian pressure in these areas, quickly saw the point. He cancelled his holiday, called in the Congressional leaders, and prepared plans for immediately taking over the British commitments. On 12 March 1947 he propounded to Congress what came to be known as the Truman Doctrine, 'that it must be the policy of the U.S.A. to support free peoples who are resisting attempted subjugation by armed minorities, or by outside pressure'.[5] To this end he asked Congress for $400 million as aid to Greece and Turkey, and the despatch to those countries of American military and civilian missions. Despite some initial bewilderment on the part of the public American opinion rapidly crystallized behind the President's

[1] On that date Truman signed an order that Lend-Lease be 'closed out'. For Truman's earlier 'cut-back', see *Memoirs* (Doubleday), I, 227; (Hodder), I, 144.
[2] By this date the wholesale price index for dollar purchases was 4 per cent higher than in 1945 (R.I.I.A. Survey for 1947–8), 68.
[3] To secure convertibility was a principal aim of American policy.
[4] Williams, 263.
[5] R.I.I.A. Survey for 1947–8, 14; *Forrestal Diaries* (ed. W. Millis), 247 seq.

move. Congress duly authorized his request. It was the end of the
Pax Britannica, and the start of establishing instead the *Pax Americana*
over what was coming to be known as the 'Free World'.

In this atmosphere Marshall returned frustrated from the Moscow
Conference, convinced that Russia would sabotage rather than help
in implementing any plans for re-starting the German economy as a
step towards reviving that of Europe as a whole. He hurried on the
creation of a policy planning staff under George Kennan, and decided
to implement the proposals which were then being formulated (May
1947) by the State Department's Committee for Foreign Aid. These
were to the effect that, while the way should be kept open for Soviet
co-operation, it should be demonstrated that the U.S.A. intended 'to
go ahead with a consistent and adequate recovery program for non-
Communist Europe with or without the U.S.S.R.' If this could be
done in a way which would help to unify the economy of non-
Communist Europe, it would give the Europeans a positive aim, that
is the building of unity, political as well as economic, which would
'help fill the present ideological and moral vacuum'. There could be
'a tremendous emotional drive in Western Europe behind the
supranational ideal of European unity'. The plan should avoid in-
juring sensitive nationalistic feelings by developing 'a European recovery plan which stresses the raising of European production and
consumption through the economic and functional unification of
Europe'.

Even if Russia refused to come into the plan there would be a
clear gain in rebuilding Europe on this basis—'it would improve
America's chances of winning a possible war with the Soviet Union.'[1]
These considerations, combined with those presented by Kennan's
staff and others, formed the ground-work of the speech delivered by
Marshall at Harvard on 5 June 1947, in which he put forward proposals for further American aid in speeding the recovery of Europe.
He stressed that this should be no one-sided affair of American
planning and giving—'the role of this country should consist of
friendly aid in the drafting of a European program and of later support for such a program so far as may be practicable for us to do so.

[1] From the memorandum by Charles Kindleberger and others in the Committee on
Foreign Aid in the U.S. State Department, of May 1947, published 12 June 1947, quoted
in Beloff, op. cit., 15–16. The preceding quotations are from the same document.

The program should be a joint one, agreed to by a number, if not all, of European nations.'[1]

Though there was little immediate reaction to this speech in America, it was at once seized upon by Bevin—'When the Marshall proposals were announced, I grabbed them with both hands'.[2] He took action with the French to prepare the ground for launching what came to be the 16-nation Organization for European Economic Recovery (O.E.E.C.) on 5 June 1948. At their end the Americans established the necessary machinery: the Economic Co-operation Administration was set up (3 April 1948), with Paul Hoffman, President of the Studebaker Corporation, as its head, and Averell Harriman, former Ambassador in Russia, as special Representative in Europe. A measure of the importance which the Americans gave to this development was that Harriman moved to this post from the Secretaryship of Commerce while maintaining Cabinet rank, as the link between the aid administration in America and the organization in Europe.

A preliminary step in setting up O.E.E.C. was the summoning of representatives of the European States to work out a suitable programme for using the promised American aid. Bevin and the French Foreign Minister, Bidault, invited Molotov to confer with them as to the mode of procedure, but in a conference at Paris (27 June–2 July 1947) Molotov made it clear that Russia would not help in drawing up a general economic programme. It was a derogation of sovereignty, he declared—each state should make up its own list of needs on the basis of its own plan (such as the Russian five-year plan), and submit it independently to America. There should be no preliminary planning among the European states or arrangements for mutual aid. By refusing to come in on an essential part of the American proposal Molotov opted out, and later the satellite countries were kept out too, though eagerly desirous of American aid. The Czech government, not yet fully assimilated to the Eastern bloc, at first accepted by a unanimous Cabinet decision. The Prime Minister, Gottwald, and several other ministers, were however summoned to Moscow, where they were instructed to send an equally unanimous refusal.

[1] Quoted from Beloff, op. cit., 22.
[2] House of Commons, 19 June 1947. *Hansard*, vol. 438, col. 2353–4.

16: Formation of the Eastern Bloc

The steps taken by Moscow, for keeping its satellites out of the Marshall Plan, heralded the final assimilation of the Eastern bloc (with the exception of the increasingly obdurate Yugoslavia). The climax of Moscow's policy was the Prague Coup of 20–25 February 1948.

Poland

Poland was perhaps the toughest nut for the Communists to crack. The Poles were almost solidly Catholic—the Jews had been eliminated by Hitler, and the Orthodox Christians had been mostly in the area which Russia had absorbed.[1] They had always been anti-Russian, and this sentiment was powerfully increased by the barbarity of the Red Army in the course of its 'liberating' progress through their country. The small group of Communists who came in with the Russian tanks had spent many of their active years in Russia and had no standing in the country.

Of all the courageous actions of a nation which had shown itself brave to the point of heroism during the war and its aftermath, one of the bravest was the decision of Mikolajczyk to return to Poland as a member of the enlarged 'Lublin' Government in June 1945. He had previously resigned as Prime Minister of the London government when his colleagues had not been willing to attempt the policy of working out a compromise with the Russians—the policy called by Churchill that of 'getting a foot in the door' with a view to forcing it open for the entrance of a truly democratic régime. In pursuit of this policy Mikolajczyk had gone to Moscow for the second time on 21 June 1945, where he was compelled to accept for himself and other non-Communist colleagues the quota of positions in the enlarged Lublin government—long since self-proclaimed as the Provisional Government of Poland—which would give it enough respectability to be recognized by the British and the Americans.

Mikolajczyk was nominated one of two Deputy Premiers, with

---

[1] The Russians had allowed those who were indisputably Catholic to leave.

the position of Minister of Agriculture and Land Reform. In a cabinet of 21 there were six non-Communists beside himself, but these were relegated by various devices to positions of little influence or power. He himself was shorn of a large part of his functions as Minister of Agriculture owing to the creation of a Ministry of Forestry under a Communist, which appropriated most of his authority.[1]

On his return to Poland there was no question where the support of the people lay. In Krakow a vast crowd of 'starved but hopeful people—men and women' lifted the entire car in which he was driven, while threatening the Communist general at his side. Then it carried him shoulder-high through the streets, 'singing the old Polish songs of freedom at the top of its lungs. . . . An ominous silence settled over the crowd as we turned a corner. Standing in the street was a knot of Red Army officers. . . .'[2]

Unanimously Mikolajczyk was elected President of the Peasant Party in place of the older leader, Vincenty Witos, who died at the end of 1945 from the effects of a bomb injury and maltreatment by the Gestapo.[3] But in pursuance of the Communist Party directive, 'Mikolajczyk must not be allowed to get too far in front,' every weapon of censorship, suppression, even terror and murder, was used against his supporters and associates. An attempt was made by a plebiscite to take the ground from under his feet, but it failed dismally. In the few districts where the Peasant Party was able to check the ballot boxes, the figures were 83·54 per cent in their favour.[4] Similar methods were used in the 'election' which followed. Even then Mikolajczyk did not give up, but led the meagre quota of Peasant Party deputies which the government allowed in unremitting criticism of Communist policy. In the end, after many threats and warnings that he was to be arrested he escaped with the aid of the American ambassador.

His compatriots who had sought refuge abroad—250,000 had joined the Polish Army abroad with its splendid fighting record, and many others had served in the Allied air and naval forces—were faced

---

[1] Mikolajczyk, 147–8.   [2] Ibid., 149.
[3] Mikolajczyk's meeting with Witos in June 1945 is not without pathos. Witos apologized for the fare he had to offer. 'My remaining chickens were stolen last night by our guests—the Reds—who are bringing us freedom and culture.' (Ibid., 148.)
[4] Ibid., 183.

with a bitter dilemma whether to return to their country or not. In the event about half of them returned to a land ravaged and wrecked by the invaders from east and west: even in the newly acquired territory of former West Prussia and Silesia, rich as they had been in agriculture and industry, a new start was necessary, as the bulk of the equipment and even houses had been stripped for transport to Russia. Few, however, had the chance of any start at all. 'Soon after their arrival most of them were quietly arrested and put into a new concentration camp in the vicinity of Hrubieszow, only to be subsequently deported to Russia.'[1]

Byrnes' Stuttgart speech (see above p. 156) did much disservice to the cause of the democratic parties in Poland by his statement that America regarded the definition of Poland's western frontier as an open question.

Bulgaria

Bulgaria, Rumania and Hungary followed a similar pattern. Bulgaria, the most Russian-oriented of the East European countries, and the one where hatred of the old régime was perhaps the greatest, experienced as harshly as any others the iron fist of Moscow. The Fatherland Front, which had seized power at the time when the Red Army entered Bulgaria (September 1944), was a combination of Communists and leftist democratic elements, the most important of which were the Agrarians led by Petkov and G. M. Dimitrov. The Communists quickly made it their business to seize control of the entire organization: according to their normal practice they were able to have one of their men at the Ministry of the Interior.

After taking revenge on the old politicians, including those who had brought Bulgaria out of the war against the Axis, the Fatherland Front split between the Communists and the rest. G. M. Dimitrov returned from exile to organize the Agrarian Union, but was forced out of the leadership of the Union. His successor, Petkov, suffered the same fate, but the mass of the Agrarians still followed him. The Socialists (Social Democrats) were similarly split, the majority continuing to follow their non-Communist leaders. With a temporary relaxation of the now entirely Communist-dominated régime after

[1] E. J. Rozek: *Allied War-time Diplomacy: a Pattern in Poland* (Wiley, Chapman and Hall, 1958), 416.

Potsdam, the opposition were allowed to publish papers, which quickly attained a circulation ten times greater than that of their Communist rivals. They were therefore soon suppressed, and faked elections were held in November 1945, after the opposition had been terrorized and had withdrawn.

The Foreign Ministers' Conference in Moscow in December took up the question of Bulgaria. The Russians agreed to the usual empty formula of broadening the government to include representatives of the opposite parties. The mission for carrying this out was entrusted solely to Vyshinsky, Moscow's principal agent for the execution of Balkan policy. Petkov and the socialist Lulchev refused to join the government on Communist terms, merely in order to give an air of respectability to it.

In September 1946, Bulgaria was, by plebiscite, proclaimed a republic; another faked election was held in October, most of the opposition leaders being by then in prison or concentration camps.

Georgi Dimitrov (not to be confused with G. M. Dimitrov), a staunch Muscovite, became Prime Minister. Petkov was arrested and judicially murdered (September 1947). Georgi Dimitrov, hero of the Leipzig trial in 1933, from which he had escaped with his life largely because of the protests on his account by the world press, declared that had it not been for the protests of the Western powers Petkov's sentence could have been commuted to life imprisonment. Lulchev, the socialist leader, who despite brutal warnings from Dimitrov, courageously continued to lead the opposition in parliament, was sentenced in November 1948 to fifteen years imprisonment. The remaining opponents of the régime were similarly liquidated or silenced.[1]

Hungary

In Hungary appalling sufferings had been inflicted on the country, first by the Germans and their Arrow Cross associates, then by the Russians. Hungary was bled white. The former had removed some 200 complete factories, and the most valuable machinery of another 300, together with hospital equipment, a third of the livestock, and the gold and bullion of the National Bank. The latter, having taken off trainloads of what machinery was left, drove away 'endless

[1] Seton-Watson, op. cit., 211–19.

columns of cattle, horses and pigs'.[1] From this denuded land the occupation army had to be fed. $300 million of reparations were demanded which, with fictitious accounting, imposed on Hungary an annual burden equivalent to 60–70 per cent of her industrial production. On top of this the Russians claimed that the Potsdam Agreement authorized them to take German property and assets to the tune of $200 million. It was a system of exploitation designed to reduce Hungary to a condition of economic slavery, entirely dependent on Russia, and this was finally organized by a Russo-Hungarian agreement.

Intervention by Britain or America in any sphere, economic or political, on behalf of the Hungarians, was completely blocked by the Russians, despite the rights which all three powers were supposed to hold equally on the Allied Control Commission at Budapest. Almost any acts of violence were permitted by the Russian authorities. When the Minister of Finance attempted to control the mounting inflation, by curtailing the quantity of roubles in circulation (which permitted the Russians to make purchases at highly favourable prices), Red Army men entered the National Bank and took away bundles of rouble notes at gun-point.[2]

On the political level a tremendous fight was put up by the Hungarians to establish and maintain democracy. Although there had been a parliamentary system, the upper and middle classes had firmly kept control, since the failure of the Communists' attempt under Bela Kun to seize control in 1919. The end of the war raised the hopes of the industrial workers and peasants that for the first time they might enjoy to the full their rights as citizens and voters. They were encouraged in this by the initial phases of Soviet policy, which demanded the establishment of several parties as a preliminary to the formation of a Communist-dominated 'government bloc'. Peasant representation came into its own in the Small Farmers' Party, which played a similar role in Hungary to that of the Peasant Party in Poland. It gained strength from the land reform, which the Russians insisted on being put through (though in a hasty, slapdash and therefore unjust fashion) in March 1945.

[1] The gold was eventually located in the American Zone of Germany and was returned in the summer of 1946. (Byrnes, 130.)
[2] Ferenc Nagy: *The Struggle behind the Iron Curtain* (Macmillan 1948), 101.

Despite censorship and other difficulties, the efforts of its leaders, notably Bela Kovacs and Ferenc Nagy, were successful. The Small Farmers' Party gained over half the votes at the elections of 1945 (the Communists and Social Democrats together polled 17 per cent).[1] For a time the Small Farmers formed the predominant element in the Government bloc, even insisting, immediately after the election, that Kovacs should hold the all-important Ministry of the Interior. But a few days later Soviet insistence forced its return to a Communist, Imry Nagy (later Premier during the 1956 revolt, and not to be confused with Ferenc Nagy). Not long after, an even more complete tool of Moscow, Rajk, took it over.

One of the Small Farmers' leaders, Tildy, a thorough-going advocate of compromise with the Communists, became Prime Minister, later becoming President when Hungary was declared a republic. His place was taken by Ferenc Nagy.[2] Though a stalwart opponent of the Communists on many issues, Nagy's strategy was one of compliance in the hope that with the eventual signing of a peace treaty with Hungary, the grip of the Russians would be relaxed and the democratic parties take over. He appeared to win some successes along this line (for instance in taking a stand against the expulsion of the entire German minority without consideration of the fact that a large number of resident Germans had an excellent record as loyal citizens of Hungary even during the period of Nazi domination—the Communists wished to get rid of them because they were a prosperous element in the state, unreceptive to their propaganda). But such successes were almost always illusory, because no matter what policy was agreed, it could always be nullified when the time came for it to be carried out.

Step by step the power of Nagy and his democratic colleagues in the government bloc was undermined. 'Fusions', as in the case of Peasant and Social Democratic parties, were engineered in a way which brought them under Communist control, and the same process

---

[1] It is uncertain why the election of 1945 in Hungary was free, whether 'because the Communists overrated their strength, because they made commitments which they could not retract, or because they wished to "impress" the West.'—P. E. Zinner: *Revolution in Hungary* (Columbia University Press, 1962), 33.

[2] The original Small Farmers' candidate for the Premiership, Deszo Sulyok, was dismissed from the party on Communist orders. Twenty-one other Small Farmer deputies suffered the same fate in the spring of 1946 (Zinner, 37).

of breaking up the unity of the democratic elements was carried on within the cabinet. Plots, either faked or greatly magnified, were made the excuse for widespread arrests by the security police, backed by the Red Army. The occasion of one such chain of arrests was the revenge taken by a lad who shot two Russian soldiers after his mother had been raped seven times by Red Army men. 'Confessions' were extorted or framed, implicating prominent democrats. Their parliamentary immunity was suspended, the first stage towards their imprisonment or complete disappearance. Such was the end of Bela Kovacs, and a similar fate would no doubt have overtaken Ferenc Nagy had he not resigned while out of the country (May 1947).

That control, from the Communist point of view, was still incomplete, was shown by the election of August 1947, when despite all the faked voting and other methods of distorting the results, 35 per cent still voted for the opposition. But a year later the process was complete. The last bastion of opposition was the Catholic Church, where the rugged Cardinal Mindszenty led an unrelenting campaign, notably against the nationalization of Catholic schools and the suppression of Church papers and associations. But at the end of 1948 he was arrested, to be sentenced to life imprisonment after a dramatically staged trial.

Shortly after (April 1949), parliament was dissolved and elections of the Soviet type were held for an assembly whose function was to proclaim Hungary a 'People's Democracy'. This time there was no opposition, and the government secured 90 per cent of the votes. The inevitable accompaniment to the Communist success, as elsewhere, was the 'liquidation' of an unknown number of opponents, and the captivity of thousands of others. Many, even among the imprisoned students, were kept for months on end in solitary confinement.

Rumania

Thanks to the skilful manner in which the young King Michael led Rumania out of the German clutches in August 1944, the country suffered less in the transition from German to Russian control than did Hungary. Nevertheless its losses were severe. Between the time of the break with the Germans on 23 August 1944 and the conclusion of an armistice convention on 12 September, the Russians seized as war-booty 50 per cent of the remaining rolling-stock on the railways, the entire navy, most of the merchant marine, and huge quantities of oil equipment.[1] Under the armistice convention the Russians claimed $300 million worth of goods (such as oil and grain) from current production—but exacting it at 1938 prices they were able to double the figure. These huge demands had to be met during a time when, on account of the looting of capital goods, total production fell to less than half the pre-war figure. This was a preliminary to the systematic milking of Rumania through the establishment of joint Russian-Rumanian companies ('Sovroms') covering every field of economic life, which was brought about as the Communist grip on power tightened.

In seizing power the Communists followed a similar pattern to that in Hungary and elsewhere. At the start their following in the country was negligible—Mrs Ana Pauker, a Communist who eventually became Foreign Minister, stated that, before the entry of the Red Army, the Communists numbered barely a thousand. Nevertheless even a tiny minority, backed by the Red Army, could extend its power over the whole body politic, when injected, like a malevolent cell, into a supposedly democratic coalition. Such a coalition was formed immediately after the King's dismissal of the Antonescus, though in the cabinets of Sanatescu and Radescu the Communists held only one portfolio. But this, together with an under-secretary-ship held by the Communist Georgescu in the Ministry of the Interior, was the growing point of their power. It was significant of future developments that when Radescu dismissed Georgescu, he refused to go and managed to retain his post.

The political climate was not propitious for the growth of Communism. Russia was hated for her seizure of Bessarabia and the Northern Bukovina in 1939, and there was little internal unrest which the Communists could exploit. They did what they could to create antagonism between the masses of solid peasantry and the town workers, and between the Hungarian minority and the rest.

Radescu, originally *persona grata* to the Russians—he had a good anti-German record—became too independent for their liking, since he wished to postpone the land reform which the Russians insisted on

[1] A. Cretzianu (ed.): *Captive Rumania* (Atlantic Press, 1956), 51.

pushing through.[1] Unable to get his own speeches reported in the Soviet-censored press, he bitterly criticised the Communists at public meetings and by broadcasts. With the country so much behind him, the Russians could not afford the gradual methods of whittling down democratic resistance which they followed in Hungary. One sharp blow was decided upon, to shatter it and so pave the way for a take-over. On 22 February 1945, the Soviet Deputy Foreign Minister, Andrei Vishinsky arrived from Moscow, and saw the King along with the Rumanian Foreign Minister Visoianu. Pounding the table, he demanded the dismissal of Radescu and the installing in his place of Petru Groza, the Communist leader of the 'Ploughmen's Front' (a Communist organisation). Groza was to head a 'National Democratic Front Government.' On the Foreign Minister's pointing out that the King would first have to consult the other political leaders, Vishinsky angrily gave him two hours and five minutes to comply, and left, slamming the door behind him. With Russian tanks parading the streets, no alternative was possible.[2]

So small was the Communist following that Groza had to pack his government with discredited politicians of the old régime, like Tatarescu, formerly Carol II's Foreign Minister, or Burducea, an ex-Fascist priest who had been prominent in the Iron Guard. Reputable politicians were harassed and threatened with violence. The National Peasant Party, which played the same role as the Small Farmers in Hungary and the Peasant Party in Poland, came most severely under fire. The General Secretary, Penescu, was wounded when trying to attend a meeting, in August 1946, and his secretary was killed. Every effort was made to break it down, and split off fractions which could be induced to join the government bloc.

This internal repression conducted in effect by the Red Army through its Soviet agents, was matched by the dreary succession of false promises and deceptions in the international sphere whereby

---

[1] The land reform produced a large number of holdings each of which was too small to support a peasant family—an arrangement possibly designed by the Communists to convince the peasants that individual small-holdings were impracticable, and so prepare the way for the later introduction of collectives (Cretzianu, 56).

[2] Byrnes, 51. According to the report of the American representative in Bucharest, B. Y. Berry, Vishinsky 'slammed the door so hard that the plaster round the door frame was cracked badly. It has never been fixed; it remained to testify of the strength of his feeling and of his arm.'

Russia eventually gained recognition abroad for the Groza régime. Hopes for freedom were aroused by the Potsdam agreements, and the King wrote to the Allied Governments requesting advice on the way to broaden his government. On Groza's refusal to include genuinely democratic representatives, the King dismissed him from the Premiership, but Groza refused to vacate his office. Thereafter the King refused to sign the decrees of the Groza government, which nevertheless put them into effect.

America and Britain, deeply concerned at these incidents, protested to the Soviet Government, but the only outcome was the agreement at the Moscow Conference in December 1945 to broaden the Groza government by the inclusion of one representative from the National Peasant Party, and one from the National Liberal Party. These men had no power, and were only included—following the same line as in Hungary and elsewhere—to gain recognition of the régime by Britain and the U.S.A. (4 February 1946). This was the prelude to months of activity by the Communists in preparation of the usual type of faked election in November 1946. Two hundred leaders of the opposition were imprisoned just before it took place, and the Printers' Union refused to print anything other than matters acceptable to the government, even in the few papers with scanty allocations of newsprint which the opposition press was permitted. Despite such efforts it was reckoned that the National Peasants polled 70% of the votes though the government bloc came out with 349 out of the 414 seats. This façade of respectability made it possible for a series of face-saving compromises to be arranged between Molotov on the one side and Byrnes[1] and Bevin on the other, which paved the way for the Peace Treaty to be signed in February 1947.

Secure in its international status, the Groza government effected its final consolidation at home. The future Prime Minister, Gheorgiu-Dej, was promoted to be Minister of Industry and Commerce. Ana Pauker became Foreign Minister, and two other Communists were given cabinet rank. The veteran leader of the National Peasant Party, Iuliu Maniu, was condemned to imprisonment for life with hard labour, along with the former Chairman of the Party, Mihalache. At

---

[1] Op. cit. 154. Even with the signing of the Peace treaties, Hungary and Rumania could not get rid of the Red Army—Russia had the right to keep garrisons in the two countries as they were on the lines of communication to the Russian zone of Austria.

the end of 1947 King Michael was forced to abdicate, and in February of the following year the National Assembly was dissolved. In March 1948 Soviet-style elections were held with no opposition candidates, and Rumania entered the ranks of the 'Peoples' Democracies'.

17: Czechoslovakia and the Prague Coup of 1948

The coup of February 1948 in Czechoslovakia whereby the Communists made their grip on the country complete, appeared to be the most dramatic of the actions which they had carried through in Eastern Europe, because so long deferred. In reality the coup marked the end of a carefully contrived strategy which the Communists had been pursuing for several years. As far back as 1943 they had secured conditions of operating which practically guaranteed their victory in advance.

The Policy of Benes

At Munich in 1938 the Czechs had been betrayed by France and Britain. None felt this humiliation more keenly than President Benes, who shortly after resigned. In exile during the war, he reassumed the functions of President and formed a government in London. He was obsessed by the necessity of gaining support from Russia—though at the time, during the period of the Molotov–Ribbentrop agreement, the Russians (and the Communists) were hostile. Their attitude changed with the German attack on Russia in June 1941. Benes built up relations with Klement Gottwald, leader of the Czechoslovak Communist Party, and the other Czech Communists in Moscow, and in December 1943 he conferred with them there, making agreements which accepted all their main points.

In return Benes gained Russian support for expelling the German and Hungarian minorities from Czechoslovakia once he had regained control. This was the policy which he eventually carried out in 1945— a policy which was a reversal of Masaryk's tolerant democracy. However much provoked the Czechs and Slovaks had been by these minorities, this policy jeopardized in advance the democratic idea for which Benes claimed to stand, and its support by Moscow put him further in its debt.[1]

[1] S. Borsody: *The Triumph of Tyranny* (Cape, 1960), 236 seq.

Among Czechs the authority of Benes was immense but he used it, at this time, in an authoritarian way, not as the democrat *par excellence* which he always set himself out to be. 'In his dealings with the Communists, Benes . . . acted as a self-appointed spokesman for the nation and for all non-Communist parties. Although no formal commitments were made at this time, the agreement in principle entailed strong moral obligations, which the democratic parties could not easily disregard. . . . He did not consult the spokesmen of the non-Communist parties before he went to Moscow. He gave the Communists an opportunity to express themselves first, and agreed to act as an intermediary between them and the democratic leaders, confronting the latter with a *fait accompli.*' [1]

Communist Strategy

The Communists therefore had a flying start in imposing their own conditions and their own personnel on a government accepted by all the Big Three before the liberation of Czechoslovakia began. Chiefly they ensured the destruction of the Agrarian Party, the equivalent of the great Peasant Parties of the other East European countries. Benes was eager to broaden his cabinet by including the Communists, but the Communists would not come in, owing to the representation of the Agrarians and other right-wing parties in the London government. They eventually entered the cabinet with five seats, after an agreement made at Moscow that these parties would be banned. The Communists hoped to be their heirs.

It was also decided between Benes and the Communists at Moscow to set up 'National Committees' in every town and district as they were liberated. These committees were to have executive, administrative and even judicial powers—instruments for taking over control of local government and (as the event showed) for exercising measures of control which were far more extensive than the old local government bodies.

As far as the central government was concerned, it was to be organized within the framework of a 'National Front', according to the same strategy as the Communists were preparing for the other East European countries. The National Front acted as a co-ordinating

[1] P. E. Zinner: *Communist Strategy and Tactics in Czechoslovakia 1914–48* (Pall Mall Press, 1963), 84.

committee representing the four parties approved by the Communists for eventually forming the government—the Communists, Social Democrats, National Socialists and Peoples' (Catholic) parties. In the government there were also representatives of the two parties approved for Slovakia, Communists (who thus had a double representation) and Democrats. Even while outside the government proper, the Communists could expect to determine policy through the National Front, which acted as an 'organism superimposed on the different parties and charged with determining their common policy in the cabinet and in Parliament'.[1]

Within this bloc the Social Democrats had the role of the Communist Party's running-mate. The pre-war parties in Czechoslovakia had tended to be somewhat left of their equivalents in other countries, and the Social Democrats (or Socialists), from whom the Communists had split in the early 1920s, were very near them ideologically. Where they differed most was in the degree of their allegiance to Moscow, and the Social Democratic Party was itself divided between its 'Muscovites' or fellow-travellers (indistinguishable from Communists) and the non-Communist remainder. The Muscovites were the channel through which the Communists could enforce their policy on the Social Democratic Party as a whole; then these two parties, presenting a solid front to the National Socialists (whose position of moderate socialism was similar to that of the British Labour Party), could expect to sway it into accepting their line.

In its turn, this 'Socialist bloc'[2] could put pressure on the People's Party, which tended to attract those right-wing elements who might escape being rendered voteless or otherwise politically null. Though not necessarily agreeing with the policy which they were compelled to accept, neither the People's Party nor the National Socialists could face the prospect of quitting or breaking up the coalition. To keep it going, however great the machinations and provocations of the Communists, was an article of faith which they maintained until overtaken by the coup of February 1948.

It was clear that they therefore had very little room to manoeuvre, especially since the one possible impartial arbiter, President Benes,

---

[1] H. Ripka: *Czechoslovakia Enslaved* (Gollancz 1950), 38.
[2] The Social Democrat 'Muscovite' leaders were aiming at an eventual fusion of the parties of the Socialist bloc, along the lines that were planned elsewhere.

was himself heavily committed to maintaining the National Front at all costs. Though democracy was regarded as their sacred creed by the non-Communists, the kind of democracy which they had a chance of restoring after liberation could only be of a limited and straitened kind. In building up the National Front it was useful for the Communists to have in the lead Zdenek Fierlinger, a Social Democrat who had become completely committed to them. The Moscow embassy became a centre of Communist intrigue.

With these close links with Moscow, it was natural that Benes should proceed to negotiate a treaty of alliance with Russia (12 December 1943), despite some misgivings on the part of the British and Americans. What, however, was still more important was that Benes was persuaded to accept the Communist plan of forming in Moscow the new government that should take over in Czechoslovakia as the country was liberated. His intention had been to proceed direct from London with members of his government, and re-form it in the liberated area, enlarging it with leaders of the resistance from within the country as well as with some of the candidates for office from Moscow. Since the Russians were likely to liberate the country, there was always the possibility that they would set up a Lublin-type government in which Benes and the non-Communists of the London government might have little or no say. By accepting that the government should be formed in Moscow and proceed thence to the homeland, Benes weighted the scales still more in the Communists' favour.

This gave additional prestige to what the Russians, and therefore their Communist instruments, could expect to gain by entering the country as its liberators. In any case they could count on immense goodwill. Russia had never invaded or oppressed the lands of Czechs and Slavs. Like them the Russians were a Slav people. They had not been compromised in the Munich betrayal. And between the wars the Communists had always been able to count on some three quarters of a million voters at the elections.

This popularity had been diminished to some extent in Slovakia owing to the failure of the Russians to assist the rising in the summer of 1944. Slovakia, being Catholic and clerical, was less oriented towards the Soviets. Something of a shock was also administered by the 'spontaneous uprising' in the Carpatho-Ukraine (Ruthenia), whose inhabitants demanded that their land should be incorporated

forthwith in the Soviet Union. Stalin indicated that this manifestation of the people's will had taken him by surprise, but as such it
could not be refused; there could evidently be no question about
leaving such a matter for the Peace Conference. But what really
caused dismay, and bitter hatred among many, was the behaviour of
the Red Army as it carried out its liberating role in a friendly country.

The Red Army in Czechoslovakia

Whether the Russians entered a country to 'liberate' or 'occupy' it,
they came in like a tide or an advancing horde of locusts—first the
tank divisions, 'well disciplined, well armed and trained . . . the
columns of guns and lorries, the parachute divisions, motor cyclists,
technical units'; then 'columns of marching soldiers, dirty, tired, clad
in ragged uniforms—tens and hundreds of thousands of columns. . . .
And columns of women and girls in military grey-green uniforms,
high boots and tight blouses, with long hair greased with goose-
fat. . . . And children, mainly small boys: the *lezprizorni* from burned-
out villages and towns. . . . Behind the first spearheads drive the
staff: they drive in German luxury cars. . . . And still more cars with
their secretaries and secretary-girl-friends and secretary companions.
And lorries laden with furniture; beds which must be taken down at
every stop and loaded again, radios, frigidaires, wardrobes, couches
. . . cars with war-booty, cases of china, kilometres of textile
materials, fur coats, carpets, silver. . . . Cars of the Agitprop Brigade
with broadcasting apparatus and theatrical properties. . . . And
further lorries belonging to the Political Commissariat, the staffs and
motorised units of the N.K.V.D. (political police), lorries with tons
of Russian delicacies, caviar, sturgeon, salami, hectolitres of vodka
and Crimean wine. . . . Behind the staffs more marching columns,
without a beginning and without an end. And finally the rearguard:
miles and miles of small light carts drawn by low Cossack horses. . . .
As the Tartars used to drive centuries ago . . . a flood from the
Steppes, spreading across Europe.'[1]
    Like the locusts they settled on the land, stealing indiscriminately.
Not even a Cabinet Minister was safe from having his watch taken in
broad daylight. Every woman was regarded as prey. Looting,

[1] J. Stransky: *East Wind Over Prague* (Hollis and Carter, 1950), 22–5.

drunkenness and raping were the order of the day, the extent of these activities varying with different units.[1] Though discipline was often severe—hundreds or possibly thousands of soldiers were shot for rape and other crimes—it happened in some villages that half the women were violated. In Brno, soon after its liberation, over 2,000 women sought hospital treatment after being raped. These were only a proportion of those who sought the help of private doctors or kept silent about their misfortune.[2]

Before the arrival of the Red Army the people were eager for friendship with Russia, but rumours of what to expect from the Army made them less eager to be liberated by it. In Bohemia the Czech National Council had organized the resistance to the Germans. Before the latter evacuated Prague they staged a rising in the city (5 May 1945) while sending emissaries to the Americans, some 56 miles away, pleading with them to come quickly to their aid. But Eisenhower had agreed with the Russians to halt the forces under Patton at that point. To the heroic resisters in Prague it was like the Warsaw rising in reverse—only now it was the Americans who held off the urgent help and even grounded the Czech-piloted planes of the R.A.F., while Koniev and his Russians dashed to the rescue. But Koniev took several days to arrive. By then (9 May) over two thousand of the resistance had been killed.[3] In the new order which was established the Czech National Council was brushed aside.

The Communists Strengthen their Grip

Despite the terrible experiences suffered by the people, the effect of the six months' occupation of the Red Army was to strengthen, not weaken, the Communist grip on the country. With the Red Army

[1] 'It would certainly be unjust to generalize and to depict the whole Red Army as a horde of wild Tartar hooligans and ruffians.' (Ibid., 35.)

[2] Ibid., 35. Among those who sought hospital treatment at Brno were 'about thirty little girls under twelve years and two women over seventy'.

[3] Ripka, 38. See Eisenhower's laconic statement in *Crusade in Europe*, 455–6: 'Patton directed the V (Corps) push eastward into Czechoslovakia. The Corps captured Pilsen May 6. In this area the Russian forces were rapidly advancing from the east and careful co-ordination was again necessary. By agreement we directed the American troops to occupy the line Pilsen–Karlsbad. . . .' In fact Eisenhower sent a message to General Antonov indicating his readiness to proceed to Prague—an offer which Antonov turned down, while reminding Eisenhower that the Russians had respected the agreement in the north to stop on the Elbe.

present it was easier to 'liquidate' or neutralize opponents—or equally to blackmail them into becoming Communist supporters or even party members, particularly if they had been collaborators with the Germans, or if the imputation of being such could be fixed on them. In this work the 'National Committees' played an essential part. These were organized by the teams of Communist agents who followed in the Red Army's wake.[1]

While establishing themselves in the towns and countryside (no local elections were held after the war), the Communists made good use of this period during which Benes had agreed not to summon parliament. Operating to the full the 'National Front' mechanism they drove through the Cabinet a number of measures, executed by Presidential decree, of which the most important was the land reform. In the view of the non-Communists this measure was not urgent and scarcely necessary, at least not in the form which it assumed, since the land-reform after the First World War had already redistributed such large estates as there had been. But a further land reform put much patronage into Communist hands (two Communist Party members were charged with carrying it through) in addition to the already vast patronage accruing through the resettlement of the rich farming and industrial areas from which the Sudeten Germans were expelled.[2] It was not surprising that when the election came the Communists received a particularly high percentage of votes in these areas. This patronage was in addition to what the Communists had been able to take over from the dissolved Agrarian Party. The effects of the far-reaching nationalization of industry were similar.[3]

It was not until a year after the liberation that the first elections took place, in May 1946. The Communists came out as the biggest single party with 38 per cent of the poll. Together with the Social Democrats they gained 51 per cent of the votes—153 seats in the Parliament, against 147 going to the other parties. The importance to the Communists of their alliance with the Social Democratic

---

[1] P. E. Zinner: *Communist Strategy*, 100.

[2] The expulsion of the 3·3 million Sudeten Germans and Germans from other parts of Czechoslovakia is another chapter of horror and suffering to be added to those for which the Nazis and Russians were responsible. See W. Jaksch: *Europe's Road to Potsdam* (Thames and Hudson, 1963), pp. 429 seq.

[3] 3,119 industrial installations were nationalized, comprising 61 per cent of the country's labour force (Zinner: *Communist Strategy*, 174).

Party was shown: many voted for the Social Democratic label, not realizing the support they were thereby giving to the Communists.[1]

The elections confirmed the Communist grip on the levers of power. In the discussions at Moscow of 17–31 March 1945 between the Communists and the non-Communists from London, it was agreed that the Communists should have eight out of twenty-five posts, including the important Ministries of the Interior, Education, Social Welfare and Agriculture. After the elections Gottwald took the Premiership in place of Fierlinger, and traded the Ministry of Education for those of Finance and Internal Trade. Within its well-defined limits, the Czechoslovak brand of democracy continued to be maintained, for the same reason that the Communists maintained it immediately after the liberation, when they could have easily imposed an entirely Communist government on the country. They wished to maintain as much goodwill as possible with the Western Allies, particularly with a view to obtaining economic aid,[2] and also because Stalin had not yet given up hope of demoralizing and dominating Germany as a whole (not merely the Soviet Zone), or of at least gaining a measure of control over the Ruhr; just as in Italy, France and other countries he still hoped to increase the Communist stake, even though obtaining full power was impracticable. To foster what was left of war-time goodwill and utilize to the full the Communist assets which were the legacy of the resistance, was obviously sound strategy. Whether on a European scale, or within Czechoslovakia alone, the line propounded by Gottwald was correct: to exploit the 'national and democratic revolution' in order to bring an effective majority into the Communist camp.[3]

This policy continued until July 1947, when the Marshall Plan made Moscow realize that the Americans were not going to permit the Sovietizing of Western Europe through any further postponement of its economic recovery. Stalin also saw in the Marshall Plan a bid by America to win over countries of the Soviet camp, and particularly Czechoslovakia. He at once showed his hand, for the first time in

[1] Between 250,000 and 300,000 Czechs and Slovaks suspected of having collaborated with the Germans were disfranchised (Jaksch, 434).

[2] As in Poland and Hungary, where Mikolajczyk and Ferenc Nagy were sent on missions to North America.

[3] Gottwald's speech to the Communist Party leadership, 9 July 1945, quoted Zinner, *Communist Strategy*, 118–19.

Czechoslovakia, as the real master of that country, by the brutal enforcement of his veto on Czech participation.[1]

Anti-Communist Moves

During the next month something of a revolt against Communist domination of the country took place, while the Communists took steps to transform the régime from one of limited democracy to a thorough-going police state under their control. In Slovakia their control had already been challenged at the election of May 1946 where the Communists received only 30 per cent of the votes. There they attempted to drive wedges, first between the Slovaks and the Czechs by encouraging a separatist movement through the 'National Slovak Council', then between the Catholics and the Protestants. Attacks on the democratic parties were accompanied by a 'plot'— and although these manoeuvres were successful in working up a crisis, the Communists stopped short of a coup. This was a postponement, because the fate of the Slovaks would be sealed when the Communists moved to take over the country as a whole, but the non-Communist parties were encouraged by what they regarded as a Communist failure. Russian torpedoing of the projected treaty of alliance with France, and the formation of the Cominform in October made the Communists in Czechoslovakia appear more plainly as the tools of Moscow. This stirred opinion more strongly against them. Even the Social Democrats began to revolt against their control; at the party congress in November 1947 Fierlinger was ousted from the leadership, and Lausman—a fellow-traveller and an uncommitted opportunist—was elected in his place. Another 'plot' which the Communists staged as part of their campaign against their democratic colleagues miscarried; the students were hostile, as was the great Sokol sports organization. Even the National Committees were passing out of Communist hands. The tide was flowing so strongly against them that their minimum requirement of a 51 per cent majority at the forthcoming elections in March could no longer be expected. The alternative was a violent seizure of power.

Preparations for the Communist Coup

For this the preparations were completed during the winter of 1947–8. Though public opinion as a whole was moving against the

[1] See p. 161 above.

Communists, the number of their party members had steadily increased (1,329,450 in the Czech lands, 210,222 in Slovakia, in
January 1948).[1] By then their control of the police was fairly complete, and the army, under a Minister of Defence and Chief of Staff
who were pro-Communists, was effectively neutralized.[2] Word came
from Moscow to go ahead—'our friends have given us guarantees
against any eventuality,' as one high official said,[3] and to reinforce
this, the former Russian ambassador, Zorin, now a Vice-Minister of
Foreign Affairs, unexpectedly arrived in Prague on 19 February
1948. Fresh Red Army units entered the Soviet Zone of Austria and
took up positions near the Czech border.

The immediate crisis was brought on by the attempt of the non-
Communists in the government to parry this threat of force. A
majority of the Cabinet demanded that the Minister of the Interior
should suspend his order to withdraw eight non-Communist divisional
police commanders in Prague (officers with wide powers) and replace them with Communists (13 March). On his refusal, backed by
the Prime Minister, the Social Democratic and People's Party
Ministers decided to resign, counting on the resignations also of the
Social Democrats. Even without the Social Democrats (for in the
event Lausman hesitated and most of them stayed in their offices),
these resignations of half the Cabinet should, according to the
constitutional rules of the game, have brought about the fall of the
government. But the Ministers who expected the game to be played
according to the rules were like flies in the web of the spider. They
counted on Benes standing firm, refusing to accept their resignations,
and bringing about a change of government in their favour, at least
after the elections which might be brought forward—but Benes was
ailing and though he inveighed against the Communists in private,
he was firmly in their grip. In any event he was not prepared to
remove the Communists from the government—even their opponents
in the Cabinet could not envisage breaking up the 'National Front'.

[1] Zinner: *Communist Strategy*, 124.
[2] The Education and Enlightenment Department in the army was completely Communist. Enlightenment Officers were posted as deputy commanders to all units of
company size and above. (Ibid., 156.)
[3] Ripka, 308.

The Coup

During the days 20–25 February the Communists completed their work. While the army was confined to barracks, armed gendarmes and security police, whom they controlled, were brought into Prague, and similar preparations were made elsewhere. The radio, controlled by the Communist Minister of Information, summoned mass meetings of workers whom they had organized. Still protesting to the Minister of the Interior, and seeking interviews with the President, the democratic ministers found their offices occupied and their party newspapers abolished. For two days the students demonstrated as they had demonstrated against the Nazis eight years before, and once again were brutally suppressed. They tried to form a solid barrier across the road to the Presidential Palace, to prevent the Communists from having access to Benes in order to force his hand. All this was unavailing. Benes had long since been their prisoner, and was obliged to accept the government of the 'Renovated National Front' as called for by the newly established 'Central Committee of Action'. The attempted suicide of the Minister of Justice, Drtina, and the death (whether suicide or murder) of the Foreign Minister, Jan Masaryk, son of the founder of Czechoslovakia, were gloomy sequels in the aftermath of terror and arrests.

A new constitution was proclaimed, and Soviet-type elections held on a joint list without opposition candidates. Benes refused to sign the constitution. He resigned in June of that year, 1948, and died the following December. The vast concourse of mourners at his funeral was a mute protest against the régime.

18: Remaking Western Germany

German Currency Reform and the Berlin Blockade

The Prague coup marked the furthest extension of Soviet power in Europe. The Soviet–Finnish Treaty of 6 April 1948 seemed to show that the Soviet tide was still rising, though this was deceptive as shortly afterwards the Finnish government managed to remove its Communist Minister of the Interior. This was the prelude to a downturn in Communist fortunes at the Finnish elections in July 1948, despite a 'carrot' from the Russians in the form of halving future reparations and the grant of a loan. The Communists stayed out of the reconstructed Cabinet.[1] During this period, too, the dispute between Tito and Moscow became public, culminating in Yugoslavia's expulsion from the Comintern on 28 June 1948.

Meanwhile the Western powers rapidly consolidated their position in Europe. While the crisis was being worked up in Czechoslovakia, the Western powers (America, Britain, France, Belgium, Holland and Luxemburg) were meeting in London[2] to consider steps for transforming Western Germany into an independent state and reorganizing its economy. The Prague coup was a challenge to America to strengthen further its position in Europe, and Truman's immediate response was to give American backing to the Brussels Pact between Britain, France, Belgium and Holland (17 March 1948). This was followed by the conference in April of the same states, for planning a constitution for Western Germany.

The Russian riposte was to consolidate their zone of Germany as a one-party state. The setting up of the German Economic Council in the East Zone (June 1947) was followed by a succession of 'People's Congresses' from December 1947 onwards. Their instrument was the Socialist Unity Party (S.E.D.), created, on their usual formula, out of Communists and left-wing Socialists. Through this organiza-

---

[1] R.I.I.A. Survey 1947–8, 159. They were offered five posts, but not the Ministry of the Interior.

[2] Representatives of América, Britain and France met on 23 February and were joined by those of Belgium, Holland and Luxemburg (Benelux) on 26 February.

tion the various steps were taken which eventually led to the creation
of the German Democratic Republic (October 1949).

More decisive even than the political moves to rehabilitate Western
Germany as a member of the 'Atlantic' bloc was its economic
rehabilitation, in which far the most important step was the reform
of the currency. On 18 June 1948 West Germans[1] began exchanging
their inflated Reichsmarks for new Deutschemarks. Each person
could hand in up to 60 Reichsmarks and obtain 60 Deutschemarks in
exchange; above that figure credit balances could be converted on a
ten to one basis, though half of each balance when converted went
into a blocked account, 70 per cent being extinguished. This meant
that holdings of Reichsmarks, above the 60 which could be immediately exchanged, could be converted at a rate of 6·5 Deutschemarks
for every 100 Reichsmarks on deposit.[2] A more serious loss was
sustained by those who had investments in public funds, for they
received nothing at all for them. Official prices and salaries continued at the old rates, but in the new Deutschemarks instead of the
old Reichsmarks. This cut out the prices of the black market, which
had previously been too high, for the most part, for workers and
salaried employees—so that these now were considerable gainers.
As usual, in such transactions, those who suffered most were people
living on savings, many of whom became destitute.[3]

The Americans and British had invited the Russians to join in this
currency reform, so that it could be extended to the whole of Germany. After the usual delays, the Russians agreed, on condition that
they could have their own set of plates for printing the notes. But
this could not be accepted by the Western Allies, since the experience
of giving the Russians their own set of plates for printing occupation
marks in 1945 had shown that they could not be trusted to print at
an agreed rate,[4] but would quickly reproduce the inflation of the
currency which the new note-issue was designed to curb.

---

[1] The currency reform was applied later in West Berlin.

[2] Clay: *Decision in Germany*, 213–14.

[3] A. Grosser: *Western Germany, from defeat to rearmament* (Allen and Unwin, 1955),
98. Although the old Reichsmarks had become nearly worthless on the free (or black)
market, they had been accepted at their pre-1945 value in payment for wage-earners'
rations.

[4] A considerable amount of the occupation marks had to be redeemed by the U.S.
Treasury. 'In the resulting wide-open money market, all Western financial assistance to
Germany was being eaten up in an inflationary spiral.' J. E. Smith: *The Defence of*

The Western Allies' decision to go ahead on currency reform for their zones whether the Russians agreed or not, was the occasion, not the cause, of the breach, which now took the form of 'cold war', between Russia and the West. The Russians were intransigent because they were reluctant to give up trying to dominate Germany by keeping her weak and impoverished. They still hoped to secure a measure of control through the considerable Communist Party, augmented in both east and west by released prisoners of war from Russia who had been through special indoctrination courses. Fusion between the Social Democratic Party and the Communists, on the model of what was carried through in Eastern Europe, was a cornerstone of their policy, but this was defeated by the obdurate resistance of Kurt Schumacher, who had been broken in body but not in spirit in a Nazi concentration camp, and would have no truck with another totalitarian régime. Control of the Ruhr through participating in a governing authority was another element in their strategy, paralleled by Communist control of the mines and other undertakings through dominating the newly-created works councils. But Western coldness towards such participation made this project doubtful of achievement, while the return of prosperity to the Ruhr, and to German industry as a whole, would end much of the discontent and bitterness on which the Communist movement throve.

The Russians had put up a fighting retreat on every Anglo-American proposal which looked like improving Germany's condition and so spoiling their strategy—on zonal fusion, on cutting down reparations, on raising the level of industrial production (the British and Americans had proposed restoring it to the 1936 level),[1] on a common policy for the railways and other services, on treating Germany as an economic unit. On the occasion of each Allied proposal there were Russian protests—in the Council of Foreign Ministers, at the United Nations, and at the Allied Control Council in Berlin. With Molotov's vituperations against the West at the Moscow Conference of November–December 1947, and with the walk-out of Marshal Sokolovsky from the Control Council on

Berlin, 106. The plates had been made available through Harry Dexter White in his capacity as Special Assistant to Henry Morgenthau, Jun., when the latter was Secretary of the United States Treasury. (For White see p. 145, note 1.)

[1] 7 September 1947.

20 March 1948, it was clear that a new chapter was opening in what had become a full-scale war, short of shooting, between East and West.

The currency reform was decisive for the recovery of Western Germany, and, along with the Marshall Plan, for that of Western Europe as a whole. But before it was applied, the Western Allies (America, Britain, France and the Benelux countries) had issued at the end of their conference in London a declaration of intent (6 March 1948). This was to ensure the economic recovery of Western Europe, including Germany, and to establish 'a basis for the participation of a democratic Germany in the community of free peoples'. Four-Power disagreement should no longer delay the pursuit of these objectives, though 'ultimate four-Power agreement is in no way precluded'.[1] Meanwhile discussions would continue among the six Allies for applying the European Recovery Programme to Germany's Western zones, and a federal constitution should be worked out for West Germany.[2]

This declaration was the signal for harassing tactics on the road and rail routes used by the Western Allies for access to Berlin. On 30 March new regulations were imposed by the Russians for halting and inspecting road and rail traffic travelling eastwards. General Clay's attempt to insist upon access rights while refusing inspection was ineffective. The test train full of soldiers which he sent, with orders not to submit to inspection, was shunted into a siding, and after staying there several days was forced to return. The question was whether to make such a test with force, by sending troops to the access point of the autobahn at Helmstedt, with orders to shoot if necessary in order to pass the pole which the Russians had lowered across the road. This question became more pressing when the Russians refused to let passenger trains leave Berlin for the west, and gradually tightened up controls on access until, on 24 June 1948, four days after the new currency was introduced, they stopped all traffic to Berlin from the west, both passenger and goods, by road, rail and canal.

Both General Clay and his political adviser, Robert Murphy, believed that the Russians were bluffing, and that they would give

[1] R.I.I.A. Documents for 1947–8, 556.
[2] R.I.I.A. Survey for 1947–8, 261–2.

way if the Western Allies insisted on their access rights with a show
of force. The British were prepared to make such a show of force,
though the French were hesitant—'not a single Frenchman would
vote to fight for Berlin' was their line.[1] The onus of the decision was
left on the Americans. For Truman, the risk was as much that of
losing votes just before the Presidential election, as of launching his
country into a war for which it was ill-prepared—though it was a
risk he was prepared to take. But Marshall, viewing the question
from a military angle, and backed up by the Joint Chiefs of Staff,
felt that in view of the vast demobilization of the American forces,
the risk of armed conflict was too great. It was estimated that eighteen
months would be required to put the American forces on a footing to
take on the Russians if they refused to yield without a fight.[2] In all
the discussions that went on 'nobody, either military or civilian, mentioned that the United States Government in 1948 possessed a
growing stockpile of atomic bombs while Russia had none yet'.[3]

Whether or not Russian intransigence was encouraged by the fact
that there were no documents in which they had made agreements
specifying Western access routes by land to Berlin, cannot be known;
nor can it be known that the existence of such an agreement defining
the air-corridors into Berlin made them hesitate to prevent the
British and Americans[4] from supplying West Berlin by air. Their
'buzzing' of British and American planes had already led to the crash
of a R.A.F. plane in April. They may not have considered it possible
for a city of $2\frac{1}{2}$ million people to be supplied in this way. Doubts also
on the Allied side about the practicability of such an operation made
many think that evacuation was the only way out of an increasingly
intolerable situation. But Clay's conviction of the need to take a
stand at Berlin in view of the Soviet advance in Europe may have
been decisive.[5] 'We have lost Czechoslovakia,' he minuted. 'Norway

[1] Murphy, 315. Murphy also says that the British were against an 'outright show of
force', though they fully supported the Americans at every point. (See Smith, op. cit.,
104, 109.)

[2] 'The United States was unable to send more than one additional division overseas
without ordering a partial mobilization.' (Smith, op. cit., 102.)

[3] Murphy, 316.

[4] The French did not take part in the air-lift, though supplies brought in by the air-
lift were made available also to their zone.

[5] In April, when the Russians were probing Allied resistance to their harassing
tactics, Clay's attitude 'seemed to settle the question for the moment' (Smith 105).
During that month and May he already had his 'little air-lift' going.

is threatened. We retreat from Berlin. When Berlin falls, western Germany will be next. If we mean ... to hold Europe against Communism, we must not budge. We can take humiliation and pressure short of war in Berlin without losing face. If we withdraw, our position in Europe is threatened. If America does not understand this now, does not know that the issue is cast, then it never will and Communism will run rampant. I believe that the future of democracy requires us to stay. . . .'[1]

Indeed there were many among the British and Americans who had their doubts, but once it had been launched the enterprise gathered strength. The brunt of the operation fell on the Americans, who possessed far more transport planes than their ally, though about a third of the planes taking part were British.

It needed all General Clay's conviction to keep the Allied governments standing firm. Truman was his strongest rock of support: both State Department and Service chiefs continued to urge caution, until by New Year 1949 the air-lift had proved its effectiveness beyond doubt. Despite Clay's objections, attempts were made to reach a compromise over the currency question, and on British insistence this was agreed at meetings of the Western representatives with Stalin and Molotov in Moscow in August 1947. The gist of this compromise was that the blockade would be lifted in return for the Western Allies accepting the East Zone currency as alone legal tender in Berlin, this acceptance being conditional on the Allies sharing with the Russians in controlling this currency. When, in Berlin, Clay tried to nail the Russians down to implementing these measures for controlling the currency, they refused to consider the proposal, and the scheme lapsed—much to the relief of the West Berlin population, who feared that the essential point, on which the Allies had so far successfully defied the Russians, would be given away.

The morale of the West Berliners and their determination to make a success of the air-lift was a decisive factor. They put up with conditions of short supplies (particularly of coal and electricity) throughout the winter; their representatives were beaten up and bullied while attending the City Assembly, located in East Berlin (an Assembly and Mayor for West Berlin became necessary in a city

[1] 10 April 1948. Clay, op. cit., 361.

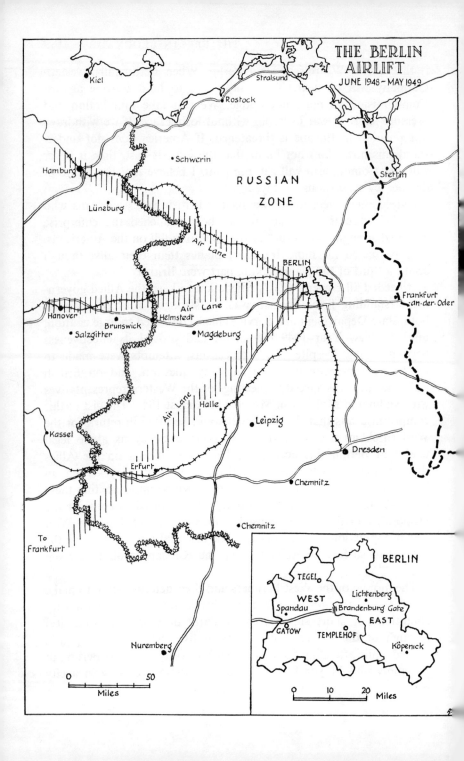

THE BERLIN
AIRLIFT
JUNE 1948 – MAY 1949

Kiel

Stralsund

Rostock

RUSSIAN
ZONE

Schwerin

Hamburg

Lüneburg

Stettin

Air Lane

BERLIN

Hanover

Air Lane

Helmstedt

Frankfurt
an-der-Oder

Salzgitter

Brunswick

Magdeburg

Air Lane

Halle

Leipzig

Kassel

Dresden

Erfurt

Chemnitz

Chemnitz

To
Frankfurt

Nuremberg

0   50
Miles

BERLIN

TEGEL

Lichtenberg

WEST

Spandau

Brandenburg Gate

EAST

GATOW

TEMPLEHOF

Köpenick

0   10   20   Miles

which was increasingly split);[1] and, except for a tiny minority, they were prepared to go without many goods rather than fall for Soviet seductions and buy them freely in the East zone. Thousands laboured at making new runways at Tempelhof and Gatow, and a completely new airport at Tegel.[2] With their extremely efficient organizing methods they worked with the Americans and British to bring about such a speedy turn-round that, at the peak, planes were departing and arriving every thirty seconds. It was at this point that the Germans became 'for all practical purposes, our allies'.[3]

Not only did the Western Allies underrate the morale of the Berliners; they underrated the capacity of the air-lift.[4] The minimum quota needed for supplying the barest needs of the population, during the winter, was 4,000 tons daily, but by December it was averaging 4,500 tons and by January 1949, 5,500. This capacity meant that coal could be brought in (though a difficult freight for a plane), and even an entire generating station. By spring 1949 the figure had gone up to 8,000 tons—as much as was being moved by rail and water prior to the blockade. On the record day 13,000 tons were delivered.[5]

Clay realized more clearly than did the authorities at home the strength of the Western position in Berlin. Twice during July 1948 he asked these authorities for permission to try breaking the blockade by bringing an armed convoy through by road. He was refused. And though on 9 May 1949 the Russians gave way, it was but a limited victory for the West. The Western Allies had not been forced out of Berlin, but they had not improved their position there, as they would have done if the Russians had been obliged by a show of force to concede the rights of access by ground which the Allies had always claimed; nor was such an agreement obtained from the Russians

---

[1] The elections were on 5 December 1948. After attacks by Communist toughs on several occasions, the Assemblymen were finally driven out of their meeting-place in East Berlin on 6 September 1948. Reuter was elected as Lord Mayor for West Berlin, after the Russians had vetoed his appointment as Lord Mayor of Berlin as a whole. Reuter had abandoned Communism after being Commissar for the Volga German Republic in the U.S.S.R., had been imprisoned by Hitler, and had escaped to Britain.

[2] 'Largely a hand job, accomplished by more than 20,000 Berlin men and women working three shifts a day.' Clay, op. cit., 284.

[3] Murphy, 322.

[4] W. Phillipps Davison: *The Berlin Blockade* (Princeton, 1958).

[5] Clay, 381–6.

when they admitted they were worsted over the blockade.[1] Because they failed to gain specific Soviet recognition of these rights, the Allies left themselves, and West Berlin, in a position to be squeezed whenever the Soviets wished to do so; and this was a tactic which the latter resorted to subsequently at such times when they required to produce a crisis atmosphere in Europe, whether to apply pressure for Western acceptance of a point of Soviet policy, or to draw attention away from activities elsewhere.

The currency issue in any case was not the real one, or at least the most important. In March 1949 it became necessary for the Western Allies to make their Deutschemarks exclusively legal tender in West Berlin (by then, after starting at parity, the East marks had sunk to being worth only four or five to one Deutschemark on the black market). The new currency had become so well established in the West zones as a whole that there was no putting the clock back. What caused the Soviets most concern was the intention to set up a separate West German government. The effect of the blockade was simply to fortify the resolution of the Anglo-Americans to pursue this aim step by step with the economic rehabilitation of West Germany—though for Germany as a whole it meant hardening and perpetuating the division between the eastern and western parts of their country.

The Making of the German Federal Republic

After the war in Germany ended, the Americans were rapidly off the mark in reviving local government in their zone. Bavaria was almost intact as the Land of Weimar Republic days, the direct descendent of the old kingdom. Württemberg-Baden was a new creation, a fusion of the two halves of the old Länder of those names which were left to the Americans after the other halves had been handed to the French for their zone. Fragments of Hesse and the former Prussian province of Hesse-Nassau formed the third Land of Greater Hesse, to which was added the Bremen enclave as a fourth in January 1947.

Under the direction of James K. Pollock, an expert on German

[1] Murphy's view is that the blockade was a defeat rather than a victory for the West. 'Our decision to depend exclusively upon the Air-lift was a surrender of our hard-won rights in Berlin, a surrender which has plagued us ever since.' When the Russians indicated that they were ready to end the blockade, the West should have insisted that the Russians no longer kept the controls (op. cit., 321).

constitutional development, the pattern of local government was reorganized. Each Land had its own government with full legislative and judicial powers. By the end of 1946 constitutional conventions, elected by popular vote, had worked out different constitutions for each of the three Länder (except Bremen). These were approved by the military government and ratified by the people at the same time as elections were held for the Land diets. 'The basic American attitude and the century-old traditions of statehood and regional autonomy [in South Germany] combined to foster a heartland of German federalism, whose state constitutions became the model for the French and British Zones and to some extent for the Basic Law.'[1]

Further development came with the addition of a body, the Länderrat (17 October 1945), composed of the Ministers-President of the two South German Länder and the Burgomeister of Bremen, each with a deputy. This was augmented by a 'modestly representative' Parliamentary Advisory Council of 24 members in February 1947.

In the British Zone the reorganization of local government was accompanied by greater upheavals in that the British insisted—to the dismay of the Germans—on importing the British model. There was correspondingly a proliferation of officials, who, however, proved useful later on in staffing the West German Government. There also the Länder were revived, though later than in the American zone. The first Land elections were in April 1947. The Länder were given constitutional powers only in 1949, with new boundaries. The biggest of the four,[2] and potentially the most powerful was North Rhine-Westphalia, including the Ruhr, and comprising half the population of the British Zone.

The impetus to further progress came from the American offer, and the British acceptance, of zonal fusion. The Zonal Advisory Council, which had been set up in the British Zone, was reorganized in October 1946 along lines which made it approximate to the Länderrat of the American Zone. At the same time a Central Economic Office was set up, while in both zones a number of 'Executive Committees' were established, composed of representatives from all the eight Länder. In May the following year (1947) the

---

[1] P. H. Merkl: *The Origin of the West German Republic* (O.U.P., New York, 1963), 9.
[2] The other three were Lower Saxony, Hamburg and Schleswig-Holstein.

Bizonal Agreement converted these various Executive Committees
into departments in an administrative body directed by a new
Executive Committee (in which was one representative for each
Land government). This was responsible to an Economic Council
of 52 members selected on a proportional basis by the Land legisla-
tures.[1]

In this way a centralized form of government was created for the
Bizone, which then only required a unified electoral system and the
appropriate constitutional arrangements to be transformed into a
democratic sovereign state. The process was completed by the
adhesion of the French Zone and the promulgation of the Basic Law.

To Lucius Clay as much as anyone is due the development of the
battered, workless, half-starved Western Zones into the prosperous
Federal German Republic of today. From 1947 until the promulgation of the Basic Law which gave West Germany her constitution, 'no man was as resolute, as informed, as clear in his conception,
or as creative in his design as Lucius Clay'.[2] It was his urgings that
brought matters to the crisis-point with Moscow, and after it was
decided to move swiftly towards rehabilitating Western Germany, it
was Clay who took the greatest share in initiating the conferences
and keeping them going. When, after Bizonal fusion had been
accomplished and the next moves necessitated agreement with the
French, it was Clay who broke the deadlock by inviting—and
fetching—Couve de Murville for talks with him at Berlin in May
1948.

From these conversations sprang the successful conference in
London between the three powers and the Benelux Countries, and
their decision to request that a constituent assembly should be
summoned by the Ministers-President. The directive was to the
effect that the assembly should 'draft a democratic constitution
which will establish for the participating states a governmental
structure of federal type'.[3] Such a constitution had already been
thought through by a meeting of experts from the Christian Democratic and its equivalent Bavarian party (Christian Social Union) in
March 1948, and this was taken as the ground-work of the Basic
Law as it came to be formulated. Much of the thinking, whose fruits

[1] E. H. Litchfield (Ed.): *Governing Post-war Germany* (Cornell University Press,
1953), 29.   [2] Litchfield, 38.   [3] Merkl, op. cit., 50.

were incorporated into the Law, sprang from the conviction that had become widespread among Catholics and Protestants as they recognized the part which they and their Churches had played in allowing Nazi demonism to have its way. The moral and religious revival which had begun during the war—particularly manifest though cut short in the Kreisau Circle[1]—was having its impact on the building of the new Germany.

The constitution that emerged was designed to correct the evils of democracy run mad—for in this light the constitution-makers regarded the Nazi era, as well as the fissiparous tendencies of the Weimar republic. There were to be no referendums, no popular election of the President. The Länderrat had considerable powers for revision and delay, and a Constitutional Court was established to review legislation, on the lines of the Supreme Court of the U.S.A.[2]

The constitutional developments brought to the fore a man who until recently had been known mainly in the context of the local affairs of Cologne and his corner of the Rhineland. Konrad Adenauer was already nearly 70 when in October 1945 a British general dismissed him from his post of Lord Mayor of Cologne (to which the Americans had appointed him a few months before) on the grounds that he was not moving swiftly enough in getting rid of the mountains of rubble that still blocked the city's streets. Adenauer had been an outstanding official in the administration of Cologne from 1906 to 1917, when he became Lord Mayor. At the end of the First World War he was a noted proponent of a federal form of union between the Rhineland and the rest of Germany. Under the Weimar Republic he was active as a member of the Centre Party, became President of the Prussian State Council, and was at one time considered as a possible candidate for the office of Chancellor. In 1933 his life was threatened by the Nazis after his refusal to have swastika flags flown from the city's bridges during the Führer's visit in that year. Obliged to live in strict retirement, partly in hiding—he was twice arrested by the Gestapo, Adenauer was 'rediscovered' by the Americans at the end of the war.

[1] See above, Chapter 10, and below, p. 380.
[2] See P. G. J. Pulzer's review of Merkl's *Origin of the West German Constitution* in *International Affairs*, July 1964, 523. West Berlin could not be included in the Federal Republic, but it was endowed with a somewhat similar constitution.

The British general's uncomprehending action in October 1945 pushed Adenauer out of local politics into the national arena. He joined the Cologne branch of the re-established Christian Democratic Union, and attended as its representative an inter-zonal conference in the British zone where, the chairman arriving late, he took the chair himself with the words 'as the oldest person here, I assume that this chair is for me'.[1] From there he progressed to being Chairman of the Parliamentary Council for working out the constitution in September 1948. This was eventually promulgated as the Basic Law in May 1949. The first Bundestag was elected in August, and in September—by one vote—Adenauer was elected Federal Chancellor.

The Recovery of Western Germany

In 1945 Germany viewed from the air was a country dying, or nearly dead. Berlin, Hamburg, the Ruhr cities showed mile upon mile of burnt, roofless houses and gaping tenements. Vast mounds of rubble and craters formed a landscape of the moon. Bombed and abandoned trains, like giant caterpillars, lay twisted or on their sides along the tracks. In the shells of factories where Krupps and other firms had poured out the steel, the tanks and the planes, acres of machinery lay silent and rusting, without protection from the elements. The only sign of life 'was the march of armies, the driblets of Germans walking back towards their homes, and the vast, pathetic aimless movement of millions of . . . displaced persons.'[2]

Statistics of damage and destruction were fearful. Even worse was the moral destruction of the nation. In the summer of 1945 'very few Germans saw further ahead than the coming winter. All the standards had fallen. The national slogan seemed to be "eat, drink and be merry and damn the expense to your honour or your virtue". The Germans did not believe "tomorrow we die". They believed something far more hopeless; that tomorrow would be worse than today. So it was not surprising that millions of Allied soldiers found Germany a combination of brothel and black market.'[3]

While the illegitimacy rate soared,[4] so did the figures for hunger-

[1] T. Prittie: *Germany Divided* (Hutchinson, 1961), 198.
[2] D. Middleton: *The Struggle for Germany* (Wingate, 1950), 13.
[3] Middleton, 19.
[4] In Western Germany 1945–53 the figure was 120,000 (Grosser, 143).

oedema, T.B. and venereal disease. In West Germany 40 per cent of the houses had been destroyed. Some smaller cities like Jülich were almost totally destroyed, a silent spectacle of weeds and desolation. In others, like Hamburg, life still continued, but for many thousands of the inhabitants in bunkers or cellars underground.[1] In Berlin '550,000 apartments had been destroyed, and 70 per cent of the remainder damaged. Of the 700,000 dwelling-units remaining in West Berlin, 50,000 were such places as cellars, ruins, garden huts, which could only be called temporary refuges.'[2] In East Berlin the situation was as bad, in some places of the East Zone, such as Dresden, perhaps worse.

People living in appalling conditions of squalor, overcrowding and promiscuity, aggravated by an acute shortage of rations, were a prey to hunger-oedema and other diseases. In Hamburg some 100,000 were sufferers from oedema in 1946. In Düsseldorf there were 13,000 people in hospital with oedema, and 25,000 non-hospitalized cases.[3]

While the black market flourished with its accompaniment of vice and crime, the rations provided by the occupying powers remained meagre—pitiful for the armies of unemployed, better though poor for most of the fortunate ones in employment. Rations were further cut in 1947, unemployment steadily increased and dismantling of factories continued. This was worsened still further by the severe winter of 1946–7. Though household fuel ceased to be delivered in October in the Western Zones, three-quarters of the industry had to be closed down because of the cold. By February 1947 production was down to 29 per cent of the 1936 figure. At least 200 people froze to death in Berlin that winter, and an unaccountable number elsewhere.[4]

But with the introduction of the currency reform in mid-1948 the picture rapidly changed. 'A chemist who on 17th June regretted to have to inform a mother of a family that the medicine she required for her sick child was unprocurable, found himself on 20th June miraculously able to provide it—although there had been no deliveries to his shop in the interval.'[5] Out came the hoards of goods

---

[1] 77,000 in Hamburg (1946)—V. Gollancz: *In Darkest Germany* (Gollancz, 1947).
[2] E. Davidson: *The Death and Life of Germany* (Cape, 1959), 288.
[3] Gollancz, op. cit., 27, 45. The incidence of oedema in Hamburg was 17 per cent for males, 9 per cent for females (24).
[4] Davidson, 157. 1936 was an average year, not so good as the boom year of 1938.
[5] Grosser, 97.

jealously guarded till this moment. Almost overnight shop-windows filled, and industrial production swiftly picked up. Enterprises, like the Thyssen steel plant at Düsseldorf employing 100,000 men, which had long been scheduled for dismantling, were now reprieved, and the ceiling for the production of steel and other commodities was steadily raised by the Allied authorities. Under the liberalizing régime of Ludwig Erhard, the Bavarian professor of Industrial Economics, who became Federal Minister of Economics in September 1949, industrial production rapidly rose. Heavy investment was channelled into the basic industries, whose production rose to the index number 220 in October 1954 (1936 = 100), while that of consumer industries was nearing 180. Despite an enormous increase in employment (800,000 more in 1948 than in the same area in 1938), that for unemployment—partly on account of the influx of refugees— mounted also, to a peak of over 2 million in February 1954.[1]

[1] Grosser, 102, 103.

19: The Resurgence of France 1940–53

The Vichy Régime

With the collapse of the French army in June 1940, the Third Republic fell into ruins. Its doom was sealed with the hurried comings and goings of Ministers at Bordeaux, when the 84-year-old Marshal Pétain—recently brought back from his embassy in Spain—was hoisted into office by those who wanted an armistice at almost any price. On this point General Weygand, the Commander-in-Chief, was insistent. Those who, like the Prime Minister, Reynaud, wanted to withdraw the government and what was left of the armed forces to North Africa, and continue the fight there, were overborne. The President, Lebrun, was tricked into staying. Some of the ministers and officials who embarked on the *Massilia* for the purpose of sailing to Africa, were brought back and treated as traitors. Only the Under-Secretary for Defence, General de Gaulle (who in May had fought one of the few successful actions of the French army during the campaign), left by air for London to raise the flag of the resistance.

Constantly active among all the Deputies[1] who could be assembled was the former Prime Minister, Pierre Laval, busily working to build up the majority which would vote the Republic out of existence and introduce the *État français*. Freed by this vote, the President transmitted his powers to Pétain, who henceforth with his decrees beginning 'Nous, Philippe Pétain' took on the airs of a monarch. The parliamentary régime was suspended. The rump of France which was left unoccupied at the armistice was for two and a half years ruled by the paternalist bureaucracy at the watering place of Vichy, presided over by the aged Hero of Verdun.

Rarely in times of crisis has France turned to younger leaders, as once she turned to Bonaparte. Usually she has called the old men to the helm—Clemenceau in the First World War, Doumergue in 1934,

[1] Members of the Chamber of Deputies in the French parliament.

Pétain in 1940.[1] Though in remarkable health for an octogenarian, an impressive figure with his still erect bearing and penetrating steel-blue eyes, Pétain could only concentrate on business for a few hours each day. He had defended Verdun magnificently in 1916 against the embattled might of Germany. Thereafter his role had been to conserve the army and restore the morale which had drained away through the prolonged carnage of Verdun and the Aisne. That role Pétain maintained in 1940, only now it was not merely the army that had to be saved—though his mind was often on the million and a half prisoners of war in Germany. His mission now, he believed, was to save France.

Momentarily, in June 1940, most Frenchmen accepted him as a father symbol or a saviour, and many continued to do so at least as long as there was unoccupied territory where the writ of Vichy could still run. His broadcast speeches with their simple themes of the earth, seedtime and harvest, were a blessed anodyne, and to many a promise not merely of physical salvation but of spiritual renewal. This mood was met by the slogan 'Work, family, fatherland' in place of the old republican battle-cry 'liberty, equality, fraternity'.

Pétain despised parliament and hated parliamentarians. He soon eliminated those of them who remained as ministers. Even Laval, to whom he owed the birth of his régime, he detested, partly on these grounds, and partly because Laval flaunted his vulgarity, and made no pretence of concealing his superior abilities and his power of doing deals with the Germans. But Laval, though dismissed and briefly put under arrest in December 1940, had to be taken back into the government sixteen months later.

Laval on his part despised 'the Marshal' and scoffed at the apparatus of moral renewal and corporative institutions which were the stock-in-trade of Vichy. Mediterranean in appearance and out-look, Laval had pursued a policy of alliance or at least entente with Mussolini's Italy, and he never forgave Britain for breaking this entente after his abortive agreement with Sir Samuel Hoare in 1935. Though no nearer Fascism in spirit—in many ways much further from it—than Pétain and the ideologists of Vichy, Laval was for full-

---

[1] 'Why is it that the old men of 80 are in power?' it was asked in 1934. 'Because none of the men of 90 can be found,' was the reply—A. Werth: *France in Ferment* (Jarrolds, 1934), 190, has a version of this joke "of Berlin origin".

scale collaboration with the Axis and the participation of a rehabilitated France in Hitler's 'New Order' in Europe. In August
1940 Laval on his own authority offered aircraft to the Germans for
use against Britain (an offer which the Germans disdainfully refused);
and in the same month he pressed for a declaration of war against
her.[1] On the occasion of his dismissal Laval said to the German
Ambassador, Abetz, 'It's no longer on the French side I must look
for friends; it's on the German side.'[2]

Laval was replaced briefly in December 1940 by the pro-British
Flandin, but the man who came to dominate at Vichy during most
of 1941-2 was Admiral Darlan. Anglophobia was traditionally
strong in the French Navy, and this sentiment, in which Darlan fully
shared, had been reinforced by the British attack on the French
warships at Oran (Mers-el-Kebir).[3] Though anti-British, Darlan was
not markedly pro-German. As the man who had brought the navy
to a high pitch of efficiency, he gave all his energy and passion to
preserving the ships which still were his, and what might be saved of
France. His record is viewed diversely,[4] but of this man, who has
been described as coarse, cold and ambitious,[5] it can at least be said
that he served his country according to his lights.

The greatest achievement of Vichy was in the first place psychological—to give a temporary though superficial sense of security,
moral and physical, to millions of French people after the Armistice,
an assuagement of their shattered pride and of other feelings
attendant on defeat, and the restoration of hope that life, and even
of a renewal of the country and its reorientation in a new order,
were possible. Secondly the *fonctionnaires* of the Republic, still for
the most part at their desks, managed to keep the economy of the
country going, even though on a low level and subjected to fearful
bleedings by the Germans. Demanding occupation costs of 400
million francs per day, the Germans bought supplies and goods on

---

[1] R. Aron: *The Vichy Régime, 1940–44* (Putnam, 1958), 207.
[2] Aron, 250.   [3] See above, p. 18.
[4] 'During the fourteen months of his government the Admiral abandoned no essential
point, neither the Empire nor the Fleet; he stood up to the Germans on many points on
which . . . Laval yielded' (Aron, 276). Compare this with: 'On the whole he compares
unfavourably with Laval, who, for all his personal ambition, seemed more obviously
than Darlan to put the interests of France first, at least as he understood them.'—
A. Werth: *France 1940–1955* (Hale, 1956), 81.
[5] Werth, 80–1.

an enormous scale, geared such industries as they could to their war effort, and let others become immobilized so that the resulting un-employment would force the workers to register for work in Germany. Ignoring the Armistice agreement, the Germans refused to allow France to be treated as one administrative unit, sealing off the occupied from the unoccupied zone for all purposes except those which suited their own economic aims (for instance they took what they wished of the products of the 'free' zone). But the economy was put back into some sort of order after the defeat, production and distribution were to some extent related to a rationing system which provided at least a minimum (normally eked out by the black market) for keeping people alive, and the other services functioned after a short period of disruption: all this meant that France was able to live.

When the Germans failed to win the Battle of Britain, and the colonies of tropical Africa began to rally to de Gaulle; when the vacillations of the Marshal—notably his meeting with Hitler at Montoire[1] and his subsequent pro-German broadcast—began to spread doubt as to his intentions; when the shabby intrigues and rivalries at Vichy came to light, and the gilt on the new ideology wore thin; when it was seen that, in pursuing an anti-Jewish policy and in licensing the French imitators of the S.S. and the Fascists, the government was falling into line with the worst excesses of a hated tyranny—then the majority of Frenchmen, even in the unoccupied area, began to waver, and before long withdrew their support. From this to resistance was but a step—clandestine papers, sabotage, assassinations of Germans and guerilla actions—the last much strengthened as younger men, to escape the dreaded deportations to work in Germany, made off to the uplands of the Massif Centrale or the Basses Alpes. This resistance for security reasons was unco-ordinated; each assassination had to be paid for by the death of anything up to fifty hostages, but the flame had been lighted which, with the Allied invasion, was to spread through France like a forest fire, to culminate in the liberation of Paris and most of the provinces in the autumn of 1944.

Before this, came the Allied invasion of North Africa in November 1942. Darlan happened to be in Algiers at the time—after some

---

[1] See above, p. 23.

shifts and hesitations, and apparently contradictory injunctions from Vichy, he agreed to a cease-fire with the Americans with respect to Algiers. Fighting, however, went on between the Americans and French elsewhere, and in Tunisia aerodromes and other facilities were turned over to the Axis. There, after an incredible series of orders and counter-orders, the troops of the Axis began to land at Bizerta and other places, whence, with a cost of thousands of French and Allied lives, it would take six months to dislodge them. But in Algeria and Morocco, Allied power was soon firmly established, thanks partly to Darlan's attitude. When he was removed by an assassin's bullet a few weeks later (24 December 1942), a bitter squabble between de Gaulle and General Giraud came to the fore. Giraud, having made a romantic escape from a German fortress, believed himself to have been promised command of the Allied armies in French North Africa, and in any case claimed precedence over de Gaulle as leader of 'Free France'. But he was less shrewd and politically minded than his rival, and before long fell into the background.

Meanwhile Laval had been consolidating his position in a France whose claims to be a sovereign state, even within the confines of the unoccupied area, were becoming increasingly empty. Though realizing that he had 98 per cent of the French people against him, Laval was determined to save them from themselves by carrying collaboration with the Axis to the limit of the possible, and so assuring some place for France within the 'new order' of Europe which he believed would be established by Hitler's victory. With this in mind, he gave a notorious broadcast (22 June 1942), in which he said that he desired victory for Germany, 'for without it, bolshevism will set itself up everywhere'.

The broadcast was partly a bid for relaxing the Germans' insatiable demand for French labour, but the immediate issue was soon obscured by Hitler's urgent insistence on the morrow of the North African landings, that the Vichy government should declare itself an ally and come into the war fully on the side of the Axis. Despite repeated threats of 'Polonising' the country, Laval had to admit the hopelessness of bringing any measurable positive response from the people to such a declaration, and in the event it was clear that nothing which he could do would prevent the complete take-over of

France by the Germans, now that the tide of war had turned against them. On 11 November 1942 the Germans sent their forces in to occupy the rest of France, with the exception of Toulon. The 'armistice army', whose officers had made secret dispositions for rising against the Germans in the event of an expected Allied landing in the South of France, had no chance of resistance. Having been kept in barracks by government order, they were ignominiously turned out of them by the Germans.

The most eloquent comment on the bankruptcy of Vichy's policy was the fate of the French fleet at Toulon. The Nazis had no intention of respecting their pledge not to enter the perimeter of the port, which they did on 27 November 1943. But their bid to seize the fleet failed, for, acting on previous orders, Admiral Laborde had just enough time to carry out the scuttling of the vessels. In this way this formidable element of the once proud navy of France—which could have slipped away to North Africa at any previous time—was prevented from joining with those 'Anglo-Saxons' whom most of the French admirals hated as much as they hated the Germans.[1]

From then on the Vichy government's existence was shadowy and unreal, centring on a few hotels within a compound surrounded by barbed-wire, access to which was closely guarded by German troops, and circulation within it scrutinized by Nazi agents. Having refused Weygand's advice to transfer what was left of his government to Africa and declare war against the Axis before the violation of the free zone, there was nothing for Pétain to do except settle down as a helpless Nazi puppet. The failure of his attempt a year later to repeat his coup of December 1940 and get rid of Laval again, was the measure of his impotence. After the Allied landings in Normandy in June 1944 he was moved around at Nazi orders, ultimately being transported to Germany along with the French Fascists Déat, Darnand and Doriot, and the remaining collaborationist ministers. At the final *débâcle* Pétain gained entry to Switzerland, whence he handed himself over to the authorities of the now liberated France. Laval, having fled to Spain, was extradited to stand his trial, along with the Marshal and other collaborationists, in France. After a brilliant defence of his policy at Pétain's trial, Laval was sentenced to

---

[1] Laval attempted to countermand the orders (issued by Darlan some two years previously). Had he succeeded the fleet would have passed into German hands.

death at his own trial, where he was not allowed to speak. Pétain passed his few remaining years in prison.

De Gaulle and the Liberation

While these events were taking place, de Gaulle was seizing every opportunity of consolidating his power wherever the French flag flew. Not that he was concerned with power for himself personally. It was power for France which he wanted—and he, de Gaulle, incarnated France as a Great Power.

His upbringing, his long meditations and his occasional writings had all prepared him for this role. Born in 1890 of an old professional family, with forebears of some eminence in learning, the law or arms, de Gaulle's background was Catholic and traditionalist, and he was himself steeped in history and a 'certain idea'[1] of the greatness of France. As a young man, he had shared in the resurgence of his country after the passions and bitterness aroused by the Dreyfus controversy had sunk her to the depths. In this spirit he entered the army, received some of his early training at the hands of Pétain, and served in the First World War. While in a German prison camp he began the first of those writings which—particularly *Vers L'Armée de Métier* (1934)—had made a name for him before the outbreak of the war in 1939.

Flying to London just as the republican régime went into its death-agonies at Bordeaux in June 1940, de Gaulle assumed the authority of France in his first broadcast over the B.B.C.—of a France which could rise again, because 'the outcome of their struggle has not been decided by the Battle of France . . . I, General de Gaulle, now in London, call on all French officers and men who are at present on British soil . . . to get in touch with me' (18 June 1940).[2] He spent his time rallying to the standard he had raised all those Frenchmen, service-men or civilians, whom the evacuation from Dunkirk and other chances had brought to England at that juncture. Despite set-

---

[1] See page 207.

[2] *War Memoirs, I, Documents* (Weidenfeld, 1959), 11–12. He was still more explicit in his broadcast of the following day: 'Faced by the bewilderment of my country-men, by the disintegration of a Government in thrall to the enemy, by the fact that the institutions of my country are incapable at the moment of functioning, I, General de Gaulle, a French soldier and military leader, realise that I now speak for France' (ibid., 13).

backs—Mers-el-Kebir cost him many followers—his position became increasingly recognized. The failure of the mixed Free French and British naval force to bring Dakar over from its loyalty to Vichy was a desperate disappointment, but other French colonies, starting with Chad, began to rally.

After the landings in North Africa in November 1942, de Gaulle was able to challenge the American desire to exclude him from power. Though never fully accepted by the Americans, the *Comité Français de la Libération Nationale*,[1] set up at Algiers in June 1943 was widely recognized not only as the government of Overseas France, but as the potential government for France itself. De Gaulle's links with the resistance in France and the control there which he exercised through the setting up of the *Conseil National de Résistance* (including the Communists among the resistance bodies), gave him the opportunity of appearing to his fellow-countrymen, at the time of liberation, as something of a saviour. The Allies' plans for governing France through their own officials were swept aside as town after town showed by their enthusiasm their underwriting of his Provisional Government, culminating in the General's progress through the vast and cheering crowds of Paris to a service of thanksgiving at Nôtre Dame (26 August 1944).

To exert this authority was not easy in a France which had been bombed and battered, and had lost a huge proportion of its utilities and rolling stock. Its communications had been practically destroyed, its ports were out of order or in enemy hands, and its people often near to starvation and with little fuel or lighting. There were so many causes of discontent or difficulty—two million Frenchmen in enemy hands as prisoners or forced workers, part of the country still held by the Germans, lynch law against collaborators mingling with private vengeance. There was also the constant challenge from the Communists who, by their record in the resistance and by their skilful and unremitting pursuit of power in it, had come to dominate the entire movement. That de Gaulle was able, in these circumstances, to exert his authority and that of his government through every corner of the land as it became liberated, was something of a miracle.

Besides taking the urgent steps of maintaining law and order, and ensuring as fair distribution as possible of such imported supplies as

[1] This succeeded the *Comité National Français* of September 1941.

could be spared from military needs, de Gaulle's main task was the assertion of his right to speak for France in the Councils of the Great Powers—his affirmation, in fact, that France, despite her defeat and losses, was still herself a Great Power.

His aim was to bring to reality that conception of France which he was to express later in the opening sentences of his *Memoirs*:

> All my life I have thought of France in a certain way. This is inspired by sentiment as much as by reason. The emotional side of me tends to imagine France, like the princess in the fairy stories or the Madonna in the frescoes, as dedicated to an exalted and exceptional destiny. Instinctively I have the feeling that Providence has created her either for complete successes or for exemplary misfortunes. If, in spite of this, mediocrity shows in her acts and deeds, it strikes me as an absurd anomaly, to be imputed to the faults of Frenchmen, not to the genius of the land. But the positive side of my mind also assures me that France is not really herself unless she is in the front rank; that our country, as it is, surrounded by others, as they are, must aim high and hold itself straight, on pain of mortal danger. In short, to my mind, France cannot be France without greatness.[1]

In pursuit of this aim he did not avoid frequent clashes with America or Britain—Roosevelt disliked him, Churchill, while respecting him, often found him insufferable ('The heaviest cross I have to bear is the cross of Lorraine'). De Gaulle deeply suspected British designs on France's position in the Levant, and resented British policy in pushing France out of her possessions, held on mandate from the defunct League of Nations, in Syria and Lebanon.[2] He was outraged at the refusal of the Big Three to invite France (in his person) to the Yalta and Potsdam conferences—and publicly refused Roosevelt's invitation to see him at Algiers in the course of the President's return journey from Yalta. He was forever striving to acquire from the Allies the means of building up the French army— which they but tardily permitted—to enable its fuller participation in the last battles of the war.

All these efforts were necessary, but they took time and energy from other problems. Partly for this reason, more perhaps because de Gaulle had little understanding of the intricacies of finance,

---

[1] C. de Gaulle: *War Memoirs* (Weidenfeld and Nicolson, 1959), *I*, 9.
[2] Duff Cooper (Viscount Norwich): *Old Men Forget* (Hart-Davis, 1953), 354 seq. See the last chapters (Ch. 24 seq.) for a picture of de Gaulle, especially the ups and downs of his relationship with Churchill.

economic recovery was delayed by wrong decisions or faulty administration. By backing Pleven instead of Mendès-France in the matter of dealing with the mountain of inflated francs left over from the occupation, a millstone was placed around the neck of all those future ministers who tried to restore France to economic health—for much of this money was in the hands of *trafiquants* or spivs, and others who would not use it productively. The exchange of old for new currency on the basis of one old for one new franc, which was Pleven's solution, was no solution at all, since the mass of money which was sustaining a continuing inflation with its concomitant of a huge black market, was still there, so that poorer people, and those on fixed incomes, continued to suffer.

Apart from the economic question (including the resettlement of returning workers and war-prisoners in conditions of grave housing shortage and unemployment) and the punishment of war-criminals by the court established for the purpose, the main concern of de Gaulle's provisional government was to work out a constitution for the future. In many ways, de Gaulle's tendencies were nearer those of Vichy than of the Republic which had passed away, and for the same reason—because the Third Republic had failed. Former parliamentarians and ministers still wanted it to go on, at least in a more or less modified form. But, for stability and a great future, France needed, so the General affirmed, a more authoritarian type of government, with power centred in a President whose position would be similar to that of the President of the U.S.A., while the Assembly's powers would be correspondingly reduced. Only so, maintained de Gaulle and his followers, could an end be made of the domination of French affairs by shifting coalitions of parties, and the resultant *immobilisme* and instability of government (from 1918–1940 France had 42 governments, while Britain had only eleven).[1] 'The political factions,' de Gaulle maintained, 'instinctively believed the state should be weak so that they could manipulate it more readily and win from it not so much the means of action as office and influence.'[2]

In the Consultative Assembly (which had originally been set up by

---

[1] D. Pickles: *France, the Fourth Republic* (Methuen, 1955), 2.

[2] C. de Gaulle, *Salvation 1944–1946* (*War Memoirs, II*) (Eng. trans. Weidenfeld and Nicolson, 1960), 252.

de Gaulle's provisional government when at Algiers, and had been enlarged on being established in France), the General's proposals for constitutional reform were rejected (July 1946). But he was at least able to prevent the Communists' proposals from being adopted, by ensuring that they should not have an absolute majority in the Constituent Assembly. He did this by arranging a system of balloting by list and proportional representation on a departmental basis,[1] instead of election by a single ballot on a constituency basis along British lines, which would have suited the Communists. Nevertheless the Communists came out of the election as the biggest single party (26 per cent of the votes and 158 of the seats), able to block, or at least hamper legislation desired by the General, but unable to govern except on a coalition basis with some or all of the remaining parties. Of these, two nearly equalled the Communists in size (Socialists 24 per cent of the votes and 142 of the seats, M.R.P.—roughly Christian Democrat—23·6 per cent of the votes and 152 of the seats).[2]

De Gaulle's strategy was to control the Communists without driving them into open opposition. Though he had dissolved the Communist-dominated militias of the Resistance, he had annulled the charge of desertion against the Communist leader, Maurice Thorez, who had absconded to Russia in 1940, and allowed him to return (to have perhaps unexpected backing from him in setting the workers on the task of reconstructing the country). He had given them places, though minor ones, in the provisional government. Now he offered them more places, but not the key ministries which they demanded (Foreign Affairs, Interior or War)—an offer which Thorez felt it wise to accept.

Both constitutions evolved by the Constituent Assembly (one rejected and the other accepted in two referendums, May and October 1945), were similar to that of the Third Republic—a weak President and a strong Assembly, with similar facilities for playing the party game which had been played with such disastrous effects between the wars. Despite this outcome of constitution-making, de Gaulle stayed on for a while, in response to a unanimous vote that he should continue as head of the state. During this last phase of power before his resignation on 20 January 1946 the government

[1] De Gaulle, op. cit., 262.
[2] Figures from Werth, op. cit., 273. M.R.P.—*Mouvement Républicain Populaire*.

carried further the programme of nationalization which had been begun during the previous post-Liberation phase (mines, gas, electricity, banks and some enterprises like the Renault works). It also laid the foundation of the Monnet plan, which was to be a powerful aid to France's economic recovery during the ensuing years.

The First Years of the Fourth Republic

After de Gaulle's retirement there followed a succession of Prime Ministers—14 in all—until, with his return, in May 1958, the transition to the Fifth Republic began. On the shifting sands of party coalitions these men strove to build their governments, the process being complicated by the need of the would-be Premier[1] to gain his 'investiture' for office with the vote of an absolute majority of the Assembly.

Until May 1947 the majorities supporting the Premier of the day had a 'tripartite' basis, consisting of the three left-wing parties, Communists, Socialists and M.R.P.—except that the two former did not consider the latter to be really a party of the Left, since being Christian in outlook, it was charged with having a 'clerical' tendency, i.e. submissive to the political influence of the Catholic Church. This division between the two Marxist parties on the one hand and the M.R.P. on the other, was not at first important, though later all the bitterness of the old quarrel of the laicizing Left against the 'clerical' Right, which had so bedevilled the Third Republic, revived to bedevil the Fourth. But in the early months of the Fourth Republic, Socialist antagonism towards the Communists—despite their partnership in government—was greater than their shared suspicion of the M.R.P. With Léon Blum, the Socialist leader, newly released from a German prison, it was an article of faith that the Socialists could never combine with the Communists, though temporarily they could act as the connecting link between Communists and M.R.P.

When, however, the international situation changed and the wartime alliance gave way to the cold war, the position of the Communists in the French government became impossible. They could no longer agree with their partners in any major sphere of policy, international, colonial or domestic—in the last of which the Renault

---

[1] The French Prime Minister is known as '*Président du Conseil*'. The investiture procedure was altered in November 1954.

strike of April–May 1946 heralded those bitter industrial struggles which paralysed for varying periods mines, factories and communications. The Communist support of the Renault strike provided the occasion for Ramadier's dismissal of the Communist ministers,[1] and the period of *tripartisme* came to an end.

This forced the government majorities farther to the right. The M.R.P. and the Radicals provided a number of Premiers, and with Bidault and Robert Schuman the M.R.P. came to have a virtual monopoly of the Quai d'Orsay.[2] Schuman was also Prime Minister during eight critical months from November 1947, when his firmness brought to an end the strikes of that winter. Strikes, though they continued to have a retarding effect on the economy, ceased to be a threat to the régime itself. This was due to a split in the working-class which developed during this time, between the Communists and the non- (or anti-) Communist workers.[3] The latter led by the Socialist Jouhaux, formed the C.G.T.-Force Ouvrière, after seceding from the Communist-dominated C.G.T. (Confédération Générale de Travail—the trade union federation). The C.G.T.-F.O. found its natural ally in the C.F.T.C. (Confédération Française de Travailleurs Chrétiens—the Catholic trade union federation), which supported the M.R.P. When Schuman was followed after a short interval by Queille, Moch, who had been his strong-man Minister of the Interior, was still there to deal with the serious strikes in the coal mines of October–November 1948.

Schuman also stayed in office, as Foreign Minister, during this period of relative stability (1947–51), when a virtual Socialist–M.R.P. alliance was supported by Radicals and elements of the Right. This combination was shaken, though not shattered, by the sudden return of de Gaulle to active politics with his founding of the R.P.F. (Rassemblement du Peuple Français, April 1947). Though not meant to be a party but a kind of informal plebiscite for de Gaulle's recipe

---

[1] These ministers left behind them a legacy in the Civil Service. 'We had civil servants who were Communists or fellow-travellers in all branches of the Civil Service, and especially in those branches where there had been Communist ministers—believe me, those ministers were not in the habit of wasting their time!' R. Schuman: *French Policy towards Germany since the War* (Stevenson Memorial Lecture No. 4, O.U.P., 1954), 7.

[2] The Foreign Office.

[3] A distinction is drawn by Werth between the 'industrial proletariat', mainly supporting the Communists, and 'the employee and the small government servant class' (*France, 1940–1955*, p. 382).

for a resurgent France, the outcome of the mass-meetings and the publicity attendant on launching the Rassemblement was a party all the same—and one that struck fear into the hearts of the established politicians, because at the Municipal Elections of October 1947 nearly 40 per cent of the votes were for the R.P.F. At the General Election in June 1951 it did less well, but still won 21 per cent of the votes, and with 117 seats was the biggest party in the Chamber (the Communists won 26 per cent of the votes, but owing to the curious system of *apparentements*, gained only 101 seats). The scare suffered by the orthodox politicians turned out after all to be groundless—for the time being—since de Gaulle soon realized that a party, even if professedly opposed to the existing régime, was likely to compromise with it and would fail to serve his purpose. Already Gaullists in growing numbers were coming forward as allies of the existing governments—32 supported Pinay in 1952. These were expelled from the R.P.F., but in May 1953 de Gaulle went further, washing his hands of the R.P.F. (it had just fared badly in the municipal elections), gave the Deputies their freedom, and went into semi-retirement at Colombey-les-deux-Églises.

By then the discontents, which had impelled so many of the voters towards a movement opposed to the régime, had abated. Food shortages ended with the glut of farm produce in 1951; spivs went out of business and the black market closed down. Though wages had long been chasing far behind prices,[1] Pinay with his right of centre government of March 1952–January 1953 at last succeeded in establishing a 'plateau'. Inflation was halted, the price of gold fell, and investments became more attractive: the hoards underneath innumerable floors began to come out into productive use, and the economy expanded accordingly. With the centre parties in the saddle it seemed as if a bourgeois counter-revolution had prevailed. The new world of the Left parties with their panacea of state control—*dirigisme*, as the French call it—had not come to birth. Nationalizations stopped in 1946. The industrial worker found himself if anything worse off, from a salary point of view, than before the war.[2]

---

[1] In the last six months of 1947, for instance, wages had risen by 19 per cent while prices had risen by 51 per cent (Werth, 380).

[2] 'In August 1948 . . . real wages were now lower than they had been since the Liberation, with the real wages of a skilled worker in the Paris area representing only one-half of his pre-war wages; and the same was true of office workers and government

But one legacy of the immediate post-war years had greatly eased the burden of the family man—a generous system of allowances which, whether or not it encouraged the impressively rising birth-rate,[1] at least made life materially better for parents who had their quivers full of children.

From a domestic angle, it was a successful solution: a working compromise between state control of utilities, mines and various enterprises on the one hand, and a considerable sector of free enter-prise on the other, the whole brought into some kind of cohesion by the Monnet Plan for the modernization and equipping of industry.[2] Business, big or small, was still very much in evidence. If the workers were dissatisfied (and the quarter of the votes at elections still given to the Communists suggested this was so), they were beginning to enjoy some of the amenities of the age of motor-scooters and tele-vision. Lengthy strikes could still break out, like the postal and rail strikes of summer 1953, but in general it was the external situation, both in Europe and overseas, which bristled with unsolved problems, and it was the growing pressure of these external difficulties on the Fourth Republic which before long led to its collapse.

The Fourth Republic's record in its European policy was marked by some impressive achievements. De Gaulle took on a difficult battle when he attempted to assert the greatness of France and her independent role in international affairs at a time when, at the war's end, she could be little more than a client of America. Dependent on vast infusions of dollars and exports of all kinds from the new world, France could not for long afford a foreign policy outside the frame-work of that constructed by America. With de Gaulle's abandonment of office the whittling away of France's independent policy towards

---

officials (except those with large families, where family allowances made a considerable difference).' Werth, 403.

[1] Some figures from a table giving the Net Reproduction Rate in France, 1911–59, illustrate this (100 means population is reproducing itself). Taken from the *Annuaire Statistique de la France, Rétrospectif* (Paris, 1961), 51, reproduced in S. Hoffman et. al. *France: Change and Tradition* (Gollancz, 1963), 133.

1937	89	1941	77	1945	93	1949	133
1938	91	1942	85	1946	126	1950	132
1939	93	1943	90	1947	131	1951	126
1940	82	1944	94	1948	133	1959	128

Figures for post-war censuses: 1946: 40,502,513; 1954: 42,777,174; 1962: 46,520,271.

[2] *Le Plan de Modernisation et d'Equipement de la France*, of which Jean Monnet became Commissaire Général (1946).

Germany proceeded apace. The acceptance of Marshall Aid and O.E.E.C., and of the policy of zonal fusion and currency reform in Germany, implied the abandonment of schemes for permanently keeping down the German economy, for controlling the Ruhr and for annexing the Saar. By 1950 the only means of control left to France was the International Authority for the Ruhr and the Saar Convention of 1947. The latter gave France economic and (to some extent) political control over the Saar, and in consequence gave her some leverage in dealing with the West German government.

The Ruhr Authority was palpably inadequate, since it was conceived as a means of restricting rather than developing production, at a time when West Germany was recovering her sovereignty, and when she was expected to contribute to the economic recovery of Europe. A new policy which would achieve the dual aims of security and prosperity was required. This was the work of Robert Schuman as Foreign Minister, leading to the Coal and Steel Pool of France, Germany, Italy and Benelux in 1951, and eventually to the Common Market.

20: The Schuman Plan and the Integration of Western Europe

The Genesis of the Plan

Robert Schuman was born in Luxemburg in 1886. His parents came from that part of Lorraine which was annexed by the new German Reich in 1871, so that Schuman passed his early years as a German subject. He went to the universities of Bonn, Munich, Berlin and Strasbourg (which, as capital of Alsace, was also in German hands at this time). During the First World War he served as an officer in the German army.

Before 1914 he had begun to practise as a lawyer, and after the war entered public life as Deputy for the Moselle. His main concern was with Franco-German relations, and the special problems of Alsace-Lorraine; on these, and on questions of Germany in general he became an acknowledged expert. At first a member of a right-wing group, in 1932 he joined the Parti Démocrate Populaire—akin to the Popular Party in Italy, banned by Mussolini, which was the forerunner of the Christian Democratic Party of that country. But both as a practising Catholic and as a member of a small party, Schuman was scarcely in the running for office, until his special qualifications brought him to the attention of the Reynaud government not long before the armistice, for the post of Director of the Office dealing with refugees. Soon after the transfer of powers to Pétain, Schuman was arrested by the Germans. He escaped in 1942, and entered the resistance movement. Although he had voted for the delegation of constituent power to Pétain in July 1940, and was therefore theoretically banned from entering Parliament again, his ineligibility was eventually removed in view of his resistance record, and he again took his seat as Deputy for the Moselle.

He quickly gained authority in the two Constituent Assemblies of 1945–6, and found his natural place in the newly formed M.R.P. The doctrine of the M.R.P., with its aim of progressive social policies based on Christian, but non-sectarian conviction, was entirely in line with Schuman's approach; and he brought to the M.R.P. his special concern in foreign policy for Franco-German conciliation. He saw this as part of reconstructing Western Europe on the foundations laid centuries before by Charlemagne, on which the states of France, Germany and Italy had eventually been built.

The axis of Charlemagne's empire had been the Rhine, prolonged into Northern Italy. Schuman as a Rhinelander and a Catholic had a fellow feeling for Alcide De Gasperi (1881–1954), Prime Minister of Italy and leader of the Christian Democratic Party.[1] De Gasperi's early experience had been similar to Schuman's: an Italian of the northern borderlands, he had sat in the Austrian Diet before the First World War; as a convinced Catholic he had taken over the leadership of the Popular Party from its founder, the priest of unusual views, Luigi Sturzo, in 1923, only to be imprisoned by Mussolini when the party was dissolved in 1926. On the intervention of the Vatican, he was enabled to leave prison and work in the Vatican Library for fifteen years, until the Duce's fall. In 1943, he refounded his party as the Christian Democratic Party, holding a similar (but more dominant) position in Italy to that of the M.R.P. in France. With Sforza, the Foreign Minister of Italy, Schuman discussed the question of Franco-German reconciliation and the integration of Western Europe. Though the immediate project of a customs union between Italy, France and Benelux came to nothing, the talks brought into view the need for a new relationship between France and Germany as the starting-point for such projects of economic and even political union, and as a means of dealing with the impending question of German rearmament, for which the Americans were beginning to press.[2]

Besides such steps taken by the leaders, many ordinary members of the Christian Democratic parties of Europe had formulated their ideas for European integration in the publications entitled *Nouvelles équipes internationales*. These helped prepare the way for the European

[1] For his outlook see Alcide De Gasperi: *Discorsi politici* (Rome, 1956), 19–20, 29–35, etc.; R. A. Webster: *The Cross and the Fasces—Christian Democracy and Fascism in Italy* (Stamford U.P., 1960), Ch. 9, 129–136.

[2] In March 1950 Churchill in the House of Commons called for the creation of a German contingent as part of a European Army, and in April the matter of Germany's entry into the Atlantic Pact was canvassed in Congress and at the State Department.

Movement, powerfully stimulated by Churchill's trumpet-call at Zürich (19 September 1946)—'We must build a kind of United States of Europe.'[1] This goal appealed to many. As Churchill also proclaimed elsewhere (Fulton, Missouri, 5 March 1946), Russia's bid to impose her system beyond her borders could only be answered by a new unity in the West. 'From Stettin in the Baltic to Trieste in the Adriatic, an iron curtain has descended across the Continent. . . . The safety of the world requires a new unity in Europe from which no nation should be permanently outcast.'[2]

Churchill was out of office, but backing for the European movement came from the Labour Government. 'The time is ripe for the consolidation of Western Europe,'[3] said Bevin in January 1948. Sforza for Italy and Spaak for Belgium—both Foreign Ministers of their countries—gave their support. In May 1948 the European Movement was officially launched, and eventually the Council of Europe came into being, with a Committee of Ministers representing the participating governments and—something of an innovation—a Consultative Assembly 'consisting not of diplomats and officials, acting on the instructions of their governments, but of members of parliament acting in an individual capacity'.[4]

The trouble was, however, that this well-devised constitution was a shadow lacking the essential substance—power. The idea of unity for Western Europe was projected, and the way seemed open towards converting the Council into an organ for exercising some degree of sovereignty over the member-states, and therefore moving towards an embryonic federation. Many of its supporters campaigned at home and at the meetings of the Assembly for 'a political authority with limited functions and real powers', and were disappointed and disillusioned when the governments dragged their feet. Britain, followed by the Scandinavian countries, blew cold on the idea.

The alternative approach was by way of inter-governmental agreements which would piece-meal turn over to the Council (or its

---

[1] He went on: 'The first step is to form a Council of Europe.' He also said, prophetically, 'The first step in the re-creation of the European family must be a partnership between France and Germany. In this way only can France recover the moral leadership of Europe.'—W. S. Churchill: *The Sinews of Peace* (post-war speeches edited by R. S. Churchill, Cassell 1948), 199, 201, 202.

[2] Churchill, op. cit., 100–1.

[3] A. M. Robertson: *The Council of Europe* (Stevens, 1956), 2.

[4] Ibid., 9.

committees) the task of co-ordinating sectors, such as transport, but without any surrender of national sovereignty, and so lead progressively towards integration in the various fields concerned.[1] This 'functionalist' approach had no more success than the 'federalist'. The real value of the Council of Europe lay in its providing a 'great forum in which the future shape of a united Europe was debated, in which . . . leading British parliamentarians could meet with other European politicians, and in which, above all, the federalists could formulate their next tactical aims and exercise pressure to translate them into reality'.[2] This was one way in which politicians and public in Western Europe became familiar with proposals for delegating to a supra-national body some elements of sovereignty over certain sectors of their affairs, especially in the economic sphere.

By 1950 it was precisely in this sector that steps urgently needed to be taken, since a business 'recession' in America was casting a threatening shadow over the returning prosperity of Europe. Marshall Plan loans had primed the pump. Such funds had enabled the Monnet Plan to be financed in France, and similar projects for modernizing industry and for developing the 'infrastructure' of communications and utilities had been set on foot with these funds, administered through the Office of European Economic Co-operation (O.E.E.C.). But, like the Council of Europe, the O.E.E.C. had no powers for imposing a co-ordinated plan for re-developing Western Europe as a whole. Each participating government had its own schemes, for a steel-works here or a power-station there, without reference to similar developments in neighbouring countries. There was much overlapping and consequent wastage, and in many cases (especially in steel production) excess capacity was being created for whose products, it appeared, no adequate markets could be found. If this occurred, and a deflationary movement resulted, with its well-known effects—reduced investment, falling production and mounting unemployment—economic depression and political disturbance would once more revisit Germany, which would become a prey to Communist subversion. Russia was awaiting the moment, as André Philip reminded the French deputies, when 'the countries of

[1] Robertson, 92.
[2] U. W. Kitzinger: *The Challenge of the Common Market* (Blackwell, 3rd edition, 1962), 9.

Europe will be enfeebled by their internal contradictions and struggles, and will collapse, to become an easy prey and fall, one after another, like ripe fruit, into the hands of those who await the moment to seize our unfortunate continent.'[1]

To forestall such developments economic policy for the basic industry of Western Europe had to be co-ordinated, and a larger market established. Capital investment would be made in accordance with an over-all plan. Economic barriers would be broken down, so that a large market could be created which would stimulate a vigorous demand.

Schuman had been confronted with these economic questions, as Minister of Finance (1946 and 1947) before having to grapple with foreign policy as Prime Minister (November 1947–July 1948) and Foreign Minister (from July 1948 onwards). The immediate problem was how to grant the newly created German Federal Republic sovereignty in the economic field, notably where the Ruhr industry was concerned. Without this its government could justly complain that it did not have the proper status of an independent power—and the same difficulty was already arising in the matter of defence. It was the same question which the victorious Allies had failed to answer thirty years before: how to impose on Germany permanent limitations in the economic and military spheres, unless by accepting similar sacrifices of sovereignty themselves.

This step was one which Schuman was now prepared to take on behalf of France. The climate between France and Germany had changed. At any earlier time after the war, such shared delegation of sovereignty and closeness of co-operation which it implied had been out of the question, owing to the gulf which Nazi aggression had driven between the two countries. Since then the liberal Christian movement in both its Catholic and Protestant forms, and often allied with a new current of socialism, had become part of the wider movement which had brought Christian Democratic governments to power in Germany, Italy and France.

This movement, basically one of spiritual renewal, was the response of Christians challenged to take action by the inhumanity, degradation and false values which they had encountered, or by which they had been overcome, during the years of war and its after-

[1] Journal Officiel (Débats parlementaires), July–August 1950, 5942.

math. It was in this spirit that Schuman—who had been thinking of retiring—resolved not to lay down office before completing his work of Franco-German conciliation, and undertook his first visit to the Federal Republic in January 1950.[1]

Schuman and Adenauer found themselves in close accord on the general lines of policy for their two countries. Immediate decisions were necessary in the light of a report just issued (December 1949) by the Steel Division of the European Economic Commission, in which the experts' cry of alarm had produced manifold repercussions,[2] alerting public opinion about the impending crisis in steel, but also proposing steps which Schuman was shortly able to put into effect. These steps had been already outlined by André Philip (one of the leaders of the French Socialist Party and Schuman's predecessor at the Ministry of Finance) in a motion adopted by the European Movement the previous April, and worked out by its Economic Commission. Since (according to the Commission) the crisis could not be overcome by a return to the anarchy of *laissez faire*, nor to the cartels and international agreements for limiting production of the inter-war years, the only way forward was by the 'harmonization' of production and investments in the steel industry. This harmonization should be the task of a 'public authority for steel' composed of delegates of the governments, with power to define the general policy of the industry, notably in the matter of investments, volume of production and prices.[3]

[1]. H. Rieben in *Des ententes de maîtres de forges au Plan Schuman* (Switzerland, 1954), 327, presents as a *'fait significatif'* of these events the support of Adenauer and Schuman for Moral Re-Armament (see below, p. 381). See also *Revue français de science politique*, VI, 1956, P. Gerbert: *La genèse du Plan Schuman*, 545. In a signed article in the *New York Journal-American* of 31 January 1960, Adenauer stated: 'Moral Re-Armament has given most valuable stimulation to the great work of uniting Europe . . . Very soon after the end of the war this ideology reached out a hand to the German people and helped them make contact again with other nations . . . We have seen the conclusion after some difficult negotiations of important international agreements. MRA has played an invisible but effective part in bridging differences of opinion between negotiating parties. It has kept before them the objective of peaceful agreement in search for common good which is the true purpose of human life." (See Note, p. 233, for Schuman's motives.)

[2] It had *'un immense retentissement'*—Rieben, 320. Europe appeared to be running into excess steel production: by 1952 production was estimated to be 69 million tons, and consumption plus exports 61 million tons—hence the danger of a cut-throat price war, or a new international cartel. (Speech of André Philip in the French Assembly, J.O., July–August, 1950, 5940.)

[3] P. Gerbet (*Revue Française de science politique*, VI, 1956), 530. 'Harmonization'

These proposals could also meet the need for freeing the Ruhr from the control of the Western Allies—depriving the Russians at the same time of the grounds for their constant pressure that they be given a share in the Ruhr Authority—while integrating the Ruhr into the Pas de Calais–Saar–Lorraine coal-steel basin and industrial complex, of which it formed a natural part. It opened the way to Germany for accepting restrictions on making the Ruhr again a potential arsenal and threat to peace—restrictions on her sovereignty because similar restrictions were accepted by France. Similarly it opened a way towards solving the Saar problem, which remained a bone of contention.[1]

During the months following Schuman's visit to Bonn, Adenauer made several declarations along the lines of mutual co-operation in those matters between France and Germany—for internationalizing the production of the Saar, for a Franco-German Union, and for a Union including Britain; and a proposal for unifying the economies of France and Germany. The Plan was however formulated in conditions of secrecy by Jean Monnet and his personal brains-trust, who had already been working on such a project. Monnet's initiative in this respect made possible the political action carried through by Schuman.

Monnet had considerable experience of these matters. Born in 1888 at Cognac, he was expected to take part in the family business trading in the brandy for which the place is famous, and in preparation for this was sent to Britain and Canada on extensive visits before the First World War. He took part in the war-time negotiations between France, Britain and America which led to the creation of the Allied Executive Council and the Allied Maritime Council, concerned with the purchase and allocation of supplies and armaments, and served on these bodies. In 1919 he became Assistant Secretary-General of the League of Nations, in which capacity he organized an international loan for restoring the finances of Austria, but had to return to the family business in 1923 on the death of his elder brother. On account of his already great experience of international finance, he was appointed in 1933 head of the China Finance

---

means co-ordination of production and investment to bring them into line so that equilibrium is achieved.

[1] See pp. 242, 294.

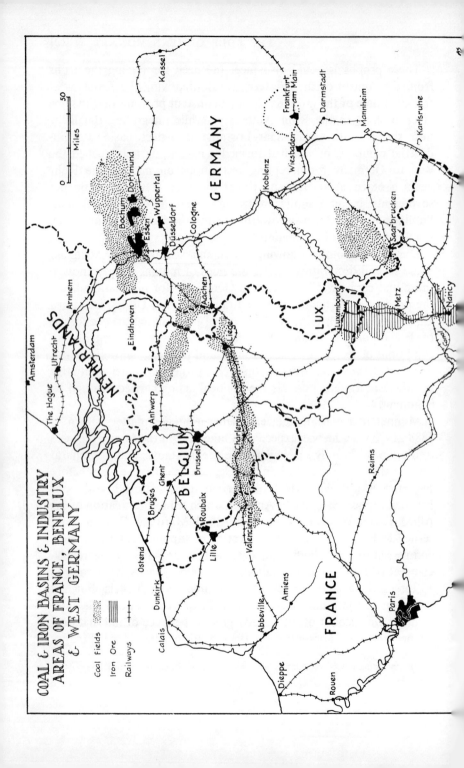

COAL & IRON BASINS & INDUSTRY
AREAS OF FRANCE, BENELUX
& WEST GERMANY

Coal Fields
Iron Ore
Railways

0   50
Miles

NETHERLANDS

Amsterdam
The Hague
Utrecht
Arnhem
Eindhoven

Ostend
Bruges
Ghent
Antwerp
Brussels
Charleroi
Roubaix
Lille
Valenciennes

BELGIUM

Aachen
Liège
Cologne
Düsseldorf
Wuppertal
Essen
Bochum
Dortmund

GERMANY

Koblenz
Wiesbaden
Frankfurt am Main
Darmstadt
Mannheim
Karlsruhe
Saarbrücken
Metz
Nancy
Luxembourg

LUX.

Kassel

Calais
Dunkirk
Dieppe
Rouen
Abbeville
Amiens
Reims
Paris

FRANCE

Development Corporation, and established a firm in New York for making capital investments in that country, at the same time re-organizing the Chinese railways and other enterprises. During the Second World War he took a major part first in the purchasing commissions for France in the U.S.A., then in the Franco-British 'pool' for co-ordinating the economic and financial affairs of France and Britain, and after the French collapse, as one of the creators of the Anglo-American 'Victory Programme' of production and supply. A thoroughgoing internationalist, he was the initiator of the plan proposed by Churchill to Reynaud in June 1940 for the fusion and common citizenship of France and the British Empire. In 1943 he entered the French Committee of National Liberation at Algiers, and was the chief organiser of Lend-Lease and other supply arrangements between Free France and the U.S.A.

By 1945 Monnet could rate as the world's most progressive and experienced supernational technocrat. He was able to look at France from a point of view clear of traditionalism or the faded glories of the past. 'France,' he said, 'is a new country for him who has eyes to see.' Reconstruction without modernization was useless. With modernization, France could be put on the level of the most economically advanced nations. De Gaulle's government accepted his propositions. Monnet was charged with drawing up a plan for the modernization and equipping of the country, which involved unifying all the plans for particular industries which had already been drawn up, and elaborating new ones. In six months the Council over which he presided had drawn up its plan. In 1947 it began to be carried out, based on a vast programme of capital investment up to 1950, under the supervision of a series of commissions concerned with every major branch of the economy, the whole being 'animated, co-ordinated, inspired and ordered',[1] by the Commissaire-General, Jean Monnet.

The outline of what became the Schuman Plan had first been proposed by Monnet to Bidault, the Prime Minister, and then—after Bidault's somewhat cool reception of it—to Schuman.[2] With Schuman's agreement, Monnet rapidly proceeded to draw up the

[1] *Dictionnaire biographique français contemporain* (Centre International de Documentation, Paris, 1950). Owing to under-investment, the period of the Plan had to be extended for most projects to 1952.
[2] Gerbet, op. cit., 543–4.

declaration of policy which was the basis of the projected Plan for the Coal-Steel Pool in Western Europe. It was ready for presentation to the Cabinet on 9 May. The moment was not to be missed since on the 10th a conference was due to meet in London for defining the position of Germany within the framework of the Atlantic Pact.

The Americans, with whose help the European economy was being maintained, could hardly be left in the dark about this momentous project, and an opportunity occurred for broaching it to the Secretary of State, Dean Acheson (General Marshall's successor) during a brief visit by the latter on 7 May to Paris, on his way to the London Conference. Acheson described his initiation into the Plan by Schuman as 'so breath-taking that at first I did not grasp it . . . [Later] we caught his enthusiasm and the breadth of his thought, the rebirth of Europe which, as an entity, had been in eclipse since the Reformation'.[1]

Only a few colleagues of Schuman's in the government had been informed of the details, and these were won over to the project by the 'tenacity and strength of conviction of M. Monnet', who had, in regard to these ministers, 'an exceptional personal authority'.[2] Even the senior officials of the Quai d'Orsay were in ignorance of their chief's impending move. For Monnet and his associates it was a day of tension as, glued to the telephone, they wondered whether Schuman would succeed in inserting his project into the crowded agenda before the Cabinet. They were relieved when, at midday, they heard that his brief outline of the Plan had been accepted almost without discussion—the Premier, Bidault, himself betraying, if anything, a marked indifference towards it. In this seemingly casual way a major turning-point in the evolution of the Continent was passed, the first entirely free act of statesmanship initiated by France since the war, 'for preparing the creation of a united Europe'.[3]

The Reception of the Schuman Plan in Germany and Britain

Before his cabinet meeting on the morning of 9 May 1950, Chancellor Adenauer was apprised by a special messenger from Schuman of the move which he was making that morning with his government.

[1] D. Acheson: *Sketches from Life* (Hamilton, 1961), 42–3.
[2] Gerbet, 546.
[3] Schuman, speech in the Assembly, J.O. (op. cit.), 5943.

By a coincidence Adenauer was holding a press conference that evening and was able to announce that, though the French project came as a complete surprise,[1] his government was giving it an immediate welcome. He hailed it as a 'magnanimous step . . . making any future conflict between France and Germany impossible. It is a step of extraordinary importance for the peace of Europe and of the entire world'.[2] The secrecy with which the Plan had been matured and the way in which it was sprung upon the world were designed to cause the maximum shock effect. Only thus, in the view of Monnet and Schuman, could negotiations be swiftly started on the right level. Its precondition was agreement on the principles between France and Germany. This was now assured, and with it the almost certain assent of Italy and the Benelux states. Britain was a more doubtful starter, though her participation by the Plan's authors was hoped for as an element which would immeasurably strengthen the foundations of the new Europe and the trend towards a federal objective.

No amount of 'psychological shock effect'[3] could however shake Bevin and his confreres in the Cabinet into acceptance. His reaction was publicly lukewarm and privately negative.[4] He was supported by Sir Stafford Cripps, now Chancellor of the Exchequer, and Hugh Dalton, who had recently exchanged that post for a ministry without portfolio.[5] 'Bevin, Cripps and I were all definitely anti-Federal,' wrote Dalton later.[6] 'We were determined not to allow interference by a European Committee with our full employment policy, our social services, our nationalized industries, or our national planning.' This was particularly the case since, as the Labour Party pamphlet *European Unity* stated, 'No Socialist Party . . . could accept a system by which important fields of national policy were surrendered to a supra-national European representative authority, since such an authority would have a permanent anti-Socialist majority and would arouse the hostility of the European workers.'[7]

[1] P. Weymar: *Konrad Adenauer* (Deutsch, 1957), 349.
[2] *News Chronicle*, 10 May 1950.
[3] *New York Herald Tribune*, 14 May 1950.
[4] A. Nutting: *Europe Will Not Wait* (Hollis and Carter, 1960), 31. See Note at end of chapter, p. 233.
[5] Chancellor of the Duchy of Lancaster.
[6] H. Dalton: *High Tide and After—Memoirs 1945–1960* (Muller, 1962), 334.
[7] National Executive Committee of the British Labour Party: *European Unity* (May 1950), 8. It was prepared soon after the publication of the Schuman Plan, and given to

Bevin, Cripps and Dalton carried Attlee along with them. An official welcome was given to the project, as a French initiative for closing the gulf between France and Germany, but the note struck was of reserve and caution. This was maintained even after Monnet's visit to London (14–19 May), when he explained in detail the implications of the scheme. 'If the French Government intend to insist on a commitment to pool resources,' stated a British memorandum of 27 May, 'and set up an authority with certain sovereign powers as a prior condition to joining in the talks, His Majesty's Government would reluctantly be unable to accept such a condition'.[1] The government held out for a meeting at ministerial level first, to discuss the principle of the Plan, since it was precisely the principle they wished to demolish: they were opposed to committing themselves to anything more than an inter-governmental committee of the European Payments Union type as the co-ordinating body for the Plan.[2] But this, as the French realized, would move matters no further than the O.E.E.C. committee had been able to do. Hence an air of unreality hung over the subsequent exchanges between the two governments, an exercise in polite fencing while formulas, supposedly for making Britain's participation possible, were exchanged. Finally the French turned down Britain's proposal for a ministerial meeting on this basis (3 June 1950), and the British accepted merely a watching brief —the French still hoping, according to their last communiqué, that 'the British Government . . . may find it possible to join or associate themselves with the common effort at the time when they judge it to be possible'.[3]

Though at the time and during the later debate in Parliament, Churchill and the Conservatives showed themselves zealous champions for participating in the conference of the six states which accepted the principle of the Schuman Plan—with a similar reservation to that made by the Dutch[4]—in reality it is doubtful whether

---

the press by Dalton, who also 'had seen it through the National Executive' (*High Tide*, 334).

[1] Cmd. 7970 (1950), Doc. 8.

[2] See Notes at end of chapter.

[3] Cmd. 7970, Doc. 17 (3 June 1950).

[4] 'In view of the fact that this Text involves the acceptance of certain principles underlying the French Government's memorandum, the Netherlands Government feels obliged to reserve its right to go back on the acceptance of these principles in the course of the negotiations in the event of their proving impossible to translate into practice.'

they, any more than the bulk of the Labour Party, were eager to bind an important area of the British economy to that of the continental states in the way the French proposed. As for the larger objective of European federation, most Conservatives agreed with Churchill that Britain 'could not be an ordinary member of a federal union limited to Europe in any period which at present can be foreseen. . . . Although a hard-and-fast concrete federal constitution for Europe is not within the scope of practical affairs, we should help, sponsor and aid in every possible way the movement towards European unity. We should seek steadfastly for means to become intimately associated with it.'[1] Britain's world role precluded, in his view, membership of a continental federation which might be exclusive in character. Western Europe was but one of the three 'circles' which Britain had to bring into closer mutual relations, the other two being the Commonwealth and the Atlantic Community.

Churchill's vision was lofty, but the practice of the Conservatives, once they were again in office (October 1951), was not strikingly different from that of their Labour colleagues. Churchill might refer to the *European Unity* pamphlet as 'Dalton's Brown Paper', but (apart from its tone of doctrinaire socialism) there was little in its conclusions with which the Conservatives disagreed. Nor could they disagree fundamentally with Cripps, who, in the debate of 26 June 1950, quoted the French government's statement[2] that the proposals would 'build the first concrete foundation of the European federation', and commented: 'this approach involves the other partners in the scheme not only in commitments in regard to the coal and steel industries, but also in commitments in regard to the future political framework for Europe. In our view, participation in a political federation, limited to Western Europe, is not compatible either with our Commonwealth ties, our obligations as a member of the wider Atlantic community, or as a world Power.'[3]

It is a question whether this was the main consideration, or whether it was the more parochial one summed up by the back-bencher who demanded that 'no supra-national authority will be allowed to

House of Commons, 27 June 1950 (*In the Balance*, 301).
[2] Cmd. 7970 (1950), Doc. 2.
[3] *Hansard*, vol. 476, col. 1947–8.

interfere with the Socialist Government's planning for full employment'.[1] Harold Macmillan later expressed much the same view: 'One
thing is certain, and we may as well face it. Our people will not hand
over to any supra-national Authority the right to close down our pits
or our steel-works.'[2]

In the welter of thinking on the subject there was one point which
might be held to have more validity than others, that European
integration might prove a weapon in the hands of those who wished
to build a 'third force' standing between the U.S.A. and Russia.
This conception to most British statesmen was unrealistic and fraught
with danger, particularly that of driving America back to her hemisphere, so leaving Europe—and inevitably Britain also—a prey to
possible Communist aggression.[3]

Negotiating the Schuman Plan

British production of coal in 1950 was half that of Europe as a whole,
and of steel about one-third. Britain's refusal to participate in the
European Coal and Steel Community was therefore a serious blow
to its creators, but they wasted no time before pressing on towards
their goal, necessarily restricted though it now appeared. On 3 June
1950 the 'Six' (France, Germany, Italy, Benelux) announced their
decision to work towards the pooling of their coal and steel industries
under a High Authority whose decisions would be binding. On the
20th conferences began between delegations from the Six, in which
the participants decided to work as experts without committing their
governments, and by March of the following year (1951) a draft
agreement was initialled by the delegations, ready to be presented to
the governments for ratification.

This stage was not reached without much intensive discussion and
give-and-take among the delegations. A French draft somewhat
elaborating the original proposals was all they had to work on.

[1] Harold Davies, *Hansard*, vol. 476, col. 38 (13 May 1950). Regarding full employment *The Economist* (17 June 1950, p. 1314) shrewdly commented: 'What has done the
trick has not been the successful application of socialist principles in Britain, but the
successful working of capitalism in America.'

[2] *Reports of Council of Europe Consultative Assembly* (Strasbourg, 1950), 7–28
August 1950, 434. Quoted in U. W. Kitzinger: *The Challenge of the Common Market*
(Blackwell, 1962), 10.

[3] *European Unity*, 9. See also *Foreign Affairs*, January 1951, D. H. McLachlan:
Rearmament and European Integration, 284.

Questions of the powers and composition of the High Authority had to be decided, and in the event a proposal was accepted to limit these by the setting up of a 'Common Assembly' whose function would be to review the work of the Authority, with power—not to interfere with its decisions—but to execute a censure by voting it out of office. Similarly the Belgians and Dutch proposed an intergovernmental body to have further functions of review: this took shape in the Council of Ministers, composed of government representatives.[1] There was also to be a Court of Justice before which cases could be brought by parties claiming that the High Authority was not conforming to the Treaty, or was acting inequitably. The 'supernational' position of the High Authority was safeguarded by maintaining the principle that no one government could have a veto over what the Authority might ordain in its territory.[2]

In the intricate questions of making the transition to free trade in coal and steel within the community, and to unifying prices and transport costs, there were many delicate points where the interest of one or other country, or of an important group of producers or sellers, was concerned. Fears that high-cost coal-mines would have to be closed were particularly daunting to the Belgians. Italian steel cost on average more than double that of other community manufacturers to produce—the consequence of Mussolini's determination to build a steel industry no matter how non-competitive, and of his post-war successors to keep it going and even re-equip it.[3]

If prices for coal and steel had dropped during this time, high-cost marginal producers would have been badly hit in any case, and once within the Community might have been obliged to accept closures of mines and scaling down of enterprises to an extent which would have seemed intolerable. But conveniently prices during this time increased, thanks to a stroke of Communist strategy which was certainly not designed to help the free world—the outbreak of the Korean War (June 1950), shortly after the negotiations about the Plan began.

The prospect of rising prices and a seller's market undoubtedly

[1] W. Diebold: *The Schuman Plan* (Council of Foreign Relations; Praeger, 1959), 63.
[2] *The Economist*, 26 August 1950.
[3] H. L. Mason: *The European Coal and Steel Community* (Nijhoff, The Hague, 1955), 5; Diebold, 131–3.

helped along the negotiations and later eased the transition period. When, after the Korean 'boom' prices temporarily fell, the Community was already firmly enough established to make adequate adjustments without strain.

It could be said of Monnet that for him the Schuman Plan was a 'prolongation of an internal French plan'.[1] For some years Monnet had presided over the Plan for Modernization and Equipment of French industry: that process had now gone so far that unless the basic French industries could be integrated in a unit larger than that of the nation, they could not be worked to capacity, nor could they be sure of receiving adequate supplies of coal now that the days of France's special privileges of access to Ruhr coal were numbered. The two new continuous wide strip mills which were being erected under the Monnet Plan were indicative of this situation. A larger export market was essential to absorb their products when the mills were running at capacity, and the extra coking coal they required would mostly have to come from the Ruhr.

Monnet and Schuman were merely recognizing the fact that in economic development, as in scientific research, no countries except possibly the largest super-states, could in the new conditions of the mid-twentieth century begin to live unto themselves. Not merely markets, but research programmes and their application, together with all the economies of scale, pointed to co-ordinated work in a dimension which exceeded those of the national state. 'For five years (1945–50) the whole French nation had been making efforts to recreate the bases of production, but it became evident that to go beyond recovery towards steady expansion and higher standards of life for all, the resources of a single nation were not sufficient. It was necessary to transcend the national framework.'[2]

Further, Monnet's experience in designing and operating the Plan for France was ideal for coping with the similar but wider problems involved in applying such a plan to the Community. There it had proved possible to bring the public sector of the economy and the—still large—private sector into a general development programme. Though the success of this depended in part on the size of the public

[1] Gerbet, 539 n.
[2] Journal of Common Market Studies, I, No. 3, J. Monnet: *A Ferment of Change*, 205.

sector—nationalized industries like coal, electricity, gas, railways, and enterprises like Renault—it was by no means due solely to the direct control which the government was able to exercise there. Whereas in Britain at this time the battle raged fiercely over the nationalization of steel—eventually accomplished by the Labour government before it fell in 1951, only to be de-nationalized a few months later by the Conservatives—in France further nationalizations were seen to be irrelevant. The ability to apply steadily a programme for both sectors of industry depended, not primarily on using investment as a bludgeon, but on seeking agreement with the heads of private businesses as well as those of the nationalized concerns for the best ways of applying investment capital in the interest of developing the country's resources.

It was true that investment in a large industry like electricity—the biggest industrial investor in France—could strongly influence the development of its host of suppliers,[1] and therefore the general development of much of the economy. It was in this indirect way, that Monnet's *Commissariat du Plan* controlled the development of France's basic industries, and eventually the whole economy—a flexible method which rarely set output targets, but (particularly where private industry was concerned) enabled objectives to be appreciated, after studies at all levels, by those who had to attain them. It was the 'indicative' rather than the 'imperative' method.

This method Monnet carried into the work of negotiating the arrangements for the difficult five-year transitional period, and later into that of the High Authority. His own *Commissariat-Général* had stood somewhat in the same relation to the French government as the High Authority came to stand in relation to the governments of the Community. Monnet had developed a system of Commissions for carrying out the detailed surveys on which the French Plan, in its successive versions, was based. These were recruited partly from high civil servants of the Ministry of Finance and other Ministries (*les Grands Corps de l'État*), from engineers, professors, jurists, economists and private industry (only a few from these two last). They formed a body, largely practical and administrative in experience, with close personal contacts with the government departments

[1] J. and A.-M. Hackett: *Economic Planning in France* (Allen and Unwin, 1963). 262–3.

and economic sectors from which they came. The Commissariat itself being small never went in for 'empire-building', but worked through the Ministry of Finance, the Economic and Social Council and other existing organs of the state.

Such was the secret of Monnet's success. Also, while Ministers came and went, Monnet went on, until he transferred his services, and those of some of the experienced officials, to the Coal and Steel Community.[1]

Though the outbreak of the Korean War helped on the negotiations in one way, in another it raised difficulties. In September 1950 the Americans proposed that in view of the new threat to the free world, the Germans be permitted to raise ten divisions as their contribution to the Atlantic Alliance.[2] If accepted, the new status of the Federal Republic would undoubtedly involve the speedy dismantling of most remaining checks on its sovereignty, and it appeared as though the Germans might gain all the freedom from post-war shackles which they wanted without incurring the obligations involved in entry to the Community.

At this point the Americans stepped in. John J. McCloy, the American High Commissioner in Germany (who had replaced General Clay) virtually took over the negotiations concerning the reorganization of the Ruhr industry. The French needed all the diplomacy and pressure which the Americans could exert to bring about the final stages of breaking up the big cartels and concentrations. Without this the French were not prepared to have Germany in the Community, and if the Schuman Plan did not go through, the French were not prepared to let Germany rearm. Particularly they were afraid that if Germany came in with its great coal marketing agency intact (the Deutscher Kohlen-Verkauf), the Germans would have too much bargaining power and would not permit them access to Ruhr coke on the terms they needed.[3]

After several months of intense diplomatic activity, with the un-faltering backing of Chancellor Adenauer, McCloy succeeded in making arrangements which the French could accept, and in in-corporating them into the Treaty. This was initialled by the delegates

[1] From 1946–62 there were 3 Commissaires-Généraux in France and 22 Ministers of Finance.
[2] See p. 238.   [3] Diebold, 73.

on 19 March 1950, and a month later signed by the Foreign Ministers of the Six.

Ratification was a lengthy process. In France the fact that the executives of the nationalized industries supported the Plan decided the Treaty's passage through the various committees (the spokesmen for private business were mostly against it), and in the Assembly the almost solid backing of the Socialists and M.R.P. eventually gave it the necessary majority (13 December 1950). This was confirmed by the Council (formerly Senate) the following April. In Germany the Christian-Democratic majority had ensured the Treaty's passage through the Bundestag, against Socialist opposition. Eventually all the other parliaments followed suit and the Treaty was signed on 18 April 1951. It entered into force on 25 September 1952, and the High Authority began its work at its Luxemburg headquarters on 10 August 1952. Six months later, on 10 February 1953 the common market for coal, iron ore, and scrap came into operation, and the common market for steel opened on 1 May.

NOTES

1. MOTIVATIONS OF THE SCHUMAN PLAN

'Why should we have recourse to this idea, to this new-fangled supra-national institution? . . . To enable Germany to accept restrictions on her own sovereignty which is being gradually and irrevocably restored to her. And if we wish to make Germany accept these restrictions, we must set her an example. . . . We want to accord Germany equality in rights and in treatment, and we cannot do otherwise. But equal treatment means that we cannot retain for ourselves more power in the sector concerned than Germany will have. This is an act of self-denial on our part; self-denial in the sense that we make sacrifices; but we have the consolation that Germany will undertake to make the same sacrifices. It will mean identical renunciation on both sides and in the most delicate matters, such as the army and the production of coal and steel, products essential to the preparation of war and for the formulation of policy.'—R. Schuman: *French policy towards Germany since the war* (Stevenson Memorial Lecture, O.U.P., 1954), 21.

2. THE REACTIONS OF BEVIN AND DALTON TO THE SCHUMAN PLAN.

Acheson describes Bevin's reaction to the Schuman Plan: 'He was in a towering rage, and at once charged that I had known Schuman's plan and kept it from him. . . . He rushed on to accuse me of having conspired with Schuman to create a European combination against British trade with the Continent. . . . He bristled with hostility to Schuman's whole idea.'

Dean Acheson: *Sketches from Life* (Hamilton, 1961), 42-3.

Dalton, at the first general debate of the Consultative Assembly of the Council of Europe (August 1950) stated (in his own summary) that 'Britain would not take the Federal road to Europe, but let others take it if they wished, and good luck to them! I reminded the Assembly of recent successes of the inter-governmental method, including the E.P.U., which I said, was triumph for the working of the unanimity rule in an atmosphere of good-will, each country having a power of veto in reserve, but none using it. . . . I urged the importance of full employment. We in Britain had kept our unemployment percentage below 2% since 1946, but some members of the Council of Europe had more than 10% unemployed.' (*High Tide*, 327.)

21: The Atlantic Alliance and the Common Market

The Atlantic Pact and NATO

The Dunkirk Treaty (March 1947) between France and Britain was the last instrument to be negotiated between two Western powers which aimed at countering a resurgent Germany as a military threat. By 1948 it was clear that such a threat was likely to come from another quarter—Russia. Ernest Bevin believed that a military framework was required to complement the economic arrangements for rebuilding Europe which, with American aid, culminated in the Marshall Plan. The rape of Czechoslovakia added impetus to the moves which he initiated.

Russia was keeping four and a half million men under arms, while those of the West had melted away. She was credited with 6,000 planes ready for immediate combat, while those of the West were scarcely a thousand. If this overwhelming force were not there for attacking the West, and bringing Communism to the Channel, what was its *raison d'être*? The surly and aggressive attitude of Moscow reinforced the sense of insecurity. Bevin sounded Washington as to what help might be expected if the Western countries began to integrate their defences. He was encouraged to proceed, but was told that the West must take further steps in self-help before American assistance for any new defence venture would be forthcoming.

At the Brussels Conference in the month following the Prague Coup these steps were taken. Britain, France and the Benelux countries signed an agreement to set up a joint defensive system (17 March 1948). In effect it was an alliance, presided over by the five Foreign Ministers. In September it created its own staff under the chairmanship of Field-Marshal Montgomery, with its Headquarters at Fontainebleau near Paris.

The Americans and Canadians had kept in touch with these developments, sending observers to the meetings of the organization. A crucial step towards Atlantic co-operation was the Resolution introduced in Congress by Senator Arthur H. Vandenberg, formerly one of the toughest of isolationists who had been converted to a 'global' view by Pearl Harbour. Now, as a senior Republican he was the great protagonist of a bi-partisan policy under the Democratic President, Harry Truman. With Secretary of State Marshall and officials of the State Department, he worked out the Resolution which recommended 'the association of the United States by constitutional process, with such regional and other collective arrangements as are based on continuous and effective self-help and mutual aid, and as affect its national security', and gave a definite warning that the United States would make clear its determination to exercise its right of individual *or collective* self-defence under Article 51 (of the United Nations Charter) 'should any armed attack occur affecting its national security'.[1]

The need was to by-pass the security arrangements envisaged by the U.N. charter, which had been negated by the Russian attitude. As the question of regional security was studied, it became clear that this would be best served by a wider association than one between the Brussels partners and the U.S.A. Canada was ready to come in, and other countries were proposed of which, by the time the Pact was signed on 4 April 1949, Iceland, Denmark, Norway, Portugal and Italy joined.[2]

The essence of the Pact was in Article 5—'an armed attack against one or more (of the signatories) shall be considered an attack against them all'—all the partners would forthwith take necessary action 'including the use of armed force, to restore and maintain the security of the North Atlantic area'. Further, their forces would be kept in a state of readiness by the provision (under Article 3) that the parties 'by means of continuous and effective self-help and mutual aid, will maintain and develop their individual and collective capacity to resist armed attack'. This pledge led on, in the words of the Organization's first Secretary-General, Lord Ismay, to 'unity of command, unified planning and uniformity of military training, procedure, and, as far as possible, equipment. And so it came about

---

[1] My italics. Full text in Lord Ismay: *NATO, the First Five Years 1949–1954*, 171. Also Arthur H. Vandenberg, Jr. (Ed.): *The Private Papers of Senator Vandenberg* (Gollancz, 1953), 407.

[2] Greece and Turkey acceded to the North Atlantic Treaty in 1951.

that by the end of 1950, sovereign states were to entrust their forces to international commanders, assisted by international staffs. Never in history have the principles of alliance been carried to such a pitch in time of peace.'[1]

Here on the military plane was a new start in the pooling of sovereignty, such as had already developed in the economic sphere, and which was about to be taken a further step forward by the Schuman Plan. So far the pattern was similar to that of the wartime 'Grand Alliance', but such a structure of relationships was new in time of peace. This reflected the fact that statesmen understood that the 'cold war' was as real as the shooting war, and that sacrifices, at least of an increasingly precarious autonomy, were necessary. Also—and this paralleled the situation in the economic field—the vast costs of modern defence made it prohibitive for the smaller powers, and far less effective even for a super-state like the U.S.A., without a pooling of productive effort and a spreading of overheads.

The Communist attack on South Korea, launched on 25 June 1950 underlined the urgency of the need. In this crisis the United States showed what could be done by collective military action within the framework of the United Nations, at a moment when the Russian veto was in abeyance. But such a contingency could not be counted upon again, in the event of a Soviet attack in Europe. By this date various agencies, which the signatories of NATO had set up—the Defence and Military Committees, the Financial and Economic Committee, and the Regional Planning Groups—had done useful preliminary work. The United States government had voted a billion dollars under the Mutual Defence Assistance Act (July 1949) 'to assist other countries in the Pact to maintain their collective security'. But matters moved slowly, the military planners were waiting for the economic planners, and *vice versa*, until Korea galvanized all parties into speedy action. At the meeting of the Council of NATO in December 1950 it was agreed to set up an integrated military force. General Eisenhower was designated as its Supreme Commander, with Paris for his headquarters.[2]

[1] Ismay, 14.
[2] In 1952 the organization was further strengthened by the establishment of a Permanent NATO Council in Paris, capable of taking decisions, with an International Secretariat.

Defence of the European continent meant the defence of Germany, and here another problem arose. The Western zones were occupied by the Allied forces without any consideration for defence, and their supply lines were highly vulnerable to any advance against them from the east. 'There would be scenes of appalling and indescribable confusion . . . if we were ever attacked by the Russians,' Montgomery reported at this time.[1] To defend Germany adequately meant arming and training Germans, yet the spectre of a reviving Wehrmacht caused dismay among many Europeans. An American proposal in the autumn of 1950 was that German forces should be raised, in units of not more than a division, each being integrated in larger Allied formations. There should be no German General Staff, and though German industry (which would have to be further freed from limitations) would be used to supply these forces, the Germans would be dependent on the other powers for equipment which, under the Allied ban, they were not allowed to manufacture themselves.

In France the government of René Pleven tried to find a formula for German rearmament, which would allay the legitimate fears of Germany's neighbours (October 1950). He proposed 'Europeanizing' the problem. German units would be raised as part of a European Defence Force; this would come under a Minister of Defence responsible to a European Assembly, appointed by the participating governments. This scheme was thrashed out with the Americans and other governments, and by the end of 1951 a draft treaty was ready for setting up a European Army. Though this was signed by the parties concerned the following year, it was never ratified. The struggle over ratification held up the integration of Germany in the Atlantic Alliance until 1955, and slowed down the movement towards the economic and political integration of the Continent which had been forwarded by the Schuman Plan.

E.D.C. and the Paris Agreements

On 27 August 1950 the French Chamber of Deputies voted in favour of the Pleven Plan 'in principle' for creating a European army in which German units would be integrated. Thereafter no majority was ever forthcoming in the Chamber for ratifying it. Every French politician knew that no such majority existed. The feverish diplomacy

[1] Ismay, 30.

which resulted, the attempts to get guarantees from Britain and America to strengthen the hands of successive French governments which wrestled with the problem, all failed.

The Pleven Plan tided France over an awkward period. France was dependent on American aid. It was unlikely that this aid would be continued, at least on the necessary scale, unless the French government accepted the urgent American demand for a German 'defence contribution'. This prospect however raised too many unpleasant ghosts of the past—a Continent dominated by Germany; Britain and America backing out of Europe (as they had backed out of the projected alliance with France in 1919), so leaving France at a disadvantage in the face of a reviving Germany. There were also the doubts understandably connected with a surrender of sovereignty over such a vital area of policy as defence, and the pull of centuries of tradition and powerful national feeling.

If Britain would come in, then all would be well—so ran the usual argument. But Britain protested that, though she would go to the farthest limit in association with the European Defence Community, she could not actually join in—her responsibilities to the Commonwealth, her island tradition and so on, made this impossible. 'If (Churchill) wants us to ratify the European Army, he only has to . . . agree to Britain's entry into the European system of integration. . . . "Impossible," says London, "we've got the Commonwealth." Quite. But France has the French Union—and the problem is precisely the same.'[1]

Churchill had become Prime Minister again in consequence of the Conservative victory at the election of October 1951, and Anthony Eden was again Foreign Secretary. While still out of office, in August 1950, Churchill had declared: 'We should make a gesture of practical and constructive guidance by declaring ourselves in favour of the immediate creation of a European army under a unified command, and in which we should bear a worthy and honourable part.'[2] But, when it came to the point, the part which Britain would play was specified as 'association' in various forms. The formula of 'all support short of membership' in fact provided valuable guarantees for France: joint training, interchange of officers, co-ordinated air

---

[1] *Le Monde*, 13 October 1953, quoted in Werth: *France, 1940–1955*, 645.
[2] Sir Anthony Eden (Lord Avon): *Memoirs—Full Circle* (Cassell, 1960), 30.

defence systems, the maintenance of British forces on the Continent 'for as long as is necessary'.[1] In the British view this close association with the European Army would be effective because the European Army, the British forces, and the American forces too, would all be co-ordinated within NATO under the Supreme Allied Commander in Europe (SACEUR).

All this was not enough for the French. They tried to obtain further guarantees, and by a series of 'interpretative texts' to gain various concessions, notably the right to withdraw units from the European Army when certain circumstances arose. During this time the French were negotiating against the background of a constant drain on their manpower and money due to the war in Indo-China, and threats of other conflicts breaking out in North Africa. They failed to obtain ratification, by their associates of the Six, of all these texts, and were deadlocked between governments who urged ratification of E.D.C. and parliamentary majorities opposed to it.

This prompted the American Secretary of State, John Foster Dulles,[2] to speak at the end of 1953 of the necessity which might face the United States of making 'an agonising reappraisal' in her foreign policy. The threat was that if France would not agree to E.D.C., either America would back German rearmament without her consent, or would retire to 'Fortress America' and concern herself only with 'peripheral defence'. At the Bermuda Conference in November 1953 the French Premier, Laniel, was treated as a good deal less than an equal by Churchill and Eisenhower (now President of the U.S.A.). 'M. Laniel, the *Premier*, was put in the same car as the *Foreign Ministers*, Number One car being reserved for Churchill and Eisenhower. Worse still, when, before that, Laniel and Churchill waited at the airfield for Eisenhower's arrival, Churchill—the French press reported—turned his back on the "unknown" French Premier, and instead stroked the beard of the regimental mascot goat of the Welch Fusiliers—"*un animal sympathique*".'[3]

Attempts to bully France were not likely to be successful—they only aroused a stronger current than ever of opposition to ratification. Eden quickly understood that the alternative was to strengthen

[1] Eden's statement to Schuman, 1 February 1952, Eden, 38.
[2] Secretary of State since September 1951.
[3] Werth, 650.

and enlarge NATO, to provide a framework for the introduction of German forces which would be acceptable to the French.

Before the inevitable rejection of E.D.C. by the French Chamber (30 August 1954), when the question was finally posed by the new Premier Pierre Mendès-France,[1] Eden had already made his plans. Eisenhower at the start had counselled Britain to stay with NATO and not go into a European Army.[2] With the Americans favouring a NATO solution of the difficulty, it became a question of timing and tactics. The idea came to Eden in a moment of relaxation—'in the bath on Sunday morning',[3] a week after E.D.C.'s demise in the Chamber—to enlarge the Brussels Treaty of 1948[4] by bringing Italy and Germany into it, and turning it into a Locarno-type mutual defence pact. With this preliminary accomplished it should be possible, he thought, to overcome French opposition to bringing Germany into NATO. He at once took off for Brussels, Bonn, Rome[J] and Paris, where he successfully 'sold' the idea—though at Paris the bargaining was hard. Mendès-France himself was partly prepared for this solution by a visit to Churchill which he made when he knew that E.D.C. was doomed.[5] But it was only after the meeting at Paris, and a sleepless night following it,[6] that Mendès agreed that Eden's arguments for Germany's entrance into NATO were decisive.

To help him gain a majority in the Chamber for the new policy, Eden stated at the Nine-Power conference (the 'Six' plus Britain, Canada, U.S.A.) in London (28 September to 1 October) that Britain would take on the 'unprecedented commitment' to maintain on the Continent indefinitely the forces which had been assigned to NATO. She would only withdraw them in the event of some acute overseas emergency; otherwise they would not be withdrawn except with the assent of a majority of the Brussels Treaty powers. At this London meeting the admission of Germany to NATO was agreed.

At another round of discussions in Paris (20–22 October) the Agreements were finally formulated. A Council of West European Union was set up to co-ordinate the defence arrangements of the Brussels powers; the occupation of Germany was to end; and a new

---

[1] Became Premier 18 June 1954. [2] Eden, 32.
[3] Eden, 151. (The date of the Brussels Treaty is misprinted as 1946.) [4] See p. 235.
[5] On 25 August 1954, just after the Brussels Conference of 19–22 August, when his attempt failed to get the other associates of the 'Six' to accept a watered-down version of E.D.C. [6] Eden, 160–1.

Statute for 'Europeanizing' the Saar was to be negotiated between France and Germany.

Even with all this preliminary work the outcome was still in doubt. On 24 December 1954 the French Chamber rejected the first paragraph of the Bill for ratifying the Paris Agreements. It was only when Mendès-France made ratification of the whole bill a vote of confidence that it was eventually passed, by 287 to 260 votes. It was a weak vote, parties being divided and 76 deputies abstaining, among them the former Foreign Minister, Robert Schuman. But with their ratification by the Council (Upper House) soon after, they duly came into force. Germany entered NATO and the Western Alliance was saved.

1954 was the year of the Hydrogen bomb, when the fearful power of this weapon, so much greater than that of Atom bombs, was revealed. Russia, having secured the secret of the A-bomb, could also, it was realized, produce an H-bomb as well. Inter-continental missiles, aeroplanes flying faster than sound, germ warfare and cobalt bombs—such means of swiftly destroying large areas of the world, perhaps of destroying human life altogether, made some of the older strategic concepts pale into insignificance. Such considerations may have played a part in swaying doubters and in accomplishing the shifts of policy which by the end of the year brought about the agreement on the vexed question of German rearmament.

The Founding of the Common Market

The Paris Agreements cleared the way for a further step towards economic and political integration, on the part of the Six who had established the European Community for Steel and Coal. Ten years after the war's end Europe had more than made good the war-time loss of production[1] (in productive capacity Western Europe had actually gained during the war). The war-time loss of manpower in the west had been more than made up during the war itself by the natural increase of population. The constant infusion of American aid had ensured a steady return to recovery, largely offsetting much of the heavy loss of capital in overseas countries,[2] which had so much changed the relation of Europe to the rest of the world.

---

[1] This had been restored by 1947.

[2] 'Rough estimates suggest a fall of over $500 million in western Europe's income from property between 1938 and 1950–51 even in money terms.'—United Nations:

Though as a whole Europe had lost income from these sources to the tune of $500 million a year, this problem was largely a British one. Britain's war-time indebtedness had grown by over £2½ billion, her borrowings from America and Canada amounted to a billion dollars, and she borrowed another $5·65 billion from these countries at the war's end. France's post-war borrowings had been much less (some $1·9 billion from America and Canada) as had those of other countries. But a new drive for strengthening Europe's economy was needed, if the balance of payments position was to be permanently improved, and the reconstruction loans paid off.

By 1954 destroyed buildings had mostly been replaced, though housing still lagged. Trade had considerably increased, but if the growth-rate of the better years was to be maintained, some new departure was needed. Hence the initiative of the Six for setting up a Common Market—in reality an economic union. On the political side, the believers in federation as the goal were convinced that a new move towards economic integration promised the quickest achievement of their objective.

During the three years since its inception the Coal and Steel Community had undoubtedly been an economic success, and it had gained much valuable experience in carrying through the necessary changes in the various fields—hitherto under exclusively national control—of prices, transport, investment, social services and the like. This experience could now be used on a larger scale, to adjust the systems of production, marketing and social welfare, along the whole gamut of economic policy of the Six, so that a genuinely free trade area could be established. Such was the aim of Jean Monnet from the economic point of view: to put into practice for the entire economy of the Six the measures of harmonization which had been worked out for the Coal and Steel Community, in order to eliminate the distortions (notably of the trade-pattern) which would otherwise take place when the common market was set up. From a political point of view, his aim and that of the other federalists of the European movement, was to establish a further range of supra-national institutions, which would integrate the Six, and eventually it was hoped Europe as a whole.

Economic Survey since the War (Geneva, 1953), 11. (Other figures from the same source.)

Since the common market for coal and steel had come into effect in 1953, there had been spectacular successes. From 1952–5 'the production of iron, and of crude steel and sheet-metal increased by about 20% to 25%, whereas trade inside the Community registered an increase of 170%'.[1] Though coal production increased by only 3 per cent, trade in coal went up by 43 per cent. This was due not so much to the abolition of tariffs and quantitative restrictions as to the suppression of various subventions, of double pricing and other discriminatory measures, and to the reduction of freight rates.

It was noticeable that the expansion of the internal market in no way affected adversely imports to and exports from the Community as a whole. Between 1952 and 1955 imports of steel doubled, while exports increased by 20 per cent. Coal imports only slightly increased, but exports were doubled. Though the steady general inflation made it impossible to lower prices, they were at least stabilized. Fears that concentration of enterprises and rationalization of production throughout the area would lead to the closing of a considerable number of mines and factories proved groundless, and where such closures took place, re-employment—sometimes with retraining—of the displaced workers presented no great difficulty.

Fortified by this encouraging experience the Six were now prepared to move towards internal free trade for all goods, in other words a complete customs union, together with the abolition of all restrictions hampering the flow of goods, capital and labour. Policies for harmonization in fiscal matters, transport, wages and social welfare which had already been tried out in the Coal and Steel Community, should also be applied.

Once again Jean Monnet was the moving spirit. 'His patience, his alertness, his untiring insistence, his curious inspired impulsiveness (and) his sense of timing'[2] bore their next crop of fruits. In November 1954 he resigned as President of the E.C.S.C. High Authority in order to devote himself more freely to the construction of a further stage of European Unity. The following October he announced the formation of the Action Committee for the United States of Europe,

---

[1] R. Racine (Ed.): *Demain l'Europe sans frontières?* (Les documents de Tribune Libre, Plon, Paris, 1958). Article: J. Kymmel: *Résultats et expériences de l'O.E.C.E. et de la C.E.C.A.*, 27.

[2] R. Mayne: *The Community of Europe* (Gollancz, 1962), 90.

'a solid and sober group of thirty-three leading representatives of all shades of authoritative political and trade-union opinion, except the extreme right and the Communists'.[1] By well-directed propaganda and by judicious prodding of the governments, Monnet and his committee played an essential part in making the integration of the Six a reality.

A start had already been made by Benelux, in February 1953, in establishing an economic union of the three countries—a logical development from the customs union which their governments had decided on while in exile during the war years. Their experts, together with those of the other three—many of them Monnet's disciples—discussed the questions involved in the economic union of the Six, and worked out blue-prints, in a number of sessions extending from the latter part of 1954 to June of the following year. By then matters were far enough advanced for the Foreign Ministers of the Six to meet at Messina, where a committee was set up under Paul-Henri Spaak, Belgium's Foreign Minister and doyen of the European Movement, to plan the further details. Though Britain sent two officials to take part in the discussions, the government's policy was to keep out of such a plan of integration, and Britain was not one of the signatories to the Treaty of Rome (25 March 1957).

By this Treaty (ratified by the end of the year) the European Economic Community (E.E.C.) was set up, together with the European Atomic Energy Committee (Euratom). The aim of E.E.C. (implicitly political) was to establish 'an enduring and closer union between European peoples'.[2] Besides a common market and common external tariff, which were to be arrived at by stages covering twelve or fifteen years, 'common policies will be devised for agriculture, for transport, for labour mobility, and for important sections of the economy'.

Euratom made a speedy start under the presidency of Louis Armand, another Monnet man best known for his spectacular modernization of the French Railways. Its business was the development of the peaceful uses of nuclear energy, under a highly qualified Scientific and Technical Committee, by stimulating investment in reactor projects, by facilitating supplies of raw and fissile materials, and by maintaining a nuclear common market.

[1] Mayne, 110.   [2] Preamble to Treaty of Rome.

The constitution of E.E.C.[1] was similar to that of the Coal and Steel Community: a Commission of nine members, appointed by (but independent of) the governments—this corresponds to the Coal and Steel Higher Authority, as the chief planning and executive agency; a Council of Ministers directly representing the governments, who had a say in the final decisions on all matters of importance; an Assembly drawn from the parliaments of the Six, with advisory powers (apart from their important right, as in the E.C.S.C., to dismiss the Commission by an adverse vote of confidence). There was also a Court of Justice, an Economic and Social Committee, a European investment bank and social fund, and an overseas development fund.

This last was related to the insistence by the French, which nearly wrecked the negotiations leading up to the Treaty, that the other participating governments should contribute to a fund for dependent overseas territories. The French were afraid that their industry would not be able to compete on equal terms with that of the other Community members if it had to bear the burden of subsidizing and investing in France's overseas territories—a financial commitment which had been a constant and a heavy one since the war. After 'a long and stormy session'[2] (for on this issue France carried her partners with her against their will) a form of association was agreed for territories which had been dependent on the Six: they would share in a common development fund, and have access to the Community market on specially favourable terms.

Britain's Ambiguous Position and EFTA

Once again, as in the case of the Coal and Steel Community, Britain was faced with an awkward choice. Should she come in and have the advantages of free access to a large and developing market (170 million population), and risk her Commonwealth preferences, her subsidized agriculture, and her special relationship with the Scandinavian countries and the U.S.A.? Or should she work out an alternative plan with her particular associates, and try to get the Six to come into that?

---

[1] That of Euratom was of a similar pattern.
[2] N. Beloff: *The General Says No—Britain's Exclusion from Europe* (Penguin, 1963), 93.

The latter was the policy she attempted in the proposals for a Free Trade Area (November 1956) covering all the O.E.E.C. countries. These, including the Six, would lower their tariffs against each other on industrial goods, and eliminate quotas, by stages until they abolished them after twelve or fifteen years. They would, however, maintain their tariffs against all other countries. Since these tariffs were of varying levels, it followed that goods from outside would be exported to the Free Trade Area by way of the country which had the lowest tariffs for the particular items concerned. This would cause distortion of existing trade patterns which could be offset, according to the British, by a system of marking the country of origin when goods were imported, and levying compensatory duties on them when they were imported into a third country for sale.

Such a scheme had been part of the proposals of the Spaak Report, which the Six had taken as their working basis at the time of the Messina Conference. It was favoured by the Dutch; the Belgians and Italians were neutral; the Germans were divided. Whereas Erhard wanted such an arrangement as best for business, Adenauer opposed it and put all his efforts into the integration of the Six, as the best solution politically. Britain, by refusing to come into the negotiations with the Six in 1956 on the basis of the Spaak Report, had deprived herself of a good deal of leverage, for lack of which she was unable to overcome French opposition. Furthermore, she had created the impression of being untrustworthy in keeping her commitments with the Continental countries: less than three years after she had promised to keep four divisions on the Continent, under the W.E.U. arrangements, until 1998, she withdrew one of them in 1957.

The French opposed the British plan in detail (the 'marking' scheme for imports seemed too cumbrous), but still more they were opposed to it in principle. The ancient rivalry between the two countries was not dead. Many Frenchmen, who had originally been luke-warm about the Common Market, became its ardent supporters when they realized that the alternative scheme might give the British an economic hegemony in Europe.

In any case the French fancied that Britain was trying to get the best of both worlds—access to low-tariff European markets while maintaining her Commonwealth preferences. Britain's refusal to consider advancing towards free trade in agricultural products seemed to underline her intentions: to keep her Commonwealth trading partners, 'featherbed' her farmers, and exclude Continental produce, just at the time when bulging French farm surpluses were beginning to need new outlets. Britain also refused to promise that she and the other Free Trade Association countries would harmonize their economic development and social welfare policies with those of the Six.[1] The failure of the other countries to adjust to the harmonization programme of the Six might undo all the good—for the Six—which that programme was designed to effect, and might give them precisely such advantages which the programme was designed to offset. If distortions of trade detrimental to that of the Six occurred, the F.T.A. countries might find themselves enjoying most of the advantages of Common Market membership without having to shoulder the commitments.

This was all part, as the Six saw it, of Britain's refusal to accept a supra-national authority where her own economy was concerned. The federalists disliked this opposition to the political aims for European integration. A further fear, on the part of the French, was that their industrial products would be swamped by those of Britain, on top of the serious challenge which they expected from German exports. But in general there was disillusionment about Britain, whose policies seemed selfishly parochial. Her 'socialism' had proved to be national[2] and exclusive, not international and European, and her free trade drive was defensive, without any of the idealism for a new order which inspired the leaders for closer integration. Robert Marjolin, who as a champion of Britain's participation in Europe had become Secretary-General of O.E.E.C., resigned from that post and took up a position with the Six,[3] in the conviction that progress towards the new Europe would go farther and faster without Britain's centrifugal interventions.

---

[1] The British plan 'included no specific provisions for freedom of movement of persons, services and capital; it did not extend to the overseas associated countries and territories; and it contained none of the other provisions . . . such as the Social Fund, the Investment Fund and the measures of harmonization'.—Kitzinger: *The Challenge of the Common Market*, 94.

[2] 'The gentle and easy-going British Labour leaders would have been shocked to be called "national socialists"; but they were in truth incapable of imagining the two adjectives apart.' (N. Beloff, op. cit., 92.)

[3] A Vice-President of the E.E.C. Commission; formerly one of Monnet's associates of the French Plan.

The matter was, however, in doubt until the end of the Fourth Republic. American insistence that the arrangements of O.E.E.C. and the principles of the General Agreement on Tariffs and Trade (G.A.T.T.)[1] be respected as far as possible, helped to keep the door open for an agreement between the Six and the 'outer Seven' (Britain and her associates). With the entering into force of the Common Market, the first round of tariff-cutting by the Six (10 per cent) was extended to all the O.E.E.C. countries. Reginald Maudling, who was in charge of the negotiations from the British side, tried to keep them going,[2] but with the installation of General de Gaulle once again in power (May 1958) they took a turn for the worse. The first of the General's famous 'No's' was spoken by his Minister of Information, Soustelle, on 14 November 1958—the British plan was flatly, even contemptuously, rejected. When, later, the European Free Trade Area (EFTA) was set up, it was without the Six. With the Communist organization of the east, Europe had already split into two economic and political areas; now it looked like splitting into three.

[1] In 1947 twenty-three member countries of a Committee of the Economic and Social Council of the U.N. entered into the G.A.T.T. 'The GATT may be described as a multilateral contract, which lays down a common code of conduct in international trade, provides machinery for reducing and stabilising tariffs and the opportunity for regular consultation on trade problems.'—*Statesman's Year Book*, 1960. (See whole article.)

[2] 'For several months this amateur diplomat brashly tried to play off the Germans against the French, and thereby piled up implacable hostility in Bonn, Paris, and, most of all, at the Headquarters of the European Community, which depended for its survival on Franco-German friendship.'—N. Beloff, 80.

NOTE

THE SAAR

Under the Statute of 1947, which gave the Saar autonomy while remaining in economic union with France, its recovery was relatively rapid, and the government of Johannes Hoffman (Christian People's Party) maintained itself until 1954. By then the demand by the Saarlanders for reintegration in Germany was difficult to resist, but as part of the arrangements for according the Federal Republic full sovereignty after the collapse of the E.D.C. negotiations, a new Statute was negotiated by Adenauer with the French Government for 'Europeanizing' the Saar. It was to be put under the newly-created West European Union (October 1954), the arrangements to be ratified after a referendum held in the Saar. In the referendum (October 1955) the Saarlanders rejected the Statute. In the following year the French accepted that the Saar should return to Germany, and this took place on 1 January 1957. In 1950 the Saar mines had been leased to France for 50 years, and after the return of the Saar to Germany France continued to exploit the Warndt coalfield.

22: Decolonization and the Return of de Gaulle

The Waning of Imperialism

The Second World War shattered the empires of the West European powers. With the war's end these empires were still in being (with the exception of the Italian), though in some places more fighting was needed if the writ of the colonial government was to run. In fact, in such places, notably Indonesia and Indo-China, the position of the former colonial régimes was never properly restored. Even those territories, like the French and British possessions in Africa, which had neither been a battleground nor occupied by another power, were feeling the blasts of the new wind of independence.

The relation of Western Europe to the rest of the world had changed. The one great colonial power of Eastern Europe, Russia, had seemingly improved its position, but not so the Western powers. The British decision to grant independence to India, resulting in the setting up of India and Pakistan (1947), undermined the hopes which were still entertained of restoring the pre-war position elsewhere.

The independence movement in the Indian sub-continent had a considerable history. In view of the acceptance in principle, before the war, of independence (in the form of Dominion Status) as the eventual outcome of British policy, it was practically inevitable that, after the war, this conclusion would not be long delayed. Independence was catching. The spectacle of Europeans indulging in another fratricidal war had lowered their prestige, while the Japanese, as the occupying power in the East Indies and Indo-China, as well as in Burma, Malaya and Hong-Kong, greatly stimulated the independence movements in those countries. This was partly by direct means (e.g. the handing over of arms to the inhabitants at the time of the Japanese defeat), partly by way of a reaction—sometimes stimulated by the Communists—against being occupied at all. The realities of the situation in India, having once been accepted, could not be denied in Burma and Ceylon. These too received their independence (1948).

These actions and reactions affected particularly the French position in Indo-China. Pushed out of their Mandates in the Levant by the British, it was a point of honour for many Frenchmen, and especially for de Gaulle, to retrieve the French Empire in the east.

Though the Japanese had occupied parts of Indo-China, and had incorporated it economically into their 'Co-prosperity Sphere', Admiral Decoux, as the Vichy representative, had succeeded in keeping the French administration intact for most of the war. It was overthrown by the Japanese in March 1945, but they did not long enjoy the advantages of direct rule owing to their surrender to the Allies the following August. Thereafter, while distributing arms to various insurgents, they handed over the territory to the British in the south and to the Chinese (under Chiang Kai-shek) in the north.

The Beginning of the Indo-China War

The French people as a whole were not greatly concerned with, and were singularly uninformed about, affairs in Indo-China. Initiative was largely left to the men on the spot. General Leclerc, the army Commander in Indo-China, was prepared to follow a flexible line and make an arrangement with the Vietnamese leader,[1] Ho Chi Minh, which would give Indo-China a considerable measure of autonomy. But the policy which prevailed was that of the High Commissioner, Admiral Thierry D'Argenlieu, who was determined to follow a tough line with the Vietnamese, in order to preserve the maximum control for France. Though Ho Chi Minh was a known Communist—he had attended the Socialist Congress in Tours (1920), where the Communists had broken away from the Socialists[2]—at this time he seemed ready to do a deal with the French. To his north were the Nationalist Chinese (Mao had not yet taken over), and to offset their ambitions regarding northern Indo-China he was prepared to make an arrangement with the French. This would have involved autonomy, preserving there the gains of the revolution which had swept virtually the whole country in 1945, getting rid of

---

[1] Ho Chi Minh had become President of the Republic of Vietnam. He was the leader of the Viet-Minh, an organization created by the Communist Party of Indo-China (of which he was also the leader), in September 1941: the 'Front for the Independence of Viet-Nam' (*Viet-Nam Doc Lap Dong Minh*, shortened to Viet-Minh).— P. Devillers: *Histoire du Viêt-Nam* (1940–52) (Editions du Seuil, 1952), 97–8.

[2] Werth: 1940–55, 327.

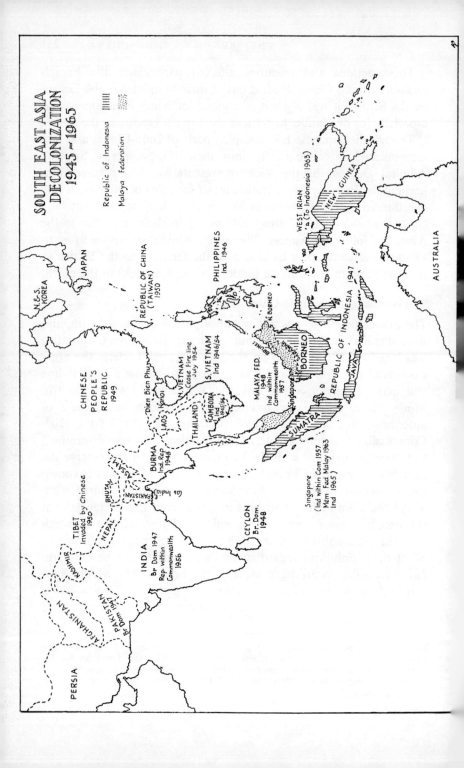

SOUTH EAST ASIA
DECOLONIZATION
1945 – 1965

Republic of Indonesia
Malaya Federation

N.&.S.
KOREA

JAPAN

REPUBLIC OF CHINA
(TAIWAN)
1950

CHINESE PEOPLE'S
REPUBLIC
1949

TIBET
Invaded by Chinese
1950

KASHMIR

AFGHANISTAN

NEPAL

BHUTAN

ASSAM

PERSIA

PAKISTAN
Br Dom
1947

PAKISTAN
(as India)

INDIA
Br Dom 1947
Rep. within
Commonwealth
1956

BURMA
Ind. Rep.
1948

LAOS
Ind.
1945/54

N. VIETNAM
Dien Bien Phu
Hanoi
Cease Fire line
July 1954

CAMBODIA
Ind.
1945/54

S. VIETNAM
Ind 1946/54

THAILAND

CEYLON
Br. Dom.
1948

PHILIPPINES
Ind. 1946

MALAYA FED.
1948
Ind. within
Commonwealth
1957

Singapore

BRUNEI

N. BORNEO

BORNEO

SUMATRA

REPUBLIC OF INDONESIA 1947

JAVA

WEST IRIAN
(To Indonesia 1963)

NEW GUINEA

Singapore
(Ind within Com 1957
Mem Fed Malay 1963
Ind 1965)

AUSTRALIA

the mandarins and notables, establishing 'People's Committees', and putting through various social reforms.

The French took over from the British in the south before the Chinese evacuated the north. Ho Chi Minh manoeuvred skilfully, using the Chinese presence to put pressure on the French, while leaning on the French to the extent that they would ensure the departure of the Chinese. This was the background of the delicate diplomacy which took place during February and March 1946, between Ho Chi Minh and the French, and between the French and the Chinese. Out of this came the agreement of 6 March 1946, which might have provided a working partnership between France and Vietnam. The accord was partly due to the absence of d'Argenlieu at Paris, so that Leclerc, as his Deputy, was able to follow his own line which he worked out with Jean Sainteny, the French pleni-potentiary at Hanoi, who was in full agreement with him.

By this the French Government recognized Vietnam as 'a free state' (un état libre), with its own government, parliament, army and finances, a member of (faisant partie de) the Indo-Chinese Federation and the French Union. The form of union of the three territories which comprised Vietnam (Tongking, Annam, Cochin-China) was to be regulated after the peoples concerned had expressed their will by a referendum.

On its side the government of Vietnam was prepared to allow free entry to the French army when it came to take over the territory north of the 16th parallel occupied by the Chinese. A further con-ference would settle outstanding questions, such as Vietnamese representation abroad, and the safeguarding of French cultural and economic interests.[1]

Both signatories would take steps to end hostilities elsewhere. This referred mainly to Cochin-China, where Viet-Minh guerillas were controlling the countryside (and continued to do so after hostilities ceased in October 1946).

Just before this agreement was negotiated, the French secured a promise from Chiang Kai-shek's government to withdraw the Chinese garrisons from the north. Once French troops had taken their place and particularly after Leclerc's departure later in 1946, d'Argenlieu and his backers among the French 'ultras' proceeded to

[1] Devillers, 205–26; Werth, 333–4.

apply their tough line. The post-de Gaulle governments in France vacillated. They were often deliberately kept in the dark by the French at the Indo-Chinese capital, Saigon, where movements of troops and naval elements were planned. During Ho Chi Minh's abortive visit to France in June–September 1946 the stage was set for action, which took the form of an 'ultimatum' presented by the French Commander at Haiphong, Colonel Dèbes, to the local Vietnamese authorities. On its expiring at 10 a.m. on 23 November 1946 French troops invaded the Chinese and Vietnamese quarters; the cruiser *Suffren* opened fire, and 6,000 people were killed or burned to death in the shelling.[1]

This massacre was followed by another, on the night of 19–20 December at Hanoi, when forty Europeans were killed by Vietnamese and two hundred seized as hostages. This was the beginning of eight years of war in Indo-China, which cost the French 95,000 men and £3,000 million.[2] There is some evidence that it could have been stopped early in 1947, but d'Argenlieu and his backers were determined to build up an area of complete French control in Cochin-China and southern Annam, under the nominal sovereignty of the former Emperor, Bao Dai. From this they hoped to expand French control northwards, linking up with Haiphong and other key points which they possessed. The Communist take-over of China in 1949 frustrated their plans. Thereafter arms and other forms of support could easily reach Ho Chi Minh and his military commander, General Giap.[3] Even without this aid to their opponents, it is doubtful whether the French could have mastered Indo-China, or having mastered it, held it for long, in the face of the rising tide of nationalism and Communism in Asia.

The French Union

What the French wished to do was to incorporate Indo-China in their new version of empire, the French Union.

On paper the French Union appeared to be more like the British

[1] Werth, 339.

[2] Of these only 19,000 were French. The remainder were men of the Foreign Legion and 'coloured' troops.—A. Werth: *The Strange History of Pierre Mendès-France and the Great Conflict over French North Africa* (Barrie, 1957), 87.

[3] His wife and small child had, in 1939, been sent to prison, where they died.—Werth, 328.

Commonwealth than the old French Empire, and that doubtless was the impression it was meant to create. In practice the element of partnership was illusory. French control—or the attempt to maintain it—remained the fact.

The French Union was set up at the end of 1946. Three institutions at Paris had a say in its affairs: the National Assembly (Parliament), among whose 627 deputies sat 53 for the overseas territories. Of these 53 a certain number were Frenchmen, representing the *colons* rather than the native inhabitants. Algeria had its representatives in the Assembly, though not included in the 53, since it was administered as a Department of Metropolitan France.

The other two institutions of the Union represented its shop-window. Overseas delegates numbered half those in the Assembly of the French Union, but it had only advisory powers and little importance. The same was true of the Higher Council, which anyway rarely met. Effective control lay with Parliament and the Ministries concerned with the various territories.

French North Africa

It was within this somewhat amorphous body that the French proposed to incorporate the states of Indo-China[1] and its other overseas territories. But though many of the pronouncements of French politicians about the Union were pleasing to the inhabitants of '*France d'Outre-mer*', the fact that the reality of power rested with the Metropolis was not. Tunisia and Morocco refused to enter the Union, taking their stand on the treaties of 1881 and 1912, which governed their relations with France. Algeria, in theory a part of Metropolitan France, was *ipso facto* in the Union already, but the Sétif revolt of May 1945, suppressed with thousands of casualties, showed the strength of the nationalist movement.[2] An attempt to satisfy Moslem (Nationalist) opinion was made by the French Government in the Algerian Statute of 1947, but opposition by the French *colons* ensured that it was never properly applied.

Algeria was France's Ireland, where a million Frenchmen lived a privileged life among a Moslem population of some 8 million in 1947 (a million or so more a decade later, owing to the high Moslem

[1] Vietnam, Cambodia and Laos.
[2] D. Pickles: *Algeria and France* (Methuen, 1963), 27.

birth-rate). This life they were, for the most part, determined to maintain in practice, whatever concessions (largely theoretical) which might be accorded their Moslem neighbours. Just as the Unionists maintained that Ireland must remain a part of Britain, so the *colons* maintained that Algeria must remain a part of France. The Moslems could have equality before the law (as well as their personal status as Moslems), they could have French citizenship and education—but when it came to questions of government, the French always had to be in a majority.

In all three North African countries the die-hards extended the days of power and privilege for the French, though briefly, and at a cost. When at last they were obliged to yield, they yielded more, and more quickly than if a policy of bringing the people of North Africa on to autonomy and partnership had been gradually and deliberately pursued. As it was, these countries achieved independence in conditions less favourable for nation-building than might otherwise have been the case.

The Geneva Conference and the Indo-China War

When Pierre Mendès-France became Premier in June 1954, he was determined to settle the outstanding questions in Indo-China and North Africa, as well as those connected with E.D.C. and the defence of Europe. The most sensational part of his investiture speech was his pledge to bring the Indo-Chinese war to an end within four weeks —if not, he would resign.

Two months previously France had suffered a crushing defeat, despite a growing infusion of American arms and money. French attempts to gain support from the local people, by recalling Bao Dai as Emperor of Vietnam, and by setting up Sisavang Vong as King of Laos, had failed in their objects. Vietnamese battalions had been trained to fight with the French, but this gain was more than counter-balanced by the fact that the French had been obliged to evacuate Langson on the northern border with China, through which, after 1948, Communist aid for Ho Chi Minh could freely pour.

The last gamble of the militarists in Vietnam was to seize Dien Bien Phu, a post well in the rear of the opposing Viet-Minh forces. It was expected to attract the Viet-Minh guerillas—once they came down from the surrounding hills, they could be got at. While destroying them in detail, the French would continually raid the Viet-Minh communications. The plan failed. Dien Bien Phu was costly to hold—it had been seized by paratroops, and could only be supplied by air. By January 1954 it was closely besieged. But the Viet-Minh did not attack in parties, risking annihilation—General Giap brought up formidable artillery, which the French did not know he possessed. When, after an artillery barrage, the first attack came (13 March) the fury of the Viet-Minh suicide-squads and of their hand-to-hand fighting brought them the capture of a French stronghold. Despite three battalions of reinforcements flying in, the French lost further strongholds, until by 7 May capitulation became inevitable. 1,220 French and 14,000 Vietnamese and other troops surrendered.

The position of the whole French expeditionary force in Indo-China became precarious. On 8 May the question of a settlement was broached at the Geneva Conference, which, since assembling on 26 April, had been wrestling with the question of Korea. The conference had been called owing to a tacit agreement between Russia and Britain that it was time to call a halt in the Far East.[1] To this agreement, and to the working partnership between Molotov and Eden (who alternated as chairmen), the conference largely owed its ultimate success in negotiating an armistice in Indo-China, and the basis of a settlement there.

At the same time even this success—necessarily limited though it was—would not have been achieved without the skill and drive of Mendès-France. The first part of the conference had taken place during the previous (Laniel) government, with Bidault as Foreign Minister. His hesitations had made it difficult for Eden to withstand the impulsive proposals made to the French by Secretary of State Dulles, for throwing in American military support. This would have risked widening (or 'internationalizing') the conflict, and would have turned India, Burma and the other Asian countries against any settlement acceptable to the West and to the security system for South East Asia, which both Britain and America had in view.[2] The threat of further American intervention may have, however, played

[1] States represented during the discussions on Indo-China were Britain, France, U.S.A., Russia, the Chinese People's Republic, Vietnam, Viet-Minh (Ho Chi Minh's government), Laos and Cambodia.

[2] Ultimately negotiated as the South East Asia Treaty Organization (S.E.A.T.O.) (September, 1954).

a part in bringing the Russians round to support a settlement: a nuclear war was a possibility which they were not ready to face. Eden's comment was that this was the first international conference at which he was 'sharply conscious of the deterrent power of the hydrogen bomb. I was grateful for it. I do not believe that we should have got through the Geneva Conference and avoided a major war without it.'[1]

Mendès-France was as hard a bargainer as Chou En-lai, the Chinese Foreign Minister. His toughness helped to bring agreement over the issue which had deadlocked the conference for weeks—the composition of the armistice commission. When it was agreed that this should be composed of representatives of India, Canada and Poland (18 July), the other matters were settled comparatively quickly, though not until a few hours after the deadline of 20 July which the French Premier had laid down.

The French had to abandon all northern Indo-China (Tongking) to the Viet-Minh, the demarcation line being fixed just south of the 17th parallel; Viet-Minh forces were to be evacuated from the south; Laos and Cambodia were to be neutralized; a general election was to take place in both zones of Vietnam in July 1956; and France's cultural and economic rights were to be preserved. It was the end of a chapter, though not of the story; but the next phase concerned France less and the U.S.A. more, with America taking France's place in another costly attempt to prevent the expansion of Viet-Minh over the rest of Indo-China.

Independence for Tunisia

Mendès-France also broke the deadlock over Tunisia. There the reforms agreed upon by Schuman in 1950 with the Chenik government had not been applied, owing to the opposition of the settlers. The latter's organization, Présence Française, had succeeded in securing the appointment of a Resident-General whom they could rely upon to maintain the *status quo*. The resulting ferment led to

[1] *Memoirs (Full Circle)*, 123. Mendès-France credited Eden with preventing this disaster. 'Eden, of course, was wonderful, and he was a great help throughout. And I honestly believe that, if it hadn't been for the British government, we might really have had World War III at the time when Bidault and Dulles and (Admiral) Radford were planning their mass raid on the Vietminh forces round Dien Bien Phu.'—Werth: *The Strange History of Pierre Mendès-France*, 92.

riots and French punitive expeditions, to the murder of the trade union leader Ferhat Hashed, and to the exile (later internment in France) of Habib Bourguiba, leader of the Neo-Destour independence party. By 1954 partisan warfare against the French was being waged by the Fellaghas.

Barely a week after securing the Indo-China settlement Mendès-France flew to Tunis (31 July 1954) where he assured the Bey that France would recognize the internal autonomy of Tunisia, 'without mental reservations or ulterior motives'. It was the first move in creating a new relationship between France and Tunisia. Before long Bourguiba returned, independence was proclaimed (20 March 1956), and—apart from the question of the base at Bizerta—most matters between the two countries were satisfactorily regulated.

Independence for Morocco

Mendès-France did not have long enough in office to do much about Morocco (he resigned in February 1955). There the independence movement (Istiqlal) had bothered the French since 1943. In December 1950 the High Commissioner, General Juin, expelled the Istiqlal members of the Conseil du Gouvernement. Since this body was dominated by the settlers, this made little practical difference, but for the progressive Sultan, Sidi Mohammed ben Yussef, it was a matter of principle. For some months he refused to sign the decrees presented to him by Juin, in effect depriving them of legality, and in 1952 he refused to endorse a plan of reforms proposed by the French.

The centre of French power was Casablanca, a modern boom town surrounded by *bidonvilles*.[1] From there the Prefect, M. Boniface, and the other diehard leaders organized a coup against the Sultan, by using his old enemy, El Glaoui, Pasha of Marrakesh, and a number of other notables, to demand his deposition (August 1953).

After two years it was clear that the Sultan's successor, an aged relative named Moulay Mohammed ben Arafa, had not the authority to fulfil the minimal role which was all the *colons* demanded of him. Unrest mounted even in the traditional pro-Glaoui and anti-Sultan areas, where the Berbers provided many of France's best troops. Some Europeans were massacred by Berbers, others—who were liberals—by diehard settlers. A firm but liberal policy embarked on

[1] Shanty towns built out of petrol cans.

by a new Resident-General, Gilbert Grandval, in June 1955, envisaging the possibility of the Sultan's return, was strongly opposed by an alliance of the diehard settlers and army. These connived at a riot of the local Europeans which threatened to paralyse Grandval's administration. Having called in the army, declaring Casablanca a Military Region, Grandval found that the generals would not co-operate. The Acting Supreme Commander, General Miguel, who was carrying out anti-terrorist drives (*ratissages*), refused even to send him reports. Other generals resigned, and the resignations only ceased (and were subsequently withdrawn) when Grandval himself resigned, and a Resident-General amenable to the diehards and generals was appointed in his stead.

This, however, did nothing to end the growing anarchy. The mass of the people still regarded the exiled Sultan as their ruler, and would accept no government in the name of Ben Arafa or a Council of Regency, which the French tried to set up in his stead. While the French were at a loss what to do, the deadlock was broken by a change of heart on the part of El Glaoui, who decided to ask for the recall of the deposed Sultan from his exile at Madagascar. On the Sultan's arrival in France (November 1955) he was reinstated with the title of King Mohammed V. El Glaoui sought his pardon, prostrating himself before his sovereign in a dramatic audience at Fontainebleau. In March 1956 Morocco received its full independence, after negotiations with France, a step which the other protecting power, Spain, was obliged to endorse. Tangier, technically Moroccan territory, though under a (preponderantly French) international régime, was reintegrated in the Moroccan Empire.

Algeria and the Return of de Gaulle

There were Frenchmen who believed that independence for Tunisia and Morocco was necessary, so that France would be free to concentrate her strength on what was most essential to her in North Africa—Algeria. Here it was not only the settlers, but the army too, which had a vested interest. Once the revolt broke out in the Aurès Mountains in November 1954, many of the officers felt emotionally involved in bringing the affair to a conclusion which would preserve Algeria for France: after the defeat of 1940 and the *débacle* in Indo-China, Algeria was the place where they must not fail. The paratroops of all ranks, who had borne the brunt of the fighting in Indo-China, shared in this attitude.

As the war went on, these elements in the army were increasingly prepared to take matters into their own hands. They had already demonstrated this during the *Affaire des Généraux* in Morocco, which was something like a dress rehearsal for Algeria. In Morocco the alliance of the army and diehards had been frustrated in their attempt to run the country themselves, owing to El Glaoui's rallying to the Sultan. In Algeria there was no such rallying-point for the Moslems. The country had no traditional dynasty. A former part of the Turkish Empire, such administrative coherence as it had was due to the work of the French. Algeria had been submitted for a longer time, and more intensively than Tunisia and Morocco, to French cultural and economic influences. Its Arab quality had weakened, whereas French education and most other elements of the French way of life were valued. Algeria was the territory where the expressed aim of French policy, assimilation, might have been achieved.

But assimilation meant, sooner or later, integration. This was accepted too late by the French, and then half-heartedly. Though in theory the coastal areas of Algeria were Departments of Metropolitan France, in practice the Moslem inhabitants were second-class citizens. They did not have the political rights nor the 'career open to talents' of the French, nor did they share their economic and social advantages.[1] Though many Algerians served in the army (60,000 in 1956), only 400 of these became officers (as against 30,000 French officers). Of the 864 high administrative posts in Algeria, only eight were held by Moslems.[2]

Even as late as 1947, if the Statute of that year had been properly applied, it might have been a sufficient instalment of equality to make the idea of integration acceptable as a policy for the Moslems. The revolt of 1954 showed that this was no longer the case. An attempt by Mendès-France to apply the Statute early in 1955 was the occasion of his fall. In September of that year 61 Moslems, mostly moderates, who were elected members of the institutions which the French had set up, declared that 'the policy of so-called integration

---

[1] Though the Jews did, except for a time when their status was altered during the Vichy régime. Moslems, for instance, did not have the social security benefits of the French.

[2] D. Pickles: *Algeria and France* (Methuen, 1963), 54.

which . . . has never been sincerely carried out, is now out of date'.[1]

The war gradually spread. By mid-1955 it was clear that there was an 'Algerian Liberation Army', whose activities were a serious threat to French rule. To the riots and massacres the French replied with the burning and bombing of villages.

Next year, 1956, with the Socialist Guy Mollet back as Premier, another attempt was made to come to terms with the Algerians. Mollet appointed the 79-year-old General Catroux as Resident Minister in Algeria, a man who was among the most liberal of the followers of de Gaulle. Before his installation Mollet visited Algiers to be greeted with boos and rotten tomatoes as he laid a wreath on the war memorial (6 February 1956). The crowd of 10,000 Europeans were only stopped from rioting when the guards threw tear-gas bombs. Mollet's 'moment of truth' resulted in replacing Catroux by the tough Robert Lacoste.

By 1958 Lacoste, the civilian diehards and the paratroop generals were running a war at £2 million a day—a war which had already cost £2,000 million, 7,000 French lives, and the lives of Algerians reckoned in hundreds of thousands. It had burgeoned into a hideous system, organized by the army and its collaborators, complete with kidnappings and tortures, both of Moslems and opposition Europeans, in approved Gestapo style. As a side-issue, more damaging for Britain than for France, it had played its part in provoking the Suez War[2] (October–November 1956), since in the eyes of the now 'converted' Mollet and his government, it was encouragement and arms from Cairo which kept the Algerian rebels fighting.

Good offices by Tunisia and Morocco had been rejected—the door on these was slammed, when, without government knowledge, the plane carrying Ahmed Ben Bella and four other Algerian leaders from Morocco to Tunisia, was diverted to Algiers where they were imprisoned (October 1956). Not surprisingly, France's relations with Mohammed V (whose guests the Algerians had been) were nearly ruptured. Relations with Tunisia were likewise threatened when the village of Sakhiet, just inside Tunisia was bombed (February 1957). It was suspected of harbouring F.L.N.[3] (Algerian liberation) fighters and being a base for their supplies—but horror was aroused, not only in Tunisia but in France and throughout the world, by the fact

[1] Pickles, 34.   [2] See following section.   [3] Front de Libération Nationale.

that half the seventy-five people killed were children whose school was hit.

The government of the day, under the premiership of Félix Gaillard, were at sixes and sevens over Sakhiet. The coalition on which it was based began to break up, and it was finally toppled by the angry speech of Jacques Soustelle, who had been High Commissioner in Algeria (January 1955–January 1956). Soustelle was a former Gaullist who, since his Algerian experience, had been converted to the 'integrationist' policy, which was now becoming fashionable with the diehard and army leaders at Algiers.

The fact that four weeks elapsed before another government was formed on 13 May 1958 underlined the instability of the Fourth Republic. Political crisis in Paris was marked by increasing ferment in Algiers. Fury had been aroused by American efforts—Robert Murphy being once more on mission, with a British colleague Harold Beeley—to mediate between France and Algeria. The Americans' threat of 'internationalizing' the affair was taken to mean that they wished to replace France in North Africa. On the day that the Pflimlin government took office the European teddy-boys of Algiers invaded the Government-General building. How far the authorities connived at this action is not known. General Massu, the paratroop commander, though possibly not privy to the coup, took over the government building and formed a Committee of Public Safety. This body, defying orders from the President and Premier, took the law into its own hands, dismissing numerous officials who did not share its views, and acted as the independent government of Algeria.

On 17 May Soustelle arrived in Algiers, after smuggling himself out of France in the boot of a car. He called for an integrationist policy for Algeria, and for de Gaulle to take over the Government of France. He evidently wished to use de Gaulle to attain his aim of *Algérie française*: in his person the army and Gaullist networks united. De Gaulle was not prepared to be used by Soustelle or anyone else. But the two main networks, together with other plotters in Algeria who favoured his return to power, formed a combination which it was difficult for the politicians in Paris, for the French people in general, and even for de Gaulle himself to resist.

For in France as well as in Algeria there were an increasing number of people who felt that de Gaulle alone could save the situation. 'De Gaulle was to become . . . a rallying point for those anxious to preserve their colonialist privileges in Algeria; for those anxious to overthrow the Republic in France; for those thinking in terms of an authoritarian or presidential régime; even for those (mostly in Algeria) who were planning a military-Fascist dictatorship in France. And, later, for all those for whom de Gaulle was a "lesser evil".'[1] At a much publicized press conference on 19 May he said he was ready to place himself at the head of the French Republic. 'Now I shall return to my village and shall remain there at the country's disposal.'[2]

He did not have long to wait. A week later the paratroop government of Algiers seized Corsica, and seemed to threaten a coup in France itself ('*les Paras à Paris!*' was the cry at Algiers). An invasion of Tunisia was threatened. Even the Communists began to feel that a stronger man than Pflimlin was needed to save the situation—and despite the considerable firmness he had shown, he was himself ready to yield his place. The various other parties had hectic consultations. The outcome was assured when Mollet and his Socialists decided to accept de Gaulle on his terms: six months of plenary powers, to be followed by constitutional reforms and a referendum. On 29 May President Coty summoned de Gaulle 'to set up a Government of National Safety and to bring about within a short time a fundamental reform of our institutions'.

De Gaulle was determined that if he returned to power it would be on a basis of strict legality. He spent time, before his investiture speech in Parliament, discussing matters with the politicians 'in an easy-going, often even jocular vein; many of them left, feeling both puzzled and charmed by the man'.[3] It was an older and more mellow de Gaulle than the President who had resigned in 1946, or the leader of the abortive 'Rally' of 1947–53. When it came to the vote on his investment, the majority was 329–224 (1 June 1958). It was a de Gaulle who would not only give France the stability she so much needed, but would end the Algerian war on conditions which neither the diehards nor the 'paras' expected.

[1] A. Werth: *The de Gaulle Revolution* (Hale, 1960), 44.
[2] Ibid., 110.
[3] Werth: *The de Gaulle Revolution*, 164.

The Suez War

The Suez War marked an important stage in the changing relations of Europe (or at least 'the West') with the rest of the world, and in the decolonization process.

Egypt had progressively gained its independence from Britain after the termination of the Protectorate in 1922. Its last vestiges were to be found in the continued existence of the British Suez Canal base, serviced by civilian technicians, in accordance with the Anglo-Egyptian agreement of 1954. By this agreement British military forces were withdrawn from the Canal Zone. Colonel Gamal Abdel Nasser, who had taken over power after the coup against King Farouk in 1952, was continuing previous Egyptian policy of making Egypt the spearhead of the Arab front against Israel, and at the same time had begun playing off the West (principally America and Britain) against Russia, in bids for their favour in return for his support. The key issue in 1956 was the financing of the High Dam at Aswan, for which there had been promises of both Russian and American (with some British) help. But when in July Nasser finally turned to America for the loan which he believed had been offered, Dulles as Secretary of State refused it, and Britain followed suit in withdrawing her offer.

A week later (26 July 1956), Nasser nationalized the Suez Canal, which was owned and operated, under a nineteenth-century concession, by the mainly French Suez Canal Company. He declared that the profits which Egypt would thereby gain from the Canal would finance the building of the High Dam. At the same time he promised compensation to the Company, while threatening imprisonment for any of the staff who left their jobs. Later when the threat was withdrawn and most of the foreign staff left, the Canal continued to function smoothly under Egyptian management, despite prophecies of disaster by the French directors and managers.

It had apparently been the intention of the Egyptian Government in any case to take over the Canal before the expiry of the concession in 1968. The foreign character of the Company, with its headquarters in France, and the large sums of interest which it furnished annually to its foreign shareholders, together with its monopolistic control of the Canal, made it appear in Egyptian eyes as just another relic of the colonial era. The view was that the Company would run down its physical assets before the eventual date for handing them over to Egypt, besides investing the bulk of its swelling capital elsewhere. It was not trusted. Embryonic staff plans were made for taking it over, but Nasser's need of a prestige blow greatly advanced the operation.

Eden, Prime Minister since April 1955, claimed that this was 'an act of plunder which threatens the livelihood of many nations', and that 'the lives of the great trading nations of the world' might be 'strangled at any moment by some interruption of the free passage of the Canal'.[1] Economic sanctions were applied, and the British and French governments prepared naval and military action, first for seizing Alexandria and striking at Cairo—which was called off—then for seizing the Canal zone, and in any case toppling Nasser.

Dulles tried to put the brake on, while yet taking steps to help the British get some satisfaction along the lines of obliging Egypt to accept some kind of international authority in place of the Suez Canal Company. He was against any resort to force. One of his proposals, the setting up of the Suez Canal Users Association, was in his view to put pressure on Egypt by virtually taking over the Canal, whereas in Eden's view it was a means of supplying the *casus belli* (in the event of Egyptian co-operation with S.C.U.A. being refused) on which Britain and France could intervene militarily.

Just as American pressure for a peaceful solution seemed to be bearing fruit in meetings of the Security Council of the U.N., where Britain, France and Egypt were moving towards an agreement, the Israelis notified the French that they were preparing a move against Egypt or Jordan, to counter the incursions and terrorism of the fedayeen (guerillas) from the Egyptian-held Gaza strip and from Jordan. At a secret meeting which Eden and Selwyn Lloyd had with the French Premier and Foreign Minister (Mollet and Pineau) on 16 October, it seems that the decision was made to intervene militarily at the time of the Israeli attack. A successful attempt was then made to persuade the Israelis not to launch their attack on Jordan, the implication being that when their expected attack took place, it would be against Egypt.[2]

---

[1] Broadcast of 8 August 1956.
[2] There were other compelling reasons why Britain and France could not countenance an Israeli attack on Jordan, notably that Jordan would claim British support in accord-

THE INVASION OF EGYPT 267

The degree of collusion between the French and the British on the one hand and the Israelis on the other cannot be known until further —and frank—memoirs of the principals are published, or until the archives of the respective states are opened. But it is known that naval and troop movements for intervention by France and Britain began before the Israeli attack was launched. By the end of October there was a formidable concentration of British and French troops, paratroops and planes at Cyprus, while the naval component of an attacking force (which could not be assembled at Cyprus for lack of harbourage) began its 1,000 mile journey from Malta on 27 October, two days before the Israelis crossed the Egyptian border in Sinai on the 29th.[1]

On 30 October the British and French governments sent an ultimatum to the Israelis and Egyptians: they were both to withdraw their forces ten miles from the Suez Canal to permit an Anglo-French occupation of Port Said, Ismailia and Suez. This occupation was to be temporary in order to separate the combatants. Although the Israelis were in process of routing the Egyptians in a lightning campaign, they were not yet in the Canal Zone, so had no difficulty in agreeing; the Egyptians were bound to refuse.

For the four following days Anglo-French air squadrons blasted aerodromes at Cairo and other targets, until the fleet carrying the ground forces arrived off Port Said. Port Said was captured and Anglo-French forces were nearing Ismailia, when the operation was halted by moves at the United Nations.

On the day of the Anglo-French ultimatum the Egyptians had taken the matter to the Security Council, just after the British and French had vetoed an American resolution condemning Israel for violating the Egyptian–Israel armistice agreement of February 1949. This use of the veto—the first time ever by Britain and France—outraged the Americans who now worked actively, along with the Canadians (through their Foreign Minister Lester Pearson) to frustrate the Anglo-French plan, of which they had been kept in the dark. They supported a Yugoslav resolution for an emergency session

ance with the Anglo-Jordanian Treaty of 1948, while the French had an understanding with Israel—Eden: *Full Circle*, 512–3. (Selwyn Lloyd was Foreign Secretary.)
[1] Israeli mobilization took place on the 27th. A report that Israel was about to mobilize reached London on the 25th, when the Cabinet decided 'in principle how it would react', including the ultimatum to Israel and Egypt.—Eden, 522–3.

of the Assembly under the 'Uniting for Peace' resolution of 1950. This was the first time a resort was made to this procedure, originally designed to nullify Russia's strategy of paralysing the Security Council through the veto, by transferring its functions in such a crisis to the Assembly. The French and British objections—which on this issue did not have the force of a veto—were disregarded, and the assembly met on 1 November. Sharply condemning the Franco-British action, Dulles introduced a resolution calling for an immediate cease-fire and repeating the demand for Israel to withdraw behind the armistice lines. In the small hours of 2 November the resolution was carried (after a sitting noted for the bitter condemnation by almost all delegates of France and Britain), by 64 votes to 5—the minority consisting of France, Britain, Israel, Australia and New Zealand.

Canada had abstained on the vote, and immediately after, Lester Pearson suggested that arrangements be made for despatching a U.N. force 'large enough to keep these borders at peace while a political settlement is being worked out'. The proposal was warmly supported by America, and when it was expressed in a concrete resolution introduced by Canada the following day, it was passed by 57 votes to none—though Britain, France and the Soviet bloc were among a group of 19 abstainers. The resolution called for the Secretary-General to submit a plan within 48 hours for setting up 'an emergency international United Nations force'.

Within 24 hours the plan was prepared and approved—the same 19 abstaining. Several of the smaller countries agreed to furnish contingents, and General Burns, the U.N. Truce Supervisor in Palestine, was appointed its commander (5 November).

Despite British abstention on these votes the British delegate had already (1 November) stated on government instruction that Britain would be delighted if the United Nations would take over 'the physical task of maintaining peace in the area'. The way was therefore open for Britain, without too much loss of face, to beat a tactical retreat, in which case France would be bound to follow suit.

The U.N. arrangements for an emergency force were passed on the same day that the Anglo-French ground forces landed. Meanwhile Nasser had signified readiness both to accept a cease-fire and receive the U.N. emergency force. Israel, too, accepted an unconditional cease-fire.

The ostensible objects of the 'police action' by France and Britain had been achieved, and this made it even more difficult for them to complete their further objective, the seizure of the entire Canal. On top of this, Egypt had blocked the Canal (locking up £50 million of shipping), while a pumping-station on the Iraq Petroleum Company pipe-line across Syria had been blown up. It was clear that Britain (and Western Europe as a whole) were to be starved of oil unless America came to the rescue—and that meant an urgent need of dollars at a time when, during October, the sterling area's gold and dollar reserves had declined by $84 million and were still declining rapidly. America would not help unless Britain quickly called off her attack. To this threat was added another from Russia, of rockets on Britain and France, and 'volunteers' for Egypt. From Eden's point of view, perhaps not the least important danger was a sizable revolt brewing both in the Cabinet and in the Conservative Party as a whole. With Britain's agreement the cease-fire came into effect in Egypt at midnight on 6 November.

During this time extraordinary efforts had been made by the Opposition in Britain—and indeed by all, of whatever party, who condemned the armed intervention—to stop the action. Feeling ran so high that the House of Commons was the scene of unprecedented verbal violence, bordering on hysteria. For the first time in 30 years, the Speaker was obliged to suspend a sitting (1 November). Anthony Nutting, the Minister of State dealing with Middle East and United Nations questions, resigned, as did a junior minister, Sir Edward Boyle. An immense crowd assembled in Trafalgar Square on Sunday, 4 November, for a protest meeting, subsequently marching to Downing Street where they practically besieged the Prime Minister with Pineau and Bourgès-Manoury (the Defence Minister), who had come over to obtain a clear decision on whether the ground forces were to go into Port Said the next day.

A breakdown in Eden's health, necessitating three weeks' holiday in Jamaica from 21 November, preceded his resignation on 9 January 1957, and the slow change of British policy under Harold Macmillan. The cost of 'Suez', far greater than the millions spent on the operation, and on taking oil round the Cape and from America, was the drop in British and French prestige throughout the Middle East (except in Israel), and its virtual extinction in Egypt.

In Egypt, French and British assets and businesses were taken over. Some of their nationals were expelled, with permission to take only a small sum and personal belongings with them; others left as soon as possible. (All but a fraction of the Jewish residents too, many of them families of long standing in the country, were obliged to leave.) This exodus, though hasty, was in the main orderly. Even during the bombings Englishmen were able to walk about Cairo in safety: order was completely maintained. But the taking over of the French and British schools and cultural institutions marked the end of an era.

The two countries and Israel attempted to bargain for guarantees concerning the future régime of the Canal and for curbing Egypt's warlike intentions against her neighbour, but these failed. The French and British withdrew their forces by Christmas 1956 without conditions, and by March the Israelis were similarly back behind the old armistice lines. The U.N. force had taken over as the ill-fated allies withdrew, and this was the only tangible guarantee which Israel had as a barrier to renewed fedayeen attacks by Egypt, or an outright war.

Not only did Nasser survive the onslaught, but his policy continued virtually unchanged both at home and abroad. Steps were taken to proceed with a modified version of the High Dam, for which the bulk of the finance and most of the technical construction staff were supplied by the Russians. Nor did the French obtain any guarantee that Nasser would disinterest himself in Algeria.[1]

[1] See R. C. Mowat: *Middle East Perspective* (Blandford, 1958), from which some portions, notably on pp. 249 and 259–62, are reproduced.

23: Cracks in the Soviet Empire

Stalin's National Communism

No sooner had the Soviet Empire in Eastern Europe been rounded off by the Prague coup of February 1948 than fissures began to appear in its apparently monolithic structure. The Prague coup brought about the inclusion of Czechoslovakia, but this was accompanied by the dispute between Moscow and Belgrade, which was made public with the expulsion of Yugoslavia from the Cominform[1] in June 1948.

Nothing showed more clearly than this event the naked basis of power on which the Soviet system rested. That power was located in Stalin. In 1936 he had set off the hideous train of purges which depleted the leaders of Russia in all branches, political, military and administrative, and left the men who remained more than ever dependent on the dictator alone. All pretences of intra-party democracy vanished. For 13 years (1939–52) no Congress of the party was held. A closely co-ordinated chain of command went from Stalin down to the lowest levels of activity, operating largely through the Communist Party. It was complemented by a system of control, headed by Lavrenti Beria, through the N.K.V.D.,[2] and an information-gathering and espionage network which swiftly brought the least whispers of unrest or criticism to the ears of the man in the Kremlin. Those through whom he worked were expected to abandon many attributes of their humanity: 'their's not to reason why, their's but to do or die.' Death, or what was often worse, years in the slave camp, was the portion of those who showed signs of independence or questioning. Those who were left were 'careerists and moral deadbeats'.[3]

The purges had been for Stalin the means of survival. During the war he found that patriotism was a powerful weapon at his disposal.

[1] See below, pp. 275–7.
[2] N.K.V.D. (People's Commissariat of Internal Affairs) was divided into two sections, one of which (N.K.G.B.) was the People's Commissariat of State Security.
[3] E. Crankshaw: *Khrushchev's Russia* (Penguin, 1964 edition), 65.

With his famous speeches of 6 and 7 November 1941, the war became
'the Great Patriotic War'.[1] Bygone heroes of Russian history were
resurrected—Tsars and saints were the exemplars and saviours of
the country, such as Stalin aspired to be, what in fact he had to be,
if he were to survive and rule. St Alexander Nevsky and Dimitri
Donskoi cast an aura round the head of the tyrant who was responsible for more murders of his fellow-men than any other ruler
in history, with the possible exceptions of Hitler and Genghiz
Khan.

Unlike these latter, however, Stalin could harness his will to constructive tasks. Everything to which he set his hand was planned on a
colossal scale. If he thirsted for absolute power, he used it to revolu-
tionize his country, and provide it with the basis for economic
growth that would bring it into the class of super-state so far represented only by America. It can be argued that, without the Bolshevik
Revolution, economic development, following the graph of its growth
in Tsarist days, could have brought Russia anyway to the point
which it had reached in 1939—and without the upheavals and waste
which had characterized Soviet history, and with a healthier and
more productive agriculture.[2] Stalin was capable only of rough
methods, and however ruthlessly he pushed through collectivization
and the Five Year Plans, the outcome was a Russia equipped with
heavy industry as never before, and a social system which contrasted
markedly with that of the West.

With the war's end this industry was in part destroyed, in part
seriously run down. Steel production which had reached 18·3 million
tons in 1940 was down to 11·2 million tons in 1945; coal and oil
production had declined respectively from 166 and 31 million tons
to 149·3 and 19·4 million tons, while the supply of electricity had
fallen from 11·3 to 10·7 million kilowatts.[3] The Donbas mines and
industrial complex had been devastated. To offset such losses new

[1] 'May you be inspired in this war by the heroic figures of our great ancestors,
Alexander Nevsky, Dimitri Donskoi, Minin and Pozharsky, Alexander Suvorov,
Michael Kutuzov! . . .'—Quoted in Werth: *Russia at War*, 249.

[2] 'There are no adequate grounds on which to compare the result finally attained by
the Soviets with that which would have evolved through a non-catastrophic process
under a democratic régime and with the aid of foreign capital. (But) there is little doubt
that the nature of the industrialization would have been different.'—R. Aron: *The
Century of Total War* (Verschoyle, 1954), 109.

[3] Crankshaw, 25, 26.

industries had been built up in the Urals and farther east, partly with machinery transported from the areas threatened by the Germans. But to bring these on to the point where they would seriously compete with America, and to provide an adequate transport system and the other elements of the needed infrastructure, was a colossal task.

In this task assistance was expected from the satellites. From some of them, such as Hungary, such machinery as the Germans had left was removed in the course of the 'liberation' by Russia (though the bulk of this particular form of loot was naturally taken from Germany). This aid to rehabilitation was, however, disappointing. It was found difficult to re-instal machinery, or even entire factory plant, once it had been moved. Losses of parts, delays and consequent rusting-up on the journey, or the deterioration which came from leaving machines for months in dumps or railway sidings—all this vastly reduced the effectiveness of this aid to economic growth.[1] Nevertheless, by October 1947 the gross production of large-scale industry in the Soviet Union had reached the average monthly level of 1940.[2]

With the establishment of the Communist bloc an integrated economic policy for the whole of its area became possible. This was applied not in the interests of the people as a whole, but in that of Russia. The economic function of the satellites was to serve as providers for the needs of Russia. The 'joint companies' which were set up, like the 'Sovroms' in Rumania, supposedly under the joint control of Russia and the country concerned, were organized solely to bring the maximum economic advantage to Russia.

So with the political control which Stalin exercised from Moscow. This was no federation of Soviet states where each had a voice in framing the policy of the whole. It was merely another manifestation

[1] The Soviet Union's capital loss through destruction, etc., during the war has been reckoned as between $13 and $16 billion; reparations collected between $13 and $20 billion. This does not include 'requisitions to support Soviet occupation forces in Europe, confiscations of industrial equipment, proceeds from the so-called "joint companies" established in the satellite countries, labour services of prisoners of war, or benefits from differential trading prices (except in the case of Polish coal)'. G. W. Nutter: *Growth of Industrial Production in the Soviet Union* (Princeton University Press), 215.

[2] United Nations: *A Survey of the Economic Situation and Prospects of Europe* (Geneva, 1948), xii.

of Great Russian chauvinism, and Stalin's ideology, far from initiating a new world society, was seen to be a form of National Communism.[1]

Thus the trends of the age were reflected in Russia. The socialism of Germany under Hitler had been superficial, but its nationalism had been real. The socialism of Britain under the Labour government had in important respects gone farther, though it too remained rigidly national. Only the socialism of the French and of some other continental countries truly transcended national boundaries, powerfully assisted by the enlightened capitalism of America and by technocrats like Monnet and Armand.

There was also a growing class[2] of technocrats in Russia. With its gigantic schemes of training —50,000 engineering graduates a year by comparison with the 5,000 in Britain—and with the emphasis on economic development, it would be clear that these people would have an increasing say in matters of policy. But as long as Stalin was alive the direction of affairs was firmly in his hands. It was only with his successors that the lineaments of a managerial society began to emerge.

Slave Labour

Slave labour was recruited from political prisoners, criminals, repatriated prisoners of war, and people of non-Soviet nationality incorporated in the U.S.S.R., who for some reason were classed as dangerous. The forced repatriation of Soviet citizens after the war, in accordance with an agreement made at Yalta, was one of the most painful episodes of a cruel epoch. Russian prisoners of war knew what their fate would be on returning 'home'. 'The summer and fall of 1945 witnessed a real struggle between the American authorities in Germany and Austria and the interned Russians; it took clubs, rifle butts, and bayonets, and shooting over the prisoners' heads, to usher them into the box cars that were to bear them to Russia. In January 1946 ten Russian soldiers in Dachau committed suicide by

---

[1] 'International Communism, which was at one time the task of revolutionaries, eventually transformed itself, as did everything else in Communism, and became the common ground of Communist bureaucracies, fighting one another on nationalist considerations.'—M. Djilas: *The New Class* (Thames and Hudson, 1957), 173–4.

[2] The word is not used in the social sense.

cutting their throats, while 21 others were saved after attempting suicide with razor blades. . . .' Such instances are legion.[1]

The camps were situated (if in towns) in dilapidated buildings surrounded by barbed wire; if in the forests, accommodation was in the form of huts or tents. The prisoners 'usually slept on the ground, without mattresses or even straw, and with only one blanket. They had no soap, towels or medicaments, not even iodine, and they were infested with lice. The food was insufficient, though there was no starvation. . . . The prisoners worked 10 to 12 hours a day, six days a week.'[2] There were of course show camps, and places where German prisoners of war were given especially good treatment along with indoctrination, so that they could be used for the Soviet cause, or even converted to Communism. Field-Marshal von Paulus and other high-ranking officers captured at Stalingrad were among those who responded as the Russians wished, forming the 'Free German Committee' who broadcast and provided other propaganda against the Nazi régime.[3]

The Break with Yugoslavia

Stalin's Great Russian nationalism was bound sooner or later to provoke a reaction among the smaller countries now tied to the U.S.S.R. The surprise was, perhaps, that the reaction began so soon.

In many fields Yugoslavia had moved faster than the other satellites in developing a Communist régime. The fact that its government owed much to British support during the war, and that it had benefited more, in relation to its size, from U.N.R.R.A. than any other East European country, in no way bound it to the Western powers. Thanks to U.N.R.R.A. it had by 1946 more tractors than at the start of the war. But Russia, not America, remained Tito's model, and his government hurried ahead with schemes of collectivization and state co-operatives. Its five-year plans, envisaging a swifter change in the ratio between the industrial and agricultural population than elsewhere, was more ambitious than its neighbours. In its

[1] D. J. Dallin and B. I. Nicolaevsky: *Forced Labour in Soviet Russia* (Yale University Press), 292.

[2] Dallin, 279. For the camps, see A. Solzhenitsyn: *A Day in the Life of Ivan Denisovich* (Praeger, 1963).

[3] Werth: *Russia at War*, 732–7. Paulus later settled in East Germany and adopted a pro-Russian line (737 n.).

dealings with education, the bourgeoisie and the churches, and in the tightly controlled expression of views, its ideological correctness could not be faulted.[1]

Criticisms which Tito and his associates held against Moscow on seemingly minor matters were conveyed to the Russians confidentially and without publicity, and with good will were capable of adjustment. But it was the fact that any criticisms were being made at all, and that any suggestion of independence was being manifested, which annoyed the Kremlin. The first rift in the lute was due to the behaviour of the Red Army in the northern part of Yugoslavia through which it passed at the end of the war. Complaints by the inhabitants brought to the government's notice 111 cases of rape with murder (and more without murder), and of 1,204 cases of looting with assault.[2] Milovan Djilas, then Minister of Propaganda, conveyed the complaint personally to Moscow, on the grounds that such behaviour should be checked in order to make the role of the Red Army as the bearer of 'socialism' more effective among the people of the countries which it occupied. The slight was resented—particularly the comparison which Djilas made between the behaviour of certain Russian officers and those of the British Mission. Subsequent apologies by Djilas failed to make Stalin forget his grudge.

Tito and his colleagues resented the Russians recruiting Yugoslav citizens to spy on their own government and army, and the brake which they put on Yugoslav efforts to foment and maintain the Communist revolt in Greece.[3] While admitting that Albania was within Yugoslavia's sphere of influence, the Russians objected to Yugoslav troop movements which could have led to Albania being 'swallowed' by her neighbour. Though they gave some encouragement to a scheme dear to Tito and his associates for a Balkan federation, starting with Yugoslavia and Bulgaria, the Russians nevertheless put the brake on it, and vetoed a customs union between these two countries and Rumania. Stalin's remark to the Bulgarian leader, Georgi Dimitrov, on this occasion, could equally have been

---

[1] Nor could it be in its dealings with Mihailovich, the former Minister of War and guerila leader, who was captured, tried and shot (July 1946). (See above, 126–7).

[2] M. Djilas: Conversations with Stalin (Hart-Davis, 1962), 82.

[3] 'The insurrection in Greece will have to fold up.'—Stalin to Djilas (Djilas, Conversations, 164). For the federation scheme see A. B. Ulam: Titoism and the Cominform (Harvard University Press, 1952), 89–95.

applied to Tito: 'Your trouble is not errors, but that you are taking a line different from ours.'[1]

Though the exchange of letters between Tito and the Kremlin which preceded the final break[2] illustrated a restrained, almost humble attitude on the part of the Yugoslavs (perhaps calculated for the record), they did in fact feel themselves other than the obedient servants of Moscow. They flattered themselves that their country, alone among those of Eastern Europe, had been liberated by their own efforts and not by the Red Army, and that the cohesion of their party derived from the comradeship in action of Tito and the Partisans throughout the war. Tito was not, like most of the other satellite leaders, a Comintern agent who had lived in Russia until sent to take over in the wake of the Red Army. He was a national leader who had earned his position by directing the resistance on the spot. But the Russians still regarded him as 'Walter' (his former sobriquet), the submissive young official whom they had placed in charge of the ailing Yugoslav Party after purges, organized by themselves, had removed his rivals.

The Comintern had been wound up in May 1943; the Cominform was founded in September 1947 with its seat at the Yugoslav capital, Belgrade. Supposedly a body for disseminating information, it swiftly showed itself to be another version of the Comintern—Moscow's agency for imposing its policy on the satellites and on the Communist Parties elsewhere. But as a means of disciplining the Yugoslavs it failed. In any event differences, which were made much of, over agricultural policy (regarding the treatment of the 'Kulaks' and collectivization) were not the real issues, for in this sphere the Yugoslavs were moving as fast as the other satellites, if not faster. Finally in June 1948 Yugoslavia was expelled from the Cominform.

Purges in Yugoslavia

A by-product of the breach between Tito and Moscow was a series of purges all round. At the moment when Moscow rejected Tito's

[1] Djilas: *Conversations*, 164. It seems that at an interview with Stalin on 10 February 1948, 'the Bulgarian and Yugoslav representatives were strongly disciplined; the union of Bulgaria, Yugoslavia and Albania was approved, but there was to be no general satellite federation and the Greek cause was to be abandoned'.—V. S. Mamatey: *Soviet Russian Imperialism* (Van Nostrand, 1964), 90.

[2] R.I.I.A.: *The Soviet–Yugoslav Dispute* (1948).

plan of Balkan federation (January 1948), Andrija Hebrang, Chairman of the State Planning Commission (in charge of Yugoslavia's economy), was demoted and subsequently arrested. The same fate befell Sreten Zhujovich, the Minister of Finance. Hebrang, who had not been in Tito's entourage during the war, was regarded as Moscow's man for replacing him, while Zhujovich, though a wartime comrade, had been passed over in promotions within the party caucus, and had begun making reports about the government direct to the Russian embassy in Belgrade. Zhujovich later recanted, but another Moscow man, General Arso Jovanovitch, was shot as he tried to abscond to Rumania.

The rest of Tito's henchmen formed a solid core with their leader, and could not be shaken by all Moscow's wiles or fulminations. At first somewhat bewildered by their situation, cut adrift from the source (as they had hitherto regarded it) of their revolution and ideology, they took some time to find their bearings. As Moscow applied sanctions, withdrawing aid and technicians, the Yugoslavs were obliged to veer towards the West, thus embarking on the course of 'neutralism'. Though finding it necessary to slow the pace of industrialization, and as a corollary to modify collectivization and other schemes in the countryside (a matter of expediency, too, for retaining peasant support), Tito and his colleagues did not cease to be Communists. With the exception of Djilas, the former Minister of Propaganda, whose thoughtful and critical attitude later cost him his freedom,[1] the Marxism and most of the methods of the Communist Party of Yugoslavia remained unimpeachable.

End of the Civil War in Greece

A by-product of the breach between Tito and Stalin was the end of the civil war in Greece. Its cessation at the end of 1945 had been temporary. At that time British intervention had just succeeded in snatching Athens from Communist control, and though Communists continued to dominate large areas, their organization, E.L.A.S.,

[1] In January 1954 Djilas was expelled from the Communist Party and kept under close arrest until his trial a year later on a charge of 'hostile propaganda'. For two years, while under a suspended sentence, he wrote *The New Class* and *Land Without Justice*, being imprisoned after a second trial in December 1956, for 'slandering Yugoslavia' in statements made to the foreign press.—See the Introduction to *Land Without Justice* [autobiography of his youth] (Methuen, 1958), 10.

made an agreement with the government (12 February 1945) which resulted in relative quiescence. It was now the turn of right-wing elements to carry out vengeance, and disturbances were endemic in many parts of the country.

Economically Greece was in a disastrous situation. One third of the villages had been destroyed, railways and bridges largely wrecked, and locomotives and rolling-stock reduced to 10 per cent and 20 per cent of pre-war numbers. Millions of olive and other fruit trees were destroyed, as were 60,000 acres of vineyards. Everyone with any property left, or any goods to sell, exchanged what they could for gold. British sovereigns took the place of the rocketing drachma, but failed to get trade and industry moving, since along with other gold they were hoarded. Merchants hoarded stocks, and people were kept alive by $358 million worth of U.N.R.R.A. supplies. Not all the politicians were corrupt or inefficient, but as a whole they failed to inspire the necessary confidence in tackling what was in any case an almost superhuman task.

Elections in March 1946 were freely conducted under the gaze of Allied observers (the Russians refused to join the observing), and a 60 per cent poll produced a right wing government. A plebiscite in September 1946 gave 89·5 per cent votes for the monarchy, but 20·5 per cent of these were against the restoration of George II. However he returned on 27 September.

This was the signal for a renewed outbreak of the civil war. The Communists took to the hills, and drawing supplies and reinforcements from beyond the frontiers in Albania, Yugoslavia and Bulgaria soon reduced government control of Greece to virtually Athens and its surroundings, and Salonika. Such chances as there had been of economic improvement vanished together with hopes of reforms (urged by the Allies) in matters like taxation, which might have eased the lot of the poor. Their plight became even worse as thousands of refugees streamed into Athens and Salonika, already fearfully overcrowded. The burden of sustaining the economy and the military effort of what was left of Greece was too much for Britain, who threw the burden on to America.

Truman's response, with his 'doctrine'[1] saved the situation, though the $300 million aid to Greece took time to bring visible results. Far

[1] See above, p. 159.

more of this had to go into the military budget than the Americans had anticipated, and meanwhile 'General' Markos continued to dominate the Grammos Mountains and other areas in the north, to recruit guerillas (many doubtless by force), and to seize children for sending abroad. In December 1947 a 'Democratic Greek Government' was proclaimed in the 'free mountains' of Greece. Markos however failed to seize any town of adequate size for his capital. One curious feature of the struggle was that, though Communists or suspects suffered at the hands of their opponents in situations where brutality was normal, two Communist papers continued to appear at Athens until October 1947.

The war might have dragged on indefinitely, while a United Nations commission,[1] appointed with teams of observers from six countries, attempted without success to limit the conflict. To terminate it seemed impracticable, until Tito's rift with Stalin threatened to deprive the rebels of one of their major supports. Stalin no longer supported the war anyway. Markos was dismissed by the Central Committee of the Greek Communist Party in January 1949, and peace-terms were offered, though not yet accepted. In February the Peloponnese was cleared of rebels, and after Tito closed the frontier in July the rebel forces collapsed. Thousands fled into Albania. That winter (1949–50) the remaining British troops were withdrawn. An election in March 1950 was a victory for the moderates, and under a new government the work of reconstruction was renewed in circumstances where genuine progress had become possible.[2]

Purges Elsewhere

For Stalin, events in Belgrade were a warning, and he took steps at once to make certain that no other satellite should become refractory. Communist Parties, whose numbers had been built up during the take-over, were now reduced, and leaders—particularly those not originally Communist, but who had entered government circles through the coalitions which it had been Moscow's policy to con-

---

[1] The United Nations Special Committee on the Balkans, set up on American initiative by a vote of the General Assembly after the Russians had steadily vetoed all proposals for such action in the Security Council.

[2] H. Seton Watson: *The East European Revolution*, 318–38; H. Seton Watson: *Nationalism and Communism—Essays 1946–63* (Methuen, 1964), 128–39; R.I.I.A. *Survey*, 1947–8 and 1949–50.

struct—were now relegated to the scrap-heap. These men had served their purpose, and being of no further use, they were, for the most part, executed. As in Russia, so now in the satellite countries, the revolution began devouring its children.

One immediate step was to take Albania out of the Yugoslav sphere of influence. The pro-Tito Deputy Premier, General Koçi Xoxe, was deposed and subsequently executed, and Enver Hoxha ruled as a despot on Moscow's behalf. In Czechoslovakia the Socialists, who had split their party to bring the Communists to power, were pushed into the background or 'liquidated'. Communists who had spent the war in London, like Clementis, were disgraced, and thoroughgoing Muscovites put in their place. Of the ordinary members of the party, some 2,300,000 strong, a quarter were purged or put on probation. The Party Congress in Prague of May 1949 was the prelude to something approaching a reign of terror.

After Mikolajczyk's departure from Poland[1] the Socialist Party, the only remaining one with vestiges of independence, was swiftly purged; in 1948 it fused with the Communists in the Polish United Workers' Party. As if this did not give Moscow enough control, Wladyslaw Gomulka, the Vice-premier and General Secretary of the Polish Communist Party, was accused of 'insufficient appreciation of the role of the U.S.S.R.', and was obliged to step down from these posts. Though he formally repented of this 'deviation', he was later charged with 'returning to his old nationalist position' and was finally dismissed from the government (December 1948).[2]

In Bulgaria, Georgi Dimitrov was too 'national' a figure for the Russians. He was in any case ailing, and his power fell to a triumvirate, Kostov, Yugov and Terpeshev. Dimitrov eventually went, or was removed to Russia for a 'cure', but the consequence was his death (which may have been from natural causes) in July 1949. The triumvirate itself did not last long. Kostov, a Communist of standing who had survived prison under the royal régime, was too fanatical for Stalin. In no country was collectivization of the peasants hurried on more ruthlessly than in Bulgaria under Kostov's direction. But he may have tried to defend Bulgaria's economic interests against the exploiting demands of Moscow. Though a known opponent of Tito

[1] See above, p. 163.
[2] H. Seton Watson: *The East European Revolution*, 314.

over the federation schemes, he was accused of collaborating with him (and also of being a British agent). In court he caused a scandal by disavowing his written confession, to the rage and mortification of his judges. 'He had been tortured before, one police questioning under the old régime leaving him with a broken back, and now the old Communist fighter, in a gesture of incredible hardness, refused to plead guilty in open court.'[1] He was duly condemned and executed (December 1949). His colleagues Yugov and Terpeshev were demoted, but Chervenkov, the Stalin man who took over power, was restrained from expelling them from the government.

In Hungary the chief victim was Laszlo Rajk, who, as Minister of the Interior, had organized the suppression of democracy. Having spent the war years in the Hungarian underground, he was a man of some prestige and standing in his country—but not in Moscow. The trial of Rajk and other prominent Communists was a tissue of inconsistencies and obvious fabrications (September 1949). They accepted without public protest to be sacrificed on the altar of Stalinism. Rakosi, who had spent the war years in Moscow, continued as Stalin's man in charge.

In Rumania no action was necessary. The one leading Communist who was unreliable from Moscow's viewpoint, Lucretiu Patrascanu, had already been disgraced. This intellectual of middle-class origins was charged with becoming 'an exponent of bourgeois ideology'. His expulsion from government and party left Gheorgiu-Dej in firm control.[2]

The Church in Russia

Parallel with the political purges in the satellite countries went the war against the Churches. This seemed to contrast with the more liberal attitude which had been prevailing in Russia since the start of the war.

There the Churches, or at least the one that really mattered in Soviet eyes, the Orthodox Church, had been bowed though not broken by the sustained campaign against it in the early 1920s. Its gesture of independence *vis-à-vis* the state, which it had made in 1917 at the time of the revolution, could not be maintained. This

[1] Ulam, 215.
[2] Seton Watson: *The East European Revolution*, 314.

gesture had taken the form of electing its Patriarch for the first time since Peter the Great had abolished the Partiarchate. The new Patriarch, Tikhon, stood out against the Soviet state's attack on the Church's position and property, but he had been worsted. During imprisonment by the O.G.P.U. he had decided to abandon his opposition, declaring that he would no longer be an enemy of Soviet power or have relations with the monarchists. Though the Church, and the other Churches and religions continued to suffer much persecution, this acceptance of the régime was to lead on eventually to collaboration between Church and state.

Anti-religious propaganda was encouraged, churches continued to be confiscated (as 'museums' they often became centres for anti-God propaganda), priests had no salaries and could undertake no teaching. Splinter-churches from the Orthodox were encouraged, especially the 'Living Church', which was given some of the finest churches which still remained open for worship. The usual avenues of promotion were blocked to believers—thousands were expelled from the Communist Party for this reason from 1929 onwards.

But when the war began, religion was found to be still a vital force in Russia. Communism had not been able to supply substitutes for Christian morality, for the sacraments (especially of baptism and marriage), and for the need of a supernatural Power at times of personal catastrophe and peril. For millions God became a security and a strength not only for themselves as individuals, but for the nation itself. Alexander Werth quotes from one of Konstantin Simonov's poems which became 'immensely popular' during the winter of 1941–2:

> . . . And it seemed that outside every Russian village
> Our grandfathers had risen from the dead,
> And were shielding us with their outstretched arms,
> And praying for us, their godless grandchildren. . . .
> Russia, our homeland, what is it? I ask you;
> It's not Moscow houses, where we cheerfully lived,
> It is rather these poor huts where our grandfathers laboured,
> And the Russian graves with their simple crosses. . . .[1]

The identification of the Church with patriotism initiated the new relation of Church and state which characterized the later Stalin era.

[1] *Russia at War*, 272.

When the war began, publication of Yaroslavsky's anti-God weekly, *Bezbozhnik*, ceased.[1] Soon the clergy were actively helping the war-effort, and raising money for defence. Stalin's speech invoking the saintly defenders of Holy Russia was paralleled by clerical exhorta-tions which led, among other things, to a presentation by the Orthodox Church of the 'Dimitry Donskoi' tank column for the army and the 'Alexander Nevsky' fighter squadron for the air force—built out of funds collected from the faithful. At the ceremony of presentation the Metropolitan Nikolay spoke of 'sacred hatred against the fascist robbers' and referred to Stalin as 'our common Father'.[2]

Stalin made good use of these sentiments. In September 1943 he received the three Metropolitans. One of these—Sergius—was per-mitted to be elected Patriarch; and the Holy Synod, through which the government of the Church had been formerly carried on, was restored. The primacy of the Russian Orthodox Church was re-established, along with that of the Georgian Orthodox Church in Georgia—the Church in which, during its time of persecution in Tsarist days, Stalin had been trained as a seminarist. This primacy did not however prevent a new measure of freedom being accorded to other Churches as well, except for the Living Church and other such splinter-sects, which were now left to wither away.

When Sergius died in 1945, his successor Alexis was elected amid scenes of splendour unknown since Tsardom, as was the celebration of the five hundredth anniversary of the autocephalous Russian Church in 1948, in the presence of a host of visiting ecclesiastical dignitaries. By this time 'the Patriarch and his closest collaborators (had) . . . moved up into the privileged classes of Soviet Society'.[3] A council for the Affairs of the Russian Orthodox Church was estab-lished (October 1943), for looking after the interests and even the comfort of the hierarchy—they were given suitable accommodation at Moscow—and also for providing the necessary link whereby the state could guide and influence Church policy. The 'ecclesiastical imperialism of the Moscow Patriarchate'[4] was encouraged as part of the Soviet diplomatic and ideological offensive. Great pains were

[1] *Russia at War*, 429. Even before the war, 'the cruder forms of anti-religious propa-ganda had been largely abandoned'.
[2] W. Kolarz: *Religion in the Soviet Union* (Macmillan, 1961), 50.
[3] Kolarz, 55.   [4] Ibid., 62.

taken by the state to make the Patriarch's visit to the Middle East in mid-1945 a success, and successful it doubtless was in winning some Arab and even Western favour for Russia and Communism. Later the Church was given a major role in the 'Peace Campaign', which became the leading theme of Moscow's anti-American offensive abroad. Eventually higher ecclesiastics were brought in to grace diplomatic occasions and impress foreigners. In return Churchmen referred to Stalin as 'the faithful defender of the Church', and when he died the Patriarch sent a message to the Soviet Council of Ministers: 'Our Church proclaims eternal memory to him with a special feeling of abiding love.'[1]

Perhaps the greatest gain for the Orthodox Church during this time was the improved facilities for training ordinands. Though the numbers of these were kept far below the actual needs for replacing the older generation of priests, the figure of 1,500 in 1955 can be considered adequate for keeping the nucleus of an educated clergy in being. Some churches which had been closed were reopened, not without difficulty; but the provision of churches remained far below the need, judging by the vast crowds who came to worship on occasions like Easter and Christmas.[2] In Moscow only 38 churches were open after the war, by comparison with the 600 of Tsarist days. In Leningrad there were only a dozen.[3] Teaching of religion was still denied in schools, and it remained rigorously excluded from the army as from all Communist organizations.

Russia's occupation of the Baltic states brought an accession of strength to the Orthodox Church, because the state needed the Church's help in absorbing the well-organized Orthodox believers. The Catholics, strong in Lithuania and Latvia, suffered savage persecution, though—partly perhaps by reaction—the devotion of the laity continued to show itself in huge congregations, even on ordinary Sundays. The German occupation of Soviet territory brought other gains, for the churches and monasteries which were reopened during that time were not closed after the German retreat. In consequence a far higher proportion of churches than elsewhere,

[1] Kolarz, 65.
[2] A reasonable guess as to the number of believers in the Soviet Union is around 45 million, and of practising Orthodox Christians between 20 and 30 million.—Kolarz, 37.
[3] Figures for 1958 in Kolarz, 80.

and virtually the only monasteries and convents in the Soviet Union, exist in these western areas.[1]

The Church in the Satellite States

In the satellites the Churches had to be broken, so that they might become submissive tools of the new régime; failing that, they had at least to be neutralized. Because the new régimes quickly took over all educational institutions, and used them as a means for indoctrinating the young with Marxism and atheism, the Churches were bound to resist.

The Orthodox Church, encouraged perhaps by the Russian example, and drawing on centuries of dealing with Turkish overlords, was prepared to yield much in order to maintain what it could of the loyalty and support of its members. In Rumania the pliable Bishop of Jassy was elected Patriarch with the name of Justinian in 1948. While the Rumanian schools were taken over by the state, the Church gained the doubtful advantage of the accession of the Uniate Church. Independent since 1596, it was now forced to fuse with the Orthodox. Minority churches both there and in Bulgaria suffered. In Rumania the Catholic hierarchy was extinguished; in Bulgaria the trial of fifteen Protestant clergy was staged in 1949. In Albania the Orthodox Church suffered most, losing its Patriarch in 1949.

The toughest resistance came from the Roman Catholic Church. In Hungary Cardinal Mindszenty showed himself to be a staunch defender of the rights and property of the Church, a fierce, unbending and sometimes bitter opponent of the Communist government. His view was that it could not be trusted: whatever guarantees the government might give would sooner or later be revoked. On these grounds he would not accept the nationalization of the schools, when the state took over half of them and left two hours a week compulsory religious teaching in the curriculum. He forbade clerical teachers to continue their functions in the schools under these conditions. He insisted that confiscated property should be returned, that Catholic books should not be censored, and that a Catholic daily paper be permitted. Though some of his senior clergy had doubts

---

[1] Figures for 1958 in Kolarz, 73. One outcome of the German occupation in the Ukraine did not however outlast their régime—the revival of the Ukrainian Autocephalous Church.

about his uncompromising attitude, they rallied round him unitedly at the height of the battle over the schools, and he became the focus of political as well as of religious opposition to the régime. But in December 1948 he was arrested, sending out a note to his friends that whatever he was forced to confess at his trial should not be taken as the truth. At his trial he indeed made confessions to the effect that his opposition to the government had been mistaken, and evidence (valid at least in Communist eyes) was produced on which he was convicted of treason and condemned to imprisonment for life.

Thereafter the main effort of the government was directed to driving a wedge between the Church leaders and their followers, clerical and lay, and to setting up a splinter 'National Church' independent of Rome. Many monastic orders were abolished, and 10,000 monks and nuns were driven out.

In Poland, which was largely Catholic, the authorities went slowly, and gained little by putting the minority Churches on an equal footing with the Catholic Church. Nor did they do better by trying to prove that the hierarchy was pro-German. The Primates—Cardinal Hlond who died in 1948, and Monsignor Wyszynski who succeeded him—showed themselves able defenders of the Church, patient and unprovocative in the face of the difficulties which the government put in their way. A Communist-engineered split failed to take effect, and laity and clergy remained solidly behind the hierarchy.

Archbishop Beran of Prague, who was consecrated before the Communist take-over of Czechoslovakia, was a survivor of a German concentration camp and a national hero. The schools had been nationalized just after the war (though provision was made for religious instruction at parents' request). Other issues were made a trial of strength: the attempt to exact an oath of loyalty from the clergy to the state, in return for higher salaries which the state would pay, and the setting up of a pro-government 'Catholic Action Committee' which claimed to represent Catholic opinion. Beran threatened 'ecclesiastical sanctions' against those who supported it, and urged resistance to the other demands.

By 1949 he was virtually a prisoner, constantly moved around since the faithful flocked to try to see him at whatever place he was. Church property was confiscated, and the monastic orders came under

attack. In 1950 ten senior members of the orders were put on trial.
Most monasteries and all seminaries were closed, and the year
ended with the trial of Beran's deputy, Bishop Zela (Vicar-General of
Olomouc) and of eight leading ecclesiastics. Next year, according to
a Vatican statement, there were seven Czech bishops in prison, and
2,000 out of 7,000 monks. Slovakia (overwhelmingly Catholic) had
fared equally badly. Three Slovak bishops were in prison with hard
labour, one of them a septuagenarian.[1]

Yugoslavia was not behind the other satellites. While permitting
the Orthodox Patriarch, Gavrila, to continue his duties, the Catholic
Church was ruthlessly persecuted. Archbishop Stepinac of Zagreb,
head of the Catholic Church in Croatia, was imprisoned, as well as
other leading clergy, ostensibly on charges—in some cases well-
founded—of collaboration with the Germans. After the breach with
Moscow persecution lessened, though Stepinac remained in prison.

In East Germany the effect of persecution was diminished by the
comparative ease of escape, via Berlin. Archbishop Preysing of
Berlin for the Catholics and Dr. Dibelius for the Protestant
Evangelical Church both took a courageous stand against the
secularization of schools, the propagation of atheism among the
young, and the other policies which were standard for the Communist
régimes.

The End of the Stalin Era

During his last years Stalin drove the Soviet people as hard as he
had ever driven them. After the destruction of war the lee-way to be
made up was colossal. The emphasis in the five-year plans was still
on heavy industry, not merely to restore the basis of the Soviet
economy for peace-time purposes, but to prepare for the next war.
The Germans, said Stalin, would recover in 12 or 15 years, Russia
would recover in 15 or 20, 'and then we shall have another go at it'.[2]

There was no question of a great abundance of consumer goods,
scarcely the chance of the 1940 position in that respect being restored
for some time. Ten per cent more of industrial production was to be
devoted to heavy industry than previously. Shortage of living space

[1] Royal Institute of International Affairs *Surveys* for 1947–8, 1948–9, 1949–50, 1951.
H. Seton Watson: *The East European Revolution*, 287–95.
[2] Djilas: *Conversations with Stalin*, 106.

in the cities remained acute, being worse in many places owing to war damage. An occasional diversion of consumer goods to the home market, or deliveries from the satellites, were made use of to allay the discontent of the masses. For those with savings the devaluation of the rouble was disastrous. By being forced to exchange ten roubles for one, many people's savings were practically wiped out. The state relieved itself of an immense burden of inflation, at the cost of more suffering for the millions, particularly the peasants.

In agriculture improvement was slow. The situation was greatly aggravated by the drought of 1946, the worst since 1890. Famine was only averted by drastic action from Moscow, and a distribution system which was much improved since the famines of the early twenties.

Stalin's only answer for deficiencies and lagging production was to drive his people harder, and when the results were still inadequate, to find scapegoats. The need for scapegoats, together with his chronic suspicions amounting almost to paranoia, drove him to further purges. Discontent smouldered throughout the country, though the only overt rebellion came from the prisoners of the Vorkuta and other concentration camps—people who had nothing to lose but their chains (1950–1).

In his old age Stalin was as opiniated and doctrinaire as ever. When Professor Eugene Varga, a leading economist, criticized the accepted view that the capitalist system as operated in the West, particularly America, was bound to collapse into another great depression, he was disgraced. The brilliant head of the State Planning Commission (Gosplan), Voznessensky, was executed for standing up to Stalin and challenging him on the priorities which Stalin had laid down for development (1949). The intellectuals were disciplined and held to an arid propagandist line under the cultural tyranny of Zhdanov. The novels, poetry and paintings of this period dealt 'not with human beings, but with the conventionalized figures of crane-operators, agronomists, capstan-lathe operators, shock-brigades in the potato-fields, and the rest'.[1] When this approach produced frustration near to rebellion Zhdanov (with or without Stalin's volition) died.

Despite this depressing background, industry forged ahead. The

[1] Crankshaw, 101.

question of dealing with the chronic lag in agriculture aroused much controversy. When the efforts of the chief of the Collective Farm Affairs Council, Andreyev, failed to raise production by cutting down the personal plots of the peasants on the collectives and increasing their work-days, he was not however dismissed. The failure was not surprising in that these small plots, though only a fraction of the cultivated land produced 20 per cent of the food supplies. The lesson was drawn to the extent of allowing each state farm worker, from 1947, to have an acre of his own land.[1]

The conflict of views over agriculture was particularly marked among two of the aspirants to Stalin's mantle, Georgy Malenkov and Nikita Khrushchev. Malenkov, young (coming up to fifty), bourgeois in origins, relatively cultured, suave and supple, had risen through the party apparatus to become, in the thirties, head of the party organization in Moscow, then in charge of the party cadres throughout the U.S.S.R. As a member of Stalin's personal secretariat he kept close to the dictator, becoming a member of the Politburo and vice-Chairman of the Council of Ministers in 1946.

The Soviet government showed itself a true heir of Byzantium in the faction fights behind closed doors, the palace revolutions, and the murders and secret executions among the group of ambitious and fearful men at the centre of government. Even the pen of a Gibbon could scarcely gild these dreary tales of furtive manoeuvres for power. When Zhdanov's star waxed that of Malenkov waned. As an opponent of Malenkov Khrushchev accordingly came more into the foreground. A different type from Malenkov and some ten years older, his chances of becoming heir-apparent seemed slender. From a peasant background and almost self-educated—he could not read or write until in his twenties—lacking the cultural advantages of Malenkov, and without the same closeness of association with Stalin, his rise to prominence had been due to his immense capacity for work and his remarkable personality. He had the ability to give himself fully to the particular person or the immediate situation, to listen with perfect concentration, 'taking in—until, like a born

---

[1] D. W. Treadgold: *Twentieth Century Russia* (Rand, McNally & Co., 1959), 459–60. 7 million farmers in the U.S.A. fed a population of 165 million and produced a surplus. In the U.S.S.R. 50 million farm workers fed a population of 200 million, at much lower living standards. For the Soviet Government's policies regarding the peasants and their plots, see A. Inkeles and K. Geiger (eds.): *Soviet Society* (Constable, 1961), 329 seq.

commander, he was ready to give out'.[1] With this went humour, quickness, originality. Djilas describes him when he was still boss of the Ukraine in the late thirties. 'Khrushchev accompanied us to a collective farm and, without harbouring in any little corner of his mind the slightest doubt of the justice of the system itself, he not only clinked huge glasses of vodka with the collective farmers, but he also inspected the garden hot-beds, peeped into the pigsty, and began discussing practical problems.'[2]

'Discovered' by Kaganovich in the thirties, he was brought to Moscow to be one of the potential replacements for the old guard whom Stalin was liquidating. Khrushchev had the toughness, adaptability and ambition for almost any job. By 1934 he was on the party's Central Committee, and took over as the boss for Moscow when Kaganovich moved up to the Politburo. He looked after the party machine there while capital and country rocked with the holocaust of Stalin's great purges. In 1938 he was moved on to the Ukraine to finish off the purges there, and then became First Secretary of the Ukrainian Communist Party. Though he crawled to Stalin along with his colleagues, his independence of mind and willingness to accept responsibility stood him in good stead as ruler of the forty million Ukrainians, many of them among the most evolved 'proletariat' of the U.S.S.R., and with long traditions of separatism.

Zhdanov died (whether naturally or otherwise) in August 1948; Malenkov resumed his place in the Soviet firmament, but Khrushchev's star did not wane. While Zhdanov's associates now suffered liquidation in the so-called 'Leningrad Case', Khrushchev moved up by taking over the task of reorganizing Soviet agriculture. His performance was by no means successful: his scheme of combining the collectives in large modern 'Agri-towns' was a failure. But at the 19th Party Congress in 1952 (the first since 1939) he was seen to be well in the running.

It was the time of Stalin's last big shake-up. Even an old comrade like Molotov—the only one whom Stalin addressed with the familiar *ty* —lost the Foreign Ministry in March 1949, and came under Stalin's suspicion with the Doctors' Plot, which immediately followed the

---

[1] Crankshaw, 58.
[2] *Conversations with Stalin*, 112. Besides his peasant background, Khrushchev had had first-hand experience of industry as a miner.

19th Congress, in November 1952. There were grounds for his fall from favour. The foreign policy associated with his name, whether his or Stalin's, had produced gains for the expanding Russian Empire —but it was a policy of diminishing returns. The West had been thrown on its guard, and had united and armed to an extent which had scarcely seemed possible in 1946 or 1947. The negative attitude to the Marshall Plan had failed to hold back Western recovery, nor had more success attended the attempt to use the Western Communist Parties to disrupt their countries' economies and sabotage the Schuman Plan, the Atlantic Alliance and German rearmament. The Communist bloc had been caught out over Korea, and the 'Peace Offensive' and the Stockholm Appeal had scarcely produced results commensurate with the effort.

Molotov's policy had failed, but Stalin's disapproval seemed to have other causes. It might be that the prospect of someone else grasping too much of his power was hateful to him. Beria, who had succeeded Yezhov as Stalin's chief security man in 1938, was now demoted (1952). Though he was not, like Yezhov, executed, he saw his successor Ignatiev purge his men[1] as he had formerly purged Yezhov's. Malenkov, whose star had been in the ascendant since just before Zhdanov's death, now seemed to be moving towards an eclipse. The Politburo and the Orgburo were closed down, being replaced by a new Presidium more than double the size of the Polit-buro (25 against 11 members). This manoeuvre, carried out by Stalin at the 19th Congress, brought in new aspirants for power. Khrushchev's position had improved, but temporarily at least control was passing into the hands of Stalin's closest henchman, Lieutenant-General Poskrebyeshev, the head of his personal staff and of his private (armed) security forces.

The purges were coming nearer the centre. In January 1953 it was reported that nine doctors of the Kremlin's staff had been charged with murdering Zhdanov and others of their distinguished patients. Six of these doctors were Jewish. Charges of 'cosmopolitanism and Zionism' were directed at Jews in positions high and low. Fears of another large-scale purge were mounting, when news came on the 4th March that Stalin had suffered a stroke two days before. It was later reported that he had died on the 5th. The anxious group at the

---

[1] The Mingrelian case.

Kremlin sent out a call that the Soviet people should avoid 'disorder and panic'. It was perhaps a reflection of their own state of mind. Among those who had seemed threatened, Molotov and Malenkov had especial cause to be relieved. But their reprieve, if such it was, was not for long.

24: The Khrushchev Era

Khrushchev Gains Power

On Stalin's death a long-drawn, largely hidden struggle for power ensued. Malenkov took over the supreme position, as both Chairman of the Council of Ministers (Prime Minister) and First Secretary of the Party. Beria resumed control of the Police. Whatever anxieties had been troubling Molotov were relieved—he was the only man to speak with feeling at his dead master's funeral. Briefly an appearance of collective leadership was presented to the world.

Stalin's body was hurried away to the embalmers and eventually reappeared by the side of Lenin in the Red Square mausoleum.[1] Even before the funeral orations were pronounced the internecine rivalry of the leadership was beginning to take its toll. Poskrebyshev disappeared without a trace. Beria, the chief gainer from his overthrow, was arrested by his colleagues a few months later (June 1953). In December he was executed. According to Khrushchev's later account, Beria 'was clearly preparing a conspiracy against the Presidium. After waiting for a favourable moment, we designated a special session of the Presidium, to which, of course, Beria was invited too. . . . We began to cross-question him. . . . For all of us it was clear that he was really guilty, and that this man could be dangerous to the party and the country. . . . We came to the unanimous decision that the only correct measure for the defence of the Revolution was to shoot him immediately. This decision was adopted by us, and carried out on the spot.'[2]

Within a fortnight of assuming power Malenkov was deposed from the headship of the party—being 'released', as he euphemistically put

[1] Stalin's death saved the doctors of the 'Plot', all of whom were now rehabilitated, except for two who had died. With the 'de-Stalinization' programme later, his corpse was moved to a more obscure position in the Kremlin wall.

[2] Statement to Senator Pierre Commin, May 1956, quoted in B. D. Wolfe: *Khrushchev and Stalin's Ghost* (Atlantic Press, 1957), 316. Beria may have been plotting a coup with the N.K.V.D. generals, who held key posts in the Moscow garrison.—J. M. Mackintosh: *Strategy and Tactics of Soviet Foreign Policy* (O.U.P., 1962), 73.

it, at his own request. This marked the first stage of Khrushchev's gaining control of the party. Malenkov had allied himself with the technocrats and top administrators in the government—he had packed the technical ministries with his supporters—while controlling (as he thought) the party as well. The party at the time was less important: it had lost ground in Stalin's last years, and the technocrats were in the ascendant. Khrushchev's aim was difficult to accomplish: to re-convert the party into a premier instrument of power, and use it to hoist himself into the supreme position. Having ousted Malenkov from the Party Secretaryship, Khrushchev, after a decent interval, replaced him in that position (September 1953). He at once began installing his henchmen in key posts in the party apparatus.

In the interval between Stalin's death and Beria's fall, Khrushchev may have allied himself with Beria in order to demote Malenkov. Molotov too was thought to be an ally of Beria's,[1] so when Beria fell, it was likely that Molotov's position would become shaky too. Meanwhile Khrushchev found new allies. Having kicked away the support of Beria, he elevated Bulganin (of the senior administrative hierarchy) and made him Minister of Defence. This gave him some control of the army, and to complete his authority in this sphere Khrushchev recalled Marshal Zhukov to be Deputy Minister of Defence. The hero of Leningrad and saviour of Stalingrad had been made practically an 'unperson' by Stalin because of his too great popularity. Now, but not for very long, he returned to the foreground.

Malenkov was challenged when Khrushchev began criticizing him publicly (though without mentioning his name) for failing to reorganize the collectives and for allowing agriculture to lag; also for the 'soft' policy of increasing consumer goods instead of continuing Stalin's line of concentrating on heavy industry—a line which Khrushchev speedily abandoned himself as soon as his power was complete. While advocating a 'hard' policy at home, Khrushchev started a 'soft' line abroad, by preaching the need of a reconciliation with Tito. In February 1955 Malenkov resigned the premiership, on account of his self-confessed 'inexperience', and his 'guilt and responsibility for the unsatisfactory state of affairs in agriculture'. (It was paradoxical that Khrushchev had in fact been responsible for agriculture for the previous eighteen months.)

[1] R. Conquest: *Power and Policy in the U.S.S.R.* (Macmillan, 1961), 202–12.

For a while the façade of collective leadership was maintained, as the rivals showed themselves together in public with every appearance of *bonhomie*. Then Molotov was replaced at the Foreign Ministry by the young and comparatively inexperienced Shepilov (June 1956). The technocrats were also under attack. Kaganovich, to whom before the war Khrushchev had owed his first promotion at the centre, was progressively demoted.

Not only Russia, but also the outside world, was beginning to feel the impact of Khrushchev's irrepressible personality. A new line was started in foreign policy in 1955, before Molotov was pushed out, which brought Bulganin and Khrushchev before the world in a remarkable two-man publicity act. At Belgrade the two talked with Tito, at the Geneva 'Summit' with Eisenhower, Eden and Faure;[1] in the winter they stormed Asia, the one with his suavity, the other with his folksiness, through India, Burma and Afghanistan. Next year it was the turn of Britain, where Malenkov was sent first to spy out the land (April 1956). His success was so much greater than that of 'B. and K.', as they were now familiarly known, that it may have caused his final eclipse. It was one of the occasions when Khrushchev's irritability projected the wrong 'image'—he answered rudely, obviously being nettled when questioned, at a dinner in the House of Commons, about the fate of certain socialist leaders in the Communist bloc. The world saw little more of Malenkov's urbanity and charm—fifteen months later he was in the wilderness.

A new act in the drama had opened with the Twentieth Party Congress in February 1956. Here in secret session Khrushchev made his famous disclosures about Stalin—for what purported to be a verbatim account soon became the common property of the world's press. Khrushchev showed himself as a ruthless iconoclast not only of Stalin—the man whom he accused of 'choking a person morally and spiritually'—but also of the 'cult of personality' as a whole. He took his stand on the example of Lenin, who, he claimed, had never allowed such a cult to develop, and who had specifically warned against the roughness and high-handedness of Stalin.

As if to prevent Khrushchev's own personality from replacing Stalin's as a cult, his anxious colleagues drew together and—briefly—appeared to be worsting their dangerous rival. The year 1956 was a

[1] The French Prime Minister.

bad one for Khrushchev. The 'thaw' in relations between East and West, together with the damning indictment of Stalinism which Khrushchev had made, combined to produce restlessness among the satellites. Explosions occurred in East Berlin, Czechoslovakia, Poland and Hungary.[1] The wooing of Yugoslavia ended in another rupture. Though by no means alone responsible for the 'softer' approach in foreign policy, Khrushchev had to bear a large part of the blame for its apparent failures.

Although Khrushchev had already packed a third of the Central Committee of the party with his followers, and had put forward more than half the candidate members,[2] he could not yet reckon on a majority there; on the highest state body (Presidium) he was in a minority. The Presidium began to curb his power. On a mission to Warsaw to deal with the Polish crisis, Khrushchev was flanked by Molotov, Kaganovich and Mikoyan, while the technocrat Pervukhin was made Chairman of the State Economic Commission with considerably broadened powers—an 'overlord of overlords', whose power over the economy went far beyond that of Khrushchev.[3]

Khrushchev's response was to initiate a devolution of responsibility on to regional economic councils, while strengthening the role of Gosplan (the State Planning Commission) and undercutting that of Pervukhin's Economic Commission. This scheme was approved by the Supreme Soviet in May 1957, and the Economic Commission was dissolved. Whereupon Khrushchev's rivals in the Presidium rose above their own internecine disputes—Malenkov, Molotov, Kaganovich, Pervukhin, and the now insecure Bulganin and Shepilov. They rehearsed Khrushchev's shortcomings and demanded his resignation. But the burly, bold fighter was not so easily unseated. He claimed the right to be heard by a full meeting of the Central Committee, where his years of patronage were at last bearing fruit. Summoning every last man among his supporters, even from the farthest points of the Soviet Empire from which they could be hurried in time, he

[1] See below, pp. 305–12.
[2] 53 out of 133 members, and 76 out of 122 candidate members. A. Brumberg (editor): *Russia Under Khrushchev* (Methuen, 1962), article by R. Lowenthal: 'The nature of Khrushchev's power', 106.
[3] Ibid., 107. On the relation between the Central Committee and the Presidium (which replaced the Politburo in 1952), and Khrushchev's manoeuvres in regard to them both, see M. Fainsod: *How Russia is Ruled* (Harvard, revised edition, 1963), 219, 323 seq., etc.

confronted his opponents with an overwhelming majority. So 'intra-party democracy' won the day for Khrushchev. The 'anti-party' group was routed (June 1957).

Heads did not literally roll—a sign of progress in the Soviet Union, but Khrushchev's rivals were safely put away. Molotov was sent as Ambassador to the Outer Mongolian Republic; Malenkov went to equally far-off Kazakhstan as manager of a power-station (he had formerly been Minister for Electric Power); Pervukhin, who had re-canted at an early stage, went only as far as East Germany as Am-bassador. Shepilov became a schoolmaster; Kaganovich had a minor appointment in the provinces. Bulganin, who also recanted, remained titular Prime Minister until January 1958: he simply dwindled away.[1]

Foreign Policy After Stalin

Stalin's death made little difference in the conduct of Soviet foreign policy, for Molotov, who took back the Foreign Ministry from Vyshinsky, was committed to the same line as his defunct master. It was the unhealthy situation in the satellites which forced a reappraisal on Moscow. The invention of the Hydrogen bomb encouraged a more flexible approach since, less than ever, could either side, if it came to a war, expect to be the gainer. Also, the long predicted economic de-pression had not yet hit the West. Instead the economic and military strength of the West was increasing. The Atlantic Pact seemed, to the Soviet leadership, a further threat to their empire, with E.D.C. and German rearmament as unpleasant possibilities which might soon be realized.

American policy was to contain Communism.[2] For the Russian leaders the time had come to break out of the circle in which America and her allies had confined them. Tentative steps in this direction were the agreement to accept an armistice in Korea, after the stale-mate of the endlessly dreary talks at Panmunjon (27 July 1953), and the withdrawal of opposition to the choice of Dag Hammarskjöld as Trygve Lie's successor in the post of Secretary-General of the United Nations.

Tito's success in maintaining himself in spite of Moscow's hostility had stirred unrest among the satellites. Dissatisfaction was rife be-cause Soviet exploitation and Communist mismanagement kept living

[1] Crankshaw: *Khrushchev's Russia*, 50.   [2] See Note at end of chapter, p. 336.

standards low, besides being an affront to national pride. The demand for freedom was building up below the surface of affairs, and might at any time break out with volcanic force. A new course in policy was necessary if these energies were to be dissipated or controlled.

Control through the party apparatus, the army and the security police was so complete throughout the satellites that organized plots against the régime were virtually impracticable. Spontaneous uprisings could not however always be checked. In June 1953 the East German government raised the work 'norms' for several industries. This was too much, coming on top of years of poor diet, rationing, queues and overcrowding. The workers of the Soviet Zone of Berlin came out into the streets (16 June). Some of the police defected to the West; others who tried to make arrests were overborne by the swelling crowds. After Western stations had broadcast news of these events, risings took place all over the zone. In Berlin 50,000 demonstrators marched on the 17th to the Potsdamer Platz, burnt pictures of Stalin and Ulbricht (the Prime Minister of the German Democratic Republic), opened the prisons and beat up security agents and party officials. A group of strikers climbed the Brandenburger Gate and tore down the Red flag while Soviet troops looked on. Elsewhere workers seized control of factories, set up their own committees, and barricaded themselves in.

On the afternoon of 17 June orders came from Moscow to put down the rising by force. Soviet troops began firing into the crowds. The workers found that with bare hands it was impossible to stop the tanks. The demonstrations were called off in Berlin, though they continued sporadically elsewhere for several days. Deaths by firing or after subsequent courts martial were over four hundred; more than a thousand people were injured, while five thousand were arrested. Such severity alternated with concessions in Soviet policy during these years. Relaxations had actually been initiated in East Germany just before the rising, and when it was over Moscow made further concessions—such as the cancellation of reparations payments—in an attempt to appease its German subjects.

Unrest had been touched off in Czechoslovakia by the currency reform of 30 May 1953 which wiped out most of the workers' savings and reduced their wages. Riots occurred in June at Pilsen and throughout the Moravia-Ostrava industrial area.

The fabric of the monolithic empire was rudely shaken. 'One of the decisive advantages of the democratic camp,' Malenkov had claimed, 'which is its principal point of difference with the imperialist camp, is that it is not torn by internal contradictions and struggles.'[1] This proud boast had to be substantiated. But attempts to keep the people quiet by relaxing control over the satellite governments, allowing each of them to find their own 'road to socialism', switching production to consumer goods and lightening the censorship—all these tended to release the pent-up tension which resulted in popular outbreaks.

The attempt to frustrate Western military policy and German rearmament failed. E.D.C. fell through, but the Paris Agreements brought Germany into NATO and confronted Moscow with a new situation. By now however Russia had the H-bomb (announced by Malenkov in August 1953), and was making great strides with rockets. A long debate took place between the soldiers and civilians as to whether mutual deterrence should be the aim, or whether Russia should prepare to wage aggressive war with these new and devastating weapons. The decision was made to prepare for taking the initiative in a nuclear war,[2] though later, when Khrushchev was securely in power, he proclaimed deterrence as the objective.

While Soviet military strength was growing, Moscow encouraged the 'thaw'. In April 1953 Churchill, sensing the new trends, had proposed a Summit meeting of Soviet and Western leaders. This was looking ahead, since even the Foreign Ministers of the Four had not met since 1949. But progress was made: a meeting of the Foreign Ministers took place in Berlin in January 1954. Though the outcome was disappointing, a further meeting was arranged, and eventually took place at Geneva. This after much travail brought forth the armistice agreement for Indo-China (April–June 1954).[3]

The Berlin Conference was deadlocked over Germany, and this proved the obstacle to progress over other matters. The Four were agreed that a government representing Germany as a whole should be brought into being when the peace treaty was finally negotiated.

[1] Speech to Supreme Soviet, 8 May 1953 (*Pravda* report, quoted in J. M. Mackintosh: *Strategy and Tactics of Soviet Foreign Policy* (O.U.P., 1962), 77.

[2] Mackintosh, 96–7.

[3] See pp. 257–8. The conference failed, however, to turn the Korean armistice into a peace settlement.

But whereas the Western powers insisted that such a government could only be set up by free elections in East as in West Germany, the Russians insisted that it be brought into being through a merger of the existing governments of the (Eastern) German Democratic Republic and the (Western) German Federal Republic. Since the former was not recognized by the Western powers, and was regarded as merely a puppet of the Soviets, they could not accept this arrangement. The Russians for their part would not allow free elections in East Germany. As Molotov put it, 'so-called free elections . . . might result in the violation of the vital interests of the working people of the German Democratic Republic, and we cannot agree to that.'[1]

Some progress was however made. After months of haggling a treaty was signed with Austria (15 May 1955). The Russians abandoned their condition that a peace treaty would have to be made with Germany first. All they specified was that Austria should be forbidden to unite with Germany, and that it should be neutralized. On this basis they, and the other occupying powers, withdrew their troops from Austria. The Austrians refused a mutual assistance pact with Russia, which Molotov ingeniously suggested might supplement and not compromise her neutrality (leaving it to Russia to decide when intervention with troops would be necessary). The Austrians however would not go beyond 'neutrality of the same type as that maintained in Switzerland', and this was written into the final treaty.[2]

The treaty would have left the Russians without any rights for keeping troops in Rumania and Hungary, because previously the excuse for this had been the necessity of defending their line of communication with the Soviet forces in Austria. But—no doubt the contingency had been foreseen—they now had the Warsaw Pact. This, negotiated in the same month, May 1955, was ostensibly the Soviet riposte to NATO. As a means of military integration it made no difference to the existing arrangements in the east, but legally it gave Russia the right to keep garrisons in the satellites. One disadvantage for Russia from leaving her zone of Austria was that it gave Hungarians an escape route through Eastern Austria. This was the salvation of many of them in the uprising a few months later.

Though Austria was now free, the German problem was as

---

[1] October 1955—Mackintosh, 113.
[2] D. J. Dallin: *Soviet Foreign Policy After Stalin* (Lippincott, 1961), 256.

intractable as ever. When the Summit Conference eventually took place at Geneva in July 1955, Khrushchev and Bulganin had no doubts about maintaining a divided Germany. They may have thought that the Western powers were now ready to accept this, in return for Soviet recognition of NATO and a measure of West German re-armament. Whether or not they expected a settlement, the conference was part of the holding operation in the West—indeed the entire 'thaw' may have been designed for this purpose—while they pro-secuted an adventurous policy in the East.

The Geneva 'Summit' produced some useful photographs for the Russians: 'B. and K.' in benign conversation with Eisenhower and Eden. Both Eastern and Western leaders learnt, if they did not know it already, that none of them wanted war. Otherwise the positions remained unaltered. The 'Geneva spirit' became a cliché of Soviet propaganda for a long time afterwards. The two leaders accepted an invitation for a visit to England, and this took place the following year.[1] But when the Foreign Secretaries met at Geneva in the autumn to continue the work of the conference, Molotov quickly demon-strated that in reality nothing had changed.

Soviet military forces had doubled during the Korean War.[2] They stayed at the higher level while disarmament was broached with the West. Proposals made in 1955 to destroy stocks of nuclear bombs and evacuate bases, while 'freezing' armed forces at their existing levels (in preparation for cutting them down), would have left the West de-prived of many of its weapons and means of delivering them. At the same time there would remain on Russia's western frontiers Soviet and satellite armies totalling a million and a quarter men against the 16 divisions or 240,000 men of the NATO forces in Europe.

At Geneva neither Eisenhower's proposal for 'open skies' (freedom to fly over and photograph each others' countries), nor Eden's for a demilitarized zone on each side of the Iron Curtain, really interested the Russians. They were preparing a breakthrough in Asia, where the Bandung conference of Asian and African states had taken place in April (1955). Though Russia had not been included, China had shown the way in developing an ideological offensive. The Soviet leaders would not be outdone, and their visit that winter to Asia was an

[1] See above, p. 296. For the conference see Eden: *Full Circle*, 290–315.
[2] In terms of manpower Soviet forces rose to 5,763,000 men under arms—Dallin, 248.

enormous personal success. The Geneva spirit was quickly forgotten as, intoxicated by the plaudits of millions of Indians, Khrushchev sweepingly rewrote history. 'The British, French and Americans started the Second World War,' he declaimed. 'They sent troops against our country, and these troops were the troops of Hitlerite Germany.'[1]

Khrushchev Woos Tito

Khrushchev's influence on Russian policy was shown in a determination to bring Yugoslavia back into the fold. Molotov accepted that Russia should reopen diplomatic relations with Yugoslavia, but he jibbed at going any further. Tito on his part insisted on something like a public apology from the Russians. Khrushchev was prepared to pay this price, in the hope of gaining control of Yugoslav policy by re-establishing relations on the party level. With a small delegation (not including Molotov) he went to Belgrade (26 May 1955) and made amends of a kind publicly in a speech on arrival at the airport.[2] The apology was coupled with an appeal to 'establish mutual understanding between the Communist Party of the Soviet Union and the Yugoslav Communist League'. Tito however remained cold to these blandishments.

The amnesty of political prisoners and the rehabilitation of those purged after Russia's break with Yugoslavia were partly due to the need to appease Tito. There was also an economic motive for releasing inmates of the slave camps. This form of labour had proved inefficient and costly, and was now regarded as out of date. Some men whose purging had led to their death would be given only posthumous rehabilitation. Those who had purged them were in some cases purged in their turn. In Bulgaria the dead Kostov was rehabilitated while Chervenkov[3] was now obliged to resign—significantly at a meeting of the National Assembly attended by a Yugoslav delegation (April 1956). The Czechs too made their apologies, as did the unrepentant Stalinite Rakosi in Hungary—but only after considerable pressure from Moscow. In both countries Communists accused of

---

[1] *Economist*, 3 December 1955; Dallin, 309.

[2] The nearest to an apology was that 'we sincerely regret' the disturbance of good relations. For the rest the blame was cast on 'Beria, Abakumov and other exposed enemies of the people'.—R.I.I.A.: *Documents on International Affairs*, 1955, where the speech is quoted in full.

[3] See above, p. 282.

Titoism were released. Another sop was the dissolution of the Cominform (April 1956).

The Twentieth Congress

The change of line was unsettling for the satellite governments. Their sense of insecurity was reflected in restlessness on the part of the people. This increased as the 'thaw' brought some relaxation of controls and expectation of further gains in the future. On top of this came the revelations made in Khrushchev's secret speech to the Twentieth Congress of the Communist Party in Moscow. By April 1956 news of this was leaking out.

Gone for ever was the myth of the infallible correctness and monolithic unity of the Communist Party. Stalin was shown to be a ruthless tyrant who flouted all the canons of Leninist leadership to seize and maintain power. By sending millions to servitude or death, especially those of the army purges, he jeopardized Russia's security, and was revealed as nerveless and defeatist when the Nazi legions, thanks to his inept strategy, advanced to Leningrad and Moscow. His reputation as a great war leader was demolished. While he tried to keep control by telephone of the fighting on all parts of the front, he made his dispositions (it was said) with the aid of a globe instead of large-scale maps.

The Byzantine struggles and intrigues—the Leningrad Plot, the 'Beria gang' and much else that was unsavoury—could hardly build respect for the Soviet régime once news of them came from this authentic source to the ears of the submerged peoples. Khrushchev's attempt to cast the blame on Stalin for so much might help him in his struggle for power within the party, but it could have dangerous consequences for the Soviet system as a whole. The peoples of the satellites could take notice of weakness in the Soviet régime from Khrushchev's account of Stalin's menaces against Tito, however much this account was designed to soothe Yugoslav susceptibilities. 'I will shake my little finger,' said Stalin (according to Khrushchev), 'and there will be no more Tito. He will fall.' Khrushchev's comment was: 'This did not happen to Tito. No matter how much or how little Stalin shook, not only his little finger but everything else that he could shake, Tito did not fall.'[1]

[1] From Khrushchev's speech to Twentieth Congress reprinted in Wolfe, op. cit., 200.

The Polish Rising

Moscow's wooing of Tito was not lost on the satellites. National Communism seemed to be paying off. Tito was offered by Russia loans of cash, credits for building factories, technicians to help build them; trade and air agreements were signed; scientific-technical co-operation was organized; Yugoslav and Soviet writers visited each other, and Russian tourists were given visas for Yugoslavia. Tito was welcomed to Moscow, Khrushchev came 'to have a rest' at Belgrade, and the two then went off to a select high-ranking conference at Yalta (September 1956). Tito was demanding a measure of independence for the satellites similar to that enjoyed by his country: this was his price for co-operating with the Soviet bloc. The Russians haggled, being unwilling to relax their grip too much on the satellites, lest they came under his, or Western influence, instead of theirs.

The satellites were increasingly posing a problem, since the process of relaxation was getting out of control. While the wooing of Tito continued, Poland and Hungary erupted. In Poland the main victim of the 'Titoist' purges, Gomulka, was released from jail at the end of 1954, though he had to wait until April 1956 for the rehabilitation process to be started. In March death had removed the Stalinist Bierut, which made it possible for the 'new course' to proceed apace. In May the remaining senior Stalinist, Berman, resigned. Thirty-thousand prisoners were granted amnesty, 40,000 others had their sentences reduced. The Chief of Police and other members of the old régime were dismissed.

Encouraged by these evident signs of de-Stalinization, the workers made economic demands, and on failure to receive satisfaction began to organize strikes. In Poznan (June 1956) the workers of the Z.I.S.P.O. (railway carriages) enterprise elected a committee to negotiate with the Minister. When it was rumoured that their delegates had been arrested they struck and began a demonstration, which soon reached mammoth proportions. People poured from factories, offices and schools, marching and chanting to the amazement of numerous Western visitors who were present for an International Trade Fair. Many troops fraternized with the mob, but enough were found loyal to the régime to stop the demonstrations after three days of fighting in the streets. The demonstrators had stormed a jail and released the prisoners. Now the government did not dare to fill the jails again. Free speech had become the order of the day, and the security agents were powerless to repress it. In all the major cities of Poland mass demonstrations took place.

Early in July concessions were made to the workers, while the government tried to pass off the riots as the work of 'foreign imperialist agents'. This was the line favoured by Moscow, but facts were too much for a majority of the Polish government. By the middle of July Ochab, the new Party Secretary, was stating that the riots were due not to imperialist agents but to 'bureaucracy and soullessness' on the part of the authorities. It was necessary, he said, to pay attention to the 'social roots' of the workers' unrest.[1]

Alarmed by this independence, Bulganin and Zhukov were sent from Moscow to bring the Polish Party to heel. Their warnings were ignored. Gomulka and other anti-Stalinists were readmitted to the party in August. Plans were made to elect a new Politburo to include Gomulka and his associates, but not the Russian Marshal Rokossovsky, who had been since Stalin's time Commander-in-Chief and Minister of Defence.

The Polish leaders refused a summons to Moscow, and asked the Russians not to send a delegation themselves until after the Central Committee had met to elect the Politburo. The Russians came nevertheless uninvited—a four-man delegation representing the chief factions at the Kremlin: Khrushchev, Molotov,[2] Kaganovich and Mikoyan. The background of the violent and stormy session that ensued was the fact that the Soviet garrisons—the nearest being already within thirty miles of the capital—were moving on Warsaw and the other centres, and that Soviet warships were heading towards the Baltic ports. Gomulka, now First Secretary, made it clear that the Polish army would fight.

Khrushchev gave up his threatening and offensive language. On their side the Poles said they had no intention of moving out of the 'socialist camp', and would keep to the Soviet line in foreign affairs. Accepting that Rokossovsky and the other Stalinists would be dropped, the Russian delegation returned to Moscow resigned to pursuing methods of co-operation rather than bludgeoning. Soviet troops

---

[1] Quoted in Mackintosh, 156.
[2] Although he had been dismissed as Foreign Minister in June.

were withdrawn to their bases; Rokossovsky and his Russian associates left the country.

Though Gomulka gained great popularity by his stand against the
Russians, the Poles were dissatisfied with his half-way policy. They
wanted complete independence, and no longer to be tied in any way to
Russia. It was all Gomulka, with his new prestige, could do, to hold
the line at the point to which the Russians had allowed it to move.
The Hungarian rising, occurring just after Gomulka took over in
Poland, strained the new government's powers of control to the
uttermost. Gomulka kept his pledge to the Russians, assented to their
decision to use force in Hungary, and ordered the Polish delegates at
the United Nations to vote with them on the Hungarian issue. A
measure of autonomy was secured, but Poland still remained firmly
in the Communist bloc.

The Hungarian Rising

In Hungary the rising began in much the same way as in Poland. But
whereas, in Poland, Communist but anti-Stalinist leadership emerged
strong enough to arrest the revolution at a certain point, this did not
happen in Hungary. There the party had been more deeply divided
than in Poland, and had become even more isolated from the people.
When Imre Nagy was eventually forced to the fore, he failed to gain
the solid backing of the remaining Communist leaders, as Gomulka
did in Poland. His government could stand neither against the rising
tide of democratic demands, nor against the threat of Soviet force.
The Nagy régime was swept far into new courses by the one before
being overwhelmed by the other.

Rakosi had not merely been Stalin's man. He was an imitator of
Stalin at all points. To the techniques which he copied from his
master he owed his success in dividing and dominating the party. The
elimination of Rajk left him undisputed ruler. Highly successful in
manipulating power, Rakosi failed disastrously in governing. The
economic situation of Hungary, after a few years of Rakosi's rule, was
most pitiful by comparison with that of other satellites and by contrast
with its former flourishing agriculture and promising industry. Here
certain observations made long before by Machiavelli, were strikingly
illustrated. By contrast with the remarkable economic development
of the free countries of Western Europe, that of Eastern Europe,

Hungary in particular, was lagging. 'All towns and all countries that are in all respects free profit by this enormously. . . . Riches abound there, alike those that come from agriculture and those that are produced by the arts. . . . The contrary of this happens in countries which live in servitude; and the harder the servitude the more the well-being, to which they are accustomed, dwindles.'[1]

Economically Hungary was important to Russia. No movement for relaxation of the régime could be allowed to jeopardize Soviet control of the uranium mines. But the conspicuous waste of Rakosi's economic policy was jeopardizing not merely the living standards but the livelihood of the workers. At vast expense an attempt had been made to build an underground railway in the capital which would redound to the prestige of the government much as Moscow's underground had redounded to that of the Soviet régime. The project had to be abandoned after more than a billion forint were spent, owing to the waterlogged subsoil which made the construction impracticable. The vast industrial complex of Sztalinvaros, designed as the centre of a new iron and steel industry, had to be left only partially built when funds for its completion dried up. Money which might have been available for easing the workers' lot was in this fashion frittered away. In any case the Korean War brought new hardships. Industrial goals were revised to meet the increased production demanded by Moscow. Work-norms, though starting low, increased in the early fifties by 50–60 per cent.

Rakosi knew how to insulate himself against the growing discontent. He built up a rootless bureaucracy, dependent only on himself, and took steps to atomize and dehumanize the population. The frenzy of industrialization in the towns, collectivization in the countryside, indoctrination courses and other organized activity of various kinds outside working hours, were designed to fatigue and deaden the people. Terror had a similar function. It 'had approximately the same effect inside as it had outside the Party. What group solidarity there was broke down. Interpersonal communications, other than of an official nature, stopped. Every individual stood alone before the impersonal monster that was the Party.'[2]

---

[1] *The Discourses of Niccolo Machiavelli* (Editor: L. J. Walker, Routledge & Kegan Paul, 1950), 365–6 (Book II. 2.10).
[2] Zinner: *Revolution in Hungary* (Columba University Press, 1962), 135.

A new course seemed to be beginning when, soon after Stalin's death in 1953, Imre Nagy was made Premier. Though a thoroughly loyal Communist, Nagy had been dismissed from his official positions at the height of Stalin's anti-Tito campaign. Returning to teaching, with a university post concerned with agriculture, Nagy won favourable opinions in many circles, among students and in the countryside. His speech in Parliament after his accession to the premiership, frankly analysing the country's ills and promising reforms, made a great impression. Though Moscow backed him on this line, Rakosi led his party colleagues against him. Still fighting a rearguard action for Stalinism, and against rehabilitating the victims of the purges, Rakosi early in 1955 for the second time secured Nagy's downfall. Later he was expelled from the party.

Among the instruments of Rakosi's power was the Writers' Association. Intellectuals, and particularly younger ones, had been built up into a privileged élite, who would popularize the régime and the 'party line' of the moment. This group, now disillusioned, turned against their patron. Information had leaked out that the evidence on which Rajk had been sent to his death was a fabrication, and that the evidence for Yugoslav plots and Titoist activities was equally groundless. At the time when Nagy was expelled from the party the Writers sent in a memorandum of protest to the party leadership. This did not raise specifically political issues, but concerned 'gross encroachments on artistic freedom'.[1] It was however the first step to a full-scale revolt by the intellectuals, from all walks of life, who found a meeting-point in the Petöffi Circle. This body, with no funds or frame-work for mass organization, attracted thousands with its programme of public debates and discussions in which the real nature of the Rakosi régime was exposed. The journalists' debate of 27 June, with an overflow of several thousand, lasted from 7 p.m. to 3 a.m. in an atmosphere of open revolution, with repeated demands for the resignation of Rakosi and the restoration of freedom of the press.

On 18 July Rakosi was dropped from the Central Committee of the party, but remained as Premier even after admitting his part in the frame-up of Rajk. So far he was backed by Moscow, where the leaders were used to relying on him as 'honest' and dependable. When at last Mikoyan arrived to dismiss him from his offices, Rakosi

[1] Zinner, 182.

could not believe the order until he had telephoned Khrushchev. He was replaced by Gerö, a man inadequate for the task, but the only Stalinist left whom Moscow trusted.

Attempts to repress the Writers failed: even non-Communists were elected to the governing body of the Association. With the opening of the universities in the autumn the students began using their organizations for anti-government work. 'In the final days before the revolution (they) seemed to be setting the tone and pace of the opposition.'[1] At the re-interment of Rajk (for which his widow had long been clamouring) everyone—students, writers, intellectuals and the masses who turned out for the occasion—all felt themselves united against the régime (6 October 1956).

On the 23rd Gerö broadcast a speech denouncing the revolutionary movement in old-fashioned Stalinist terms. People surged into the streets. A vast concourse at the City Park pulled down the huge metal statue of Stalin and broke it into pieces. Another crowd besieged the Radio Building, and were fired upon by the hated A.V.O. (security police). On their attempting to make arrests, the A.V.O. men were beaten up. Arms were looted from factories and distributed. The crowd called repeatedly for Imre Nagy, who was at last fetched and with evident unwillingness made a brief speech from a balcony.

The Communist Party, unnerved by these events, almost disintegrated. Soviet troops were moved into the capital. Too few to quell the mobs, they aggravated the trouble. Some of them on the 25th in Parliament Square, fired on the crowd, with many casualties resulting. Mikoyan and Suslov, who had just arrived to patch something up, reprimanded Gerö for involving Soviet troops. Next day he was replaced by Nagy as Premier, while retaining the post of First Secretary, which later he handed over to Kadar.

On the 26th, Mikoyan, Suslov, Gerö and some other leading Communists left Budapest. Nagy took up his quarters in the Parliament building. As the hectic days succeeded one another with constant pressure for radical changes in the régime, he gradually moved towards accepting a situation in which one by one the democratic freedoms were restored until, on 30 October the one-party system was abolished. By then a cease-fire had been arranged, after 250 people had been killed and a further 3,000 or more wounded. Cardinal

[1] Zinner, 226.

Mindszenty was released; educational freedom was declared. On 3 November a coalition government was set up of the Communist Party with the three democratic parties which it had formerly suppressed. It existed for only 24 hours.

Nagy had little time except for sanctioning these changes and receiving delegations, until he had to give most of his attention to one overriding need, that of effecting the withdrawal of the Soviet army from Hungary. With shouts of 'Russians go home!' ringing in their ears, the Soviet tanks at last rumbled away from their stations in front of public buildings. But while this was happening Russian troops were pouring into Hungary, and the garrisons in Buda were not evacuated. The Soviet army sealed off Buda's airport, and later seized the others in the country. That same day (31 October), Mikoyan and Suslov left after a second brief visit to the capital, having given fair words to the new government in an atmosphere described as amicable.[1]

On 1 November Nagy remonstrated with the Soviet ambassador about the continued troop movements, and received an unsatisfactory reply. Nagy then abrogated Hungary's membership of the Warsaw Pact, and declared her neutrality. He telegraphed the Secretary-General of the United Nations asking first that 'the defence of this neutrality by the four great powers' be placed on the agenda of the General Assembly.

It was a vain plea. Kadar, though a member of the inner cabinet, disapproved the length to which concessions had gone. On 1 November he and some other Communists slipped across the border into Soviet territory, to wait for the Red Army to do its work. The Soviet Ambassador assured Nagy that all that was needed was for two commissions to be set up for negotiating with the Soviet authorities, the one on the political aspects of abrogating the Warsaw Treaty, the other on the technical matters concerned with the withdrawal of troops. On 3 November a mixed Hungarian-Soviet committee met to deal with these technical matters. After an adjournment it was due to reconvene that night, but this time at the Russian headquarters outside the city. The Minister of Defence and the Chief of Staff drove there to continue the talks. They were arrested and never heard of again.

[1] Zinner, 223.

Next morning, fifteen armoured divisions, including 6,000 tanks, 'launched their attack on the unsuspecting country. Thunderous gun-fire boomed out from the hills of Buda and shells began to fall in the middle of the city'.[1] At 5.20 p.m. Nagy announced the attack over the radio. 'Our troops are fighting. The government is in its place. I hereby inform the people of Hungary and world opinion of the situation.' Further appeals were broadcast, ending with one from the Writers' Association. At seven minutes past eight the radio station fell silent.

The Aftermath of Hungary

The events in Poland and Hungary marked a severe setback for the Communist world. In both countries, and more particularly in Hungary, the Communists had been faced with popular risings. In Hungary the workers of Budapest and other cities turned out to fight Soviet tanks with home-made bombs, sometimes practically with their bare hands. For weeks after the Russian re-occupation of Hungary strikes continued under local factory committees. Attempts were made, with partial success, at a general strike (21 November, and 9–11 December 1956), but the workers' organizations were so harried and hampered by the agents of the restored Communist régime that such demonstrations had to be abandoned. The vast crowds of women who came to mourn silently at the tomb of the Unknown Soldier and other places were an impressive tribute to the depth of feeling of the entire nation. In the end hunger and the onset of winter forced the workers to resume production.

This was the moment of 'agonising reappraisal' for thousands of Communists, both within and without the Soviet bloc. Those within, like the students of Moscow University, could do little more than raise awkward questions. Those without, especially in Western Europe, abandoned the party in large numbers.

The casualties and damage, particularly in Budapest, were considerable—about 2,800 dead and 13,000 wounded. Many buildings were demolished by the Red Army in the course of its 'police operation'. A later casualty was Imre Nagy himself. Having been granted asylum at the Yugoslav Embassy for himself and other colleagues and their families, he was given an assurance that he could return to his

[1] G. Mikes: *The Hungarian Revolution* (Deutsch, 1957), 148.

home under a safe-conduct. But he, along with others of his party, were taken by Soviet Security agents from the coach in which they were travelling and disappeared. They were next heard of months later when they were put on trial. Nagy was executed in June 1957.

Kadar was persuaded by the Russians to take on the thankless task of heading a new Communist régime in Hungary. This convinced anti-Stalinist—he had been horribly tortured under Rakosi—now showed himself a true Moscow man. Without a shred of support in the country, he dutifully carried out Moscow's bidding. Repression of the remnants of liberty was the line, while luring the workers with material baits. The Writers' Association was suppressed, but work-norms were lowered, loans were offered by Russia, the current five-year plan was abolished, and provision for more plentiful consumer goods made instead.

While suffering a severe loss of prestige in Hungary, Russia had not done much better over Suez. The Anglo-French-Israeli attack on Egypt took place at the same time as the Hungarian rising. Had it not been for that rising, indeed, the Soviet government might have been tempted to intervene actively in Egypt, whose largely Soviet-armed forces were routed in Sinai, and whose MIG jets had been obliged to fly off ignominiously,[1] and avoid combat. Threats of rockets did something to save Soviet prestige in Asia and Africa, but had little effect elsewhere. Meetings of the satellite leaders with the Russians were called to give mutual support and a united front, but most timely for the Russians was the expression of solidarity accorded by the Chinese People's Republic. In January 1957 the Premier, Chou En-lai arrived in Moscow with a government and party delegation. He obligingly put his signature to a Sino-Soviet-East German communiqué endorsing the Soviet line on Hungary and calling for unity among the Communist countries.

Foreign Policy After Hungary

The immediate tasks facing Khrushchev after Hungary were the recovery of prestige for the Soviet Union, and the consolidation of his own régime. The latter was achieved in June 1957 when he won

[1] The related question as to whether the Western powers might have intervened in Hungary had they not been preoccupied with the Suez crisis must be answered in the negative. See Note at end of chapter, p. 336.

his majority in the Plenum of the Party Committee against the Anti-Party group. For a short time it seemed that the best strategy for recovering Russia's international position was in exploiting the gap which had opened between America and Britain over Suez. But with the healing of this breach at Eisenhower's meeting with Macmillan (now Premier in place of Eden), at Bermuda in March 1957, it was clear that other tactics were necessary.

The plan Khrushchev adopted was to win world recognition for the Soviet Union as a great peace-loving power, and himself as the architect of peace, by working for a Summit meeting. This was part of the atmosphere of *détente* which Russia needed. It was no time for adventures. The restlessness of the satellites had to be calmed. More food and consumer goods would help attain that object. The same prescription would suit the Soviet people equally. Khrushchev made lavish promises and, in fact, for many the situation improved.

Prestige was also to be gained by rockets and space-craft. The whole world was indeed amazed when the first Sputnik went into orbit in October 1957, and a second carrying a dog the following month. The first, weighing 180 lb., was ten times heavier than had been thought possible by Western scientists, and the second weighed half a ton. The launching of these space-craft by three-stage rockets of great power, showed that Russia had a startlingly long lead over the West in rocket techniques, and that her leaders were determined that Russia should pioneer the exploration of space. The military aspects of this achievement were also formidable.

The space programme, I.C.B.M.'s, nuclear developments, supersonic aircraft, these and the host of modern technical developments deemed necessary for defence, called for vast expenditures. The defence budget was 9·3 billion rubles in 1961; it was raised to 13·4 billion rubles for 1962. The announcement of this astonishing increase was made by the Finance Minister, V. Garbuzov, before the Supreme Soviet. 'No question was asked, no doubt was expressed.'[1] Some saving to balance this enormous expenditure could be achieved by reducing the number of men under arms, but there was a limit to which this could be done.[2]

[1] Foreign Affairs, April 1964. T. Sosnovy: *The Soviet Military Budget*, 494. I.C.B.M.'s were first tested in 1957.
[2] In January 1958 there was a cut of 300,000.—Mackintosh, 212.

Khrushchev's Strategy in the Cold War

These reductions presupposed a continuation of the détente. In 1957 Soviet reactions were gentler than might have been expected to the American proposal for providing nuclear war-heads for NATO tactical weapons, and for acquiring bases in a number of countries from which long-range missiles could be launched. In May 1957 Khrushchev called for bilateral negotiations with America: a *rapprochement* between the two countries, he told an American reporter, would open the way to solving all world problems. It was a theme to which Khrushchev reverted from time to time over the ensuing months. In the intervals he would remind the West of Russia's growing strength by a succession of nuclear tests, each series culminating in a blast in an even higher range of megatons. He would also remind the West of Russia's advancing technical expertise, as she steadily kept ahead of America in the space-race.

Long-distance control of satellites had so far been perfected by the Russians that in August 1960 it was possible to put Sputnik V into orbit and recover it with two dogs and other creatures alive. In February 1961 an attempt to probe Venus was made with a projectile weighing 1,418 lb. from a six-ton satellite as a launching station. After several more experiments with satellites carrying dogs and other living things, Major Yuri Gagarin became the first man to orbit the earth (12 April 1961). Shortly after (5 May), the American, Commander Alan Shepard, made a space-flight in a 115-mile ballistic trajectory, followed by a similar American flight in July by Captain Virgil Grissom. These were however outshone by the seventeen orbits achieved by Major Herman Titov in the Russian space-ship Vostok II (6 August 1961).

Just as it seemed as though the totality of aggressiveness and competitiveness in the two power-blocs was being happily redirected (even if at vast expense) by competing in the race for the moon, it seemed politic to Khrushchev to bring the conflict of the two super-states down to earth with a bump. Berlin provided him with the means he required for doing this. His periodic demands for altering the status of the city, launched sometimes as ultimatums against the West, were apparently designed to 'soften up' the Western powers and induce them to accept a settlement for Germany along Soviet lines.

This involved recognition of the East German régime, handing over to it the rights and duties which the Soviet Government had been exercising, ending the Four-Power occupation of Berlin, declaring it a free city, and replacing the existing garrisons by a token force under the United Nations.

Such a settlement was unacceptable to the Western Powers, since they stood firm for the policy (which was also that of Chancellor Adenauer), of reunification of East and West Germany after free elections. Until then there was to be no recognition of the East German régime, and no change in the status of Berlin.

The limits on Khrushchev's freedom of manoeuvre in pursuing his policy were quickly shown. The Western Powers were convinced that the only way to maintain Berlin as a 'bastion of freedom' was to keep their garrisons in the city. Russia could not try to force them out, whatever ultimatums were launched threatening such action, without risking the Third World War. This Khrushchev was not prepared to do. What was true of Berlin was also true of 'trouble-spots' elsewhere. Co-existence, constantly preached by Khrushchev, was an inescapable need if the nations, and civilization itself, were to survive.

If force were ruled out, the alternative means of achieving the Soviet objective was to build a society which would have a greater power of attraction over the 'uncommitted' peoples than the Western version. Khrushchev had no doubts as to the outcome of such a competition. During a visit to the United States he told Americans with great conviction that their grandchildren would be Communists. He told Western visitors to Russia, 'We will bury you', and later explained that he meant the inevitable burial of the Capitalist system as Communism took its place, in the same way that feudalism had been previously buried by Capitalism.[1]

Though the outcome was regarded as inevitable, constant activity was nevertheless necessary to achieve it. This was to be carried out in three ways—first, by raising living standards in the Soviet 'world' until they rivalled or surpassed those of America; second, by maintaining Russia's lead in some technical fields, such as that of space-craft and rockets; and third, by using all available means—propaganda, loans, military support, development projects—for winning friends and influencing people, especially in uncommitted or recently

[1] See Mamatey, op. cit., pp. 182–184.

liberated states. Besides this Khrushchev naturally made use of the historic weapons of diplomacy to split the opposing 'camp' and win some of its members if possible, while causing others to waver.

In pursuing this strategy there were three limiting factors: its vast expense; the size of the gap to be closed both in production and raising living-standards; and increasing competition from the other Communist great power, the Chinese People's Republic.

The Material Basis for Soviet Policy

The billions spent on defence and the space programme took away resources which could have been used for raising the living-standards of the Soviet people. Though these had improved considerably over those of the Stalin era, at least for wide categories of officials, professional people and workers, they still lagged far behind those enjoyed by the vast majority of the peoples of the West. In the cities housing remained desperately short, while the cost of many articles increasingly enjoyed by Western workers, such as cars and washing-machines, put them out of the range of their Soviet counterparts. Ordinary household goods, footwear and clothes tended to be far more expensive, less readily available, and in much less variety than in the West. Many kinds of food, especially meat and milk products, were scarce and expensive in Russia.

Yet the attempts made by the post-Stalin governments, and particularly by that of Khrushchev, to remedy these defects were disappointing. A plan for a great increase of house-building could not be fulfilled, and was revised downwards drastically in 1963 in the interests of financing a continued high rate of industrial expansion. While objectives of overtaking America *per capita* industrial output by 1970 continued to be announced (1961), that of overtaking American meat-production—which had been optimistically hoped for by 1960—was abandoned indefinitely. Projects of improving the diet and providing abundant food, after a seemingly good start, ceased to bring improvement and led to a serious disaster.

Failure to improve the output of consumer goods was not due to a failure to increase production. This had risen steadily, 1958 witnessing a growth of 11 per cent, considerably more than the planned 7·7 per cent,[1] and contrasting favourably with the average of 9·7 per

[1] Annual Register, 1959, 213. For the difficulties of interpreting Soviet statistics see

cent for the total period, 1928–57.[1] This steady increase of productivity could not be used much to benefit the consumer, even in the field of housing where the need was so urgent, because of the omnivorous demands of defence, and the necessity of devoting a high proportion of resources to improving the infrastructure—notably in communications—of the Soviet Union, if its economic development was ever to have a chance of catching up with that of America.

In food production the failure lay deeper. Ever since Stalin had forced collectivization on the peasants, the incentive to produce had diminished, and no way of restoring it within the framework of collectivised agriculture had yet been discovered by the Soviet rulers. It was only outside this framework that incentives appeared to be adequate, as witnessed by the disproportionately high contribution to total food production made by the individual plots of the peasants and by the gardens and back-yards of urban workers. Production for family or the free market proved a far greater stimulus than production for the state—especially when the state insisted on deliveries at low and often quite uneconomic prices. The bureaucratic organization of farm production, and the planning methods which were involved, all militated against efficiency, economy of effort, and the desire to produce. Yet Khrushchev persisted in continuing along the same groove, and even digging it deeper. Efforts were made to reduce the size of peasant plots and the hours that could be spent working on them, and to transfer to state-ownership as much as possible of the livestock which was in private hands (such as the cow which many a factory worker kept in his back-yard).

A much-needed reform was the abolition of the Motor Tractor Stations (1958), which had a monopoly of selling, hiring and servicing farm machinery, as well as being the centres for party control of the countryside. They were for the most part inefficient and corrupt. The M.T.S.s were turned into R.T.S.s (Repair and Servicing Stations), which evidently were no more efficient than their predecessors. An

---

Soviet Survey (Congress for Cultural Freedom), October–November 1958, 9–14, N. Jasny: *Interpreting Soviet Statistics*; also Jasny: *The 1956 Soviet Statistical Handbook—a commentary*, (Michigan State Press, 1957).

[1] Series of D. B. Shimkin, used by G. Grossman: *Thirty years of Soviet Industrialisation* (*Soviet Survey*, op. cit., 15–21). At this level Soviet industry was still producing rather less than half as much as American industry, while labour productivity per man-hour was 'substantially less than half the American level'.—Ibid., 16.

excessive amount of agricultural machinery was out of use at any time owing to breakdowns, lack of servicing and repairs. In Kazakhstan 32,000 combine harvesters were out of order in 1959, 60,000 in 1961. The sale of their stock of tractors and other machinery to the collectives often involved much hardship in paying by the latter. Though the peasants lost in the reduction of their private plots from 1½ acres to ¾ acre, they gained through the increase of prices for dairy products (150 per cent) and meat (more than 400 per cent) decreed in 1953. On balance the earnings of individual farm-workers increased by some 50 per cent.[1] But since the results in total production continued to be well below what were anticipated, Khrushchev attempted to apply tighter controls and create larger administrative units. Collectives were combined, and the top-heavy bureaucratic structure further weighted by a partial reversion to his favourite scheme of 'agri-towns'.

His most spectacular and publicized programme was for the cultivation of the virgin lands (and of much grassland besides), though this bringing of marginal land into the cultivated area was likely to yield only temporary advantages and rapidly diminishing returns. In 1953–6 territory in Kazakhstan, in West and Central Siberia, to the east of the Volga and in the Southern Urals was taken into cultivation. This equalled the entire cultivated area of Canada—'an expansion in so short a period (which) has no parallel in agricultural history'.[2] A vast labour force was deployed, in which young Communist volunteers played a conspicuous part, alongside less advertised methods of recruitment. The *sovkhoz* (state farm) was the unit of production for these lands, instead of the *kolkhoz* or collective. The lands were ploughed up, spring wheat planted, and initially heavy yields secured. The yields formed part of the increasing grain production which marked the period 1953–8, when the annual rate of growth of gross agricultural output was said to be 8·6 per cent. For the rest these good yields derived from larger investment in agriculture, from higher income and better incentives for the farm workers, and from such reforms and new methods as were introduced. But by 1958 a 'plateau' in grain-production was reached. The crops

---

[1] Figures in *Soviet Survey*, October–December 1958, W. K.: *A Review of Soviet Agricultural Policy* (22–7).

[2] *Foreign Affairs*, July 1962, A. Nove: *Soviet Agriculture Marks Time*, 578.

of the three years after 1958 showed no appreciable increase. Diminishing returns from the virgin lands may have already set in, while reducing 'the private sector' (such as farm workers' plots) correspondingly tended to lower incentives as well as restricting production for home-consumption or the free market. Little improvement had been gained after a decade of effort: one Soviet farmworker was still producing only enough for a monotonous diet for his own and one other family, compared with the norm in Western industrialized countries where one farming family produces a varied diet for some ten families.[1]

This static situation was succeeded by one of veritable disaster, when a severe drought struck the Soviet Union in 1963. Production from the virgin lands dropped to 5 million tons (14 million in 1958), while the total Soviet harvest at 118 million tons was 20 per cent below that of the year before, and the average yield per acre the lowest since 1954. Far from overtaking America in food-production and bringing variety to the larder, Russia was forced to import grain —largely from the free world [2]—on a hitherto unparalleled scale. The programme for increasing maize-production and therefore raising pig-production—for long one of Khrushchev's favourite subjects of exhortation—had to be abandoned.

Détente to Deadlock, 1958–60

The road to the second Summit was not always easy. Nineteen-fifty-eight was a good year for Russia. The troubles arising out of the Hungarian revolt had mostly been overcome. Even if the Hungarian people were not much happier, though materially they were better off, the Soviet people were both better off and happier. Thanks to the virgin lands and good harvests, for beet and cotton as well as for grain, Soviet man was better fed and better clothed than he had ever been. He was said to be eating three times more meat and drinking four times more milk than in 1952.[3] Sputnik III showed that Russia

---

[1] *Soviet Survey*, op. cit., 22.
[2] *Annual Register*; *The Times*, 1 March 1965.
  The free world could well afford to export. Americans spent £189 million ($530 million) on feeding their dogs in 1963, some 50 per cent more than they spent on feeding their babies. The bill for cat-food was £44½ million ($125 million).—*The Times*, 18 August 1964.   [3] *Annual Register*.

was well ahead in her lead over America in rockets. Trouble with China was showing as a cloud in an otherwise halcyon sky, but was seemingly under control.

While bringing Nasser into virtually the position of a client,[1] and extending Soviet influence in Asia and Africa, Khrushchev showed his determination to bring about a Summit meeting, and settle matters over Germany with the West. This took the form of requests for a meeting of the governmental Heads, followed by a jab administered over Berlin. The Western Powers, according to Khrushchev's pronouncements in November 1958, had lost all rights for keeping troops in Berlin. Earlier agreements were void, Western forces were to be withdrawn, and Berlin was to be declared a 'demilitarized free city'. If this radical change of status were not agreed by the Western Powers within six months, Russia would turn over the access routes to the control of the East German Republic.

This challenge produced the alarm in Western circles which was intended. A conference of Foreign Ministers was proposed by the West to discuss Berlin. In February 1959 Macmillan came to Moscow to smooth the way towards the Summit. In May the Foreign Ministers' conference opened in Geneva. The sparring positions of East and West remained the same. Russia stood for German reunification through confederation, then withdrawal of Russian and Western forces, and a nuclear-free zone in Europe.[2] The Western powers stood for free elections in East as well as West Germany first, then disengagement, etc. Though this match might be considered a draw (the conference adjourned in August), it was played in a spirit which suggested readiness to compromise. The 'ultimatum' over Berlin was forgotten. Khrushchev had his eyes on a personal move with Eisenhower, and the prestige for himself and the Soviet régime of being received as the President's equal—as well as the opportunity of spreading the impression of the up-to-date progressive Soviet Union and its rulers as human beings. This aim was achieved in Khrushchev's visit to America (September 1959), and his meetings with Eisenhower at his Camp David residence near Gettysburg.

The generally friendly reception accorded to Khrushchev in the

---

[1] He made two visits to Moscow in 1958, and received a £4 million ruble loan for the building of the first stage of the Aswan Dam.

[2] Along the lines put forward by the Polish Foreign Minister, Rapacki, in October 1952.

United States (together with some rudeness and indignities),[1] and the reports of the cordial man-to-man talks at Camp David, produced anxiety in two different quarters. In Berlin and West Germany it was feared that some deal might endanger the existing position, unsatisfactory though it was, for the sake of adjustments which would jeopardize the long-range aim of unification on a democratic basis. In China, the unprecedented spectacle of a Soviet leader accepting the hospitality of capitalist America, aroused alarm lest a policy of appeasement should lead on to co-existence as a permanent objective instead of as a revolutionary tactic. Khrushchev's first move after his return from America was to visit Peking to assuage these anxieties. In this he was not wholly successful. It was noticed that silence reigned at Peking on his departure: the usual communiqué announcing solidarity was not issued.

This agreement to differ (if no more) from his great eastern ally did not deter Khrushchev from proceeding with the next steps in pursuit of his chosen line—the Summit meeting, and the possible visit of Eisenhower to the Soviet Union. But objections against going further in this direction were coming from other quarters besides Peking. Despite the immense popularity in Russia which his foreign visits brought him, enhanced by the ebullient speeches which he made on his return, Khrushchev was ever aware of a group in the government representing a real, or at least potential, opposition. Such critics took issue at times with the policy itself, at times with the manner and style in which Khrushchev conducted it.

Though preparations for the Summit continued, some cooling-off in the expectations of its outcome was noticeable on both sides. Christian Herter, who succeeded Dulles in April 1959[2], stated in February 1960 that he expected no agreements of substance from the Summit. Though endless discussions had proceeded at the long-drawn Geneva Conference on disarmament, even a ban on nuclear test explosions seemed difficult to achieve, and this difficulty was underlined by the explosion of the first French nuclear device in February, followed by another in April. But from the Russian point of view the sign of American unwillingness to make any substantive

---

[1] For example, being treated—to his disgust—to seeing the *Can-Can* at Hollywood; being refused entrance to Disneyland at Anaheim, California; and being obliged to listen to a rude and aggressive speech by the Mayor of Los Angeles.

[2] Dulles died the following month, 24 May.

concessions was shown by the continuation of 'spy-flights' over the Soviet Union, linked with the existence of bases around the Soviet perimeter from which such flights could be made, and from which in the future rocket and nuclear attacks might be launched.

That the summit meeting scheduled for 19 May 1960 was only part of a wider global strategy, was shown by Khrushchev's visit to Indonesia in March 1960. This intrusion into what the Chinese regarded as their sphere of influence marked a challenge to the People's Republic—a policy of assertion in the East which, according to Khrushchev's plan, required a continuation of the atmosphere of *détente* in the West. The failure to maintain this *détente* and the subsequent reversion to outright cold war tactics against the West, culminating in the challenge to America over Cuba, signified the failure of Khrushchev's world strategy. He was in a position similar to that of the German General Staff when obliged to fight their wars, not as planned against first one enemy then another, but as two-front wars with the danger of being forced everywhere on to the defensive.

Khrushchev's major preoccupation was with China, and with winning the uncommitted world in the face of her growing and successful competition. Berlin, Germany and Western questions generally could be safely put back 'on ice', even if this action was accompanied by a renewal of the cold war against the West. A tough line with the West could persuade doubters in his own camp and strengthen his hand in dealing with China. It was a second-best to the freedom of manoeuvre which Western concessions and a further *détente* would have given him, but was the only alternative if his other objectives, with China and the uncommitted countries, were not to be put in jeopardy.

The U-2 incident provided the opportunity for Khrushchev's change of policy. On 1 May one of these high-flying unarmed American planes, equipped with photographic apparatus, was shot down near Sverdlovsk in the Urals. At first Khrushchev took the line that flights by these planes, long known and resented in the U.S.S.R., were carried out by agencies hostile to Russia without the knowledge of the President—at this point Khrushchev seemed not to have abandoned his policy of *détente*—but Eisenhower's statement that he knew of these flights made the continuation of this line impracticable. On arrival in Paris on 14 May Khrushchev told de Gaulle that he would insist on cancellation of the U-2 flights, an apology from Eisenhower, and the punishment of those responsible. Though Eisenhower had already stopped these flights, he did not make this public until the 16th. By then, in an exasperated mood, Khrushchev had decided on the switch in policy. In a meeting with de Gaulle and Macmillan at the Elysée he again insisted that his conditions be fulfilled before he would start discussions.

His own position meanwhile had been strengthened, at least in some sections of world opinion, by the launching of Sputnik IV on the night of his arrival. The only meeting of the Four (which Khrushchev insisted was a preliminary and not the Summit) was therefore a complete fiasco. Khrushchev repeated his demands to Eisenhower, who said that though he had cancelled the U-2 flights he could not bind his successor on this point. He accused Khrushchev of coming to Paris and using the U-2 incident as a deliberate means of wrecking the conference. Khrushchev withdrew the invitation for his visit to Russia, and afterwards rubbed in this snub at the angry press conferences which he held before returning, via East Germany, to Moscow.

The Renewed Cold War and Cuba

In the subsequent renewal of the cold war Khrushchev had the edge over Eisenhower. The President's visits to eleven countries, including India, in the previous winter (December 1959) had shown that he was a less skilful propagandist than his rival, however much of a personal success in other respects. Next year a Communist-inspired agitation prevented one important visit, that to Japan, altogether. American propaganda had built up the President, but neither he nor the State Department had a policy, or the means of 'getting it over' which could inspire support from the uncommitted world. By autumn 1960, after the *débâcle* of 'the Summit that never was', American policy was in disarray.

Despite this apparent advantage to Russia, Khrushchev could make little real progress, and he threw away some of his advantages by his extraordinary performance at the General Assembly of the United Nations. In September he set out on board the *Baltikum* with a retinue of satellite leaders—Kadar, Gomulka, Gheorgiu-Dej, and others, to be joined at New York by the 'neutralist' but friendly leaders, such as Nehru, Nasser, Tito, Sukarno and Nkrumah. The West had to bow to Khrushchev's initiative. Eisenhower was put up to make a speech of ponderous platitudes on the day before Khrushchev took the rostrum, Menzies was sent for from Australia to put 'guts' into the Western case, and Macmillan arrived reluctantly to try to keep the temperature down and inject some common sense into the proceedings. Only de Gaulle was conspicuous by his absence.

Whereas Macmillan had two meetings with Khrushchev, and took steps to keep the neutralists friendly, the attitude of the Americans was glacial. An attempt by Nasser, Nehru, Nkrumah, Tito and Sukarno to bring Eisenhower and Khrushchev together in order to restart talks was rebuffed. On his arrival at New York, the usual courtesies were denied Khrushchev, his movements were restricted and other leaders were treated with similar lack of respect. Khrushchev, not to be repressed, seized the headlines, visiting Castro in his third-rate Harlem hotel.

At the United Nations, however, Khrushchev's tactics were faulty. His demand for abolishing the office of Secretary-General and substituting a commission of *troika* or tripartite type (representing the West, the Communist bloc, and the neutralists, each with a veto on the other), had little appeal for the large and growing number of post-colonial states, while Mobutu's military take-over from Lumumba somewhat spoilt his violently expressed denunciation of the policy towards the Congo voted by a majority of the member-states.[1] He spoilt his case entirely by making a bitter personal attack on the Secretary-General Dag Hammarskjöld himself in this connection. His policy for disarmament commanded little more interest than that of America, his heckling and interruptions failed to make a good impression, and the scene when he banged the desk with his shoe (and the President of the Assembly broke his gavel trying to quell the disorder), seemed designed to bring all procedure for mutual understanding into disrepute, without winning points in the struggle for supremacy.

This spectacle of chaos in the world body which had been founded

[1] The policy was to restore order by means of a U.N. force, in whose composition the great powers would not have a part, and that no power should intervene in the dispute between Premier Lumumba and President Kasavubu (the Russians were sending arms and other assistance to Lumumba).—See A. Dallin: *The Soviet Union and the United Nations* (Methuen 1962), 135 seq.

for the orderly resolving of disputes, was depressing, particularly for the smaller nations, and a possible source of satisfaction only to de Gaulle and the Chinese Communists. Instead of the remarkable gathering of statesmen being an occasion for rising above the deadlock of the cold war by beginning to pool expertise and resources for the solving (as had now become practicable) of all the pressing problems of hunger, housing and disease, the cancerous tumour of ill-will between the powers, and more especially those called 'great', showed itself in all its naked ugliness. It was not difficult to predict that shortly this might burst in the overwhelming catastrophe of a nuclear war.

Though the election of John F. Kennedy as President of the United States in November 1960 was regarded by Khrushchev as preferable to that of the former Vice-President, Nixon, the meeting of the two leaders at Vienna (June 1961) was little more than an occasion of sparring. Laos on one side of the globe, Cuba on the other, were becoming the tenderest points of confrontation between East and West, rivalling that of Berlin. At Berlin the familiar policy of obstruction and pressure was pursued, this time by building a wall, in places of solid concrete blocks, along the border dividing the East Zone from the rest of the city. All forms of communication, such as the underground, were stopped (the telephones had been cut long since). Allied military personnel and officials were still allowed in the East Zone (as were Soviet personnel in the West), but the citizens themselves no longer had any communication between the two parts of their city.

This barbarous anomaly completed the system of modern defences and electrified obstructions along the entire border between the Russian Zone (now the German Democratic Republic) and Western Germany. Though not a gap geographically in that line, Berlin had been an escape-hatch by which 4,000 East Germans per week (or a quarter of a million per year) had been making their way to freedom. Being unable to vote in the East they had voted (to use Lenin's phrase) with their feet. In this fashion some 3 million East Germans had shown what they thought of the Ulbricht régime. The population of the G.D.R. was now only 16 million against the 53 million of the German Federal Republic. Thus Berlin became the second case of the monstrous division of a capital city by a practically impassable frontier.[1] This vivisection of a complex organism, as of the country itself, was the more savage in that it involved the murdering and maiming by frontier guards of people who still staked everything on making their bid to reach the West.

As if to brandish his bludgeon, the Soviet leader authorized another series of nuclear tests with explosions up to the colossal power of 50 megatons (September–October 1961). These were but the preliminaries for a direct challenge to the security of the United States. The failure of the new Kennedy administration in April 1961 to dislodge Castro by the Bay of Pigs invasion had brought about the contrary effect of binding Castro closer to Russia and humiliating the United States. Secretly Cuba began to be built up into a base from which the whole Western Hemisphere could be brought under attack. Russian jet bombers and rockets were brought in, and launching-pads were covertly constructed. Inevitably the United States reacted forcibly, as soon as these preparations came to light. During a week of crisis (22–28 October 1962), when the world was at the threshold of thermonuclear horror, the wills of two men representing two great nations, were in conflict. The steady nerves of the younger man and his colleagues held. Khrushchev was forced to bow to the ultimatum—to stop his ships from trying to pass the American naval force now quarantining the island, to agree to withdraw the jets and rockets, and to dismantle the bases.

Détente in the West

After Cuba came a perceptible *détente*. Khrushchev and Kennedy now had each other's measure. Talks were initiated between their governments, with Britain joining in, for bringing about a partial test-ban treaty. This was accomplished in August 1963.

A further move towards sanity was the installation of the 'hot line' (June 1963) between the White House and the Kremlin—an instant means of radio-telephonic communication to be used in an emergency such as the need to avert hasty military action on either side in the event of some crisis or misunderstanding. Khrushchev accepted Kennedy's invitation that their two countries should co-operate in a project to put a man on the moon—though later the Soviet government stated that it was no longer interested in this

---

[1] Jerusalem is the other.

enterprise. Russia's successful 'moon-probes' with unmanned space-craft showed however that she was well advanced in this field of endeavour, as did the 'rendezvous in space' by Major Nikolayev and Lieutenant-Colonel Popovich (August 1962) and the later space-meeting, famous for the achievement of the first woman cosmonaut, Lieutenant Valentina Tereshkova (16 June 1963).[1]

Too many hopes were built on the personality and leadership of President Kennedy. On 22 November 1963 he was assassinated. Though the Vice-President, Lyndon Johnson, who took over the Presidency, at once showed himself to be a man of outstanding political ability—at least in the field of home affairs—a serious gap was left in the younger generation of leaders now emerging to replace the veterans of the troubled past. In October 1963 Adenauer, who had held on as Chancellor until the advanced age of 87, at last resigned. In the same month ill-health compelled Macmillan's resignation also. Old men in the smaller countries, like Franco and Salazar in Spain and Portugal, still kept their grip on affairs. France still had de Gaulle, but in Russia, Khrushchev's days were numbered.

The Fall of Khrushchev

On 13 October 1964 Khrushchev fell from power. He came under criticism from his Presidium colleagues for many reasons—his autocratic behaviour, the failure of his agricultural policy, the inept handling of Cuba, his nepotism. He had made his son-in-law Adzhubei Editor of Pravda and his personal emissary. He had given Nasser the order of Hero of the Soviet Union and the promise of a £100 million loan without consulting his colleagues. Above all he was challenged on the failure of his policy towards China.

Khrushchev tried to defend himself, with familiar bluster and vituperation. Before resigning he demanded a vote of the full Central Committee of the party—the same procedure which he had used to secure himself in power in 1957. But this time the vote went against him. Khrushchev resigned as Prime Minister and Party Secretary, though still remaining a member of the Central Committee. These offices were taken by A. N. Kosygin and Leonid Brezhnev. Both were Deputy Premiers. Brezhnev had been relieved of the Presidency in July 1964 to be Deputy to Khrushchev in his capacity as Party

[1] She met Lieutenant-Colonel V. F. Bykonsky.

Secretary (not that Khrushchev had any intention voluntarily of letting him step into his shoes).[1] Both men were creatures of Khrushchev, more particularly Brezhnev, who had followed him up the same ladder of party offices in the Ukraine. Kosygin as a specialist in light industry had a particular concern for consumer goods which the new leaders, like their fallen master, soon emphasized as a feature of their régime.

In July, Brezhnev's place as President was taken over by Mikoyan —the man who had risen along with Khrushchev step by step to the top of the Soviet hierarchy, and with whom Khrushchev had been on close and familiar terms. A joke which he had once made with Mikoyan had been noted. Mikoyan, at a diplomatic luncheon, had banteringly warned Khrushchev against visiting the United States, since he might like it so much he would want to stay there—to which Khrushchev retorted, 'I know what you want, Anastas—my job'.[2] At the time Khrushchev had roared with laughter at his own joke. Now he may ruefully have thought that Mikoyan, of all those who had dispossessed him, was most likely to step into his shoes.

Khrushchev's huge portrait, which had replaced that of Stalin on the Kremlin wall, was taken down, but for some days no word of the transfer of power was uttered by the Soviet press. When the news leaked out the reactions of Russians were remarkably indifferent. Khrushchev's popularity had ebbed away from its high point in the autumn of 1959. His kind of showmanship had palled, and there was much resentment over the failure of agriculture: the shortages in the towns and the real hunger in some parts of the country.[3] At the same time the manner of his going was disliked. Russians felt that since Stalin's day they had reached a stage of political maturity which should be reflected in some system designed to give them a share in such decisions, instead of old-style palace revolutions. Though there was now a quasi-democratic procedure in the Central Committee,

[1] He said to the French Minister of Atomic Science, Gaston Palewski, who visited him at his Black Sea retreat just before the decisive Presidium meeting (à propos of de Gaulle), 'A political leader should never leave power of his own free will.'—*Sunday Times Magazine*, 13 December 1964. Brezhnev had taken over the Presidency from Frol Kozlov, whom Khrushchev regarded as his Deputy and probable successor, after he had been incapacitated by a stroke.

[2] *Sunday Times*, 12 April 1964. Suslov, the chief party ideologist, was also thought to be in the running for the leadership, in combination with Mikoyan.

[3] *The Times*, 17 December 1964.

where decisions were made by vote, this scarcely began to supply the new structure needed to bring the people, at their more mature stage of development, into relation with their government.

Dissatisfaction with Khrushchev was as much with the system as the man. He had presided over a difficult time of transition, both as regards the Soviet Union's internal development and its relations with the satellites and the outside world. But in no direction had the transition to any fundamentally new and stable system been effected. Some of the worst features of the Stalinist autocracy had disappeared —the N.K.V.D. empire with its concentration camps had been largely dismantled—but in its place there had been administrative improvizations, not radical structural reforms. Khrushchev's 'unending series of organizational expedients—the decentralization and recentralization of the economy, the changes in regional administration and in planning, the division of the party into two parallel hierarchies for industry and agriculture—left untouched the root of the difficulty, which is that the inflexible political structure designed for the Russia of 1917, embodied in the party dictatorship, is an anachronism for the Russia of 1964'.[1]

Even the cultural thaw, which appealed to so many of the educated people had not gone far enough. Dudintsev's *Not By Bread Alone* had a tremendous vogue after it was published in 1956. Under Stalin it could not have appeared at all, and doubtless was allowed to circulate on the scale it did because it accorded with the trend of de-Stalinization. But it went further than de-Stalinization. It tilted against all bureaucratic controls, all the vast congeries of hierarchies, all the petty monopolists of power, who still flourished in the Soviet realm. Lopatkin, the independent-minded inventor, who gave up position and material rewards to create the best possible machines for a Russia which should take the lead among modern countries, had been persecuted and degraded by the second-rate incumbents of the establishment. Many a Russian man and woman saw themselves as at least potential Lopatkins. They welcomed de-Stalinization, but resented Khrushchev's continuation of the worst features of the old establishment in its rule over the sciences and culture. Lysenko, known to be bogus by all qualified biologists, still held his position under Khrushchev as the doyen of plant-breeding for agriculture.

[1] *The World Today* (R.I.I.A.), December 1964.

Modern art was dismissed as rubbish, while a young poet like Yevtushenko or an old one like Akhmatova came under official fire. Pasternak, at the end of his days, was threatened with expulsion from the Soviet Union for accepting a Nobel Prize for *Dr. Zhivago*, and in order to stay in his home had to refuse the prize and make a humiliating apology to the authorities.[1]

Not that disillusionment with Khrushchev for failure to dismantle the establishment was the main cause of his downfall. This was the dispute with China, in which Khrushchev was confronted with a situation baffling to a statesman of the highest calibre.

The Sino-Soviet Dispute

There was a certain inevitability about this rupture between the two greatest Communist states. The one was European, the other Asian. The one was becoming rich, the other was miserably poor. The one had a developed technology, the other was dependent on more advanced countries for developing its own technology. The one had passed through its revolution and had (more or less) arrived; the other was at an early stage of the revolution and therefore had a revolutionary outlook.

Stalin had been doubtful about supporting the Chinese Communists, as if he foresaw their victory as a challenge to Soviet power. But once their victory had been achieved, China was regarded rather like another satellite, a client country dependent on the Soviet Union. So in fact it was, and the Chinese were willing to admit this fact— up to a point. They were willing to admit Soviet supremacy in the Communist world, and to take their cue from Stalin just as they took their technicians from Russia. But they continued to be strongly conscious that they had achieved power through their own efforts, and with little support from Stalin. In their own minds the relationship of their party with that of the Soviet Union was one of an association freely entered into. Russia was the senior partner, but the compact was based on nothing except a shared ideological commitment.

Paradoxically it was Khrushchev's soft line towards Tito, as they

---

[1] 'Educated people resent increasingly that they cannot travel freely abroad, that they cannot meet whom they like, read what they like, dance as they like, and make up their own minds about abstract art.'—*The Times*, 17 December 1964.

considered it, which first annoyed the Chinese. They could not accept the formula with which Khrushchev's peace-making mission to Belgrade in 1955 terminated—'the roads to socialist development in different countries in different conditions are different'. They were further irritated by Khrushchev's anti-Stalin revelations at the Twentieth Congress next year, not only by the matter but by the manner. Such a major shift of policy as de-Stalinization represented should not have been decided unilaterally in Moscow—consultations with other parties, and notably theirs, should first have been carried out.

When the unsettling effects of de-Stalinization were apparent, the Chinese improved their position *vis-à-vis* the Russians by their support of Khrushchev over Hungary. At this moment such support was, indeed, almost indispensable to Khrushchev to maintain his precarious position. The squeeze for the Chinese came soon after, when, to consolidate Russia's position in regard to the satellites, Khrushchev reversed the policy of milking them and poured aid of around six billion dollars into them—money which had to be taken, in part, from that which would have gone to China.

The Chinese, forced to a greater economic independence, assumed a more independent attitude in other respects also. Against Soviet advice they tried to overcome their economic problems by the 'great leap forward' of 1958, proclaiming that by rapid collectivization they could jump straight into Communism without passing through the intermediate stage of socialism. The Russians rejected this claim, seeing it as a bid for the leadership of world Communism.

To the Chinese, Khrushchev's claims to be building socialism by developing the Soviet Union's productive forces indicated that the Russians were gripped by a bourgeois ideal—that they had fallen for the white man's materialism. Their aim of overtaking American productivity and living-standards, and enjoying these fruits themselves (without a mention as to how the Chinese and others would benefit) put them into the camp of the rich Europeans. It was therefore not surprising, though deplorable, to see them making up to the Americans. Khrushchev's visit to Eisenhower in 1959, his angling for that invitation and his long pursuit of the Summit, above all his friendly remarks about Eisenhower on his return from Camp David, were outrageous to the Chinese.

Linked with this was Khrushchev's concept of co-existence. War had ceased to be inevitable, even between capitalist countries. The development of nuclear weapons had made nonsense of the old dogma. Peaceful evolution was the theme, a doctrinal revision, which in Chinese eyes, brought Russia near to co-operating with the capitalists. 'Our country,' said Khrushchev, striking a typically nationalist note in a speech in July 1959, 'and the United States are the two most mighty powers in the world. If other countries fight among themselves they can be separated; but if war breaks out between America and our country, no one will be able to stop it. It will be catastrophe on a colossal scale.'[1]

The conflict, long looming, was kept out of view until 1959. In 1958 Khrushchev's position was not yet so assured that he could risk a breach with China. After the Iraqi revolution of that year when America put troops into the Lebanon, Khrushchev negotiated for a Summit with Eisenhower to settle the crisis, but backed out after Chinese opposition. His wrecking of the Summit in 1960 may have been, in part, for the same reason—a last attempt to come to terms with Peking, by appeasing the Chinese over the issue of conflict versus co-operation with the capitalist powers.

By then it was already too late. The issue had been made public at the Third Congress of the Rumanian Communist Party, at Bucharest in June 1960. Khrushchev's tirade at the leader of the Chinese fraternal delegates, Peng Cheng, was expressed with the full vigour of his invective. Specifically (among other things) he assailed China for its policy of attacking India, embarrassing the Soviet Union in its task of bringing that country towards socialism, for the sake of a national issue. He accused Mao of being 'a left revisionist', implying that his type of unrealistic dogmatism and objection to opportunist policies came under the heading of Lenin's definition —'left-wing communism, an infantile disorder'.

From then on both sides quoted Lenin at each other, but Russia could apply the squeeze. In August 1960 aid to China stopped. The technicians were withdrawn, taking their blue-prints with them. The building of plants and factories came to an abrupt halt, at least for the time being. China was left deprived of even the physical conditions of survival for millions of people at a time when droughts,

[1] E. Crankshaw: *The New Cold War, Moscow v. Peking* (Penguin, 1963), 85.

aggravated by the effects of over-hasty collectivization, had drastically reduced the crops.

After weeks of disputation that autumn a compromise seemed to be patched up at Moscow (December 1960), but in reality the debate raged on. At Bucharest only Albania had spoken up for China. Now the charges were levied indirectly—by Russia against Albania 'and other dogmatists', by China against Yugoslavia 'and other revisionists'.[1] In 1961 the Soviet Communist Party programme—the third since that of 1903—came out flatly for economic advance, not political action, as the road to the Communist millenium.[2] Comecon, originally designed as a weapon against Yugoslavia, was reactivated towards this end: partly too for strengthening the Soviet Camp, by applying the idea of the Common Market, so successful in the West, to the needs of the Soviet hegemony. An invitation to China was even tried, perhaps for the record rather than anything else, but China declined to enter the Soviet Common Market. This paralleled her refusal to enter Russia's copy of NATO, the so-called 'Malinovsky strategy': an integrated defence structure of which the outcome would have been to reduce Soviet commitments in the Far East and 'to inhibit any independent Chinese action'.[3] It would underline Chinese military dependence, made clearer by the Soviet refusal, much resented by the Chinese, to share with them its nuclear 'know-how'.

Independent action was indeed China's intention. Russia had promised MIGs to India, hence China's invasion of India in the autumn of 1962 was a kind of 'dare' to see whether Russia would really give India support. The Cuba crisis, occurring at the same time, anyway inhibited Russian action farther east, and left Khrushchev more dependent on his allies. The state visit of Tito to Moscow followed (December 1962), marking the renewal of the relations between the Yugoslav and Russian Communist Parties for the first time since 1948. This was another slap to China.

Khrushchev's bungling over Cuba brought out the weakness of Russia's world-position, and encouraged the trends towards independence not only in China, but in the Communist Parties everywhere. In economic affairs the satellites were increasingly following

---

[1] Mamatey, op. cit., 106.   [2] Crankshaw, 139.
[3] *International Affairs* (R.I.I.A.), January 1964, John Gittings: *Co-operation and Conflict in Sino-Soviet Relations*, 70.

their own 'roads', Rumania conspicuously building its own trading-pattern with Western countries and in other ways emancipating itself from Soviet control.[1] The fraternal parties (in non-Communist countries), such as those of Italy, France and Sweden, were following an increasingly 'reformist' line. As Longo said, representing Togliatti at Moscow in November 1962, the aim to be pursued was a better life for the masses. This was not to be achieved by the victory of the Communist Party as such, but rather by 'the creation, with the help of all men of good will . . . of a new kind of international society'.[2]

Togliatti's memorandum, written just before his death in August 1964, and taken as his last testament, presented the full logic of this view, and played a part in leading to Khrushchev's fall. Togliatti had already dubbed the new tendencies 'polycentrism'. 'The autonomy of the parties', he wrote, 'which we champion decisively, is not just an internal necessity of our movement, but an essential condition of our development in the present circumstances. We will therefore be opposed to any proposal to create once again a centralized international organisation. . . . Even in the Socialist camp perhaps . . . it is necessary to be on one's guard against uniformity imposed from without, and to believe that the unity which must be established and maintained must respect the diversity and full autonomy of different countries.'[3] There was no longer any question of smashing the bourgeois state, but 'of the working class capturing the positions of power within a state that has not changed its bourgeois nature, and therefore . . . of fighting for its progressive transformation from inside'.[4]

Both the programme and the methods were at the opposite pole to those of the Chinese. Khrushchev was the man who had fostered this approach, and who had to be sacrificed if any reconciliation with the Chinese was to be possible. His attacks on Mao had become increasingly personal: it was noted at the Soviet-Polish Friendship meeting at the Kremlin in April 1964 how he spoke of him with sarcasm and

[1] In spring 1964 Rumania rejected the Soviet plan for economic integration, declared neutrality in the dispute with China, and asserted that no party could claim a privileged place or impose its opinion on others—See *The Times*, 11 December 1964.

[2] Crankshaw, *The New Cold War*, 148. Togliatti was leader of the Italian Communist Party.

[3] Keesing's Contemporary Archives, 3–10 October, 1964, 20332.

[4] Ibid., 14.

contempt.[1] His plan for another conference of the parties at Moscow in December, designed for the excommunication of the Chinese, was regarded by most parties to be a dangerous manoeuvre. Half of the twenty-six parties invited accepted the invitation, six refused, and the rest did not reply.[2] Togliatti's negative on creating again a monolithic organization marked the end of Khrushchev's policy of salvaging what could be saved of the old-time Leninist and Stalinist centralism. Politically it sounded the death knell of Khrushchev himself.

[1] *The Times*, 16 April 1964.
[2] *Survey* (a journal of Soviet and East European studies), January 1965, L. Labedz: *The End of an Epoch*, 21.

NOTES

1. THE AMERICAN POLICY OF CONTAINMENT

The containment policy of the U.S.A. was publicised in an article in *Foreign Affairs* for July 1947, p. 566, under the title of *The sources of Soviet conduct*. Its author was given as 'X', which concealed the name of the State Department expert George F. Kennan. The article was later reprinted in his book *American Diplomacy 1900–1950* (Secker and Warburg, 1953). Its key phrase was 'a policy of firm containment, designed to confront the Russians with unalterable counter-force at every point where they show signs of encroaching upon the interests of a peaceful and stable world'. (p. 581 in *Foreign Affairs*).

2. THE POSSIBILITY OF WESTERN INTERVENTION IN HUNGARY AT THE TIME OF THE RISING

'Since the outbreak of violence was not related to any specific impulse from the outside, it caught the Western governments by surprise. The confused and rapidly changing situation could not be evaluated reliably and with sufficient dispatch to cause a responsible government to remonstrate with the Soviet Union. For several days there was nothing about which to remonstrate.

'By the time the need for rescue became urgent it was too late, not because the Anglo-French-Israeli adventure in Egypt had given the Soviets a free hand, but because the Soviet Union had built up a military force in Hungary far superior to anything the West could marshal. This deployment, which began before the Suez adventure was precipitated, gave Russia an advantage that could not be challenged without the risk of general war.

'The psychological optimum moment for the West to intervene with any hope of effectiveness would have been before October 30, when the revolution was still an internal Hungarian affair, and when the Soviet Union was hesitating as to the proper course of action. The purpose would have been to warn the Russians against invading Hungary, thereby transforming the internal conflict into an international war, and to reassure them that the West would not exploit events in Hungary for any further inroads against Soviet security interests.

'This type of intervention by the United States was clearly unthinkable, irrespective of the approach of the presidential elections. Neither the administration nor the public was psychologically or otherwise prepared for it.'—Zinner, 362–3.

25: After Empire: Power and Welfare

The Algerian Settlement

De Gaulle returned to power twice as the accepted head of the French nation. He has described how, on the first occasion, when Paris was liberated, he headed the march down the Champs Elysées, with the sense of the history of France and all her great figures crowding on him.

> I went on, then, touched and yet tranquil, amid the inexpressible exultation of the crowd, beneath the storm of voices echoing my name, trying, as I advanced, to look at every person in all that multitude in order that every eye might register my presence. . . . This was one of those miracles of national consciousness, one of those gestures which sometimes, in the course of centuries, light up the history of France. . . . At each step I took along the most illustrious avenue in the world, it seemed to me that the glories of the past were associated with today's. . . . On his pedestal, Clemenceau, whom I hailed in passing, looked as if he were springing up to march beside us. . . . The Tuileries, which framed the majesty of the state under two emperors and two monarchs; the Place de la Concorde and the Place du Carrousel, which had observed the frenzies of revolutionary enthusiasm and the reviews of conquering regiments; the streets and the bridges named after battles won; on the other bank of the Seine, les Invalides, its dome still sparkling with the splendour of Le Roi-Soleil, the tombs of Turenne, of Napoleon, of Foch; and the Institute, honoured by so many illustrious minds—these were the benevolent witnesses of the human stream that flowed between them. Here was the Louvre, where the succession of kings had succeeded in building France; on their mounts, the statues of Joan of Arc and of Henri IV; the Palace of Saint Louis, whose anniversary had occurred the day before; Nôtre-Dame, the prayers of Paris, and the Ile de la Cité, her cradle—all shared in the event. History, gathered in these stones and in these squares, seemed to be smiling down on us.[1]

When de Gaulle returned to power the second time, in May 1958, it was with the same sense of history, of the greatness of France and of her destiny. His own purpose, as part of this history and this

[1] De Gaulle: *War Memoirs*, I, 1942–4, 312–14.

destiny, was clear—to bring France back to the position which she ought to occupy in the affairs of Europe and the world.

To this end he had to deal with the Algerian question. As long as this vast unsolved problem hung round the neck of France, she could not be free to play her part in the world.

De Gaulle had been borne into power on the conviction of millions of Frenchmen that he could solve this problem, and that in so doing he could restore direction and strength to the government of France. But different groups looked to different solutions of the Algerian question. The 'Paras' thought in terms of *Algérie Française* and 'integration'. Others were prepared to see some much looser form of association between an autonomous Algeria and France. Almost everyone was agreed that de Gaulle alone had enough authority to impose a solution, whatever it might be.

It is possible that the General himself had no particular views on this matter. What he wanted was a solution, to get the Algerian question out of the way, and then proceed to policies which would enable France to find her rightful place in the world. Not that his guiding lines were merely expediency. If one of de Gaulle's most powerful motives has sprung from his sense of history, another has been the desire to see that justice is done.

During the months after he resumed office he therefore seemed to lean first towards one solution then another. His observations on the subject of Algeria were contradictory. They gave hope both to the integrationists under the leadership of Soustelle and Generals such as Salan and Jouhaud, and also to those who had little sympathy with the passionate proponents of *Algérie Française*, and who looked rather to negotiations with the rebels for finding a solution along the lines of autonomy.

De Gaulle did not fail to make conciliatory gestures towards the rebels, though he seemed at first to favour an integrationist solution. In France, Soustelle was given a Cabinet post. In Algeria, Salan was made Delegate-General and Commander-in-Chief, directly responsible to de Gaulle—but the Committees of Public Safety, set up during the revolt of April–May 1958, were deprived of all political and administrative powers. Algerians were to have the full status of French citizens, there was to be a ten-year programme of economic development. Elections should be held, and Algeria's future determined through negotiations with her elected representatives. Meanwhile the fighting went on, with serious allegations of torture and maltreatment levelled against the French command.

Next year, 1959, the future of Algeria still seemed to be in the balance, with municipal elections successfully carried out in all the larger communes, two-thirds of the elected councillors being Moslems. This took place in the face of attempts by the rebel organization, the F.L.N., to persuade the voters to keep away from the polls. At the same time talks continued between the French government and the F.L.N., who agreed in principle to a cease-fire.

The pace was too slow and the outcome too uncertain for the French 'Ultras', who staged an insurrection in Algiers in January 1960. Some paratroops fraternized with the insurgents, but most of the army remained loyal. Within nine days the insurrection was suppressed. These events were an opportunity for de Gaulle—who received massive backing from the public in France—to demand special powers for a year to maintain order in Algeria.

His own attitude remained thoroughly ambiguous: he spoke at one moment of '*francisation*', at another of 'Algerian Algeria'. He entered into negotiations with the rebels, but also spoke of the possibility of a long war. Meanwhile (June 1960) negotiations with the rebels broke down. With Egypt, Russia and China supporting the F.L.N., it was difficult to keep Algeria as a purely French concern, though de Gaulle stood firmly against intervention through the United Nations. The effects of the revolt spread into France itself, where at least one murder a day took place, usually of one Algerian by another.

Among the Algerians the trend was strongly towards the F.L.N. and independence. Seeing de Gaulle going in this direction the advocates of *Algérie Française* resorted again to demonstrations and riots. Soustelle secretly broke with de Gaulle and joined with former Premier Bidault to organize opposition from the civilian side, and to link up with Salan and other generals in revolt. At a great demonstration in Paris which they organized in October 1960, which was banned by the government, there were 100 casualties and 500 arrests, and a further 123 were killed during de Gaulle's visit to Algeria in December. But de Gaulle's policy was endorsed by a majority of the electorate, both in Algeria and France, in referendums held at the beginning of 1961, and a last insurrection by the Ultras in Algeria failed (April 1961). To take part in this, Salan returned to Algeria from Madrid, whence he had been organizing the opposition. Though some of the other generals concerned surrendered, Salan escaped again, and along with his accomplices in the Organisation de l'Armée Secrète (O.A.S.) stirred up terrorism and race riots in Algeria.

In France huge demonstrations of Algerians, of whom there were 125,000 in the Paris region alone, backed de Gaulle. In May 1961 his representatives began negotiations with the F.L.N. whose leaders now constituted the Algerian Provisional Government, at Evian. Six thousand Algerian internees were released, but progress towards a settlement was held up by such questions as the future of those parts of the Sahara which lay within Algerian territory. The Sahara had now become important owing to the oil and natural gas which had been discovered there, and which the French were beginning to exploit. In September de Gaulle conceded Algerian sovereignty over the Sahara. He was not deflected by a crisis which arose in neighbouring Tunisia, where Bourguiba demanded instant French evacuation of Bizerta. Diplomatic relations were broken off between France and Tunisia, and fighting began, but when in September Bourguiba restarted negotiations it was clear that both in Tunisia and Algeria a final solution was in view. Secret talks with the F.L.N. continued during the winter, and in March 1962 the Evian negotiations were resumed. On 18 March an agreement was signed, and the next day the cease-fire came into effect.

Independence was to be granted to Algeria; the form of its association with France was to be negotiated after a referendum. Until this was held France would maintain a caretaker government in Algeria to look after local affairs. The principles for dealing with such vexed questions as the positions of French nationals in Algeria were agreed, the details were to be settled later. A referendum in France in April gave de Gaulle conclusive support for this policy, and it was endorsed by another in Algeria in July. There, over 91 per cent of the electorate came out in favour of Algeria becoming an independent state 'cooperating with France in accordance with the conditions defined by the declarations of 9 March 1962'.

On 3 July 1962 Algeria was declared independent and the Provisional Government took office. Owing to disputes within the F.L.N.

it was some time before it was well established. Ben Bella and five other leading rebels had just been released from confinement in France, and their claims for cabinet posts had to be settled. Finally in August Ben Bella assumed control, held elections on a single list—thus making Algeria a one-party state—and in September took over the Premiership. At the beginning of the next year, 1963, along with the settlement of questions of French nationals and other matters, France accorded a programme of aid of 1,700 million francs (over £120 million). A last flare-up of terrorism organized by the O.A.S. took place in France—plastic-bombs were a favourite method. De Gaulle himself was fired at, but escaped. With the arrest of ex-Generals Salan and Jouhaud, and the kidnapping of another terrorist leader, Colonel Argoud, from Germany, serious danger from the O.A.S. could be considered as over.

De Gaulle, Macmillan and the Nuclear Deterrent

To restore the greatness of France General de Gaulle had to pursue a flexible strategy. In dealing with the situations which he had inherited from the Fourth Republic there were many ways to the desired end. There was the question of the alliances, and particularly France's place in NATO; there was the new relationship with Germany; and there was the Common Market.

De Gaulle brought about no sudden changes. He accepted the new relationship with Germany. An exchange of visits with Adenauer brought the two together as firm political friends, and the warmth of the reception which each had from the other's people during their respective state visits showed how much the old enmities had given place to a genuine reconciliation. NATO was accepted, and German rearmament within it. But then came the rub: in the *direction* of NATO de Gaulle demanded an equal place for France along with Britain and the U.S.A. In letters to Macmillan and Eisenhower he demanded a tripartite directorate of U.S.A., Britain and France for Western military strategy and the pooling of nuclear information. Pending a favourable decision on these proposals—which was not given—he refused to have NATO rocket-sites or atomic material on French soil, and vetoed France's participation in the Tactical Air Force pool (1958). In 1959 he refused participation for France in an integrated NATO command.

If France could not have an equal voice in the direction of NATO, the alternative was to reduce her NATO commitments and build up her own defences. The decision to produce nuclear weapons had already been made under the Fourth Republic. De Gaulle accelerated the work and began to create the *force de frappe*, or striking force, capable of delivering a nuclear bomb. He was the more ready to take this step because it would bolster the army's morale, which had been reduced to a low level by the succession of failures in Indo-China and North Africa. But the expense of these projects was enormous, particularly since neither America nor Britain would share their nuclear 'know-how' with France, and it was only by costly research leading to processes, already in some cases obsolescent, that France could begin to catch up.[1]

The new prosperity of France made such expenditure possible, and to de Gaulle it was worth while because only so could France become a member of the 'nuclear club' and maintain the stance of a great power. When the Americans pointed out that any deterrent which France could create by herself would be so meagre by comparison with the destructive power of Russia as to be negligible, the General was no whit abashed. His view was that America would not use nuclear weapons except in the case of a threat to her own territory— the nuclear 'umbrella' which America held over Western Europe was largely useless.

He was fortified in this view by the Cuban crisis. Though approving of President Kennedy's firmness, he noticed that a nuclear war, which might have engulfed France along with the other members of the Atlantic Alliance, had been risked by America without consultation with her allies. They had, it is true, been informed, but in a crisis it was clear there would be no consultation. It would be the American President's finger on the nuclear trigger and no one else's.

Equally de Gaulle believed that France, to be a great power, had to have her own means of attack as well as defence. It was because France had been content with a purely defensive posture, based on the Maginot Line, that (in his view) she had not been able to make her influence felt during the Hitler era: she had had no means of delivering a blow against Hitler in support of Czechoslovakia, and her inability to come to the aid of Poland had been patently shown in 1939.

[1] The diffusion plant at Pierrelatte is a case in point.

Was de Gaulle thinking in the 1960s in terms which had been relevant enough to the situation of the thirties, but were now superseded by the vast and terrifying equipment of nuclear war? Could a French deterrent ever be 'credible'? The British experience indicated that it never could.

In 1955 the British began reducing their conventional forces to a minimum in order to put everything into their own nuclear deterrent (even to the point of forfeiting the goodwill of their European allies by withdrawing a division from Germany).[1] No sooner had the British tested their H-bomb (1957) than they began to have doubts on this point, not primarily because the destructive power which they now had available might prove insufficient to deter an aggressor, but because the means of delivering such weapons might prove inadequate. The V-bomber force which was built for delivering atomic weapons in the fifties was seen to be losing its potency as the defensive power of guided missiles increased, and though devices like the American air-to-ground 'Skybolt' seemed to prolong their usefulness, by the sixties it was clear that the long-range rocket, launched from the ground or sea was the only dependable missile for the future.

Hopes of Britain's keeping ahead in developing her own ballistic missiles had been fostered by the agreement between the American and British governments for co-operating in research on these projects in 1953, but the resulting 'Blue Streak' liquid-fuel rocket was a disappointment. Its slowness in warming up and the fact that even the underground sites from which it could be launched had become vulnerable to a direct hit from a Russian counter-missile indicated its inadequacy. Early in 1960 it was cancelled.

Though cancellation of Blue Streak appeared virtually to bring an end to Britain's independent status as a nuclear power, in reality the decisive step had been taken two years before. The agreement, published in July 1958, by which America would share her nuclear 'know-how' with Britain, though seemingly enhancing Britain's position as a nuclear power, had in fact shown that her nuclear independence was ending. For the previous twelve years, since the MacMahon Act (August 1946) had banned the transmission of secret nuclear knowledge, Britain had been forced to be an independent nuclear power, if she wished to be one at all. Now that Britain had come so far on as a

[1] See p. 247.

nuclear power, the Americans realized that it would be best to share all their 'know-how' in order to bring Britain fully into their nuclear strategy. With the resumption of close interchange of information, such as had taken place during the war, the co-ordination of the defence strategies of the two powers was the next logical step. 'It became desirable to adjust British operational procedures and targets so that in practical terms the two forces [of Britain and the U.S.A.] almost became one.'[1]

The integration of the striking forces of the two countries was displeasing to de Gaulle. He would much have preferred that the British should share their deterrent, even if 'puny',[2] with France. The two countries, in his view, could build up a nuclear force together, pooling their knowledge and resources for what would still have been a costly enterprise, but one more efficient and economical than if France continued her nuclear adventure alone. His readiness for such co-operation was shown by the agreement for the joint development of the *Concord* supersonic airliner.

Despite the drawing together of Britain and America for nuclear defence, de Gaulle did not abandon hope that Britain might come round to becoming a partner with France in this sphere. In 1958 Macmillan had assured him of British support for France's nuclear ambitions; he had spoken to the French Ambassador of the 'logic of an Anglo-French nuclear partnership'.[3] Various *démarches* from the British side had seemed to make it plain that Britain's intended entry into the Common Market (the European Economic Community) implied her willingness to develop the nuclear partnership also. With this possibility in view de Gaulle did not oppose Britain's application for entry, and during most of 1962 continued to expect that the lengthy negotiations at Brussels would lead to Britain's membership of E.E.C.

[1] Journal of Common Market Studies, I, No. 3, A. Buchan: *Europe and the Atlantic Alliance: Two Strategies or One*, 235.
[2] When Britain agreed to give up Skybolt and accept American nuclear submarines instead (Nassau, December 1962—see below), de Gaulle is reported to have said, 'Britain has decided to hand her puny deterrent back to the Americans. She could equally well have shared it with the Europeans. Well, she's made her choice.' Journal of C. M. Studies, II, No. 1, J. Bruce-Gardyne: *Outbidding de Gaulle for the Soul of Europe*, 17.
[3] N. Beloff: *The General Says No*, 150.

The General's 'No'

By 1960 the Common Market (the European Economic Community) had so far proved itself that to join seemed to be a necessary safeguard for Britain's own future economic development. The rate of investment, notably American, was running much higher in the Community countries than in the rest of Europe; between 1957 and 1960 their gross national product had increased 15 per cent (for Britain it was 10·8 per cent during this period, for the U.S.A. 8·2 per cent).[1]

Macmillan had to edge slowly towards this radical change of policy without splitting his party and antagonising the Commonwealth. As a market for British goods the European continent was developing far more quickly than the Commonwealth, and its trade with Britain surpassed that of the Commonwealth in 1961. Economically it was sensible to 'go into Europe', but the trade preferences for Commonwealth countries were still important for them. For Australia and New Zealand it had been worth while having a protected market in Britain for their agricultural products, even if it meant subsidizing exports, as had been the case in recent years.[2]

By skilful diplomacy Macmillan kept his party with him in moving towards applying for entry to the E.E.C., sufficiently to neutralize the opposition to the new policy from the Commonwealth countries. Britain then applied for membership of E.E.C. and entered upon months of bargaining with the Six at Brussels on the terms for her entry. The maximum conditions for her entry, which Britain would have liked to obtain, were put forward by Edward Heath, the minister in charge of the negotiations, on 10 October 1961. These included the association of EFTA and Commonwealth countries with E.E.C. making 'a wider trading unit', and for prolonging the transitional period before the common market for farm products came into operation. Any losses in trade resulting from the raising of a united tariff against Commonwealth exports should be compensated by 'comparable outlets' (markets of comparable size) in the E.E.C.[3]

These conditions were put forward as bargaining counters. Each

[1] J. F. Deniau: *The Common Market* (Barrie and Rockliff, 1960), 143.

[2] 'It has been calculated that the exporters were contributing an average of a thousand million dollars a year to Britain's upkeep.' Beloff, 121.

[3] Beloff, 116, 118; *The Times*, 11 November 1961. See above, pp, 247–9

one of them, even if only accepted in part by the Six, meant considerable adjustments in their own arrangements within the Community. Every proposal put forward by Britain had therefore to go through two sets of discussions—those of the representatives of the Six as to what these adjustments would be, and again between the Six and Britain in reaching a further adjustment between what they would offer and the British position.

An immediate challenge, which the Six had to accept, was to formulate their own agricultural policy, something which they found extremely difficult to do. The Germans wanted to go on protecting their farmers, relatively less productive than those of France or Denmark who wished to have expanding markets for their more abundant and cheaper produce. Since settling this matter was a precondition of continuing the talks with Britain, the French were in a strong position to put pressure on their German colleagues (who wished to leave agriculture out of the Common Market for as long as possible) to agree to their own scheme. 'But for this, it is highly doubtful . . . whether, in the two hundred hours' marathon meeting which ended on 14 January 1962, they could have obtained terms so advantageous to their own farmers and taxpayers.'[1] According to this agreement, food imported from outside the Community would pay duties corresponding to the difference between the world price and the price inside the Community: from the fund so accumulated compensation would be paid to farmers within the Community whose earnings would have dropped after losing their protected positions.[2]

Britain had to consider how entry into the Community would affect not only Commonwealth producers but those of the other EFTA countries. The latter had agreed to let Britain negotiate alone with the Six, on the understanding that arrangements for her entry would be valid also for themselves so that all the Seven would go into the E.E.C. at the same time. On this point, the Six, under the leadership of Couve de Murville for France, were as helpful as could be. Britain's entry would have to be negotiated first, but she could come into E.E.C. without imposing tariffs against her EFTA partners, in order to allow time for terms to be made with them.

---

[1] N. Beloff, 121. I have adjusted the date which is misprinted 1963.

[2] 'This would mean that the big importing countries would pay a lot and that the money would probably be used to help subsidise the exporters: it was obviously immensely to France's advantage.'—N. Beloff, 129.

As for the Commonwealth, an agreement about industrial commodities was the easiest to negotiate, and this was completed by the end of May 1962, followed by an outline scheme for future trade relations between the enlarged E.E.C. and the Asian Commonwealth countries. An agreement was also made for associating the African and Caribbean territories of the Commonwealth with the E.E.C. on terms highly advantageous to them, similar to those which had been negotiated for France's former overseas territories. Each of the Commonwealth countries however flatly rejected association, following Ghana's assertion that the plan was a 'neo-colonialist' plot to exploit them, as a condition of Britain's entry into the E.E.C.[1]

There remained the question of foodstuffs from the old Dominions, notably Australia and New Zealand (South Africa had withdrawn from the Commonwealth in 1961), and related to this was the removal of the high price-supports enjoyed by British farmers. Many difficult questions were involved in this negotiation, and to get it through quickly, concessions by Britain were necessary. These Heath was ready to make, but the strategy employed by the British government was to hold them up in the hopes of making a big 'package deal' later. This delay 'may have been the key blunder of the negotiations'.[2] If Britain could have reached agreement on these issues before the Brussels conference adjourned for the holidays in August 1962, she could almost certainly have secured entry into E.E.C.

After that it was too late. Whereas up to midsummer de Gaulle had considered Britain's entry as inevitable, later in the year he changed his mind. There were two reasons for this. One was that he thought that the Conservative government would soon fall: the Labour Party, under Hugh Gaitskell's leadership, were opposed to Britain entering E.E.C. The other was that his hopes of nuclear partnership with Britain were disappointed. Britain, becoming increasingly integrated with America for defence purposes, would merely be a Trojan horse for increasing America's influence in Europe. Further, the long-drawn negotiations and haggling on the

[1] 'Cabinet Ministers who had worked hard and long to overcome the Community's reluctance to extend to the Commonwealth Africans those same trading privileges and economic aid as the Six were committed to giving French-speaking Africa failed to conceive how anyone could credit such a ludicrous proposition. Here was a measure of the Government's total failure to explain to the Africans what they had been doing at Brussels.'—N. Beloff, 138.   [2] N. Beloff, 122.

part of Britain had raised the question as to whether, once within the Community, she might prove to be too 'un-European', too awkward a partner—and in any case a challenge to the hegemony which France had so far exercised there.

Britain's entry might certainly have slowed the evolution of the Six towards a political federation, which had been the object of the initiators of E.E.C. It was because this had been their objective, and because de Gaulle disliked supranational institutions which would limit France's freedom of action, that he had originally been opposed, first to the Schuman Plan and then to E.E.C. He had come round to supporting E.E.C., partly because, as a realist, he was ready to accept its existence when it had proved a way of building a 'Europe' in which French hegemony would be certain, and which could be a power-focus independent of America. To get Britain further away from America and into this kind of Europe was, from the General's point of view, worth while, even at the risk of Britain challenging French hegemony in Europe. But it was precisely because Britain could be a counter-balance to France that her partners were eager to bring her into E.E.C.

Whereas France's partners were looking to the political consummation of E.E.C. as a federation, from de Gaulle's point of view Britain's entry might prevent, or at least delay this development, since she had always favoured a looser kind of association. This was in line with de Gaulle's thinking about a *'Europe des patries'* as the pattern to aim for, which Macmillan had specifically approved. Some organization which could bring the states of Europe together in a way which would make them 'the world's most powerful, prosperous and influential political, economic, cultural and military *'ensemble'*[1] was favoured by de Gaulle, but only on condition that the states which composed it, and specifically France, remained 'the only entities that have the right to make decrees and the authority to act'.[2]

France and her partners had in fact different reasons for wanting Britain to join the Community. When however it became clear that Britain, by seeking to come 'into Europe' was not at the same time leaving America, but was instead strengthening her links with her,

[1] *Le Monde*, 7 February 1962, quoted in Journal of Common Market Studies, I, No. 2, C. Johnson: *De Gaulle's Europe*, 171.
[2] Quoted in above source, 160.

the reasons for her entry had, from de Gaulle's point of view, practically disappeared. This came home to him when Macmillan negotiated new defence arrangements with Kennedy at Nassau in December 1962, without consulting with him first, although Macmillan had visited him just before proceeding to his rendezvous with the American President (17–19 December 1962).

At the meeting with Macmillan on 15 December 1962, de Gaulle had expressed doubts as to whether Britain was ready to enter E.E.C. At this stage, to show willing, Macmillan could have offered joint development of nuclear weapons. De Gaulle was ready for an offer, but his pride forbade him to make a request. Macmillan did not even inform him of the projected moves with America, involving the cancellation of Skybolt and the offer of nuclear submarines and Polaris missiles. This lack of trust was aggravated by the fact that the Americans had made an offer of nuclear submarines to France in September, but had soon afterwards withdrawn it.

By the Nassau agreement, Britain was more firmly than ever in the American orbit. Three nuclear submarines were to be made available to Britain, along with Polaris missiles for which Britain would supply the war-heads. This nuclear force was to take its place within NATO, under (ultimately) American command.

With the fading of any prospect of Britain bringing her nuclear force to build up a 'European deterrent', her entry into E.E.C. lost its attraction for de Gaulle. President Kennedy's plan for a 'multilateral' NATO naval force, equipped with nuclear missiles, had no appeal for him. According to this plan officers and men, together with naval units, from the various NATO countries, would be fused into a single fighting force, but this would, in de Gaulle's view, have simply reinforced American control. Already he had begun withdrawing the French units from the NATO naval forces.

According to the constitution of E.E.C. each participating country had a veto on the entry of a new member. This veto the General proceeded to use. At a press conference which he called on 14 January 1963 he explained his reasons for this step. Recalling Britain's earlier refusal to come into the Community while it was being built, and her attempt to kill it in the germ by the organisation of EFTA, he expressed his doubts as to whether Britain was yet ready to take the decisive step. Britain, he said, was a different country from those of the Six—'insular and maritime, linked by her trade, her markets and her supply routes to often very varied and often very remote countries'. The 'long, long, so long, so long Brussels conversations' had shown how difficult it was for Britain to come into another economic system. Her entry would endanger the orientation of the existing Community. In the enlarged Community 'the cohesion of its members, who would be very numerous and diverse, would not endure for long, and ... ultimately it would appear as a colossal Atlantic community under American dependence and direction, which would quickly have absorbed the community of Europe'.[1]

The General's 'No' was at first received with incredulity by France's partners, and attempts were made to continue the negotiations at Brussels, which had now reached an advanced stage. The difficulties over Commonwealth agriculture seemed on the point of being overcome, after long and intricate bargaining covering the smallest details and individual items. A few days after the fatal press conference Dr Adenauer was at Paris for signing the Franco-German Treaty of co-operation and friendship, and did his best to persuade the General to continue the negotiations. Instead he sent his emissary to wind them up. It was an embarassed Couve de Murville who pronounced the sentence of execution in a meeting of the Six. The reactions of France's partners were almost violent—'the rumpus was indescribable. All the ministers lost their tempers.'[2] Pleas to France, threats, a special visit from the German Foreign Minister, Dr Schroeder, were all to no avail. The General was adamant. On 29 January 1963 the Conference was indefinitely adjourned.[3]

The French Community

To build nuclear armaments and take a line independent of America and NATO was one way in which de Gaulle claimed for France the status of a great power. Another, and one perhaps more relevant to the modern world, was the new relationship which he pioneered between France and her former colonies, building on the 'outline-law' (loi-cadre) passed under the Fourth Republic in 1956. This had provided for assemblies in each territory, elected by

[1] The Times, 15 January 1963.
[2] N. Beloff, 167.
[3] A later evaluation of these events is to be found in P. Reynaud: The Foreign Policy of Charles de Gaulle (Hamlyn, 1964), 75 seq.

universal suffrage, with powers over matters of predominantly local concern.[1]

Soon after resuming power in 1958 de Gaulle went on tour to Madagascar and the colonies of West and Central Africa. He proclaimed their right to independence, and arranged for a plebiscite in which a 'Yes' would give them membership of the French Community (a looser entity, superseding the Union), with augmented powers of self-government, and the possibility of evolving towards independence. In the event all these dependencies except Guinea voted for membership of the Community on these terms,[2] (October–December 1958).

Not only did de Gaulle thereby move France's African territories on to something near the 'Commonwealth' relationship of Britain and her former colonies; the programme of aid which he approved for these territories continued the tradition of the Fourth Republic in this respect. It was on a generous scale, more than double that of Britain for her ex-colonies,[3] and was now augmented by the funds contributed for the purpose by France's partners in E.E.C. This type of aid was, according to de Gaulle, another function of France as a Power. There was an obligation upon her to help bring all peoples to modern civilization, by means of 'developing her own economic, technical and cultural capacities in such a way as to provide a large measure of assistance to others'. France's 'historic vocation would be carried out henceforward by co-operation'.[4]

Decolonization: Holland and Indonesia

Other countries had not been so successful in carrying out decolonization. While Portugal still continued as if the mid-twentieth-century 'wind of change'[5] had never blown, and managed to retain all

[1] D. Pickles: *The Fifth French Republic* (Methuen, 1960), 151.

[2] In East Africa French Somaliland voted for the alternative status of being an Overseas Territory, with an elected assembly but only a limited degree of self-government.

[3] Between 1956 and 1959 France contributed 2·7 per cent of her national income in public and private aid to underdeveloped countries (Britain 1·3 per cent, U.S.A. 0·9 per cent)—Kitzinger: *Challenge of the Common Market*, 79, 81.

[4] Quoted from de Gaulle's message to the National Assembly, 11 December 1962, by A. Grosser (*International Affairs*, April 1963), whose comment is: 'To be able to substitute decolonisation and aid for colonisation and domination as a national objective—that indeed is an extraordinary intellectual feat!' (p. 202).

[5] The phrase given currency by Macmillan in a speech at Cape Town, 3 February 1960. R.I.I.A.: *Documents on International Affairs* (1960), 344.

her colonies except Goa, Holland and Belgium found it impossible to resist the pressures of the new age.

For Holland the abandonment of her wealthy domains in the East Indies was made practically inevitable by the Japanese wartime occupation. Just before defeat, the Japanese came out in support of the independence movement, whose leaders like Sukarno had already been, before the war, a considerable thorn in the side of the Dutch. Having received military training from the Japanese, and administrative and technical experience in posts never open to them under the Dutch, these leaders proclaimed the Indonesian Republic two days after the Japanese collapse (17 August 1945).

Battles were fought against the troops of the British South-East Asia Command, and subsequently against the Dutch. By keeping up a continuous guerilla struggle, and by mobilising world opinion against Holland, especially through the United Nations, the Indonesians made it impossible for the Dutch to restore their sovereignty except over part of the archipelago. An attempt to transform the islands into a federation under Dutch control was a failure, and after intervention by the U.N. Security Council independence was granted at the end of 1947.

Political and economic troubles however persisted. A Communist rising had to be put down in Madiun, while battles were fought with insurgents led by Dutch nationals, of which the most formidable was in defence of Bandung against Captain R. P. Westerling and the remnants of the Netherlands Indies army which he had collected. Further friction was caused with Holland by Indonesian claims to New Guinea (West Irian), though it was neither geographically nor ethnographically a part of the Malay archipelago. Once again Indonesian pressure, by means of the Afro-Asian bloc in the United Nations, was successful, and Holland transferred this territory to the new Republic in 1963.

Not content with these gains, Indonesia attempted military action against the Federation of Malaysia immediately after its establishment in 1963. It charged that the Federation was dominated by Britain and subject to neo-colonialist influence. When the Federation's case went against Indonesia in the United Nations, Sukarno declared its resignation from that body. Afflicted by galloping inflation

and racked by corruption, Indonesia was obliged to lean heavily on
the People's Republic of China.

Decolonization: Belgium and the Congo

If Belgium's hold on her vast Congo empire was more quickly
loosened when the time came, the fighting and upheavals which resulted were equally disastrous. Presenting an outwardly calm
appearance, the Congo had not seemed destined for independence, at
least for many years, until the wind of change blew it with a vengeance
into the turmoils of the mid-twentieth century.

With independence being granted by Britain and France to their
colonies, it became increasingly difficult for Belgium to ignore the
demands for independence by the more articulate of her Congolese
subjects. In his tour of the Congo early in 1960 King Baudouin frequently encountered jeering demands for this boon which had been
promised the year before.[1] Suddenly reversing the policy of decades,
the Coalition government of M. Eyskens decided to grant independence forthwith, despite the almost total lack of preparation for
the inhabitants in the arts of administration and diplomacy. A handful of Congolese, among them the President and Vice-President of the
Mouvement National Congolais, Patrice Lumumba and Cyrille
Adoula, had some experience of trade union affairs, and some practice of politics on a tribal rather than national basis. The same applied
to M. Kasavubu of the rival Abako Party. A professional élite with a
higher education, such as existed in the French and British territories,
was almost totally lacking. The Lovanium University near Léopoldville had been founded only just before independence. At this time
there were only twelve Congolese medical doctors. For its administrative, professional and technical services, for most of its education
and much else besides, the Congo depended almost entirely on the
Belgians.

Although in the view of British administrators overseas, progress
towards independence in the colonies had been much too fast to
ensure a smooth and efficient transfer of power, in the Congo it was
accomplished at breakneck speed. A few months was all that intervened between the calling of the round-table conference at Brussels

[1] Though the Congolese peoples were to be 'led forward towards independence . . .
without undue haste'.—R. Slade: *The Belgian Congo* (O.U.P., 1960), 50.

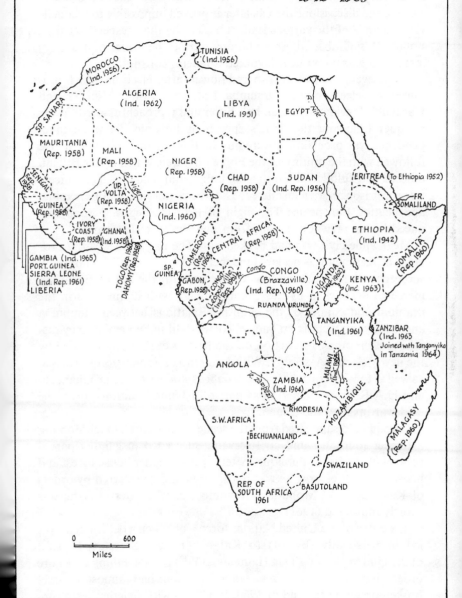

AFRICA ~ DECOLONIZATION
1942 ~ 1965

TUNISIA (Ind.1956)

MOROCCO (Ind. 1956)

ALGERIA (Ind. 1962)

LIBYA (Ind. 1951)

EGYPT

SP. SAHARA

MAURITANIA (Rep. 1958)

MALI (Rep. 1958)

NIGER (Rep. 1958)

CHAD (Rep. 1958)

SUDAN (Ind. Rep. 1956)

ERITREA (To Ethiopia 1952)

FR. SOMALILAND

SENEGAL 1958

GUINEA (Rep. 1958)

UP. VOLTA (Rep. 1958)

NIGER

IVORY COAST (Rep. 1958)

GHANA (Ind.1958)

NIGERIA (Ind. 1960)

CAMEROON (Rep. 1960)

CENTRAL AFRICA (Rep. 1958)

ETHIOPIA (Ind. 1942)

GAMBIA (Ind. 1965)
PORT. GUINEA
SIERRA LEONE (Ind. Rep. 1961)
LIBERIA

TOGO (Rep. 1960)

DAHOMEY (Rep.1958)

SP. GUINEA

GABON (Rep. 1958)

CONGO (Leopoldville) (Ind. Rep. 1960)

Congo

CONGO (Brazzaville) (Ind. Rep. 1960)

UGANDA (Ind. 1962)

KENYA (Ind. 1963)

SOMALIA (Rep. 1960)

RUANDA URUNDI

TANGANYIKA (Ind. 1961)

ZANZIBAR (Ind. 1963
Joined with Tanganyika in Tanzania 1964)

ANGOLA

R. Zambezi

ZAMBIA (Ind. 1964)

MALAWI (Ind. 1964)

MOZAMBIQUE

MALAGASY (Rep. 1960)

S.W. AFRICA

RHODESIA

BECHUANALAND

SWAZILAND

REP. OF SOUTH AFRICA 1961

BASUTOLAND

0   600
Miles

in January 1960 and the grant of independence at the end of June. During the discussions then as later it proved impossible to reconcile the demands of the various leaders backed by their respective tribes, notably Lumumba, whose ambitions were to be leader of a unitary state, and Kasavubu who favoured a federal constitution.

In the event the two men shared power, after elections which produced no clear result, Lumumba becoming Prime Minister and Kasavubu President. Lumumba's bitter and reproachful words at the banquet following the King's speech in Léopoldville when independence was proclaimed, were humiliating for the Belgians. Worse followed with the mutiny of the Force Publique, which under Belgian officers had fulfilled the duties of police and soldiery. The officers were imprisoned, then dismissed. The troops ran riot, looting, raping, and beating Europeans. The flight of Belgians began, partially reduced by the arrival of troops from Belgium to restore order.

Meanwhile civil war had broken out. The huge and wealthy province of Katanga was declared independent by Moise Tshombe, who succeeded in maintaining law and order with the aid of European mercenaries, backed by the Union Minière with its interests in the uranium and copper of the country. Relations between Lumumba and Kasavubu went from bad to worse, until in September they dismissed each other, this action on the part of each being annulled by the newly elected Assembly. With Lumumba's application to Russia, as well as to Western countries for support, and with Indian, Ghanaian and U.A.R. troops entering as part of a United Nations force, the cold war invaded the Congo.

Lumumba disappeared from the scene soon after Colonel Mobutu, a former journalist and civil servant, succeeded in gaining partial control of the Force Publique. After a period under house-arrest and his subsequent escape, he was re-captured and transferred by orders of Kasavubu and Mobutu to Tshombe, in whose territory he was shortly murdered (1961).

The entry of the United Nations force—of which a detachment was led in personally (by air) to Katanga by the Secretary-General of the United Nations, Dag Hammarskjöld—did something to restore order, but over large areas administration had almost entirely broken down by the end of 1960. Relations with Belgium were ruptured, and Belgian administrators and technicians were only partially replaced by some brought in by the United Nations. Supplies imported through the U.N. averted famine, but for the following years the Congo remained at a low economic ebb, a prey to tribal war, anarchy and violence. The resumption of diplomatic relations with Belgium at the end of 1961, and the continued work of numerous Belgians in the Congo, showed that the relationship between the two countries had not been severed—a relationship which might eventually help the young Republic to emerge from the appalling difficulties with which it was struggling.

Britain After Decolonization

Though decolonization as carried through by Britain proceeded along more orderly lines than in the case of Belgium and Holland, it could not be completed so quickly. The Indian Empire had been dismantled in 1947. With the independence of Ghana, Malaya and Singapore in 1957, Nigeria in 1960, Sierra Leone and Tanganyika (1961), and her remaining East African colonies in the two following years, Britain was left with relatively few of her former possessions. Yet these still imposed considerable preoccupation and expense: in the far East, Hong-Kong and a base at Singapore; in the Middle East, Aden and the remnants of dominion in the Persian Gulf; in the Mediterranean, a base at Cyprus (independent 1959), a colony at Gibraltar, and obligations demanding financial outlay and defence commitments in both those places, as well as at Malta and Libya.[1] Militarily Britain was obliged to intervene both in East Africa and Cyprus in 1962. In the latter the quarrel between Greeks and Turks had not been finally settled, after years of civil war, with the Greeks still working for *Enosis* (union with Greece). Relations between Greece and Turkey had been more than once near a point of complete rupture, and the arrangements of NATO (of which both countries were members) had been consequently jeopardised in the Eastern Mediterranean.

Britain might have acquired an empire in a fit of absence of mind, but a great deal of hard thought and hard cash went into getting rid of it. Her participation in the Korean War not merely signalized her support of the United Nations; it underlined her commitments east of Suez. The independence of Malaya did not free her from the

[1] Malta independent 1964. Libya independent 1951, after being liberated from Italy during the war. Southern Rhodesia (now Rhodesia) still remained a Colony (1965).

obligation of protecting the infant Federation of Malaysia from the threats of Sukarno's Indonesia. The attempts to steer Aden and its hinterland towards independence on a federal basis involved troubles with the Adenis themselves and clashes with tribesmen from Nasser-dominated Yemen.

While carrying the defence burden which all these commitments necessitated, maintaining her garrisons in Germany (though in reduced numbers and with German support), providing her former dependencies with a measure of financial aid and continuing (as was the British tradition) a high level of investment overseas, Britain still managed to maintain a rising standard of living. In this last respect Britain did not differ from her continental neighbours. But she was obliged to finance her multifarious expenditure out of production which was rising more slowly than most of theirs. This fact, together with her still heavy overseas commitments, made it difficult for her to pay her way. The illustration of this was her chronic balance-of-payments difficulties: she was importing more than she could pay for by her exports, both visible and invisible.[1]

Entry into the Common Market might have led to expanding trade and a greater challenge to modernization and efficiency. As it was, Britain in the 1960s had taken France's place as the sick man of Europe.

Adenauer and Germany

West Germany, by contrast, was booming as the fifties ended. Being forbidden nuclear forces by treaty, and with practically no air force or navy[2]—her army had been rebuilt by Adenauer under protest—her expenses in the matter of defence were relatively small.[3] Her rubble was almost cleared away, her cities rebuilt, and her factories and mines re-equipped along the most modern lines.

Politically she had shown a great deal more stability than might have been forecast from the record of the Weimar Republic. This was

[1] Invisible exports: receipts from investments abroad, banking, insurance and shipping services, etc. See Table at end of chapter, p. 374.
[2] In the early 1960s a German Air Force, at the disposal of NATO, was being built up towards a strength of 28 wings. The new German Navy at the end of 1961 consisted of six destroyers and six groups of minelayers and landing craft, together with supporting vessels, submarines, etc., being planned. For the army, see p. 363.
[3] See below, p. 374.

in large measure due to Konrad Adenauer, who in Churchill's view can be regarded as the greatest German statesman since Bismarck. History may well record that the achievements of Adenauer were more durable and more firmly based than those of his famous predecessor.

When Adenauer came to the fore in 1948 he was accepted as a provisional leader for a transition period. Few had expected that this survivor of the Wilhelmine era, already a decade beyond the age at which most men retire, could be anything more than the leader of a caretaker government. Few realized how much political expertise—shrewdness, cunning, resourcefulness and patience had matured in Adenauer's character during his long experience as Oberbürgermeister of Cologne and his shorter, but also important, presidency of the Prussian Council of State.[1] Few realized the toughness of the man—his steadfast adherence to principle combined with flexibility in practice, his paternal and sometimes high-handed authoritarianism combined with respect for forms and procedures.

As Oberbürgermeister he had formed the habit of briefing himself thoroughly on every question which might arise, on being able to out-argue his opponents on every issue, of tenaciously sitting out the meetings until his colleagues through sheer weariness conceded the point—yet doing it in a way which caused the minimum divisions and created at least the illusion of unity. 'When everyone was dog-tired from the endless pro and contra of debate, he would finally come out with his own motion or proposal, which to hazy and sleepy minds would then appear like a summary of their own views, and they would adopt it without further ado.'[2]

The combination of authority and respect for the new constitutional forms brought the Germans into the way of working a democratic system. At the general elections since the founding of the Federal Republic over 80 per cent of the citizens have steadily voted. The polarization of the Christian Democratic Union (C.D.U.) round

[1] As Oberbürgermeister (Lord Mayor), appointed for successive periods of seven years, handling a large budget, and combining with his office positions such as Town Clerk, Commissioner of Police and permanent head of every municipal department in Cologne, Adenauer was used to exercising wide powers. He was also the highest paid official in Germany, drawing more than the Reich President.—C. Wighton: Adenauer—*Democratic Dictator* (Muller, 1963), 52; G. A. Craig: *From Bismarck to Adenauer* (John Hopkins Press, 1958), 126–8.
[2] P. Weymar: *Konrad Adenauer*, (Deutsch, 1957), 95.

Adenauer and of the Socialist Party (S.P.D.) round Schumacher[1] helped to bring about the formation of a two-party system, akin to that of Anglo-Saxon practice. This was helped by a wise provision of the constitution which excluded any party with less than 5 per cent of the popular vote from obtaining a seat in the Bundestag.

The Socialist challenge was powerful and sometimes bitter, particularly over foreign policy issues: in the debates on Germany's entry into E.D.C. Schumacher accused Adenauer of being 'the Chancellor of the Allies'. Whether a more 'non-aligned' attitude between East and West could have attained the goal desired by all Germans, the re-unification of their country, is doubtful. Adenauer's persistence in building links with the West, his belief that a united Germany could only be attained if 'it were the goal not only of the Federal Republic but of the entire Western Alliance',[2] ultimately carried conviction to most of his compatriots. In reality the issue— though ostensibly kept as alive as ever—receded into the background, as Germans in the Federal Republic increasingly found a measure of satisfaction in the rising standards of living and growing affluence brought about by the 'economic miracle'.

Ludwig Erhard, who shared with Marshall (and the American administrators of the Aid programme) the credit for the economic transformation of West Germany, was not among the Chancellor's closest colleagues. The bulky ex-Professor, who became Minister of Economics, with his jovial cigar-smoking ways, was a contrast with his grave ascetic senior.[3] Erhard was not Adenauer's discovery. His rise had been due to the Americans who, in May 1945, to his own surprise, fetched him by jeep to be economic adviser in one of the embryonic institutions of their zone. But having shown his mettle both there and on the inter-zonal bodies to which he was later appointed,

---

[1] Dr Kurt Schumacher had been a Prussian officer in the First World War, when he lost an arm. In 1933 he refused to go into exile, and after ten years of maltreatment in Nazi prison-camps he lost a leg. He was post-war leader of the S.P.D. until his death in 1952, opposing all Adenauer's European policies. (R. Hiscocks: *Democracy in Western Germany* (O.U.P., 1957), 82–4). Schumacher's successor was Erich Ollenhauer, followed by Willy Brandt, Lord Mayor of West Berlin.

[2] W. Stahl (ed.): *The Politics of Post-War Germany* (Praeger, 1963), 39; for E.D.C. see above, p. 238.

[3] Not that Adenauer lacks humour. 'Son sens de l'humeur est vif, ilaime plaisanter . . . il sait faire rire un auditoire populaire. . . .'—A. Grosser: *La démocratie de Bonn* (Paris, 1958), 259. The concluding chapter, *Konrad Adenauer et la démocratie de Bonn*, 255–63, gives an excellent picture of the man and his style of government.

Erhard could not be dispensed with. So great was the success of his 'free market economy' as Minister in the Federal Government that his vote-getting powers made him a fixture in all the cabinets of Adenauer, and despite the old Chancellor's objections, his inevitable heir.

The 'miracle' was also due to the traditional German love of work. From the squalor of 1948 there was only one escape for the Germans —to 'work their way out of the rubble'. The high proportion of skilled workers made the return to an economy based on the most advanced technology a matter of almost months once the upswing had begun. The equally traditional discipline of the race was apparent, notably in the trade union movement. In 1949 sixteen unions federated to form the six million strong Deutsche Gewerkschaftsbund (D.G.B.). The strike weapon has scarcely been used, and the amount of production lost through strikes has been negligible. In the interests of national revival the unions 'pursued a policy of restraint both as to wages and hours, and attached importance rather to steady prices and full employment, and to securing a share in industrial management'.[1]

The latter was achieved with the co-determination law of 1951 (*Mitbestimmungsgerecht*) in the iron, steel and coal industries. Though some inflation took place, price increases over the years were in general moderate. Despite a high investment rate, *per capita* consumption soon passed the pre-war standards, and the vast pool of unemployment which existed in 1949, and which thousands of refugees continued to fill, was completely absorbed by the mid-1950s—this after a migration of eight million 'expellees' from Eastern Germany, Poland, Czechoslovakia and the Balkans, together with three million refugees from the Eastern Zone (German Democratic Republic). In 1950 there were fifteen million unemployed, in 1962 there were twenty-one million in employment.[2] Since the late fifties there has been a chronic labour shortage.

On its territory, considerably diminished from that of the Third Reich, without the Silesian mines and industrial complex, the Republic shot ahead in production, surpassing in 1960 the production rate of the Germany of 1936, and becoming the world's third

[1] R. Spencer in R. Flenley: *Modern German History* (Dent/Dutton 1963), 454.
[2] Stahl, 59.

producer after the U.S.A. and the Soviet Union. The working day was reduced, pensions adjusted to rising living-costs, half a million houses built annually (though here the backlog after the war-time destruction was not yet fully made up by the mid-sixties), and family allowances and other welfare schemes introduced.

This solid economic foundation has helped to ensure stability, despite setbacks and disappointments in foreign policy, and shocks arising from Adenauer's occasionally excessive authoritarianism. Adenauer had his triumphs—the virtual achievement of complete sovereignty by the 'Bonn Convention' of 1952;[1] the immense prestige conferred on him and the new Germany by his visit to the U.S.A. in 1953 (similar to that secured by Khrushchev with his Camp David visit six years later); and the firm integration of the Federal Republic with Western Europe through the Schuman Plan and E.E.C.; and—as part of this—the reconciliation of Germany with France crowned by the Franco-German Treaty of 1963.

He also had his failures and near disasters—the collapse of E.D.C.; the meagre results of the diplomatic link re-established with Moscow (1955) in the way of gains beyond release of a few thousand war-prisoners; the failure of integration with the West to bring about the 'roll-back' of Soviet power and the freeing of Germany's former eastern territories; his decision to stand for the Presidency on the retirement of Theodor Heuss in 1959, and its cancellation when he announced to his frustrated colleagues his determination to continue as Chancellor (he was already 85). Whereas his earlier achievements had led to the C.D.U. gaining an absolute majority in 1953 (244 out of 487 seats), and more than 50 per cent of the popular vote in 1957, his vacillations in 1959 and the general view that he was clinging to office reduced the C.D.U. vote by 5 per cent in 1961. The S.P.D. gained a third of the popular vote, and the Liberal Party (F.D.P.) revived with 60 seats. Once again, however, Adenauer imposed his will on his party, and succeeded in bringing the F.D.P. into a coalition with the Christian-Democrats. After seven weeks without a government, Adenauer was re-elected Chancellor by a small majority (November 1961).

---

[1] No final peace treaty was made, however. The Western Allies continued to keep troops in the Republic and West Berlin, and the Republic was bound to the Western alliance through E.D.C. and later NATO.

His acceptance of the candidature for President had been due to his belief, into which he was persuaded, that he could run foreign policy from that office. Had he attempted to do so, the Presidency might well have been transformed and a constitutional crisis created. Adenauer's failure to find an alternative to Erhard in his place as Chancellor, who would be acceptable to his party and the public, brought about this change of mind. He believed that Germany's future was only safe if firmly integrated with France and the E.E.C., and he realized that Erhard was far from sharing all his convictions.

Though he continued to regard de Gaulle as Germany's greatest friend, there were unresolved chords in the apparent harmony established between the Chancellor and the President—the *Europe des Patries* was a different conception to the integrated Charlemagne's Europe of Adenauer's vision. The high-tide of co-operation between the two countries had receded before the Franco-German Treaty was signed—a symbolic treaty of friendship, without important provisions. Coming so soon after the General's No to Britain over her entry to E.E.C. it seemed to make the Federal Republic an accomplice in that act. After Adenauer's retirement in October 1963 relations with France cooled while those with Britain became increasingly cordial, culminating in the immensely warm welcome given to Queen Elizabeth II on her state visit in May 1965.

The Chancellor's last twelve months in office were overshadowed by the *Spiegel* affair, when the review of that name published criticisms of the new Germany army which the government regarded as treasonable (October 1962). The arrest of its editors and the occupation of its offices provoked almost universal protest.

The army (Bundeswehr) had been rebuilt painfully and rather slowly in the face of the *ohne mich* (count me out) attitude of many Germans, and the repugnance of Adenauer, despite his recognition of its necessity. On the failure of E.D.C. he stated (privately) that 'the national army to which M. Mendès-France is forcing us will be a great danger for Germany and Europe'.[1]

The army consisted of 375,000 men in nine divisions in 1962, planned to rise to 500,000 in 1965 with another 500,000 in reserve. It was built up by former career officers, notably General Adolf Heusinger, who was Chief of Operations, O.K.W., until arrested for

[1] G. A. Craig: *From Bismarck to Adenauer* (John Hopkins, 1958), 140.

complicity in the attempt on Hitler's life of 20 July 1944. He became military adviser to the government in 1951 (later Chairman of the Military Advisory Council). A break with old army usages and 'corpse obedience' has been made, and the fostering of a new attitude among soldiers based on 'inner leadership'.

The army has been recreated specifically as a contribution to NATO, of which General Heusinger became Chairman of the NATO Military Committee in Washington. General Hans Speidel, also arrested as one of the senior officers suspected after the July 1944 plot, has been Commander of the Northern Army Group.[1]

The trial and execution of Adolf Eichmann, a Gestapo leader, in Israel in 1962, brought to the fore the relations of West Germany with Israel and reopened the entire question of de-Nazification. On the former issue, it had been the policy of the government to make what restitution to Jewry that it could. Among other acts of policy was a considerable provision of aid, and later of arms, to Israel.[2] On the question of retribution for the Nazis, most Germans hoped that enough had been done by the trials of leading Nazis carried out by the four-power International Military Tribunal in 1945–6 at Nuremberg, and the time and effort spent by the Allies and German courts during the following years in tracing and penalizing the lesser fry.[3]

With the reopening of the question by the Eichmann trial, prosecutions increased in number, and demands were made for abolishing the ruling that such cases would be considered void twenty years after the ending of the war.[4] In the prosperous Federal Republic of the

[1] H. zu Löwenstein and V. von Zühlsdorff: *N.A.T.O. and the Defence of the West* (Deutsch, 1963), 156–7, 205–16.

[2] This provoked recognition by Nasser's Egypt of the (East German) D.D.R. and a rupture of diplomatic relations with the Federal Republic in 1965, thus putting to the test the 'doctrine' formulated by State Secretary Walter Hallstein that the Federal Republic would neither recognize the D.D.R. nor have diplomatic relations with any country which recognized it.

[3] The juridical validity of the Tribunal was a much discussed matter. Its aim was to fulfil the war-time pledge of the Allies to bring all 'war criminals' to punishment. Ribbentrop, Keitel, Sauckel, Rosenberg and others were executed. Goering escaped the hangman by taking poison; Bormann, though convicted, was never found. Speer, Raeder, Dönitz, Hess and others were committed to varying terms of imprisonment. As part of the de-Nazification process all Germans over eighteen in the American and British zones had to answer a questionnaire under 133 heads. Many Germans who had been in favour of bringing the leading Nazis to book thought the Nuremberg trials the wrong way of doing it, and believed that it would have been done more effectively and with greater impact on the German public if the trials had been carried out by German courts.   [4] The period for continuing prosecutions was extended by four years.

1960s, where a new generation had grown up without any recollection of the 'Hitler time', on which their elders had long since turned their backs, there were perhaps advantages as well as disadvantages in these grim and sordid reminders of the dark side of Germany's history.

The Recovery of Italy

The recovery of Italy was as steady as that of West Germany, if less spectacular. Her immediate handicaps were fewer, but she was encumbered by persistent economic and political difficulties, ante-dating the war and the régime of Mussolini.

Having worked her passage (in Churchill's phrase) by a policy of 'co-belligerence' with the Allies, leading to an eventual declaration of war against Germany, Italy could not be treated merely as a defeated country. Though this fact, and the very real services performed by the Italian guerillas (Partisans), particularly in the North, against the Germans, were not, in Italian eyes, given adequate recognition in the treatment their country received at the war's end, it was nevertheless a great deal better than that meted out to Germany. Destruction of homes and industry, though on a considerable scale, was for the most part restricted to certain zones, and, thanks to Partisan action, the important northern industrial area fell into Allied hands almost intact.

U.N.R.R.A. supplies of food, raw materials and equipment saved the people from starvation and helped put industry on its feet. When this ended its place was soon taken by massive aid under the Marshall Plan. Finally, another boost to the economy came through Italy's entry into the Coal and Steel Community and then into E.E.C.

Politically a measure of stability was provided during the immediate post-war years by the predominance of the Christian Democrats, by far the largest party in the state.[1] When Alcide De Gasperi was able to emerge from the Vatican library in 1943, he restored the Popular Party in a new form as a progressive Catholic party, with social welfare as its main concern—a parallel movement to that of the M.R.P. in France and the C.D.U./C.S.U. in Germany.

[1] For its origins see above, p. 216; also R. A. Webster: *The Cross and the Fasces—Christian Democracy and Fascism in Italy* (Stanford University Press, 1960), Ch. 9, 129–36, *De Gasperi: The Exile of the Vatican.*

As in France, the most powerful rival force to this movement was the Communist Party, and for the same reasons, notably the great part played by Communists in the resistance movement. The shrewd leadership of Palmiro Togliatti, with its appeal even to practising Catholics because of its moderation and realism, secured the party a large stake in affairs in the immediate post-war period, and brought the numbers of its members up until it was reckoned the largest outside the Soviet Union and China.[1]

Despite this challenge the Christian Democrats came out on top at the first post-war election (June 1946) with 207 seats and over eight million of the popular vote. Though the Socialists scored more than the Communists (115 and 104 seats), they were soon riven between their Communist-oriented left under Nenni and the moderates under Saragat. In January 1947 Nenni led more than half the Socialist Deputies to join the Communists, while Saragat's group moved towards alliance with the Christian Democrats. The Communists were strengthened, but for the time being the Christian Democrats under De Gasperi were able to consolidate their position.

Although the Christian Democrats secured the biggest vote at the 1946 elections, the Premier who headed the government of that date, Ferrucio Parri, was a non-party man who had made his mark as a resistance leader. His coalition government included the Communists. They were not however given key positions, and in May 1947 they resigned. Parri's government fell and De Gasperi took his place.

During this immediate post-war period a new constitution was framed. The colourless King Victor Emmanuel II abdicated; his more lively heir Prince Umberto failed to be confirmed on the throne in consequence of a plebiscite (June 1946), which declared in favour of a republic by twelve million against ten million votes.

At the first election under the new constitution (May 1948) the Christian Democrats gained an absolute majority with 307 seats. De Gasperi decided to include some of the smaller groups in his government—Social Democrats, Republicans and Liberals—since he wanted them to provide a balance against the clerical forces in his ranks. From his own Catholic stand-point the main requirements were met by the confirmation of Mussolini's concordat with the Vatican, by which religious teaching in state schools was safeguarded.

[1] It now (1965) comes after that of Indonesia.

De Gasperi's eight-year régime played a similar role in Italy to that of Adenauer's government in Germany. Though shorter in duration, it saw the re-establishment of Italy's international position, and the groundwork laid for her economic advance. 'In eight successive coalitions this great statesman showed himself to be the most astute and courageous parliamentary leader since Cavour himself, and one of the most high principled.'[1]

The frustrating Paris Peace Conference of 1946 at least saw the preparation of drafts for the Italian peace treaty, which was later signed in February 1947.[2] Italy's African empire was not immediately liquidated. Ethiopia had regained its independence, Libya had become a kingdom under British sponsorship, Eritrea went to Ethiopia, and Somaliland remained temporarily under Italian rule, though since 1949 as a Trusteeship of the United Nations for ten years as a preliminary to independence. The islands of the Dodecanese went to Greece. The Allied claims to reparations were waived, with the exception of those of Russia, who insisted on taking certain Italian vessels and a payment of $100 million.

One outstanding question was left unresolved, that of Trieste.[3] The two Zones, occupied by the Yugoslavs and the Anglo-Americans, had been given a separate status as the Free Territory of Trieste by the Italian Peace Treaty of February 1947, but this had proved unworkable. Temporarily the two Zones had remained under their respective occupiers who continued to face one another across the boundary dividing Zone A from Zone B. While the stock of the Allies in Italy rose through their declaration of March 1948 that the whole of the Free Territory of Trieste should go to Italy, thereby increasing the electoral chances of the Christian Democrat and moderate parties, Tito continued to assimilate Zone B to the rest of Yugoslavia. With the break between Tito and Stalin hopes of settling the Trieste question rose, but it was not until October 1954 that an agreement between Italy and Yugoslavia was finally reached. With a small adjustment favouring Yugoslavia Zone B went to that country and Zone A returned to Italy. A free port which was established by the Peace Treaty was to be maintained; by this it was hoped

[1] D. Mack Smith: *Italy* (University of Michigan, 1959), 496.

[2] Though regaining her sovereignty, Italy was prevented by the Soviet veto from joining the United Nations.

[3] See above, p. 130.

that trade from the now divided hinterland would re-establish the city's prosperity.

Christian Democratic dominance and De Gasperi's statesmanship brought Italy firmly into the Western camp. His Foreign Minister Count Sforza[1]—also a convinced 'European'—had talks with Robert Schuman in December 1948, followed by a conference of De Gasperi and Sforza with Schuman and Pleven in February 1951. These talks prepared the way for the Schuman Plan and Italy's adhesion to the Coal and Steel Community and later to E.E.C. and the Atlantic Alliance. Cordial relations were developed with West Germany, marked by Adenauer's visit to Rome in June 1951 and De Gasperi's reception at Bonn, in September of the following year, of the Charlemagne Prize for his work in building European unity. With the ending of aid under U.N.R.R.A. in June 1947 Italy was threatened with grave economic difficulties. Like Adenauer's later visit to the U.S.A., that of De Gasperi to Washington in January 1947 marked a milestone in his country's post-war history. It is probable that 'De Gasperi's masterly presentation of his country's situation played an important part in convincing the American authorities of the need for continued aid to war-torn European countries after U.N.R.R.A. should come to an end, thus preparing the way for General Marshall's offer of aid in the following June which Italy was among the first to accept.'[2]

This aid, plus Italian hard work and expertise, led the country from its post-war slough of near-starvation, astronomical inflation and massive unemployment to a recovery which bore the character of a 'take-off' on to a new level of economic production. By 1954 industrial production was running at 71 per cent above the rate of 1938. The ratio of gross investment to gross national product was averaging 20 per cent or more—'not far below West Germany and the Netherlands, above France and well above the United States and the United Kingdom'.[3] In this effort only Canada and Japan were markedly outdistancing Italy. During the fifties exports rose faster than imports. Helped by an average of eleven million tourists a year, Italy's balance of payments showed, by 1960, a substantial surplus,

---

[1] Foreign Minister 1947 to 1951. From 1951 to 1953 De Gasperi was Foreign Minister as well as Premier.

[2] M. Grindrod: *The Rebuilding of Italy* (R.I.I.A., 1955), 47.

[3] V. Lutz: *Italy: a Study in Economic Development* (O.U.P. and R.I.I.A., 1962), 310.

and large gold and foreign exchange reserves had been accumulated. Great entrepreneurs like Enrico Mattei undertook boldly the opening of new fields for Italian industry and trade.

The advantages of this rising prosperity were however offset by several limiting factors. Unemployment remained around the two million mark, and considerable under-employment persisted particularly in the South. The lack of training was underlined when, by 1960, skilled manpower was practically all absorbed, still leaving a large pool of unskilled labour. Secondly, the lag in the development of education, particularly at the higher technical and university levels, resulted in a lack of skilled manpower, of engineers and other technicians, and of managerial personnel. For these reasons 'the full growth potential' of the economy could not be achieved.[1]

An obsolete social system also persisted: the gulf between rich and poor remained far too wide. The wealthier classes tended to invest too much of their money in real estate and in other assets of little benefit to the economy, while flaunting their means in various forms of conspicuous waste or prestige spending. Though real wages for the workers increased by some 15–30 per cent during the period 1950–9, this advance was much less than the average in Western Europe (in Britain it was about 80 per cent). Average income was still low in 1959—45 per cent of that in Britain, half that of France and West Germany.[2] Part of the workers' gains were derived from post-war social legislation, which brought many of them substantial benefits. Labour costs for the employer were correspondingly raised, by 45 per cent in the case of family allowances.

Progress was most evident in the North. The South had long been a depressed area, since the days of the Kingdom of Naples. Poor resources, soil erosion, lack of industry and over-population combined to keep the Mezzogiorno at a lower economic level than the rest of the country. Italy's post-war governments made heroic attempts to fill this gap. 'The effort made after the Second World War to promote industrialisation in the South of Italy and to raise living standards there to parity with those in the North, has exceeded, in respect both of the financial resources devoted to it, and the variety of the methods used, all previous attempts in this direction.'[3] A land-reform provided small-holdings for over 92,000

[1] Lutz, 316.   [2] Lutz, 312, 319.   [3] Lutz, 101.

families by 1955, and the Cassa per il Mezzogiorno, set up in 1950, channeled funds into the South under a far-reaching twelve-year plan.

Nevertheless there was little sign of congruence between the two parts of the country. Average income remained, during the fifties, less than half of that in the North; population in the South increased at a more rapid rate, while in the North the birth-rate fell. The most hopeful trend for the South lay in the increased openings for employment in the North, and even outside Italy altogether. An imaginative scheme for employing Italian labour in the British coalmines to raise the limits on production resulting from falling manpower, had been baulked by trade union obstruction; but the entry of Italy into the European Coal and Steel Community, and later into the E.E.C., provided greatly increased opportunities for employment in France, Germany and the other Community countries. In addition the boost to her economy resulting from entry into these Communities went far towards putting the 'Italian miracle' on a lasting basis.

These advances continued despite a recurrence of political instability. Economic progress may have helped to hold the Communist advance in check in the North, but despite all the efforts for development in the South, the Communist vote there showed an increase of 200,000 in 1953. The general election of that year was held under an amendment to the electoral law, passed only after the most violent scenes in Parliament (particularly in the Senate), by which any party winning more than half the popular vote would gain two-thirds of the seats in the Assembly—a measure by which the Christian Democrats hoped to obtain a substantial working majority. In the event they and their allies missed gaining the coveted 50·01 per cent of the votes by a mere 57,000. The failure was a blow to De Gasperi's prestige, and his defeat in Parliament in July 1953 began a lengthy crisis, during which for four weeks Italy was without a government. Eventually Giuseppe Pella took office, but the coalitions through which the still dominant Christian Democratic Party continued to manage affairs became increasingly precarious. Although the left-wing vote in the North began to fall off at this time, and the Communist hold on the trade unions weakened,[1] the total Communist vote continued to increase.

---

[1] By 1965 losses of working-class membership were marked in the most modern sectors of industry, the lowest percentages being in factories in Turin (1·9) and Milan (4·8). Only one worker in seven among those subscribing to party funds could be con-

With De Gasperi's death in August 1954 the Christian Democrats were deprived of the leadership they so badly needed. The party split and split again, until in 1959 it was composed of some dozen warring factions. The individualism and factionalism in Italian life, so evident in all phases of her history since the fall of Rome, appeared in the mid-twentieth century to be reasserting themselves in fullest vigour.

The Progress of Benelux

Like Italy, the smaller countries in E.E.C. benefited considerably from their membership. Loss of colonies made little difference to the prosperity of Holland and Belgium. The revolts in the Congo immediately after independence threatened a loss of trade which would cut Belgium's gross national product by 3 per cent, with a consequent balance of payments crisis. This, adding to the burdens of an economy which had been stagnating for some time, aggravated by political troubles—notably the constant quarrels between Flemings and Walloons over the language issue—made the future appear grim indeed. Belgium's lowest point was reached with the widespread strikes of 20 December 1960 to 23 January 1961, organized by the General Federation of Belgian Workers, in protest against the *Loi Unique*. This was an austerity plan to counter the economic difficulties arising out of the rupture with the Congo: resentment was caused by its provisions for adding 6,600m. francs to taxation, which was to fall largely on the ordinary consumer.

Belgium lost five billion francs through the strikes, and took three months to recover from them. But from mid-year 1961 improvement was rapid. The benefits arising from membership of E.C.S.C., from the conversion of Benelux into a full economic union (November 1960),[1] and from the rapidly increasing activity of the Common Market, led to expansion in trade and industry at a rate unknown for years. In consequence industrial activity in 1961 as a whole was 5 per cent more than that of 1960, and a similar rate of growth was maintained during 1962. By 1963 the economy was at full stretch, with new

---

sidered militant, according to a report submitted to the Italian national convention of Communist factory cadres in May 1965. *The Times*, 31 May 1965.

[1] The stages of co-operation leading up to the economic union are documented in J. E. Meade: *Negotiations for Benelux: An Annotated Chronicle 1943–1956* (Princeton University, 1957).

output records being set in several industries, and the former stagnant sectors, notably coal and textiles beginning to boom like the others.

The loss of Indonesia was only one of the set-backs suffered by the Dutch economy on account of the war. Damage to industry, housing and livestock, as well as to other resources, had reduced Holland's wealth by 30 per cent in 1945. In addition the country had to feed a population which was growing more rapidly than any other in Western Europe. But a large-scale industrialization programme, together with a policy of austerity, brought about a remarkable improvement. High prices for raw materials during the Korean War put the country badly in debt, but by 1951 it was earning a large surplus (1,800,000 gulden). Membership of E.C.S.C., the Benelux Economic Union and E.E.C. brought further improvements, which more than offset the loss of practically all remaining assets in Indonesia during the dispute over Dutch New Guinea (West Irian).[1] The boom of the fifties continued into the sixties—production in 1960 was running at a level some 14 per cent higher than that of 1959, and there were three times as many vacancies as unemployed. Further prospects of rising prosperity were opened by the discovery of vast reserves of natural gas, second only to those in the U.S.A.

Luxembourg shared in the prosperity of its neighbours and of E.E.C. generally, with its steel industry in 1960 running practically at capacity.

Britain's EFTA Partners and Finland

In the sixties the countries associated with Britain in EFTA continued to build up their economies, though not at such a rapid rate as those of E.E.C. Those hardest hit by the war—Norway and Austria—had made a remarkable recovery; Denmark, which had also suffered considerably during the German occupation, regained its pre-war levels of production in the latter half of 1948. Sweden had helped to finance the recovery of her less fortunate neighbours to the tune of $600 million (mostly loans), and Marshall Aid had also been an enormous boon.

[1] The policy of the United States was much resented in putting pressure on Holland to turn over the territory to United Nations administration as a preliminary to handing it to Indonesia, and lack of support from Britain over this issue was also regretted. However 'the loss of a territory that cost the Dutch taxpayer $36 m. a year and took only a minute proportion of Dutch exports was hardly to be mourned'. *Annual Register*, 1962, 255.

Sweden's brilliant progress as an industrial nation owed much to the soundness of her collective bargaining arrangements and codes for industrial relations developed by the trade unions and management. These preceded the war, the most important being the Basic Agreement of 1938 between the Confederation of Swedish Trade Unions (L.O.) and the Swedish Employers' Federation (S.A.F.). This 'marked a milestone in the evolution of the trade union movement from a predominantly defensive collective bargaining agency to a mature and socially conscious power group, aware of its responsibilities in the new welfare state. . . .'[1] By 1961 sixteen L.O. unions had accepted the Basic Agreement. Strikes and loss of working days since 1945 dropped to an almost negligible quantity.

Denmark, Norway and Sweden formed a solid bloc in EFTA, though following divergent courses in other aspects of affairs: Norway and Denmark had entered NATO in 1949, while Sweden maintained her traditional neutrality, to be defended at need by some of the most advanced types of weapons and aircraft, developed and manufactured in that country. Finland resumed her old connection with her neighbours when she joined the Nordic Council in 1955—the same year in which Russia permitted her to join the United Nations.

For the rest Finland had been kept by Russia in a semi-dependent position, although the attempt to transform her into a Soviet satellite had not succeeded: the army and police had never come under Communist domination despite the fact that from 1946 to 1948 both the Prime Minister, Mauno Pekkala and the Minister for the Interior, Yrjö Leino, were Communists. In the five years ending in September 1952 she paid off the huge sum of $300 million as reparations to Russia, in goods valued at 1938 prices, and did this with a territory reduced by 10 per cent due to cessions to the Soviet Union, including the Arctic port of Petsamo with its large nickel industry.

Two of the most incongruous partners in EFTA were Switzerland and Portugal: the one being Europe's (and almost the world's) banker, and a thriving centre of tourism and specialized industry; the other enjoying a certain stability under Dr Salazar's long dictatorship, but relatively poor and burdened by an ancient colonial empire. The loss of Goa to India (1962) benefited neither that country nor the

---

[1] T. L. Johnston: *Collective Bargaining in Sweden* (Allen & Unwin, 1962), 18.

COMPARATIVE TABLES FOR CONSUMPTION, GROWTH-RATES
AND PRODUCTIVITY, 1960

U.S. Government Printing Office:

Dimensions of Soviet Economic Power (1962).

1. *Gross National Product by end use (percentage of total in factor cost).*

	Private consumption	Government consumption	Defence	Gross capital investment	Investment	Foreign balance	Total
France	58·3	10·7	6·6	20·7	2·3	1·3	100
Germany (F.R.)	50·4	11·9	3·9	28·0	2·6	3·2	100
Italy	58·7	13·7	—	25·2	1·8	0·4	100
Britain	61·3	11·8	7·1	18·3	2·7	−1·2	100
Japan	48·9	9·6	—	35·4	5·5	0·6	100
U.S.S.R.	47·1	10·1	10·2	31·3	1·3	?	100
U.S.A.	60·4	9·8	10·1	17·9	0·9	0·9	100

2. *Average annual rates of growth of Gross National Product.*

	1950–5	1955–60	1950–60
France	4·5	4·2	4·3
Germany (F.R.)	9·0	6·0	7·5
Italy	6·0	5·9	5·9
Britain	2·6	2·7	2·6
Japan	7·1	9·4	8·8
U.S.S.R.	7·0	6·5	6·8
U.S.A.	4·3	2·3	3·3

3. *Roles of increase in employment and labour productivity in comparative growth of Gross National Product:*

	G.N.P. Annual rates of growth	Employment	Productivity (per man-year)
France	4·3	0·4	3·9
Germany (F.R.)	7·5	2·2	5·2
Italy	5·9	1·6	4·3
Britain	2·6	0·6	2·0
Japan	8·8	1·9	6·7
U.S.S.R.	6·8	1·9	4·7
U.S.A.	3·3	1·2	2·1

Goanese. Portugal's extensive African territories continued to be a target for nationalists and Communists throughout Africa.

Once again, in another balance of payments crisis in the autumn of 1964, Britain showed that she scarcely as yet qualified as a good European in de Gaulle's sense of the word. Without consulting its EFTA partners the new Labour Government under Harold Wilson suddenly imposed a 15 per cent surcharge on all manufactured or semi-manufactured imports (26 October 1964). Under the G.A.T.T. rules, which Britain had accepted, the government could not make exceptions for a particular group of countries such as EFTA (the Commonwealth was relatively little affected),[1] but the manner of Britain's proceeding, as much as the policy itself, showed the Continental countries that Britain was still far from accepting any genuine unity with themselves.

[1] The surcharges affected 13 per cent of the imports from Commonwealth countries, 57 per cent from E.E.C. countries (according to the E.E.C. commission 64 per cent), and 36 per cent from EFTA countries. It 'unilaterally more than offset the tariff cuts that have been made (within EFTA) since its inception'. *Economist*, 31 October 1964, 511.

NOTE

DE GAULLE AND THE FIFTH REPUBLIC. On achieving power in May 1958 de Gaulle at once initiated the transition to a presidential régime. The new constitution, mainly the work of his Minister of Justice, Michel Debré, was ratified by a referendum on 28 September 1958. The elections in November provided a majority for a coalition of the Union pour la Nouvelle République (a newly founded Gaullist party), the M.R.P., and conservative Independent groups. De Gaulle was elected President by a large majority in the electoral colleges set up by the constitution, formally entering office in January 1959, while Debré took over the Premiership. De Gaulle's position was enhanced by the limitations placed on Parliament's sphere of action under the constitution and the corresponding strengthening of the executive; also by his deciding policy for Algeria on his own responsibility from September 1959 onwards, and by the grant of special powers in February 1960 for settling the Algerian crisis, endorsed by the referendum of 1961. Another referendum, in October 1962, gave approval (though with many abstentions) to a system for electing the President by universal suffrage. Parliament was dissolved after a majority of Deputies voted that Parliament alone could effect such a change, but at the subsequent elections in November 1962, the U.N.R. secured an absolute majority.

26: Motivations

During the war most Europeans had one obsessive desire—to see the last of Hitler's tyranny. With his removal many found they had exchanged one tyranny for another, that of Moscow. Twenty years after the war ended they still looked for freedom as the goal beyond all others to be prized.

Those who enjoyed freedom were subject to other motivations. Security and affluence could be defined as the principal aims. By harnessing the drives which men were able to put into attaining such objectives, statesmen were able to begin building some of their most imposing constructions such as NATO and E.E.C.

The urge to satisfy basic human wants will always supply a large part of the dynamics of society. Primarily, in the case of individuals, it is the demand to satisfy one's own wants and those of one's family and other near dependants. To satisfy people's wants on a wider scale than this is the concern only of a minority.

To say as much is to accord a special value to this minority, whatever the motives impelling its members to the fulfilment of their necessary function in society. It need not imply anything especially altruistic and therefore virtuous on their part. Statesmen and administrators in the U.S.A. who dispensed U.N.R.R.A. and various other forms of aid around the globe were not for that reason particularly righteous men. Motives of self-interest played their part in great policy decisions: the need to prevent revolution or Communism; the need for security; the need to open markets and to dispose of surpluses.

The functions are important, but motives matter. It was important that millions were saved from starvation and disease and that economies, derelict or at a low ebb, should be restarted. But the extent to which motives mattered may be assessed from a glance at the treatment by the S.S. of the people in the occupied zones which they controlled, together with their longer-term plans for colonizing them, and the treatment—more in the long-term than the short-term—

accorded by the Western Allies to the peoples whom they liberated or occupied.

This was not, of course, because the Allies belonged to inherently superior nations. It was because their outlook and policy were shaped in part by a clearer sense of their interests, in part by a more humane tradition. This was proved by those Germans who followed a different course to that laid down by Hitler and his minions. A German commandant, who was a sincerely practising Christian, like von Thadden-Trieglaff at Louvain, could win golden opinions from the inhabitants.[1]

Traditions can be guides to sanity, but the 'conventional wisdom'[2] easily becomes an excuse for abandoning the thought which new situations urgently require. In every generation men arise who question the assumptions of their time, and who pioneer new trends of development, and even initiate new types of society. The attempt to do this has been the strength of Marxists whether they have called themselves Communists or socialists. The extent to which it has failed to achieve its objectives has prompted a change in thinking among Marxists—even if the sanctity of the Marxian doctrines is not called openly in question. In Russia, Lenin and his successors, having defeated Tsarism, attempted to apply new doctrines in government and economic policy. The result was, in part, a failure. Recently much in those doctrines has been called in question, and they have been revised—despite Soviet rebuttals of charges of 'revisionism'. The consequence has been new policies. Examples are the tentative application of the Libermann system, which is a recognition of the necessity of profit as a regulator; and the reversal by Brezhnev and Kosygin of Khrushchev's policies for whittling down the private plots of peasants on the state farms and collectives.

'Freedom is the recognition of necessity,' said Engels, and by recognizing certain necessary facts, and by initiating practical action accordingly, the leaders of Russia have taken a large step in the direction of freedom.

To allow room for individual choice as regards the goods for which a man may exchange his labour, is a part of freedom, and it is more effective to organize production on a rational principle rather than

[1] W. Hühne: *A Man To Be Reckoned With* (S.C.M. Press, 1962), 62 seq.
[2] The phrase used by J. K. Galbraith in *The Affluent Society* (Hamilton, 1958).

by the whim or guesswork of small bodies of men acting as the agents of the state. This freedom, though valuable, is of a minor kind. Of a different kind is the freedom of a peasant to spend time and labour on a plot which is large enough to give him and his family real satisfaction in their work. Family endeavour has been the mark of a prosperous peasantry in Denmark or wherever they are to be found, rather than the regimented labour of kolkhozes, feudal estates or slave plantations. The free release of creative energy, with consequent good production, is related to the family sense of partnership. This principle also applies in industry: where good management–labour relations exist, and a sense of community in the enterprise is created, as in Sweden or Germany, production is high. This point has been taken in eastern Europe, where the reversal of at least the worst of the Stalinite policies and the application of genuine principles of co-operation in Comecon has led to a growth-rate which, in East Germany as an instance, now rivals that in the Federal Republic.

The Soviet Dilemma

In forbidding everything approaching pornography,[1] in legislating to strengthen marriage and the family, and in excluding from advertising and similar media the incentives to eroticism which are a constant background to life in the West, the Soviet Union might be charged with diminishing freedom, not increasing it.

It was not on account of any principle of freedom that the Soviet government so legislated, but for purely practical reasons. Legislation of earlier years had facilitated quick marriages and easy divorce, and had placed no stigma on passing and irresponsible unions. The consequence had been an alarming increase in unstable, shiftless and virtually unemployable people, together with aggravation of problems such as drunkenness and hooliganism.

Those who control the Soviet state believe that it should have a monopoly of power in every human domain. Monopolies of economic power cannot officially be built up by individuals or groups, even though in practice, under the auspices of 'His Majesty *blat*'[2] they

---

[1] D. and V. Mace: *The Soviet Family* (Hutchinson, 1964), 81. For a critical account see A. Inkeles and K. Geiger: *Soviet Society*, (Constable 1961), article by V. S. Dunham: *Sex: From Free Love to Puritanism*, 540–546.

[2] A system of corruption, black market and the equivalent of the 'old boy net.' See Ch. 11 with this title in D. J. Dallin: *The New Soviet Empire* (Hollis and Carter, 1951), 182.

sometimes are. To give the state a monopoly of power in legislating about sex and morals brings with it the disadvantages of a censorship, and of an attempt to regiment writers and artists, which reduces creativeness to zero. Though the governments of Russia and other Communist countries have been relaxing controls in this domain they are uncertain and hesitant about their new approach.

The Soviet state, in allowing more freedom, has to try to reconcile it with authority. To reconcile these two principles is the concern of every state. The most radical experiment in western Europe during the last twenty-five years in reconciling these principles may well be the European Economic Community. It may be that the creation of an economic community with political implications, on an international basis, and on principles of organization and control differing both from *laissez-faire* liberalism and autarchic totalitarianism, marks the emergence of a new kind of society. But in this respect men's hopes are likely to be as disappointed as they were in the case of those who believed in Communism or Nazism, unless a new enthusiasm, maintaining the motives of its initiators, comes to replace the present growing disillusionment.

Changing Motives in Germany

Nazism seemed to many to be a powerful ideology, but when the Nazis were defeated in battle the ideology, to the surprise of the victors, practically vanished away. Some Germans who were not too dazed by the catastrophe, nor merely preoccupied by the exacting task of living, came with pain and difficulty to new insights through the religion which they had denied. Some who had maintained their faith, as had the surviving members of the Kreisau circle,[1] tried to build it into the fabric of Germany's post-war political and social life. Such men, lay and clergy, were the support of the leaders who attempted to place on a Christian basis the constitution of the new republic and its policy.[2] Karl Arnold, the first Minister–President of North Rhine-Westphalia (which included the Ruhr), was a Christian-Democrat who, because of his Christianity, was a socialist. His followers, together with the Catholic trade unions under Jakob Kaiser, formed a strong group whose aim was 'socialism based on a Christian sense of responsibility'. Arnold worked out the original

[1] See above, pp. 98, 195.   [2] See above, p. 195.

social and economic policy for the British Zone, pioneering important developments such as workers' participation in management.[1]

The extent to which a change came over the Germans during the war and its aftermath may still be difficult to assess.[2] The powerful role which spiritual forces played in this change is unquestionable. Men who had stood firm against the tyranny gave by that very fact a powerful witness to their faith—Archbishops and Bishops, both Catholic and Protestant: von Galen, Faulhaber and Preysing; Dibelius, Meiser and Wurm; also those of lesser rank but equally known like Pastor Niemöller. These could proclaim with greater force their faith because others, like Bonhoeffer and von Moltke, had died for it. Laymen who had survived perils and persecution, like Reinold von Thadden-Trieglaff, moved mountains with their determination that there should not die away 'the promising beginnings of revival that were clearly manifest during the decades of resistance to Hitler's new paganism, during the sufferings of the war-period [and] . . . after the German collapse'.[3] From this determination came the great project of the Kirchentagen, culminating in the enormous gathering of 650,000 people at Leipzig (East Germany) in 1954. The movement of moral and spiritual renewal owed much to Frank Buchman, an American of Swiss ancestry, who in 1946 founded, at Caux in Switzerland, the European Centre for Moral Re-Armament. This provided a meeting point for Europeans of all backgrounds with people from overseas, and to it came Adenauer, most of the Ministers-President, and other leaders from politics, management and trade unions, in the years after 1945.[4]

The new spirit in Germany, matched by a corresponding change of outlook in France, made possible the *rapprochement* of the two countries, which has been mentioned above.[5] Whatever may ultimately

[1] R. Hiscocks: *Democracy in West Germany* (O.U.P., 1957), 75. The Christians in the C.D.U. were by no means all Catholics. In the first Bundestag 40 per cent of the C.D.U. Members were Protestants.

[2] The assessment of Professor Hiscocks is rather gloomy, but he notes the emergence of 'a small minority . . . the salt of the earth,' which 'has faced the implications of its country's past with uncompromising courage and honesty.'—Ibid., 229.

[3] Quoted by Hühne, op. cit., 101.

[4] See above, p. 280. For the work of Moral Re-Armament in Germany, notably that of Mme. Irène Laure, former Socialist Deputy for Marseilles and leader of the Resistance, see L. Hovelsen: *Out of the Evil Night* (Blandford, 1959), especially for developments in the Ruhr, 45 seq.; also Gabriel Marcel: *Un Changement d'Espérance* (Plon, 1958), 3–19.

[5] See p. 220.

happen to the European Economic Community, it is clearly in line with the needs and potentialities of the age. Its success, even during the short term of its existence, has demonstrated the truth of the statement, that 'the economic problem is not . . . the permanent problem of the human race'.[1] What has proved valid for a sizable body of people in Europe, may be presumed valid on a global scale. Technology has supplied the means, and a new type of economic organization has shown the way. In this instance the essential element of *will* was also applied. As Professor Galbraith says in another context, 'the question is less one of feasibility than of will'.[2]

Sartre and Existentialism

This question of will—of motive and aim—has been the concern of religious leaders and philosophers down the ages. In our own day it has been the concern of existentialists, of the Vatican Council, and of radicals, religious and secular. In probing motives Kierkegaard, in his time,[3] cut away the stifling layers of old formulas and traditions. His work has provided the foremost inspiration for many thinkers of today. Whatever differences there are between those thinkers who are called existentialists, whether they accept or repudiate the label, they have in common the attempt to strip away ruthlessly all assumed or preconceived ideas concerning the nature and destiny of man.

They are also the champions of freedom, in full revolt against determinism, whether the historical and economic determinism of Marx, or the determinism of personal conduct popularized by certain psychological thinkers and psychiatric practitioners. 'There is no determinism,' asserts Sartre. 'Man is free, man *is* freedom.'[4]

Restating the Kantian imperative, Sartre further affirms, 'I cannot make liberty my aim unless I make that of others equally my aim.'[5]

---

[1] J. M. Keynes: *Essays in Persuasion* (Macmillan, 1931), 366; Galbraith, 118. Keynes' point is that wants 'which are relative in the sense that we feel them only if their satisfaction lifts us above, makes us feel superior to our fellows . . . may indeed be insatiable'. But 'absolute needs' are now capable of being satisfied for mankind.

[2] Galbraith, 258.

[3] 1813–1855.

[4] J. P. Sartre: *Existentialism and Humanism* (Methuen, 1948), 45. Born in 1905, Sartre's career as a Professor of Philosophy at Paris was interrupted by the war. He was made prisoner during the German advance, and on his release in 1941 became a member of the resistance movement. His autobiography was published in 1964.

[5] Ibid., 30.

Because man is free, responsibility, like choice, is squarely on the individual, and this responsibility is total, for all men not merely for self. 'I am thus responsible for myself and for all men, and I am creating a certain image of man as I would have him to be. In fashioning myself I fashion man.'[1]

The *aim* is of paramount importance, because man is only man in action; abstract philosophising is meaningless—it is man grappling with his day-by-day decisions, trivial or agonizing as they may be, who *makes himself*. It is because he is moving somewhere that man has life at all. 'Man is, before all else, something that propels itself towards a future and is aware that he is doing so. . . . Man is a project which possesses a subjective life.'[2]

The goal towards which man is projecting himself becomes therefore supremely important. The goal is not determined. There may be indications, but the choice is man's alone. The indications are formulated by the philosophers in the systems of values which they present. An atheist like Sartre says that 'our aim is precisely to establish the human kingdom as a pattern of values in distinction from the material world'. For Christians like Heidegger, Jaspers or Marcel, the pattern of values is not human but transcendent. No matter which, the aim, as indicated by the particular pattern of values, must be discovered and tested through action, and pursued with a dedicated sense of commitment (*engagement*).

Affluence and the World's Needs

A survey of national policies during the post-war era indicates however that they are not yet determined by values, in the Sartrian sense, but by instinctive reactions. For this reason the richer communities go on getting richer, and although the poorer ones may not get poorer, the merely slight increases in their wealth and well-being leave them ever farther behind their richer neighbours. Though American aid on an immense and unparalleled scale sufficed to restart the economy of Europe, it has not been nearly enough to cure the economic ills of Asia and Africa, or of the rest of the American hemisphere.[3] Europe is now booming, and is investing and giving

---

[1] *Existentialism and Humanism*, 30. He speaks of 'man's complete and profound responsibility'.   [2] Ibid., 28.
[3] Related to this is the fact that the depressed areas of the United States itself continue to be depressed.

considerable sums overseas, but these are again totally insufficient to bring the underdeveloped countries into line with the richer ones.

The applications of Keynes' formulas have proved effective in preventing depressions from developing within America and other countries, though at the cost of steady and continuous inflation. Unemployment has been, generally, kept at a low level. Can such boons be extended to the world as a whole? Professor Galbraith is confident that it can be done within America, and on the same principle it can be done in the world—'to eliminate poverty efficiently we should invest more than proportionately in the children of the poor community'.[1] Do this on a sufficient scale in countries where industrialization alone will provide employment and good living-standards, and their 'take-off' into this desirable stage of development will be assured.[2]

At present the wealthier countries cannot do this because they are spending astronomical sums on satisfying an increasing number of wants developed by their own peoples, on fantastically expensive defences, and equally expensive activities which certainly bear on defence, but which also contribute to prestige—something for which people will pay heavily—notably the exploration of space. The urge for security is behind much of this expenditure, not merely for defence, but for maintaining jobs and living-standards. For this reason the vast mechanism of advertising is constantly stimulating new wants, to satisfy which ever higher wages and salaries have to be paid, ensuring that as high a proportion of production is consumed as before (or even higher), without the possibility existing of the massive investment required to bring all people to conditions of decency and opportunities for progress.[3] New inventions, like television, which came into its own during the post-war decade, have been directed in large part towards this end.

Pope John and the Oecumenical Movement

To counter this trend an incentive is needed powerful enough to provide a decent life with the fullest opportunities for all men in every land. This is faith as much as conviction—'do unto others as you would

[1] Galbraith, op. cit., 257.
[2] According to the process expounded by W. W. Rostow: *The Stages of Economic Growth* (Cambridge, 1960).   [3] Galbraith, 120.

384

they should do unto you'. Many pronouncements have been made in
recent years, by those qualified to speak in matters of faith, about the
world and its needs. Pius XII, in his great encyclicals, struck a note
of agonized warning, in the face of a Europe plunging to barbarism.
John XXIII stressed rather the unprecedented possibilities facing
mankind. His appeal was 'to all men of good will' to go forward
together, 'in confidence building afresh and building better'.[1] Pope
John was aware too of the wrath of God, and that in a physical sense
it might be manifested in the dropping of nuclear bombs, but he
believed that, whatever appearances to the contrary, men were open
to the appeal of undertaking great enterprises together. 'All the
world is my family,' he wrote in his diary in December 1959. 'This
sense of everybody belonging should colour my mind, my heart and
my actions, and give them life.'[2]

This new attitude on the part of the leader of the largest body in
Christendom gave an immense stimulus to the oecumenical movement and new hopes for unity, as well as opening up fresh possibilities for co-operation between the Churches in many fields. This
linked with the Protestant oecumenical movement, in which the
Dutch leader, Dr. W. A. Visser't Hooft, Germans like Niemöller and
von Thadden-Trieglaff, and others of many nations had played a
part, notably in the formation of the World Council of Churches.
Five Catholic theologians attended as observers its Assembly at New
Delhi in November 1961.

Before he became Pope, Angelo Roncalli (1881–1963) had been
used to mingling with men of all faiths and backgrounds, both in east
and west. Born the son of a peasant in the North Italian village of
Sotto il Monte, with twelve brothers and sisters, his early life was
hard—'sometimes he could not write his diary for lack of a candle to
see by, sometimes for lack of ink'.[3] As the bright boy of the village, at
the age of eleven he was sent to begin his training as a boarder in the
seminary at Bergamo. There he later became a member of the staff,
professing ecclesiastical history and other subjects. After being
President of the General Council for Italy of the Congregation of
Propaganda (Missions), his real launching into the non-Catholic
world came with his appointment in 1925 as Apostolic Visitor in

[1] E. E. Y. Hales: *Pope John and his Revolution* (Eyre and Spottiswoode, 1965), 38.
[2] Hales, 126.   [3] Ibid.. 8,

Bulgaria, followed by that of Apostolic Delegate in Turkey and Greece (1934), a post which he held throughout the difficult war years, much of them in German-occupied Greece, until his appointment in 1944 to be Apostolic Nuncio at Paris. After nine years in France, dealing, among other matters, with the question of the worker-priests, he was appointed Cardinal and Patriarch of Venice (1953), and in 1958 was elected Pope at the age of 77.

This man, who had won golden opinions from Moslems in Turkey and Orthodox Christians in Bulgaria and Greece, as well as from secularists like Kemal Atatürk, was in a good position to rise above barriers of creed and race. He discovered 'real spiritual goodness in all sorts of men, of all sorts of belief, Christian and non-Christian'.[1] It was the vision of the unity of all Christians, consecrating the aspirations towards a better world of all men of good will, which prompted him to call the Vatican Council of October 1962. Here Cardinals and bishops from all over the world, including Poland and other countries of Eastern Europe, attended. The note for the Council was struck by the Pope in a broadcast, shortly before its opening, in September 1962. It was, he said, to give enlightenment to the world and guidance to Christians. In practical terms, the Christian was to win others by his example, and on the social plane 'to take stock of what he has in excess of his needs, giving thought to the needs of others, and to strive most strenuously to ensure that the development and distribution of the resources of creation redound to the benefit of all men'.[2]

The Ultimate Need

Besides security and wellbeing—vast armaments and the welfare state—men want meaning for their lives. They need an aim which is a challenge, and the opportunity for pursuing it. Each generation makes this demand, even if the opportunity for great living involves the likelihood of speedy dying. The appeal of certain types of war was less evident in 1939–45 than in 1914, but to fighter-pilots and others it was still immense. The demand for adventure and risk-taking is insatiable, even if it means hooliganism and law-breaking, as much in the Communist lands as in the West. Schemes for voluntary service

[1] Hales, 16.   [2] Ibid., 136.

overseas in countries like Britain and Germany have attracted those who want to do something towards building new nations.

In an age in which the extremes of brutality and self-sacrifice have coexisted, the words written by Simone Weil in 1943 are relevant: 'Germany is a mirror for all of us; what looks to us so hideous is our own features, but magnified.'[1] Heroic self-sacrifice was not lacking in Germany. If we look only on the better side of our achievements, whether in the last war or of any other time, we fail to see the barbarism which still lies near the surface.

The need is the moment of truth, experienced once and if possible repeated. The atheist may experience it, finding thereby community with the man of traditional faith. Though Meursault rejected the prison chaplain at the moment when he accepted reality, it was the chaplain's challenge which brought him his moment of truth and the return of peace.[2] For the man of faith reality is more than this: 'truth is Thyself',[3] the vision of God which brings not merely peace but meaning and a goal. Lopatkin in Dudintsev's *Not by Bread Alone* was professedly an atheist, but in fact he was a man of faith. His vision was concerned with machines for producing pipes, but it was a vision of truth which he could not live without. For him it lit the way towards serving humanity and building a better world.

[1] S. Weil: *Selected Essays*, 1934–43 (O.U.P., 1962), 214. Simone Weil, born at Paris 1909, died at London 1943. An outstanding student, she graduated in Philosophy in 1931. After teaching for a few years she took work in the Renault factory; fought on the Republican side in Spain in 1936; and joined the French resistance in 1942. Her writings became well known only after her death.

[2] A. Camus: *L'Étranger* (English translation, *The Outsider* (1946)).

[3] St. Augustine.

Bibliography

MANY books and articles are referred to in footnotes. A selection of other books and documents appears in the following list, together with some of the sources referred to in the footnotes in cases where comments about them seem necessary.

Some general histories of Europe include part of the period 1939–65, e.g. David Thomson: *Europe Since Napoleon* (Longmans, 2nd ed. 1962). A book which contains contemporary European history in a wider range of world history is D. Donnelly: *Struggle for the World* (Collins, 1965). History shades into journalism—John Gunther: *Inside Europe To-day* (Hamilton, 1961) is a sequel to his pre-war *Inside Europe*. A recent book covering a large part of the ground is J. Freymond: *Western Europe Since the War* (Pall Mall Press, 1964).

Source-books and Documents

Royal Institute of International Affairs: *Surveys* and *Documents*; also *Documents on Germany under Occupation 1945–54; The Annual Register* (Longmans); London Institute of World Affairs; *Year Book of World Affairs* (Stevens)—since 1947; *Documents on German Foreign Policy 1918–45* (H.M.S.O.)—the outbreak of war comes with Vol. 7 of Series D; publication complete (1965) to end of 1941 (Vol. 13).

Origins of the War

W. N. Medlicott: *The Coming of War in 1939* (Routledge and Kegan Paul for the Historical Association, 1963). Also printed in W. N. Medlicott: *From Metternich to Hitler*, p. 231 (Bibliography, p. 255).

A. J. P. Taylor: *Origins of the Second World War* (Hamilton, 1961).

Past and Present, December 1964: T. W. Mason, 'Some Origins of the Second World War' (criticism of A. J. P. Taylor's book).

K. Feiling: *Neville Chamberlain* (Macmillan, 1946).

Sir Nevile Henderson: *Failure of a Mission* (Hodder and Stoughton, 1940). By the British Ambassador to Germany at the time of the outbreak of the war.

The War

Official Histories: History of the Second World War (United Kingdom Military Series), editor Sir James Butler (H.M.S.O.). *Victory in the West* Vol. I: Major L. F. Ellis: *The Battle of Normandy*, S. W. Roskill: *The War at Sea;* Sir Charles Webster and Noble Frankland: *The Strategic Air Offensive 1939–1945* (each in several volumes). There is also the Civilian Series, editor Sir Keith Hancock, with valuable material on the economic blockade (two volumes by Medlicott), on American aid, Lend-Lease, shipping, etc., in volumes on *The British War Economy* (W. K. Hancock and M. M. Gowing).

H. A. Jacobsen: *1939–1945: Der Zweite Weltkrieg in Chronik und Doku-menten* (Wehr und Wissen Verlagsgesellschaft, Darmstadt, 1959). Contains chronicle of events, documents (Hitler's addresses to the army commanders, etc.), maps, bibliography.

W. S. Churchill: *The Second World War* (Cassell, 1948). Besides being Churchill's own account of events, it has useful maps and documents.

F. Halder: *Hitler as War Lord* (Putnam, 1950). A highly critical assessment by Hitler's one-time Chief of the General Staff. (Halder's war diary has not been translated.)

L. P. Lochner (editor and translator): *The Goebbels Diaries* (Hamilton, 1948).

R. Macleod and D. Kelly (editors): *The Ironside Diaries* (Constable, 1962). General Sir Edmund Ironside was Chief of the Imperial Staff during the first nine months of the war, after which he commanded the Home Forces until July 1940. He was later promoted Field-Marshal.

E. von Manstein: *Lost Victories* (Methuen, 1958) is useful for the Battle of France as well as the war in Russia.

A. Bryant: *The Turn of the Tide 1939–1943* (Collins, 1957) and *Triumph in the West 1943–1946* (Collins, 1959) are based on, and contain large extracts from, the diaries and autobiography of Sir Alan Brooke (Lord Alanbrooke), Chief of the Imperial General Staff, 1941–6.

The Trial of the German Major War Criminals—Proceedings of the International Military Tribunal sitting at Nuremberg, Germany (H.M.S.O., 1951). One of the most important sources. There is also *Trial of the Major War Criminals before the International Military Tribunal, Nuremberg.* (Published at Nuremberg—Official Text, English edition.)

P. Calvocoressi: *Nuremberg, the Facts, the Law and the Consequences* (Chatto and Windus, 1947). Useful information about Himmler, the S.S., war-crimes, etc., as well as a study of the proceedings from the juristic point of view.

L. L. Snyder: *The War: A Concise History 1939–1945* (Hale, 1962). A good introductory survey of the war as a whole.

J. F. C. Fuller: *The Second World War* (Eyre and Spottiswoode, 1948).

A. Goutard: *The Battle of France, 1940* (Muller, 1958). A concise and thorough analysis.

K. Demeter: *The German Officer-Corps in Society and State 1650–1945* (Weidenfeld and Nicolson, 1965). A translation recently published of the book mentioned on page 1.

W. Görlitz: *The German General Staff* (Hollis and Carter, 1953).

M. Heppell and F. B. Singleton: *Yugoslavia* (Benn, 1961). For the background of Hitler's attack.

D. J. Dallin: *Soviet Russia's Foreign Policy 1939–1942* (Yale, 1942).

A. Werth: *Russia at War 1941–1945* (Barrie and Rockliffe, 1964) contains extracts from the official Soviet *History of the Great Patriotic War of the Soviet Union*; also material from the same author's *The Year of Stalingrad* (Hamilton, 1946).

P. Carrell: *Hitler's War on Russia* (Harrap, 1964).

M. P. Gallagher: *The Soviet History of World War II* (Praeger, 1963).

G. Martel: *The Russian Outlook* (Joseph, 1947).

D. D. Eisenhower: *Crusade in Europe* (Doubleday, 1948). Extracts in the text reprinted by permission.

W. Bedell Smith: *Eisenhower's Six Great Decisions* (Longmans, 1956)—by Eisenhower's war-time Chief of Staff.

H. W. Baldwin: *Great Mistakes of the War* (Redman, 1950).
N. Frankland: *The Bombing Offensive against Germany* (Faber, 1965).
S. E. Morison: *The Two-Ocean War* (Little, Brown, 1963). The U.S. Navy in the war.

The Churches and the German Resistance

G. Lewy: *The Catholic Church and Nazi Germany* (Weidenfeld and Nicolson, 1964).

War-time Diplomacy

G. F. Kennan: *American Diplomacy 1900–1950* (Secker and Warburg, 1952).
The Memoirs of Cordell Hull (Hodder and Stoughton, 1948, two volumes).
Stalin's Correspondence with Churchill, Attlee, Roosevelt and Truman (Secker and Warburg, 1952).
E. R. Stettinius: *Roosevelt and the Russians* (Cape, 1950). The Yalta Conference by the Secretary of State at the time.
J. R. Deane: *The Strange Alliance* (Murray, 1947).
Ciano's Diplomatic Papers (ed. M. Muggeridge, Odhams Press, 1948).
Ciano's Diary 1939–1943 (Heinemann, 1947).
F. Maclean: *Disputed Barricade* (Cape, 1957). For Trieste, see p. 302 seq.

Post-war Diplomacy

President Truman's *Memoirs* are incomplete in the English version (Hodder and Stoughton, 2 vols., 1955, 1956). Chapter 9 on Truman's early life is missing. The American version is by Doubleday (1955, 1956).
R. Payne: *General Marshall* (Heinemann, 1952)—no index.
F. C. Pogue: *George C. Marshall: Education of a General* (Viking Press, 1963), while excellent for an understanding of Marshall's personality, stops short of the period concerned.
W. Miles (editor): *The Forrestal Diaries* (Cassell, 1952).
F. S. Northedge: *British Foreign Policy 1945–1961* (Allen and Unwin, 1962).
W. Bedell Smith: *Moscow Mission 1946–1949* (Heinemann, 1950).
A. Grosser: *La IVe République et sa Politique Extérieure* (Librairie Armand Colin, Paris, 1961).
Dean Acheson: *Sketches from Life* (Hamilton, 1961). Material on origin of Schuman Plan, etc., and portraits of Schuman, Churchill, Vandenberg, Marshall, Adenauer.
J. W. Spanier: *American Foreign Policy since World War II* (Praeger, 1960).

Germany

M. Dill: *Germany: A Modern History* (Michigan, 1961).
F. Meinecke: *The German Catastrophe* (Harvard University Press, 1950).
J. F. Golay: *The Founding of the Federal Republic of Germany* (Chicago, 1958).

390 BIBLIOGRAPHY

W. Philipps Davison: *The Berlin Blockade* (Princeton, 1958).
A. J. Heidenheimer: *Adenauer and the C.D.U.* (Nijhoff, The Hague, 1960).
K. Bölling: *Republic in Suspense—Politics, Parties and Personalities in Post-war Germany* (Pall Mall Press, 1964).
A. Grosser: *The Federal Republic of Germany—a Concise History* (Pall Mall Press, 1964).
J. Mander: *Berlin: Hostage for the West* (Penguin, 1962).
H. Fraenkel: *Farewell to Germany* (Bernard Harrison, 1959). Reports on Germany after the war.

France, the Schuman Plan and the European Economic Community

P. de Beaumont: *La IVᵉ République: Politique Intérieure et Européenne* (Editions de la Librairie encyclopédique S.P.R.L., Brussels, 1960).
E. B. Haas: *The Uniting of Europe* (Stevens, 1958).
M. Beloff: *Europe and the Europeans* (Chatto and Windus, 1957).
O. Wilcox and H. F. Haviland (editors): *The Atlantic Community* (Praeger, 1963).
M. Einaudi and F. Goguel: *Christian Democracy in Italy and France* (Notre Dame, Indiana, 1952).
C. Ledré: *Robert Schuman* (Éditions Spes, Paris, 1954).
Robert Schuman: *Pour l'Europe* (Nagel, Paris, 1963). Selections from his speeches and writings.
'Adstans': *Alcide De Gasperi nella Politica Estera Italiana* (Mondadori, 1953).
Maria De Gasperi: *De Gasperi, Uomo Solo* (Mondadori, 1965).
The Economist Intelligence Unit: *The Commonwealth and Europe* (1960).
British Iron and Steel Federation pamphlets, e.g. *A European Steel Programme* (1949), *The Schuman Plan and Britain* (1952).
R. Pryce: *The Political Future of the European Community* (Marshbank, 1962).
J. Pinder: *Europe Against de Gaulle* (Pall Mall Press, 1963).
Drew Middleton: *The Supreme Choice* (Secker and Warburg, 1963).
Archives Diplomatiques et Consulaires (Geneva). Supplement: *Pour l'Europe* (October 1964).
F. V. Meyer: *The European Free-Trade Association* (Praeger, 1960).

France: The Return of de Gaulle

A. Siegfried: *De la IVᵉ a la Vᵉ République* (Grasset, 1958).
J. H. Meisel: *The Fall of the Republic—Military Revolt in France* (Michigan, 1962).
E. Ashcroft: *De Gaulle* (Odhams, 1952). One of a number of biographies in English.
R. C. Macridis and B. E. Brown: *The De Gaulle Republic* (Dorsey Press, Illinois, 1960).
P. M. Williams and M. Harrison: *De Gaulle's Republic* (Longmans, 1960).

U.S.S.R. and Satellites

W. B. Walsh: *Russia and the Soviet Union* (Michigan, 1958). A general history of Russia with the focus on the more recent period.

C. E. Black: *The Transformation of Russian Society* (Harvard, 1960).

J. Gunther: *Inside Russia To-day* (Hamilton, 1958).

H. Seton-Watson: *From Stalin to Malenkov* (Praeger, 1953).

H. Seton-Watson: *The New Imperialism* (Bodley Head, 1961).

H. Seton-Watson: *The Pattern of Communist Revolution* (Methuen, 1953).

V. S. Mamatey: *Soviet Russian Imperialism* (Van Nostrand, Anvil paper-back, 1964). (Appendix contains treaties and other documents, e.g. Nazi-Soviet Non-aggression Pact of 23 August 1939.)

W. Lippmann: *The Communist World and Ours* (Hamilton, 1959). An interview with Khrushchev.

N. Jasny: *The Socialized Agriculture of the USSR: Plans and Performance* (Stanford University Press, 1949).

N. Jasny: *The Soviet Economy During the Plan Era* (Stanford University Press, 1951). Contains summary of the position towards the end of the Stalin era, with statistics for consumption, investment and defence.

N. Jasny: *The Soviet 1956 Statistical Handbook: a Commentary* (Michigan State University Press, 1957). 'Its purpose is to examine the impossibly large rates of growth claimed in official Soviet statistics and to reduce them to their real proportions . . . to determine the periods in which these large rates of growth occurred . . . and, finally, to designate the areas in which these large rates of growth are found. . . .'

Doris Scarlett: *Window onto Hungary* (Broadacre books (Bradford), n.d. apparently 1959). Cyclostyled. Eye-witness account of the 1956 rising. The author was at the time a Communist and worked in the Budapest Radio.

L. B. Bain: *The Reluctant Satellites* (Macmillan, New York, 1960). Eye-witness account of the Hungarian rising.

Motivations

K. Jaspers: *Reason and Anti-reason in our time* (S.C.M. Press, 1952). A short exposition of his thinking.

F. J. Copleston, S.J.: *Contemporary Philosophical Studies of Logical Positivism and Existentialism* (Burns and Oates, 1956).

H. Arendt: *The Burden of Our Time* (Secker and Warburg, 1951). A study of totalitarianism and its challenge to civilization (especially of the West); in particular the relation between anti-semitism, nationalism and Nazism.

A. Hatch: *His Name Was John: A Life of Pope John XXIII* (Harrap, 1963).

Reviews

In addition to those referred to in footnotes there are many others which are valuable sources, e.g. *Political Science Quarterly; Journal of the Royal United Service Institution; Time; Le Monde* weekly edition.

Index

Reval 118
Reykjavik 33
Reynaud, Paul, Prime Minister of France 14, 17, 199
Rheims 80
Rhine 4, 70, 73, 75, North Rhine-Westphalia 193, 379
Rhineland 1, 3, 195, 216
Rhodes 59
Ribbentrop, Joachim von: Ribbentrop-Molotov Agreement 1, 3, 96, Vienna Award 25, 122, Nuremberg Trials 364 n.
Rimini Brigade 133
Rockets 344, 350
Röhm, Captain Ernst 99
Rokossovsky, Marshal 306-7
Rome 58, Treaty of 245-6
Rommel, Field-Marshal Erwin 27, 37, 39, 57, 67, 69, 71, 100
Roncalli, Angelo (*see* John XXIII)
Roosevelt, Franklin D., President of the United States: aid to Britain (Lend-Lease) 32-3, Atlantic Charter 34, Allied strategy 36-41, 56, Teheran (Stalin and Churchill) 59-61, 108, Casablanca 62, Poland 63, 138, United Nations 65, occupation zones 78, evaluation of Stalin 136-7, Yalta 139, 145 n., and Truman 143, and de Gaulle 207
Rosenberg, Alfred 118, 119, 364
Rostock 85, 90
Rostov 31, 47, 50
Rotterdam 11, 82, 83
Rouen 14
Royal Air Force 16, 20, 26, 178, 188
Ruhr: German defeat 76, Russian claims 144, 156, 180, 186, North Rhine-Westphalia 193, destruction 196, Authority 214, 221, Schuman Plan 230, 232; *also* 380, 381
Rumania: German control 25, army at Stalingrad 49, 50, Russian claims on 56, Allied strategy 61, Red army enters 62, Vienna Award 122, end of war 124-6, Sovietization 168-72, Peace Treaty 171, purges 282, Churches 286, Warsaw Pact 301, rejects Soviet economic plan 335; *also* 133, 140, 152, 164, 273, 276, 278
Rundstedt, Field-Marshal Gerd von 14, 31, 47, 67, 71, 74
Russia (U.S.S.R.): Molotov-Ribbentrop Agreement 1, 28, Finnish War 6, Hitler prepares to attack 23-7, German invasion 28 seq., aims (Poland, etc.) 55-66, 77, Berlin and zones 76-8, German surrender 79-80, bombing policy 83, 87, 90, 92, German resistance and Russia 105, Baltic states 109-10, Hitler's aims 111, German occupation 113, 118, 119-20, Balkans 123-6,

and Yugoslavia 126-9, and Greece 132-3, 280 n., Yalta and Potsdam (Poland, etc.) 136-47, cold war 148-61, and Bulgaria 164, and Hungary 165-8, and Rumania 169-72, and Czechoslovakia 173-7, Soviet-Finnish Treaty 184, post-war policy in Germany 185-8, currency reform 189, Berlin blockade 192, Iron Curtain 217, aims in Germany 218-19, and Ruhr 221, NATO 236-8, A-bomb/H-bomb 242, Geneva Conference (1955) 257-8, Suez War 265-70, Stalin's post-war empire 271-3, slave labour 274-5, and Yugoslavia 276-8, purges 281, Churches 282-6, economy 288-90, end of Stalin régime 292-3, rise of Khrushchev 294-8, foreign policy after Stalin 298-303, Polish rising 305-7, Hungarian rising 307-11, Hungary and Suez War 313, agriculture 290, 318-20, industrial production 317-18, 20th Congress 332, and Algeria 340, reparations from Italy 367, sex and family life 378; *also* 343, 362, 373, 377
Rutherford, Lord 93

Saar, 214, 221, 242, 249
Sahara 341
St Lô 71
St Nazaire 67
Sakhiet 262-3
Salan, General 339-42
Salazar, Dr, Prime Minister of Portugal 328, 373
Salisbury, Lord (4th Marquess) 83
Salmi 30
Salonika 25, 133, 279
Sanatescu, General 169
San Francisco Conference 140, 142, 152
Saragat, Giuseppe 366
Sartre, Jean-Paul 381-2
Sauckel, Fritz 115, 364
Saxony (Lower) 193
Scandinavia 142, 217
Scharnhorst 5
Scheldt 73
Schlabrendorff, Fabian von 101-7
Schleswig-Holstein 193
Schlieffen Plan 11
Schlusselburg 52
Schneider, Pastor Paul 97, 106
Scholl, Hans and Sophie 96
Schönfeld, Dr Hans 100
Schroeder, Dr Gerhard 351
Schumacher, Kurt 186
Schuman, Robert, Prime Minister and Foreign Minister of France 211, career 214-15, European Movement 216, Plan 219-37, 292, 349, 362, Paris Agreements 242; *also* 258, 292, 349, 362, 368
Scobie, General 133, 134

COLOPHON BOOKS ON EUROPEAN HISTORY